Fighting for Ireland?

Fighting for Ireland?

The Military Strategy of the Irish
Republican Movement

M.L.R. Smith

London and New York

First published 1995
by Routledge
11 New Fetter Lane, London EC4P 4EE

Simultaneously published in the USA and Canada
by Routledge
29 West 35th Street, New York, NY 10001

Typeset in Times by LaserScript, Mitcham, Surrey
Printed and bound in Great Britain by
Mackays of Chatham PLC, Chatham, Kent

British Library Cataloguing in Publication Data
A catalogue record for this book is available from the British Library

Library of Congress Cataloging in Publication Data
Smith, M. L. R. (Michael Lawrence Rowan), 1963-
   Fighting for Ireland? : the military strategy of the Irish
   Republican movement / M.L.R. Smith.
   p. cm.
   Includes bibliographical references and index.
   ISBN 0–415–09161–6 (HB)
   1. Irish Republican Army–History. 2. Ireland–History,
Military–20th Century. 3. Northern Ireland–History,
Military–1969– 4. Insurgency–Ireland–History–20th Century.
5. Violence–Ireland–History–20th Century. I. Title.
 DA963. S625 1995
941. 60824–dc20

ISBN 0–415–09161–6

For my parents

Contents

Figures and tables

FIGURES

TABLES

Acknowledgements

This study would have been nothing without the Linen Hall Library in Belfast. To all of the staff there, my warmest thanks. To Robert Bell, former Supervisor of the Political Collection at the Linen Hall, for his help, advice and friendship, I am especially grateful. I greatly appreciate the assistance received from all the many libraries in which I worked while researching this project: Belfast Central Library; the British Library of Political and Economic Science; the Library, King's College London; the University of London Library; the Institute of Historical Research; the Library, The Queen's University of Belfast; the Hugh Owen Library, University of Wales, Aberystwyth; the Library, the International Institute for Strategic Studies; the Press Library, Royal Institute of International Affairs; the British Newspaper Library at Colindale; and the Westminster Reference Library. The Central Library of the National University of Singapore also deserves mention for helping me out in times of need.

In the course of my research there were many individuals who showed me immense kindness. Many gave generously of their time to meet me. Some I met only fleetingly. Some I never met in person at all. But all went out of their way to facilitate my progress. In this regard, special thanks are due to David Bloomfield, Adrian Guelke, Alvin Jackson, the Northern Ireland Office, Joe Austin, Jonathan Stephenson, Mairtin O Muilleoir and the RUC Information Office. I would also like to thank those who provided me with information on a confidential basis.

I gratefully acknowledge the role of the Economic and Social Research Council for its generosity in helping to fund this work. I also wish to express my appreciation to Professor Lawrence Freedman for his guidance between 1987 and 1991, in particular for his help in clarifying my thoughts about strategic theory. My sincere thanks are extended to Keith Jeffery and Brendan O'Leary, from whose constructive comments and criticisms I learnt much. Gordon Smith, Caroline Wintersgill, Leigh Wilson and James Whiting at Routledge always showed tolerance towards and understanding of my work on this study for which I am profoundly grateful.

Associate Professor Edwin Lee showed every kindness in affording me the time off to complete this study. Malcolm Murfett has been a constant source of friendship and encouragement, as well as a professional inspiration. Shirleen Wong Su-Lynn provided some much valued assistance, shouldering a number of burdens on my behalf which enabled me to progress that little bit quicker. I owe

Peter Andrews, Barry Lee and Rohan Harith special thanks for their invaluable technical help.

During the course of my work on this project I derived both inspiration and enlightenment from many of those with whom I had contact, but, as always, it is important to state that I alone am responsible for the interpretations and arguments set down here. I apologise to anyone who in my thoughtlessness I have omitted to mention. However, to all of those who I have chanced across in this continuing odyssey through the academic study of Irish history and strategic theory, in whatever capacity, named or unnamed, my sincere thanks.

Abbreviations

AP/RN	An Phoblacht/Republican News
ASU	active service units
CRA	Committee for Revolutionary Action
GHQ	General Headquarters (IRA)
ICA	Irish Citizen Army
INLA	Irish National Liberation Army
IPLO	Irish People's Liberation Organisation
IRA	Irish Republican Army
IRB	Irish Republican Brotherhood
IRIS	Irish Republican Information Service
IRPB	Irish Republican Publicity Bureau
IRSP	Irish Republican Socialist Party
MP	Member of Parliament
NICRA	Northern Ireland Civil Rights Association
NIO	Northern Ireland Office
OIRA	Official Irish Republican Army
PIRA	Provisional Irish Republican Army
PSF	Provisional Sinn Fein
RAC	Relatives Action Committee
RIC	Royal Irish Constabulary
RSF	Republican Sinn Fein
RUC	Royal Ulster Constabulary
SARAF	South Armagh Republican Action Force
SAS	Special Air Service
SDLP	Social Democratic and Labour Party
UDA	Ulster Defence Association
UDR	Ulster Defence Regiment
UFF	Ulster Freedom Fighters
UK	United Kingdom
UVF	Ulster Volunteer Force

Chronology

1791		Society of the United Irishmen founded in Belfast.
1798	23 May	United Irishmen launch rebellion.
	July	Rebellion around Wexford defeated at Battle of Vinegar Hill.
	19 November	Wolfe Tone commits suicide following his capture after the French invasion force in which he is sailing is intercepted by Royal Navy in September.
1800		Act of Union between Britain and Ireland.
1803	23 July	Robert Emmet leads attempt to seize Dublin Castle. Rebellion collapses immediately.
	20 September	Emmet executed.
1823		The Catholic Association formed by Daniel O'Connell.
1842		Foundation of the Young Ireland newspaper, *The Nation*, edited by Thomas Davis.
1845		John Mitchel takes over the editorship of *The Nation* on Davis' death. Beginning of potato blight, which becomes known as the Great Famine, 1845–49. Nearly a million perish and another million emigrate, mainly to the US, Canada and Australia. Over the next fifty years the Irish population is halved, due mainly to emigration, from over 8 million in 1841 to 4.5 million in 1901.
1846		Young Irelanders split from Daniel O'Connell's Repeal Association.
1846	January	Young Irelanders set up their own organisation, the Irish Confederation.
1848		Early in the year John Mitchel leaves *The Nation* to found *The United Irishman*. Young Irelanders mount short-lived rebellion under William Smith O'Brien, defeated after skirmish at Ballingarry, Co. Tipperary, 5 August.
1858	17 March	Foundation of the Irish Republican Brotherhood, also known as the Fenians, led by James Stephens in Ireland and John O'Mahoney in USA.
1867	March	Fenian uprising.

	November	Execution of three Fenians – the 'Manchester Martyrs' – following the killing of policeman during rescue of two IRB prisoners in Manchester.
	December	Fenian bomb outside Clerkenwell prison kills a dozen people.
1870		Home Government Association formed under Isaac Butt to campaign for return of self-government to Ireland.
1879		Land League formed by Michael Davitt and Charles Stewart Parnell.
1881	January	Fenian bombing campaign in England, sponsored by the American arm of the Fenians, the Clan-na-Gael, begins with attack on Salford Barracks. The bombings continue intermittently until 1887.
	April	Land Act introduced following widespread agitation on the land organised by the Land League.
1882	6 May	Secretary of State for Ireland, Lord Frederick Cavendish, and Under-Secretary, T.H. Burke, stabbed to death in Dublin by the Irish Invincibles, known as the Phoenix Park Murders. Gaelic Athletic Association formed.
1886		First Home Rule Bill defeated in House of Commons.
1893		Second Home Rule Bill defeated in House of Lords. Gaelic League formed.
1907		Sinn Fein formed under leadership of Arthur Griffith.
1912		Third Home Rule Bill passed. Ulster Volunteer Force formed to oppose imposition of home rule.
1913		Irish Volunteers formed to resist threat from UVF. Irish Citizen Army formed by James Connolly.
1914		Outbreak of First World War. Irish Volunteers split over attitude to First World War with majority following call of John Redmond to enlist in British Army, leaving smaller group under Eoin MacNeil opposed to involvement in the war.
1916		Easter uprising in Dublin.
	May	Leaders of Rising, such as Patrick Pearse and James Connolly, executed.
1917		Eamon de Valera elected President of Sinn Fein. Sinn Fein win a number of by-elections.
1918	December	Sinn Fein win 73 seats in general election.
1919	21 January	Dail Eireann formed. Two policemen killed at Soloheadbeg, Co. Tipperary, signalling the start of the Anglo-Irish war.
1920		Widespread violence. Attacks on police and army by units of Irish Volunteers, increasingly known as the IRA. British introduce Auxiliaries and 'Black and Tans' to support security forces.

	December	Government of Ireland Act provides Northern Ireland with its own assembly and government at Stormont.
1921		Violence continues.
	7 July	Northern Ireland parliament opens.
	11 July	Truce declared between British and IRA.
		Negotiations on peace settlement arranged.
	6 December	Anglo-Irish Treaty reached between British and Irish delegations.
1922	7 January	Dail approves Anglo-Irish Treaty, 64 votes to 57.
	March	IRA splits into pro- and anti-Treaty factions.
	April	Anti-Treaty IRA or 'Irregulars' set up headquarters at Four Courts in centre of Dublin.
	June	The pro-Treaty party, Cumann na nGaedheal, win large majority in elections to the first Irish Free State parliament.
	28 June	Free State forces attack IRA Irregulars at Four Courts, signalling start of Irish civil war.
		Widespread violence ensues.
	11 September	Free State parliament, or Dail Eireann, opens.
	October	Free State government introduces severe measures to curb IRA violence.
1923	27 April	IRA orders ceasefire bringing civil war to a close.
		Sinn Fein wins 44 seats in general election.
1926	16 May	De Valera and some of his colleagues in Sinn Fein split from the anti-Treatyites to form Fianna Fail.
1927	12 August	Fianna Fail deputies enter Dail for the first time.
1931		Saor Eire, a republican-socialist group, is formed.
	October	Free State outlaws IRA and Saor Eire.
1932		Fianna Fail wins general election. De Valera becomes Prime Minister.
1933	9 September	Fine Gael Party formed out of old Cumann na nGaedheal.
1934		Peadar O'Donnell and George Gilmore set up short-lived Republican Congress.
1936	June	De Valera government declares IRA illegal.
1937		New Constitution changes name of Free State to Eire and claims territorial jurisdiction over Northern Ireland.
1938	April	IRA Convention approves a bombing campaign in England.
1939	12 January	IRA ultimatum threatens to declare war on Britain unless its forces withdraw from Northern Ireland.
	16 January	IRA begins bombing campaign in England.
	August	Five people killed by IRA bomb in Coventry.
1940	January	Irish government passes Emergency Powers Act to intern IRA suspects.
		IRA bombing campaign in England peters out.
1946		Clann na Phoblachta, a small group of disaffected republicans, is formed.

1948		A Fine Gael/Clann na Phoblachta coalition wins power from Fianna Fail.
		Irish government declares the country a full republic.
		British government passes Ireland Act in which Northern Ireland's position in UK guaranteed so long as the Stormont parliament wishes.
1953	July	Sean MacStiofain and Cathal Goulding gaoled for abortive arms raid in Felstead, Essex.
1954	June	IRA mounts arms raid on Gough Barracks, Co. Armagh.
1955	May	In British general election Sinn Fein gains 152,310 votes in Northern Ireland and wins two seats for its abstentionist candidates.
1956	11 December	IRA launch border campaign against Northern Ireland.
		Northern Ireland government introduces internment.
1957	March	Fianna Fail returned to power in Irish general election.
	July	De Valera introduces internment in Irish Republic.
1959		Sean Lemass replaces de Valera as Irish premier.
	October	In British general election Sinn Fein vote halved to 73,415.
1962	26 February	IRA calls off border campaign.
		Cathal Goulding becomes Chief of Staff of IRA and embarks on reassessment of IRA strategy.
1963	March	Terence O'Neill becomes Prime Minister of Northern Ireland.
1964		Campaign for Social Justice formed to lobby for civil rights reform.
1966		Series of UVF killings – organisation declared illegal in Northern Ireland.
1967	January	Northern Ireland Civil Rights Association formed.
1968	August	First Civil Rights march from Coalisland to Dungannon.
1969	January	Civil Rights march from Belfast to Derry attacked by loyalist crowd at Burntollet Bridge.
	19 April	Rioting in Bogside, Derry.
	28 April	Terence O'Neill replaced as Northern Ireland Prime Minister by James Chichester-Clark.
	12–14 August	Severe rioting in Bogside, Derry.
	14 August	British troops sent onto streets of Derry.
	15 August	British troops also enter Belfast to quell disturbances.
	December	Extraordinary IRA Convention approves ending of abstention. Opposition delegation form PIRA Army Council.
1970	11 January	Split between Official and Provisional wings of IRA confirmed at Sinn Fein Ard Fheis when a third of delegates opposed to the ending of abstention walk out to form Provisional Sinn Fein.
	March/April	Widespread clashes between British Army and young Catholics in West Belfast.

	1 April	Ulster Defence Regiment formed to replace RUC B Specials.
	July	Curfew imposed by British Army on Lower Falls area of West Belfast.
	21 August	Social Democratic and Labour Party formed.
	October	PIRA begins sustained bombing campaign, mainly against commercial targets.
1971	6 February	First British soldier killed by PIRA.
	20 March	James Chichester-Clark resigns as Northern Ireland Prime Minister and is replaced by Brian Faulkner.
	June	PSF issue Eire Nua programme.
	9 August	Stormont government introduces internment.
	September	PIRA set out five-point peace plan.
		Ulster Defence Association formed.
	4 December	Fifteen people killed by UVF bomb at McGurks Bar, Belfast.
1972	30 January	Parachute Regiment shoot dead thirteen men during a civil rights demonstration in Derry, the incident becomes known as 'Bloody Sunday'.
	22 February	Official IRA bomb kills seven people at Parachute Regiment's headquarters in Aldershot.
	10 March	PIRA call three-day ceasefire.
	20 March	Six people killed by PIRA car bomb in Donegall Street, Belfast.
	24 March	Stormont parliament suspended. Direct rule from Westminster introduced. William Whitelaw appointed Secretary of State for Northern Ireland.
	20 May	OIRA announces ceasefire.
	14 June	Whitelaw grants special category status (political status) for prisoners convicted of paramilitary offences.
	22 June	PIRA announces ceasefire.
	26 June	Ceasefire comes into effect.
	1 July	UDA erect 'no-go' areas in loyalist districts to match those in nationalist areas of Derry and Belfast.
	7 July	PIRA delegation meets William Whitelaw in London. Nothing is agreed.
	9 July	Ceasefire collapses over PIRA claims that British Army have broken truce during incident at Lenadoon, West Belfast.
	21 July	Nine people killed in PIRA bombing assault in Belfast, the incident becomes known as 'Bloody Friday'.
	31 July	British army launches Operation Motorman to retake 'no-go' areas of Derry and Belfast. Eight people killed in car bomb in Claudy, Co. Londonderry.
	24 September	Whitelaw initiates conference at Darlington to consider political options for the province.

	19 November	PIRA Chief of Staff, Sean MacStiofain, arrested in Irish Republic and sentenced to six months for IRA membership. His arrest ends his involvement in PIRA activities. Seamus Twomey becomes new Chief of Staff.
1973	8 March	Border poll in Northern Ireland produces large vote for staying in UK. PIRA car bombs in London kill one person and injure 180.
	28 June	Voting for new Northern Irish Assembly. PSF call to boycott elections ignored.
	December	Sunningdale Conference agrees to establish a Power Sharing Executive for the province.
1974	January	Power Sharing Executive takes office under leadership of Brian Faulkner. Immense unionist objections to Executive, especially to Council of Ireland.
	5 March	Following Labour victory in British general election, Merlyn Rees made new Secretary of State for Northern Ireland.
	15 May	Ulster Workers Council (UWC) strike aimed at bringing down Power Sharing Executive begins.
	17 May	Thirty people killed in Irish Republic by UVF car bombs in Dublin and Monaghan – highest loss of life in any single day of conflict to date.
	28 May	UWC strike causes collapse of Power Sharing Executive.
	4 July	Secretary of State, Merlyn Rees, announces the setting up of a Constitutional Convention to work out a new form of devolved government for the province.
	5 October	Five people killed by bomb explosions in two pubs in Guildford.
	21 November	Twenty-one people killed by bomb explosions in two pubs in Birmingham.
	25 November	Home Secretary, Roy Jenkins, announces introduction of a series of anti-terrorist measures. The Prevention of Terrorism Act makes the IRA an illegal organisation in Great Britain and extends the powers of arrest and detention.
	December	Irish Republican Socialist Party formed by OIRA breakaway group led by Seamus Costello. Over the next few months the IRSP establishes a military wing – later known as the Irish National Liberation Army.
	10 December	PIRA announces a ceasefire to run from 22 December to 2 January 1976.
1975	2 January	PIRA ceasefire extended.
	16 January	PIRA calls off ceasefire.
	10 February	PIRA suspends operations against security forces after new ceasefire negotiated. Incident centres set up by PSF to monitor ceasefire and liaise with Northern Ireland Office.

	February	Violent feud breaks out in Belfast between OIRA and INLA.
	1 May	Polling takes place for Northern Ireland Constitutional Convention.
	24 July	Rees promises to release internees by end of year.
	31 July	Three members of Miami Showband killed in UVF ambush, two UVF men also killed by their own bomb during the attack.
	September	Five Protestants killed at Tullyvallen Orange Hall by South Armagh Republican Action Force, widely believed to be a cover for PIRA's units in the area.
	11 November	Rees closes down incident centres.
	5 December	Last series of internees released.
1976	4 January	Five Catholics killed in shooting incidents near Whitecross, South Armagh.
	5 January	Ten Protestant workmen killed by SARAF attack on their minibus outside Kingsmills, South Armagh.
	7 January	Prime Minister, Harold Wilson, announces SAS to move into South Armagh, though SAS widely suspected to be there already.
	1 March	Special category status ended for those convicted of paramilitary offences.
	9 March	Northern Ireland Convention dissolved after failure of participants to agree on a form of power-sharing.
	10 August	Three children killed in Andersonstown, West Belfast, when car pursued by British Army careers out of control after the driver had been shot dead. Incident provides impetus for the establishment of Peace People. Next few months sees large-scale demonstrations calling for an end to violence.
	September	Protest in Maze Prison against the ending of special category status begins when Ciaran Nugent refuses to wear prison uniform.
	10 September	Roy Mason, new Secretary of State for Northern Ireland.
	28 October	Maire Drumm, Vice-President of PSF, shot dead by UVF.
	25–27 December	PIRA Christmas ceasefire.
1977	3 May	Loyalist strike launched as protest against the British government's security policy and to demand return of majority rule in Northern Ireland.
	13 May	Loyalist strike called off after failing to rally support and in face of the British government's determination to resist strikers' demands.
	June	Jimmy Drumm tells PIRA supporters at Bodenstown that previous strategy was mistaken.
	27 July	Four people killed in PIRA/OIRA feud.

	5 October	IRSP leader, Seamus Costello, shot dead, almost certainly by OIRA.
1978	17 February	PIRA fire bombs kill twelve people at the La Mon Hotel, Co. Down.
	30 November	PIRA says it is preparing for a long war after widespread fire bombing campaign throughout province.
1979	20 February	Eleven Protestants known as the 'Shankill Butchers' sentenced to life imprisonment for series of sectarian murders carried out in mid-1970s.
	30 March	Airey Neave, Conservative shadow spokesman on Northern Ireland, killed by INLA car bomb in House of Commons carpark, London.
	5 May	Humphrey Atkins made new Secretary of State for Northern Ireland following election of Conservative government on 3 May.
	2 July	INLA declared illegal.
	27 August	Lord Mountbatten and four of his companions killed when PIRA bomb planted on his boat explodes off Mullaghmore, Co. Sligo. Eighteen soldiers killed in double-bomb ambush at Warrenpoint, Co. Down – biggest daily loss suffered by Army in Northern Ireland to date.
	29 September	On visit to Ireland, the Pope appeals for an end to violence.
	2 October	PIRA rejects Pope's appeal, claiming only force can remove the British.
1980	7 January	Constitutional conference convened at Stormont to debate forms of government for the province.
	27 October	PIRA prisoners in Maze prison begin hunger strike to demand the restoration of political status.
	18 December	Hunger strikes called off.
1981	21 January	Former speaker of Stormont parliament, Sir Norman Stronge, and his son James killed by PIRA gunmen.
	1 March	Second hunger strike begins in Maze prison.
	9 April	Hunger striker, Bobby Sands, elected MP for Fermanagh and South Tyrone following the death of the sitting member, Frank Maguire, in April.
	5 May	Bobby Sands dies on 66th day of his hunger strike causing widespread rioting in Belfast and Derry.
	12 May	Second hunger striker, Francis Hughes, dies.
	19 May	Five soldiers killed in land mine attack near Bessbrook, South Armagh.
	20 August	Owen Carron, Bobby Sands' election agent, elected MP for Fermanagh and South Tyrone in the by-election caused by Sands' death.
	13 September	James Prior becomes Secretary of State for Northern Ireland.

3 October	Hunger strike called off after ten republican prisoners in all have died.
10 October	PIRA bombs kill two civilians and injure twenty-three soldiers outside Chelsea Barracks in London.
14 November	PIRA kill Reverend Robert Bradford, Official Unionist MP for South Belfast.
23 November	Loyalist day of action to protest at British government's security policy – rallies and marches all over province.
1982 April	James Prior issues White Paper on proposal for 'rolling devolution' Assembly which would agree on measures of self-government for the province.
20 July	PIRA bombs in London kill eleven soldiers.
20 October	Voting takes place for 'rolling devolution' Assembly. PSF gain 10.1 per cent of the vote in Northern Ireland compared to the SDLP's 18.8 per cent.
27 October	Three RUC officers killed in PIRA booby trap, near Lurgan, Co. Armagh.
6 December	Eleven off-duty soldiers and six civilians killed by bomb planted by INLA at the 'Droppin Well' pub at Ballykelly, Co. Londonderry.
1983 April	Conclusion of first 'supergrass' trial when fourteen UVF men convicted on evidence of Joseph Bennett.
24 May	PIRA bomb Andersonstown RUC Station, West Belfast, causing extensive damage to neighbouring houses.
9 June	British general election. PSF gains 13.4 per cent of the vote and Gerry Adams wins the seat of West Belfast. The unionist parties win fifteen seats and the SDLP one seat.
5 August	Thirty people convicted on evidence of PIRA 'supergrass' Christopher Black.
25 September	Thirty-eight PIRA prisoners escape from Maze prison, during which a prison officer is killed.
13 November	Gerry Adams elected PSF president.
7 December	Official Unionist Assembly member, Edgar Graham, shot dead by PIRA in Belfast.
17 December	Five people killed when PIRA bomb explodes outside Harrods department store in London.
1984 14 June	European election poll. PSF gain 13.3 per cent of vote in Northern Ireland.
10 September	Douglas Hurd appointed new Secretary of State for Northern Ireland.
12 October	PIRA bomb planted at Grand Hotel, Brighton, explodes during Conservative Party Conference. Conservative Prime Minister, Margaret Thatcher, narrowly escapes death but five others killed.

	2 December	SAS soldier and PIRA member killed during shoot-out at Drumrush, Co. Fermanagh.
	6 December	Two PIRA men shot dead by SAS soldiers in Derry.
1985	28 February	Nine RUC officers killed in PIRA mortar attack on police station at Newry, Co. Down.
	20 April	Four leading PIRA members expelled from organisation after alleged disagreements over movement's new political orientation.
	20 May	Local government elections – PSF wins 11.4 per cent of vote in the province and fifty-nine seats.
	2 September	Tom King becomes new Secretary of State for Northern Ireland.
	15 November	Irish Prime Minister, Garret FitzGerald, and British Prime Minister, Margaret Thatcher, sign Anglo-Irish Agreement at Hillsborough, Co. Down.
	16 November	Unionist MPs say they will resign their seats in protest at the Anglo-Irish Agreement in order to cause a series of by-elections over the issue.
	23 November	Large loyalist demonstration held in Belfast to protest at Anglo-Irish Agreement.
1986	23 January	In the fifteen by-elections caused by the resignations of unionist MPs, the unionist parties increase the size of their vote (71.5 per cent) from their 1983 general election performance (62.3 per cent), but lose the seat of Newry and Armagh to the SDLP. PSF gain only 6.6 per cent of the vote.
	26 February	Loyalist day of action against the Anglo-Irish Agreement causes widespread disruption to most areas of the province.
	31 March– 1 April	Serious loyalist rioting in Portadown, Co. Armagh.
	15 May	Renewed loyalist protests to mark six-month anniversary of Anglo-Irish Agreement.
	29 May	Tom King announces that Northern Ireland Assembly will be dissolved.
	6–16 July	Serious loyalist rioting in Portadown.
	2 November	PSF Ard Fheis votes to end abstention from the Leinster House parliament in the Irish Republic. The vote causes some former PSF members to break away to establish Republican Sinn Fein.
	10 November	New unionist paramilitary style grouping, Ulster Resistance, formed to oppose the Anglo-Irish Agreement.
1987	19 February	In general election in the Irish Republic, PSF gain 1.9 per cent of the vote and fail to win a seat.
	26 March	Announcement of end of internal feud within INLA which claimed a number of lives over the previous year.

11 April	Muted response to loyalist 'Day of Defiance' to protest at Anglo-Irish Agreement.
25 April	Lord Justice Maurice Gibson and his wife killed by PIRA car bomb at Killeen, Co. Down, close to border with Irish Republic.
8 May	Eight PIRA men killed in SAS ambush as they try to place a bomb at Loughall, RUC station, Co. Armagh; a civilian also dies in the shoot-out.
12 June	In British general election PSF gains 11.4 per cent of the vote in Northern Ireland. Gerry Adams retains his seat.
8 November	PIRA bomb kills eleven people at a Remembrance ceremony in Enniskillen, Co. Fermanagh.
30 November	New Extradition Act comes into effect in Irish Republic.
22 December	Deputy leader of UDA, John McMichael, killed by PIRA car bomb.
1988 January	PSF–SDLP talks begin.
6 March	Three PIRA members shot dead by SAS in Gibraltar.
16 March	Three mourners killed at Milltown Cemetery, West Belfast, by loyalist gunman during funeral of PIRA members killed in Gibraltar.
19 March	Two army corporals attacked and killed when their car is caught up in funeral cortege in Andersonstown, West Belfast.
1 May	Three RAF men killed in gun and bomb attacks in the Netherlands and West Germany.
15 June	Six off-duty soldiers killed by bomb planted under their van in Lisburn, Co. Antrim.
23 July	PIRA bomb intended for High Court judge kills all three members of the Hanna family as they were crossing the border from the Irish Republic.
20 August	Eight off-duty soldiers killed by PIRA bomb attack on their bus at Ballygawley, Co. Tyrone.
30 August	SAS shoot dead three PIRA men in ambush near Drumnakilly, Co. Tyrone.
2 September	PSF–SDLP talks end.
19 October	Home Secretary, Douglas Hurd, announces restrictions on the broadcast of interviews with members of paramilitary organisations and their supporters.
1989 January	PSF President, Gerry Adams, publicly cautions PIRA over increasing number of civilian deaths caused by its operations.
17 May	Local elections in Northern Ireland sees PSF win 11.3 per cent of vote.
16 June	In general election in Irish Republic PSF gain only 1.2 per cent of the vote.

	20 June	Polling in European elections sees PSF gain 2.3 per cent of vote in Irish Republic and 9.2 per cent in Northern Ireland.
	24 July	Peter Brooke becomes new Secretary of State for Northern Ireland.
	14 August	Twentieth anniversary of introduction of British Army onto streets of Northern Ireland.
	22 September	Ten Royal Marines bandsmen killed when PIRA bomb explodes at their base in Deal, Kent.
	17 October	Four people imprisoned for the Guildford pub bombing in 1974 released on appeal on the grounds that their convictions were unsafe when the Director of Public Prosecutions withdrew evidence against them.
	25 October	PIRA shoot dead an RAF serviceman and his six-month-old daughter in Wildenrath, West Germany.
1990	9 January	PSF publicity director, Danny Morrison, charged along with four others of conspiracy to murder and membership of IRA.
	9 April	Four UDR soldiers killed by PIRA landmine outside Downpatrick, Co. Down.
	27 May	Two Australian tourists shot dead by PIRA in Roermond, the Netherlands.
	24 July	Three RUC officers and a Catholic nun killed in PIRA bomb attack outside Armagh City.
	30 July	Ian Gow MP, former parliamentary private secretary to Margaret Thatcher, killed by car bomb at his home in Hankham, Sussex.
	9 October	Two PIRA men shot dead by SAS near Loughall, Co. Armagh.
	24 October	Six soldiers and a civilian killed in two simultaneous PIRA human proxy bombs which are driven into border checkpoints at Coshquin, near Derry, where five soldiers and the civilian are killed, and at Cloghoge, near Newry, Co. Armagh, where one soldier dies.
	29 October	PSF publicity director, Danny Morrison, committed for trial along with eight others accused of unlawful imprisonment and PIRA membership.
	10 November	Four people, 2 off-duty policemen and two civilians, shot dead by PIRA at Castor Bay, near Lurgan.
1991	7 February	PIRA mount mortar attack on Downing Street, London, while (Gulf War) War Cabinet is in session; no one is injured.
	18 February	PIRA bomb at Victoria Station, London, kills one person and injures forty others.
	3 March	Four people killed by UVF attack on a bar in Cappagh, Co. Tyrone.

14 March	Six men imprisoned for Birmingham pub bombings in 1974 released on appeal on the grounds that their convictions were unsafe and unsatisfactory.
30 April	Inter-party talks on the political future of Northern Ireland involving the constitutional parties in the province get underway at Stormont.
8 May	Former PSF publicity director, Danny Morrison, found guilty of unlawfully imprisoning a police informer, though he and six others acquitted of conspiracy to murder. He is sentenced to eight years in prison.
4 June	Three PIRA men killed in SAS ambush in village of Coagh, Co. Tyrone.
3 July	Following protracted procedural difficulties the inter-party talks in Northern Ireland brought to an end.
23 July	Secretary of State for Defence, Tom King, announces that the UDR and the Royal Irish Rangers are to be merged to form the Royal Irish Regiment (RIR).
28 July	Seven UFF firebombs explode in shops and bars in the Irish Republic.
2 November	Two British soldiers killed by a PIRA bomb planted at the Musgrave Park Hospital, Belfast.
13 November	Four Protestants killed in three separate PIRA shootings in Belfast.
14 November	Three men, two Catholics and one Protestant, killed in a UVF attack near Lurgan, Co. Armagh.
15 November	Two PIRA members killed by their own bomb which they were attempting to plant near a concert hall in St Albans, Hertfordshire, where a military band was playing.
1992 17 January	Eight Protestant men killed by a PIRA bombing attack on their minibus at Teebane Cross, Co. Tyrone, because their employer carried out maintenance work for the security forces.
5 February	UFF gun attack on a betting shop in the Ormeau Road, Belfast, kills five Catholics in retaliation for the Teebane Cross minibus massacre.
16 February	Four PIRA members shot dead by undercover soldiers at Clonoe, Co. Tyrone.
28 February	PIRA bomb at London Bridge Station injures twenty-eight people, and severely disrupts the London commuter rail and underground network.
10 April	PIRA bomb outside the Baltic Exchange in the City of London kills 2 people.
	Westminster General Election result returns the Conservative government of John Major to power. In Northern Ireland PSF's share of the vote declines to 10 per cent. Gerry Adams loses the seat of West Belfast to Joe Hendron of the SDLP.

11 April	Sir Patrick Mayhew appointed Secretary of State for Northern Ireland.
6 July	Political talks among the constitutional parties in Northern Ireland opened at Lancaster House in London.
10 August	Secretary of State for Northern Ireland, Sir Patrick Mayhew, announces the proscription of the UDA under the Emergency Provisions Act.
14 November	Three Catholics killed in UFF attack on a betting shop in North Belfast.
1993 27 February	Eighteen civilians injured by a PIRA bomb in Camden, north London.
20 March	Two young boys, one aged 3 and the other 12, killed and fifty-one others injured after two PIRA bombs explode in Warrington, Cheshire.
25 March	Four Catholics, including one PIRA member, killed in UFF shooting at Castlerock, Co. Londonderry. Another Catholic also killed in second UFF attack in West Belfast.
11 April	John Hume, leader of the SDLP, and PSF president, Gerry Adams, meet each other in the first of a series of meetings which become known as the 'Hume–Adams' talks.
24 April	A large PIRA bomb at Bishopsgate in the City of London kills one person, injures forty-five others and causes extensive damage to the surrounding financial district.
21 May	Local elections in Northern Ireland result in PSF winning fifty-one council seats with 12.5 per cent of the vote, on a 58 per cent turnout. This represents a rise of 1.2 per cent in PSF's vote since 1989.
23 October	PIRA bomb placed in a fish shop on the Shankill Road, West Belfast kills ten people, nine Protestants and the PIRA member who was attempting to plant the bomb.
26 October	Two Catholics shot dead by the UFF in Belfast.
28 October	Two Catholics shot dead by the UFF in Warrington, Co. Down.
30 October	Seven people, six Catholics and a Protestant, killed in UFF gun attack on the Rising Sun bar in Greysteel, Co. Londonderry.
15 November	Gerry Adams, president of PSF, reveals that his party has been in prolonged talks with the British government.
5 December	Two Catholics shot dead by UFF in Belfast.
12 December	Two RUC officers shot dead in PIRA attack at Fivemiletown, Co. Fermanagh.
15 December	The British and Irish governments announce a joint statement on Northern Ireland which becomes known as the Downing Street declaration.

1994	11 January	The Irish government lifts the Republic's broadcasting restrictions on PSF.
	9 March	PIRA launch mortar attack on Heathrow airport, London. All five mortar bombs fail to explode.
	11 March	PIRA launches second mortar attack on Heathrow airport. None of the four mortar bombs explode.
	13 March	Four more mortar bombs fired at Heathrow airport by PIRA, though none explode.
	5 April	PIRA begins three-day ceasefire in order to facilitate clarification of the Downing Street declaration.
	24 April	Two Protestants shot dead by PIRA in Garvagh, Co. Londonderry.
	13 May	PSF submits questions for clarification to the Irish government.
	17 May	Two Catholics killed in UVF shooting in Belfast.
	18 May	Two Catholics shot dead by loyalist paramilitaries in Armagh city.
	19 May	Northern Ireland Office publishes response to PSF's list of clarification questions.
	2 June	Twenty-five senior intelligence officials, ten from RUC Special Branch, nine from army intelligence and six from MI5, along with four RAF crew, perish when the helicopter transporting them to a security conference crashes into a hillside in bad weather on the Mull of Kintyre, Scotland.
	13 June	European Parliament elections result in PSF gaining 9.9 per cent of the vote in Northern Ireland, representing a 0.7 per cent rise on the party's performance in the previous European election in 1989.
	24 June	PSF conference in Letterkenny, Co. Donegal, rejects key sections of the Downing Street Declaration.
	31 August	PIRA announces indefinite ceasefire.
	13 October	The Combined Loyalist Military Command declares a ceasefire.

Introduction
Developing a strategic approach to the Irish republican movement

The Provisional Irish Republican Army's (PIRA) motto, *Tiocfaidh ar la* (Our day will come), would seem to demonstrate the sense of inevitability that many Irish republicans feel towards the eventual achievement of their goal; an end to British rule in Northern Ireland and the political unification of the island of Ireland. Yet the past twenty-five years of PIRA activity reveal that republican faith in the historical tide is not so certain. Not certain enough for republicans to believe that they simply need do nothing and that one day the wave of the future will fall to the irresistible idea of Irish unity. For republicans, the goal of unity is a vision for which plans need to be made, campaigns organised and, in particular, armed force employed. Today, republican policy marches on a wide front, encompassing electoral participation, economic and social agitation and propaganda. But the focus of republican action has remained the unswerving commitment to the armed struggle. How the republican movement came to see the practice of military force as an effective instrument of policy is the subject of this study.

How has the republican movement viewed the role of armed force in the political process? What are the factors which condition republican strategic analysis? How effectively has the movement applied military means to reach political objectives? Does the movement possess a firm grasp of the limits of its military capabilities? Are there tensions between ideology and the practical considerations regarding the use of force? These are the sorts of questions which will be explored. In essence, this study is about the composition and evolution of the Irish republican movement's strategic thought.

Throughout, the term 'republicanism' will refer to that section of Irish nationalism which has supported and organised military operations in order to end any form of British rule in Ireland. Where the terms have become common descriptions – the Irish republican movement, the IRA and PIRA (or the Provisionals) – they can, except where specified, be taken to be synonymous. Obviously, this study cannot consider every twist and turn in the republican movement's long and varied military history. Therefore, the focus of this analysis will be on the main agencies of republican violence throughout the years, like the IRA, and not recent or ephemeral splinter groups like the Irish National Liberation Army (INLA) or the Irish People's Liberation Organisation (IPLO).

In the debate over the controversies in Ireland the usage of particular expressions are sometimes taken to indicate political preferences. As a general rule, official place names will be used, though there will be a number of variations and exceptions. The term the 'Republic' will refer to the Republic of Ireland created in 1949. Before 1949 the 'South', as the Republic of Ireland is still called, was known as the Irish Free State. Republicans frequently refer to the South as the 'Free State' or the 'twenty-six counties'. Northern Ireland will occasionally be referred to as the North or Ulster. Republicans and nationalists often dub Northern Ireland the 'six counties' or the 'North of Ireland'. The name Derry will be used to distinguish the city from the county of Londonderry. In discussing the conflict in Northern Ireland, the terms Catholic and Protestant will be used interchangeably with the respective descriptions nationalist and unionist/loyalist. Admittedly this is a simplistic formulation since it does not reflect the diversity of opinion in the province. The point is that the terms Catholic and Protestant do provide convenient shorthand which most people can comprehend.

DEVELOPING A STRATEGIC APPROACH TOWARDS THE IRISH REPUBLICAN MOVEMENT

Conceptually, strategic theory is all about the 'use of available resources to gain any objective'.[1] The way the term 'strategy' has grown up often expressly denotes the use, or threat of use, of organised armed force in politics. The broadest but perhaps the most acceptable definition of strategy in this respect was that given by Basil Liddell Hart, who described strategy as the 'art of distributing and applying military means to fulfil the ends of policy'.[2] Strategic theory is formalised in the sense that it usually carries a series of explicit assumptions which govern the way strategists view the role of military power.

Fundamentally, strategic theory accepts war as an instrument of policy. To put it crudely, military power, as T.C. Schelling recognised, is about the capacity to hurt and destroy, to inflict 'shock, loss and grief, privation and horror'.[3] Although war is usually an ugly and unheroic enterprise, one of the principal assumptions of strategic theory is that military force is a functional aspect of power, deliberately employed to achieve political objectives. For strategists, 'war', in the words of the Prussian philosopher, Carl von Clausewitz, is 'a continuation of political intercourse, carried on with other means',[4] and the deed of war itself, *'an act of force to compel our enemy to do our will'* (emphasis in original).[5]

In the abstract, war, in its absolute form, is a single, instantaneous, blow to wipe out the enemy. Clausewitz argued that in theory all wars will work their way to an extreme where each side operates to the limits of its endurance. In reality, of course, war is limited from the absolute by any number of variables, both tangible and intangible; finite resources, difficult terrain, limited objectives and so on. Therefore, war is never a single act, but usually consists of a series of engagements.[6] This insight is important because it emphasises that real war is not simply about the crude application of military might but is a more calculating and competitive environment. This understanding helps to introduce us to the concepts of bargaining in war and limited war. Thomas Schelling takes the view that conflicts are usually bargaining situations where the 'ability of one participant to gain his ends is dependent to an important degree on the choices or decisions that the other participant will make.'[7]

The concept of limited war is useful in that it helps us to comprehend those conflicts which exist between unequal participants. This is particularly relevant to the Irish republican case as its strategic history has largely been about how the movement has tried to circumvent the superior power of the British. For groups like the IRA, coercive bargaining will normally involve indicating to the adversary, through military action, that the costs of not acceding to its political demands will outweigh the costs of concession. In this sort of conflict the weaker party may not be able to achieve any tangible military objectives, such as securing a piece of territory. Instead, as Clausewitz observed, 'another military objective must be adopted that will serve the political purpose and symbolise it in peace negotiations.'[8] In this regard, a belligerent may feel, for example, that given the means at its disposal, trying to exhaust the enemy's patience with a series of small-scale attacks would be a more appropriate military aim. When political actors seek these types of intangible military objectives strategic planning takes on an even more intriguing dimension as it requires the weaker side to possess, amongst other things, both a highly sophisticated understanding of the utility of the military instrument (particularly how it may be exploited in a psychological sense) and a careful appreciation of adversarial power.

Underpinning the assumption of the instrumentality of war is the notion of power politics. It is an idea which is often closely associated with the so-called realist school of international political theory.[9] To simplify the arguments of the realist tradition, it can be said to represent a view which accepts a world of competing political entities, each pursuing their interests, as the chief regulator of the international system. Political actors within the system will seek to enhance their power relative to others in order to defend their interests.[10] Thus, war is regarded as a liability of the political system, in both the international and domestic environments, because clashes of interest will, from time to time, lead to military hostilities.

One of the basic tenets of the discipline of strategy is that political actors are behaving rationally. F. Lopez-Alves has described rational action simply and effectively as conduct which 'is determined by the endeavour to relate means to ends as efficiently as possible'.[11] How one calculates whether an actor is behaving rationally is altogether more difficult. To behave in a completely rational fashion requires perfect information and total objectivity. For strategists to pontificate on rationality might suggest that they are somehow enriched with remarkable powers of reasoning denied to all other human beings. Such hubris would devalue any analysis. The assumption of rationality 'does not suppose', as Lopez-Alves comments, 'that all rational decisions are right ones', merely that an 'actor's decisions are made after careful cost–benefit calculation, and the means chosen seem optimal to accomplish the desired end.'[12] Strategists assume rationality because they cannot really assume anything else. One may conclude after surveying the evidence that an actor is misapplying the military instrument. But it cannot be assumed at the outset that the actor is irrational. This would be a job for the psychiatrists, not the strategists.

Closely connected with the assumption of rationality and the relationship between means and ends is the idea of the primacy of political control in war. Clausewitz argued that war is not simply a sustained burst of violence to achieve the political ends sought, but is a more variable phenomenon.

> War moves on its own goal with varying speed, but it always lasts long enough for influence to be exerted on the goal and for its own course to be changed one way or another – long enough, in other words, to remain subject to the action of a superior intelligence.[13]

As war results from a political purpose it is this element which will 'remain the supreme consideration'[14] in its conduct. 'Policy, then, will permeate all military operations, and in so far as their violent nature will admit, it will have a continuous influence on them.'[15] This observation is crucial to our understanding of rationality within strategic theory as it recognises that the correlation of ends and means can shift in war. If the ends are proving unobtainable the political actor may seek to reformulate his strategy either by changing the means or moderating the objectives. Clausewitz was not saying that this is an inevitable process in warfare, merely that wars are sufficiently drawn out affairs for the political authority, if it so wishes, to calibrate the war to ensure that the overall aims do not outrun the means to achieve them. In this way, the conduct of war can be kept within the realms of rational activity.

Strategic theory is not about the study of war per se. It is only one branch, arguably even just a sub-branch, of a much wider study of military power. The strategic approach is not an explain-all theory. It is just one approach among many, with limited terms of reference. The essence of the strategic approach is simply to trace the line of thinking of a particular political entity in order to comprehend how it proposes to achieve its objectives; and also to look at the ideological assumptions and values that underlie that entity's thinking and how this informs the way it formulates its strategy. Like most analytical frameworks, strategic theory offers a way of reducing an amorphous mass to manageable proportions and of imposing intellectual structure and discipline where there may well be none. No single theory can deal with the complex reality of Irish republican violence in its entirety. The use of strategic theory in this study is designed to help investigate, understand and explain some of the questions arising from the republican movement's practice of military force. The strategic approach is not a rigid concept. Because each situation varies so enormously in both time and place, it is impossible to elaborate durable and all-embracing strategic models. Strategic theory can only delineate norms of expected logical behaviour within any specific situation. The accent in this study will therefore be placed on viewing the evolution of republican strategy as a process unique within its own historical context while the effectiveness of the movement's military conduct will be interpreted through the broad principles of strategic evaluation set down here. This allows the analysis to unfold without suggesting either that Irish republican strategy is somehow exceptionally deficient in the annals of warfare or that the methods of analysis constitute immutable principles of strategic law. As Carl von Clausewitz well-recognised: 'In war, more than elsewhere [analytical] criticism exists only to recognize truth, not to act as judge.'[16]

The bulk of this analysis is based on the material published by the Irish republican movement. This material is supplemented by a review of the Irish, British and international press, as well as the wide range of secondary sources. This study covers events up to summer 1994, concluding with the declaration of the Provisional IRA's ceasefire in late August of that year. Given the limitations of time and access to data, it should be noted that the work that informs the detailed strategic analysis extends only to 1992.

One difficulty confronting students of Irish republican history is the problem of obtaining reliable evidence. J. Bowyer Bell has summarised well the problems of gaining accurate information.[17] The IRA is an army on the run. On the military side there is no such thing as any collection of records and documents. The little that has been committed to paper has often been lost, seized or destroyed. The republican press is useful though offers only a partial insight. Little of substance is mentioned on the IRA and, as Bowyer Bell says, 'divisions over policy and personality are argued out of print if at all possible'.[18] As a con- sequence, it is impossible for anyone not privy to the movement's internal machinations to write as if they were looking over the shoulders of the IRA's Army Council. So while this analysis will always try where possible to get behind the military rhetoric, the intention is also to take the Irish republican movement at its word and assess its pronouncements, with reference to strategic theory, to see how they stand up under sustained scrutiny. There is no doubt, however, that we are still left with a very incomplete picture. That is why emphasis has been placed on viewing the republican movement's utilisation of the military instru- ment through an evolutionary perspective. On this background, one can attempt to trace lines of continuity and build up an impression of the process of republican strategic formulation.

1 The Irish republican military mind

The evolution of a strategic tradition

The true cultural and psychological origins of republican strategic thinking stretch back to the outer reaches of Irish history, and even to mythic prehistory. It is impossible to do justice to even a fraction of the republican movement's rich historical inheritance in the space available here. So, the intention of this analysis is to analyse schematically the evolution of a number of ideological themes within the republican tradition which have a bearing upon the employment of the movement's use of armed force.

Modern republicanism draws its inspiration from a tradition of conspiracy which centres on a number of rebellions, most notably the revolts of the United Irishmen in 1798, the Young Irelanders in 1848, the Fenians in 1867 and, most importantly, the Easter rising of 1916. Although the movement claims this heritage of revolt to represent a direct line of succession with the modern era, it would be wrong to speak in terms of a clearly defined republican strategic legacy. For example, it is doubtful whether those like the United Irishmen or the Young Irelanders considered themselves republicans in any consistent sense. As is so often the case, interpretations of history are used to support political positions in the present.[1] Indeed, this is the process in which we are interested for the purposes of this chapter. We are not concerned here with the exact nature of the events as they unfolded but with perceptions of the past and the effects they have on the republican movement's strategic analysis.

THE RELATIONSHIP WITH BRITAIN – THE COLONIAL ANALYSIS

'British soldiers and British administrators have never brought anything but death, suffering, starvation and untold misery to the people in this country. They will never bring anything else until they get out.'[2] These sentiments, expressed in one small Provisional Sinn Fein (PSF) publication in the 1970s, capture the emotional core of republicanism. Wolfe Tone, one of the figures in the rebellion of the United Irishmen in 1798 and hailed in the modern era as the founding father of the republican tradition, declared: 'From my earliest youth I have regarded the connection between Ireland and England as the curse of the Irish nation.'[3] From this assumption, later republicans would claim, Tone concluded that England was the 'party solely responsible for all the ills afflicting Ireland'.[4] It is the root rejection of British, or more particularly English, influence in Ireland which remains the most distinguishing feature of republican thinking. Why should this be so? To comprehend republican practice of the military instrument it is necessary to understand the reason for this perception as the answer provides the intellectual basis upon which the movement has sought to define relevant strategies.

The republican view of the relationship between Ireland and Britain was stated forcefully by Provisional Sinn Fein in 1988 during a series of meetings held with the main constitutional nationalist party in Northern Ireland, the Social Democratic and Labour Party (SDLP). 'British interference in Ireland', PSF exclaimed, 'has and continues to be malign because its presence has and continues to be based on its own self-interests.'[5] The history of British involvement in Irish affairs is seen in terms of Britain's attempts to use its power systematically to drain Ireland of its human and material resources through underdevelopment, restricted markets, famine and emigration, and the imposition of alien institutions. The present situation in Northern Ireland is deemed to play a key role in Britain's continuing imperial design. Republicans see the province's existence as an artificially manufactured political arrangement to preserve British domination of the whole island. One republican writer compared it to a robber, who, having broken into someone's home and 'while leering at the householder, he tells you, look get on with your own business, I am occupying only one room'.[6] In this way, republicans allege that the British presence distracts and divides the people and disfigures all aspects of political and social life in Ireland. It prevents the emergence of a mature class-based polity, retards economic progress and distorts social and cultural values, thereby leaving the British in the North, and their neo-colonial business allies in the South, to carry on making their mint out of the exploitation of the Irish people.[7]

The notion of colonial subjugation is the strongest theme in Irish republican nationalism. The contention that Ireland remains at the mercy of an exploitative foreign power, with all the attendant suffering it causes, forms the central hypothesis of republican political analysis. In Wolfe Tone's opinion, the 'bane of Irish prosperity is the influence of England'. 'I believe', Tone went on, 'that influence will be ever extended while the connection between the countries continues.'[8] It was this impression of the fixed nature of British interests in Ireland that convinced the United Irishmen that they could never be masters of their own destiny. The movement's 1797 constitution proclaimed:

> We have no National Government; we are ruled by Englishmen and the Servants of Englishmen, whose Object is the Interest of another country, whose Instrument is corruption and whose Strength is the Weakness of Ireland.[9]

The republican diagnosis of Ireland's predicament was straightforward. Echoing the words of Tone, an article in the republican newspaper, *An Phoblacht*, declared that 'Ireland would never be free, prosperous or happy until she was independent and that independence was unattainable while the connection with England lasted.'[10] The consequent belief that the British have no moral right to govern or have any influence in Ireland provides the basis of republican strategic thought, as it helps to define both the political object to be gained and the military goal with which to achieve it. The political object as described by Tone was 'to break the connection with England, the never failing source of all our political evils and to assert the independence of my country'.[11] The demand for independence only became entrenched in republican philosophy after the emergence in the mid-nineteenth century of the Irish Republican Brotherhood, also known as the Fenians. The IRB was established by a small group of nationalists to coordinate conspiratorial efforts in Ireland. Unlike the United Irishmen and the Young Irelanders before them, who had initially tried to work within the constitutional process but had felt pushed into rebellion as an act of desperation, the IRB from the outset repudiated British rule and dedicated itself to conspire against Britain as a first resort.[12] Since the time of the Fenians the aim of complete British disengagement from Ireland has remained the foremost goal of the republican movement. In the view of the present president of PSF, Gerry Adams, 'British withdrawal is a necessary precondition if we are to secure the basis upon which peace can be built in Ireland.'[13]

The military objective by which Irish republican violence would seek to expel the British is an altogether more problematic affair. Part of the answer as to how and where to apply violence in republican strategy was supplied by the conciseness of the movement's analysis in clearly identifying the enemy. 'British imperialism' is cast as the general shape of the threat to Ireland[14] and the British government, as the main regulator of imperial policy, as the central authority to be coerced. Daithi O Conaill, a founder member of the Provisional IRA, made this point explicit in 1974 when he declared that 'the British Government . . . hold[s] the key to peace and war'.[15] The clear belief of such a statement was that attacks on the symbols and structures of British authority would be able to alter governmental attitudes towards Ireland.

By the late nineteenth century a pattern of republican–nationalist military activity was beginning to emerge in a form which in certain ways would be recognisable today. For instance, one of the first major acts of political assassination was carried out in May 1882 by a group calling itself the Invincibles when they murdered the Secretary of State for Ireland, Lord Frederick Cavendish, and his Under-Secretary, T.H. Burke, in Phoenix Park in Dublin. The motives for the murders remain obscure and similar acts were not repeated for many years. The Invincibles were a shadowy nationalist grouping, seemingly comprised of ex-Fenians, but whose immediate political origins appeared to reside more in the land agitation campaigns of the time.[16] However, some years afterwards one minor figure in the Invincible conspiracy, P.J.P. Tynan, explained the rationale for the murders as the 'removal' of those who upheld Britain's 'illegal and alien administration' and described political assassination as a 'species of guerrilla warfare' to be employed so that 'these ferocious offices should be kept vacant by the continual suppression of their holders'.[17]

Besides the Phoenix Park murders, the 1880s also saw the outbreak of Fenian dynamiting campaigns in England. The bombings began in January 1881 and concentrated mainly on targets like military barracks and public offices. The

Byzantine nature of republican politics at the time makes it difficult to fathom the precise purpose of the bombings as they were undertaken by rival factions of the American arm of the Fenian movement, the Clan-na-Gael, though the original intention was apparently to distract Britain from a general insurrection in Ireland.[18] The bombings continued intermittently with little effect until 1887. Nevertheless, the depiction of British colonialism as the main adversary in Ireland's fight for independence had been pressed to its logical military end. Along with the assassination of important figures in the British establishment, 'bringing the struggle to the enemy's backyard'[19] was to become a mainstay in republican military doctrine because it was through these means that the movement could hope to gain the greatest influence over British policy.

The strength of republican analysis is that it presents a powerful and easily comprehensible argument. Yet its strength in this respect is also its main theoretical weakness. The image of complete British culpability risks promoting tunnel vision as it narrows the scope of republican analysis by excluding a multiplicity of other factors which might also have some bearing on the Irish context and affect strategic calculations accordingly. For example, the main reason for Ireland's relative economic underdevelopment probably owes less to British domination and far more to the simple geographical fact that Ireland is an isolated part of Europe bound to be disadvantaged because it is caught inescapably in a structural relationship where wealth gravitates towards the more densely populated heartlands of the continent. The republican perspective would tend to rule out, at least as a primary factor, any such interpretation of Ireland's predicament and place the blame squarely on British influence. The pitfall with any mono-causal explanation is that it can rigidify thinking to a degree where the analysis itself is elevated to a point of dogma.[20] If this happens it may well create an unstable intellectual platform on which to base assessments of the value of military force. In the extreme, this can lead force to be applied out of blind hatred, where violence is seen not in functional terms but purely as a means of striking a righteous blow against an enemy perceived to be responsible for centuries of oppression. The lack of a wider consideration of influences may make the process of strategic formulation inflexible and unself-critical, unable to take account of changing circumstances, thereby guiding and reinforcing other inaccurate or outmoded assumptions which may flow from a highly restrictive analysis.

THE NATIONALIST VANGUARD AND APOSTOLIC SUCCESSION

One obvious corollary of the republican movement's colonial analysis is the cultivation of an idealised alternative to the despoliations of British rule. Emphasis on asserting Ireland's cultural achievements has played a major part in the development of this theme in republican ideology. The Young Irelanders were significant in this respect as they believed that cultural rejuvenation was a prerequisite to substantiate any claim for independence. Through the promotion of Irish culture and history the movement sought to build a distinctive and integrated national identity.[21] In the pages of the Young Ireland newspaper, *The*

Nation, under its editor and intellectual mentor of the movement, Thomas Davis, Ireland's claim to autonomy was advanced through the portrayal of a vigorous, self-reliant and disciplined cultural inheritance capable of resisting the corrupting values and oppression of foreign intervention. Davis announced:

> And now, Englishmen, listen to us! We tell you, and all whom it may concern, come what may – bribery or deceit, justice, policy or war – we tell you, in the name of Ireland, Ireland shall be a Nation![22]

It was in the early years of the twentieth century, against the background of an upsurge of interest in Gaelic culture, that the concept of Irish nationality was further enhanced within the republican tradition through the writings of Patrick Pearse. Pearse's visions of nationhood were quasi-religious. He rejected the view that independence was something to be decided empirically in terms of economic viability, ethnic homogeneity and the ability to maintain sovereignty. The Irish nation he believed to be a mystical entity, a unified whole embracing all men and women in Ireland, something 'holy in itself'.[23] 'Freedom' in Pearse's view, was conceived as 'a spiritual necessity' which 'transcends all corporeal necessities'.[24]

There is no doubt that the belief in Ireland as a single political unit which can only attain 'true justice, peace and happiness'[25] with the overthrow of British rule remains the object of devotion within the modern republican movement. The intensity with which this goal is held has endowed republicans with a strong sense of conviction in the correctness of their motives and intentions. The impression is one of a nationalist vanguard that sees itself as the embodiment of the true spirit of Ireland's destiny. Intellectual elitism has been a notable feature of the republican tradition. The Young Irelanders, for example, saw their role as that of tutors to the masses in order, in Davis' words, to 'spiritualise and nationalise them with higher and nobler aims'.[26] Tom Garvin suggests that after the Irish civil war in 1923 this strand of moral elitism bred a particularly puritanical republican persona which saw the Irish people as a largely impassive mass who had been deflected from following the true path to freedom by British and Irish Free State propaganda.[27] Such attitudes were detectable in republican rhetoric around this time. For example, in 1926 the Sinn Fein leader, Eamon de Valera, expressed the hope that after the damage caused to republican unity by the civil war the movement 'would receive back all those of the rank and file who had been misled in the recent years'. He continued: 'Republicans must be prepared to recognise that error is a human failing and make the necessary allowances.'[28] In a similar vein, one republican advocate writing in the early 1970s reminded his readers that, as one of the 'minority revolutionary movements', republicans were 'fighting against conservative odds to keep the real needs and most urgent social and political problems before the people'.[29] Implicit in these sorts of statements is a disposition which regards the bulk of the people as rather guileless, capable of being manipulated and unable to determine their 'real needs'. Deviation from the republican line results not from differing perspectives and analyses but from 'human failing'. The debasement of those who do not follow the republican course is mitigated only by the prospect that they will return to the fold having seen the futility of the alternatives and having finally recognised their own gullibility. In the recent past, the republican movement has had occasion to proclaim openly that the IRA 'has a monopoly on true Irish patriotism'.[30] This type of thinking underlines the fact that the movement's conception of the political arena is not one where men and women are invited to choose freely between competing ideas and visions through argument and debate, but is one characterised by a series of unmovable truths to which people should owe allegiance.

The effect of republican elitism on the employment of the military instrument has been to furnish the movement with a firm belief in the power of exemplary violence to awaken the nationalist consciousness of the Irish people. Explaining the motives for his involvement in the Fenian conspiracy, the Irish Republican Brotherhood leader, James Stephens, wrote that 'if another decade was allowed to pass without an endeavour of some kind or another to shake off an unjust yoke, the Irish people would sink into a lethargy from which it would be impossible for any patriot to arouse them'.[31] The notion that a republican uprising could lift the people out of their apathy and goad them into action remained a pervasive theme in the movement's thought. Moreover, demonstrative action was seen as a method to crystallise public disaffection into a mass effort to overturn the status quo. Stephens' sentiments in this respect found their echo decades later in the twentieth century when one republican writer suggested that the 'nationalist atmosphere needs a stimulus which will reinvigorate and free the hitherto muffled, thwarted and psychologically repressed youth of Ireland to play their part in the rebuilding of a new Ireland'.[32]

Evidence of the influence of the nationalist vanguard on the use of force is discernible in the republican tradition of attempted rebellions. All of them, to some degree, were premised on the hope that local risings would encourage a mass revolt. The rebellion of the United Irishmen of May 1798, though reliant on French intervention, was equally dependent on a countrywide uprising. Only in Wexford were a significant number of rebels prepared to rise up along with two smaller risings in Ulster, but by early July these had been suppressed. The tiny conspiracy led by Robert Emmet in 1803 had hoped to excite the population through the seizure of Dublin Castle, the seat of British government in Ireland, but it failed in this objective and collapsed immediately. Neither did many feel willing or able to follow the rebellions of the Young Irelanders in 1848 or the Fenians in 1867, both of which were put down in a matter of days.

That these risings failed to incite popular revolt emphasised the fact that they were the work of a conspiratorial elite. Not that military defeat acted as any kind of deterrent for a determined minority. As the Fenian John O'Leary argued, it was 'ridiculous' to believe 'that if any people fail to reach their goal, they prove thereby that they were never on the right path'.[33] Out of the failure of republican insurrection grew the image of what Pearse called the 'apostolic succession'.[34] This notion held that uprisings could act as nationalistic statements to keep the republican ideal alive so that it 'passes down from generation to generation from the nation's fathers'.[35] None of the rebellions mentioned were ever intended merely to be futile dramatic gestures. Their organisers hoped on each occasion that they could mount a serious challenge to British rule. However, as John Devoy commented after the debacle of the 1867 rising, little purposeful rationale could be claimed for the lack of success other than to pass 'on the "burning brand" to the generations that followed'.[36] The concept of the apostolic succession still plays a central role in sustaining the idea of a direct linear connection between the republicans of the present and the history of Irish resistance extending back, not just to Wolfe Tone and the United Irishmen, but beyond to all the other rebellions ever since the Norman invasions of Ireland in the twelfth century.[37] The continuity of revolt is important in republican heritage as a source of inspiration. For many republicans, the significant fact has not been that the rebellions did not succeed, but, in the words of Pearse, that the 'chain of the separatist tradition has never once snapped during the centuries'.[38]

Alongside the idea of the resuscitation of republicanism through exemplary military action exists a potent self-sacrificial motif. Those who are seen to have given their lives for Irish freedom are held up in the present, not just for admiration as past heroes, but to inspire emulation. Shortly after the rebel forces in Ireland had been defeated in 1798, Wolfe Tone proclaimed: 'From the blood of everyone of the martyrs of the liberty of Ireland will spring, I hope, thousands to revenge their fall.'[39] The essence of this entreaty for Tone's future disciples has been to harness the emotional power of martyrdom in order to draw people into the republican fold and create a forceful rejuvenating dynamic which can carry the movement forward to its objectives. For example, speaking of the influence of the executions of three Fenians in 1867 for their part in the rescue of two IRB men in Manchester in which a policeman was killed, the republican socialist, James Connolly, declared that 'the echo of those blows has for a generation been as a baptismal dedication to the soul and life of thousands of Irish men and women, consecrating them to the services of Irish freedom.'[40] Connolly's words illustrate the strong transcendental element contained in the appeal to martyrdom. Pearse invoked the memory of Emmet, who was hanged after the 1803 rising, describing his death as a 'sacrifice Christ-like in its perfection'. He affirmed: 'Be assured that such a death always means redemption. . . . His attempt was not a failure, but a triumph for that deathless thing called Irish Nationality.'[41] The call is for individuals to submit themselves to a higher purpose. Sacrifice perpetuates the spirit of rebellion and achieves a form of national catharsis. Death is not considered to be an end but a continuation by laying the foundations for others to follow. The belief in redemption through violence and sacrifice reached its height in the few years preceding the 1916 uprising. Patrick Pearse and his co-conspirators feared the slow extinction of Irish national identity if nothing was done to challenge British domination. Uninhibited by the failure of past rebellions, they wanted to launch a strike for Ireland, regardless of the immediate military outcome, in order to liberate a new generation to fight for Ireland's independence. As Thomas Clarke, a veteran IRB man and oldest of the 1916 rebels explained: 'We want a kind of spiritual dynamite to blow sky-high the chains of England on our minds and hearts.'[42]

The self-sacrificial image is a compelling symbol of republican ideology and something from which the movement continues to draw much of its inner strength. The ardent commitment to the republican ideal expressed through the actions of a nationalist vanguard is perhaps the main reason for the movement's longevity. It also goes a long way to explain the movement's tenacity even when confronted by vastly superior forces and, as often as not, public hostility or incomprehension. These emotional undercurrents remain pertinent to the contemporary era in reinforcing the movement's own sense of legitimacy, as one grassroots PSF publication reiterated: 'It must be made clear to all that it is the Republican movement which has done the struggling, which has suffered the pain, which has kept the hope and the vision, which has kept faith with the past and the future.'[43]

Dogged determination is a vital ingredient for success in any strategy and in the capacity for sheer endurance the republican movement possesses a highly valuable resource. However one danger of this emphasis on commitment and willpower engendered by the sacrificial tradition is that it can encourage rather aberrant forms of elitist violence which are not apparently related to the achievement of political objectives. At worst, the rationale for bloodshed can slip into existentialist justifications where the cathartic element of martyrdom becomes the end in itself and the continuation of violence is seen as virtuous for its own sake. On certain occasions such emotional impulses are detectable in republican literature. For instance, one newsletter from the mid-1970s, harking back to an earlier epoch recalled: 'Pearse wrote . . . "To fight is to win, not to fight is to lose." Sixty years later, his words are just as relevant now as they were then. No matter how long it takes, as long as we are fighting we are winning.'[44]

For the most part, though, the republican movement has stressed that the mystical appeal of self-sacrifice is a means to an end. Sacrifices in the present may not immediately achieve the republican dream but they are aimed at building momentum and gaining support so that one day the movement will be sufficiently strong to realise its ends, as the following passage reveals:

> The road before us lies clear and unmistakable. . . . The Irish Republic for which all the generations have died . . . lies at the end of that road. It is a hard road to travel, because for many it may yet mean persecution, sacrifice, death, but it is the only road to freedom. Let us achieve unity of purpose to travel that road together in company with our comrades of a new generation who will complete the task of liberating this country from her dark night of bondage.[45]

It is not the intention of this study to dwell on the metaphysical aspects of republican thinking. The theme of self-sacrifice can be noted here as an important factor which sustains the movement's purpose and cohesion. The significant feature from a strategic point of view is that the concepts of the nationalist vanguard and the apostolic, or generational, succession can condition the use of violence independently of any large-scale popular backing. But, as Richard Kearney argues, in the Irish context this does serve a wider functional role for the republican movement. It is at times when republicans can portray themselves as sacrificial victims in the face of overwhelming odds that military failure can assume a certain mystique, thereby awakening the latent sympathies of the Irish people and from which the movement can hope to mobilise support and so increase its power.[46]

THE PRIMARY MEANS OF VIOLENCE

Republican literature on the subject of physical force often exhibits a highly power-orientated view of a world of competing political interests which rarely give way to each other except under the threat, or as a result of, military coercion. Conversely, scepticism towards more peaceful methods of persuasion is also clearly visible. Writing in the mid-nineteenth century, Father John Kenyon, a supporter of the Young Ireland movement, asked: 'What is there in political rights more than any other rights that they should all be attainable by moral force alone?' He concluded:

> Moral force may obtain some rights . . . because some men are honest and intelligent, but it cannot obtain all rights, personal or political, because it is the fatal destiny of the earth, that many men will always be ignorant and vicious.[47]

No doubt, most strategists would identify in this type of remark a strong 'realist' position. Indeed, the acceptance of the inevitability of violent clashes of interest to resolve political struggles has been a consistent feature of republican belief, being reflected in declarations such as that made at the 1863 Fenian National Convention in Chicago which stated that 'no enslaved people ever regained independence' except by methods deemed 'in the enslaver's sense rebellious and illegal'.[48]

Given this background, it is not surprising that, in the words of one republican writer in the 1930s, the 'use of physical force' is regarded as 'the only instrument which would (or ever will) get rid of all these Anglicised forces in Ireland'.[49] The staunch belief in the utility of the military instrument has helped elevate the concept of physical force to the high ground of republicanism. 'Arms are the badges of freedom,'[50] as Thomas Davis put it. The firm adherence to the principle of force has bestowed republican doctrine with a strong predisposition to engage in armed conspiracy, an imperative encapsulated by John Mitchel, who continually exhorted his colleagues in the Young Ireland movement to make military preparations: 'Instead of "Agitate, agitate" I would say to the people "Arm!, Arm!"'[51] Contained in this imperative lies the crux of the movement's dedication to the use of force as the primary means to dislodge perceived entrenched British colonial interests. It is not simply that republicans believe that the British remain unimpressed by peaceful political gestures, but that the entire constitutional arena is a deliberate British creation to frustrate and restrict Irish nationalist aspirations:

> Over the centuries [Britain] has persuaded many brave and trusting Irishmen to use peaceful political methods to attain their ends, or in other words, to play the game by her rules. What chance do you have playing against an opponent

who dictates the rules? How can you beat a stacked deck? None of them ever did.[52]

In effect, those who pursue the peaceful road in good faith are seen as misguided and their efforts as wasted in a fruitless search to overcome the inspired obduracy of the British political system. In this sense, republicans reject the notion of constitutionalism. Ireland has no constitutional history, they argue, merely a series of externally imposed laws which act as a vehicle to sustain the interests of British colonialism. Consequently, many republicans feel that the concept of the '"Constitution" is a thing that has no place in the minds of those who think of a free Ireland'.[53] Republican antipathy towards the political process is fortified by another common suspicion that constitutional participation really conceals a lack of commitment to the goal of independence. According to Terence MacSwiney, Lord Mayor of Cork, who died on hunger strike in 1920, 'Moral force has been used persistently to cover up the weakness of every politician who was afraid or unwilling to fight for the whole rights of his country, and confusion has been the consequence.'[54]

Therefore, republicans feel that only by acting outside the realms of established peaceful political conduct can British rule be seriously challenged. This conclusion is based not merely on a series of intellectual postulations about the nature of British colonialism but on what republicans perceive as hard practical experience. They look back to the failure of Daniel O'Connell's efforts, in the years between 1823 and 1843, to repeal the 1801 Act of Union, and later to the blighted hopes and eventual demise of the Home Rule movement in the early twentieth century, as manifestations of the futility of the constitutional path. On the other hand, violence, even on a small scale, has been seen to yield results and act as an engine for political change. For example, in the wake of the IRB's bid to rescue its members in Manchester in October 1867, followed a few weeks later by the killing of a dozen civilians in a bomb explosion in Clerkenwell, England was gripped by a wave of public anxiety over Fenian activities.[55] The political reverberations enabled William Gladstone, when he became Prime Minister in 1868, to turn his mind to Irish issues. 'These phenomena', Gladstone said, referring to the incidents at Manchester and Clerkenwell, 'brought home to the popular mind . . . the vast import of the Irish controversy.'[56] The next few years saw the disestablishment of the Protestant Church of Ireland and the beginnings of the Home Rule movement. Britain had been seen to concede to, or at least have a policy partially dictated by, the threat of violence. The point was not lost on the Fenians, causing John Devoy to observe that Gladstone's remarks had 'proved a stronger argument in favour of physical force – and even of terrorism – than any Irishman ever made'.[57]

Republicans can point to the agrarian violence of the land war in the early 1880s, which produced a commitment from the government to introduce fundamental land reform in Ireland, and later to the IRA's campaign in the Anglo-Irish War between 1919 and 1921, which secured the independence of the Irish Free State, as further proof to sustain the principle that: 'Spokesmen and negotiators are only effective when they can say: "We have guns to back our words." ' [58] The adage that 'armed force is the only language which Britain will listen to'[59] is uttered almost as a republican mantra. The strategic reality behind such apparent clichés, as one republican editorial of recent times grimly admitted, has been that 'in the absence of any credible alternative to the armed struggle, we accept that bloodletting, however regrettable, will continue.'[60]

When republicans in this day and age pronounce upon the efficacy of violence, few if any of them have sufficient faith in the movement's military abilities to believe that Britain can be physically ejected from Ireland. 'I cannot imagine the IRA driving the British Army into the sea, or anything like that,' acknowledged the one-time president of PSF, Ruairi O Bradaigh, in 1971.[61] The recognition of the disparity in power has necessarily entailed modifications in the nature of both operational conduct and the military objective sought in war. Prior to the twentieth century, however, republicans clung to very conventional ideas of revolt. The rebellions of 1798, 1848 and 1867, for example, all hoped to gather sufficient men and material from within Ireland, or in the case of 1798 by seeking direct outside assistance, to defeat the British through force of arms and literally push them out of Ireland. Despite a record of unremitting defeat, the mainstream of the republican movement remained devoted to old style insurrection throughout the nineteenth century. However, by the mid-nineteenth century, there were those ready to accept the implausibility of all out military confrontation. The radical nineteenth century thinker, and associate of the Young Ireland movement, James Finatan Lalor, was edging his way to what would be a more realistic military posture for those wishing to challenge superior British force when he wrote:

> To be successful, your fight must be a *defensive* one. The force of England is *entrenched and fortified*. You must draw it out of position; break up its mass; break its trained line of march and manoeuvre – its equal step and serried array . . . . You must . . . nullify its tactique and strategy, as well as its discipline, decompose the science and systems of war, and resolve them into their first elements. You must make the hostile army a mob, as your own will be; force it to act on the *offensive* and oblige it to undertake operations for which it was never constructed.[62]

> (emphasis in original)

That Lalor's statement contains the main structural prerequisites of a guerrilla war theory indicates the transitional nature of republican strategic thinking in the era. For though the movement's military doctrine was to remain largely under-developed until the Anglo-Irish war, by the late nineteenth century a distinctive modus operandi was beginning to take shape. We have mentioned already in this regard that from the 1880s political assassination and bombing campaigns were to become an established feature of republican activity. In tandem with these developments the outline of a low intensity warfare doctrine also started to emerge. This was noticeable during the planning of the dynamiting campaigns by the Clan-na-Gael. One of the leading advocates of attacks against Britain, Patrick Ford, argued that: 'A few active, intrepid and intelligent men can do so much to annoy and hurt England. The Irish cause requires Skirmishers. It requires a little band of heroes who will initiate and keep up, without intermission, a guerrilla warfare.'[63] Originally, a Skirmishing campaign was envisaged only as a series of diversionary attacks as a prelude to a general insurrection in Ireland, though this never materialised. The significant point is that some Fenians were prepared to entertain the thought of military action within an extended time frame, rather than concentrating all efforts solely upon building up resources for a single, violent outburst of rebellion.

The gradual movement towards the acceptance of a more protracted war scenario would, in time, supplant the means of revolt as the primary military objective. As preparations for the dynamiting campaign progressed this shift became more discernible. James McDermott, one of the protagonists of the Skirmishing faction under O'Donovan Rossa, sketched out the purpose of the campaign: 'We don't mean to meet England on the open battlefield – that would be folly; but we do intend to carry on a warfare on the principle of nihilism. . . . What we want to do is to free Ireland from the cruel yoke of British oppression.'[64] Perhaps the misleading use of the term 'nihilism' illustrates that the process of change was essentially one of groping erratically towards new concepts of military thinking. Nonetheless, McDermott caught the spirit of the changes taking place and, though the dynamiting campaigns were largely ineffective in terms of producing any tangible political results, they did mark out the future course of republican strategy. Henceforward, there was a greater willingness to consider military acts on the basis of their political impact. No longer would warfare be conceived entirely in its conventional sense where there could be little doubt that the stronger side, the British, would always win.

Modern republican strategic thought focuses on the proposition that small-scale destructive acts can be used, not to reach any conclusive decision through force of arms, but to extend the duration of the conflict in order to wear down the morale of the opponent. Exponents of this military philosophy, like Robert Taber, have been cited regularly in the past to support IRA actions. According to one republican periodical, the 'revolutionary principle' revolves around Taber's thesis that 'the object of the guerrilla is not to win battles, but to avoid defeat, not to end the war but to prolong it, until political victory, more important than any battlefield victory, has been won'.[65] It is within this sort of strategic format that the combination of the republican movement's trenchant belief in the utility of violence and the total dedication to the purity of the national object can form a potentially valuable weapon. It is the fusion of these two elements which has given the movement the ability to maintain a continuous level of operational activity over a considerable length of time, thereby denying the complete victory it is believed the British seek. Through these means, the republican movement can aim to confront the British with the prospect of an interminable conflict involving a costly and open ended commitment. In so doing, the movement can hope to outlast Britain's will to hold on.

A writer in the republican press in the early 1970s probably best described the basic premise of the movement's attitude towards the use of force by claiming that 'almost all civilisations on Earth owe their continued existence during conflicts to the success of violence. I don't think the fact that the use of violence can bring success is at issue.'[66] It is this kind of prominence accorded to the subject of violence in politics which brings with it a series of potential hazards for republican strategy. The adoption of a rather unquestioning approach towards the functionality of violence risks concentrating all attention on violent means to the exclusion of other methods which might also enhance the movement's effectiveness. This exclusivism was encapsulated by Lalor's appeal to Irishmen to defend their rights:

> Let men differ as they may about other principles, there is one principle that admits no dispute . . . the first principle of BLOW FOR BLOW; blow for blow in self-defence – no matter for who or wherefore, no matter for risk or result.[67]

An even more serious potential problem, and an accusation which the movement has had to periodically fend off, is that when unstinting faith in the value of violence blends with the more mystical elements of republican ideology, violence can cease to be regarded as an instrument of policy and, instead, be treated as an object of reverence in its own right. Predictably, perhaps, it is Patrick Pearse who is most often viewed as the main proponent of a cult of violence.[68] In one of Pearse's most notable statements he argued:

> We must accustom ourselves to the thought of arms, to the sight of arms, to the use of arms. We may make mistakes in the beginning and shoot the wrong people: but bloodshed is a cleansing thing, and the nation which regards it as the final horror has lost its manhood. There are many things more horrible than bloodshed and slavery is one of them.[69]

Easy as it is to imagine Pearse as a lurid militarist, it should be said that the belief that martial values were virtuous and ennobling was thoroughly in keeping with the spirit of the Edwardian years prior to the First World War. Furthermore, Pearse's remarks were made in response to the mobilisation of the UVF – in nationalist eyes a highly belligerent act of militarisation itself. In general terms, though, the republican movement has shown itself to be aware of being seen as exalting in physical force and is careful to deny any emotional attachment to violence. For instance, Terence McSwiney stressed that in the cause of freedom *'war must be faced and blood must be shed, not gleefully, but as a terrible necessity'* (emphasis in original) and that 'the mind must guide and govern our passion'.[70] Sensitivity to this issue is also reflected in the recent age of republican violence. All the same, the following passage indicates that while republican rhetoric tries to refute any image of a devotional commitment to violence, there is still a hint, in the final sentence, of what one may call a 'Pearseite' subtext which sees fighting as more laudable than mere passivity:

> The IRA know that physical force is not the sole means of revolutionary social change. Guns do not have political principles. The Republican movement is agonisingly aware that armed struggle without a just goal, and based on a

reasonable chance of achieving either [sic] defence of a beleaguered community or the liberation of our country, is monstrously without merit. Possession of arms is no certain test of patriotism, but . . . the IRA believe that the risks of a carefully planned and principled armed struggle are nothing to the shame of slavery.[71]

The basic difficulty about the republican attitude to the military instrument concerns the inherent limitations of armed force when viewed within a complete conflict scenario. If one recognises the unique coercive qualities of violence in its proper strategic sense as a rational policy instrument, then presumably one's adversary is also likely to see the functional benefits of violence. This poses a problem if the adversary happens to be more powerful than oneself. The danger exists of a discrepancy appearing between the scale of political demands and the capability of achieving them through the coercion of the enemy. The most assured way to obtain victory will be through the destruction of the enemy's forces. To ensure success in war presupposes that one possesses the necessary strength to defeat the enemy.[72] Rarely are wars so clear cut. That is why many, if not most, wars are uncertain undertakings. But for a demonstrably weaker side the issue is even more problematic, for no matter how skillful its military blows may be, they will be no guarantee of political victory. Here lies one of the key questions: how has the republican movement sought to manipulate the military instrument to compensate for its limited capacity for physical denial vis-à-vis British power? Resolving this question poses republican strategy with a great challenge, as it requires a subtle understanding of the delicacies involved in applying military means to confront the superior power of an opponent.

ABSOLUTISM AND ABSTENTIONISM

One effect of the intensity of the republican movement's commitment to its vision of an Ireland free from British rule has been the desire to see this goal transformed into reality in its complete form. Pearse argued 'that no "half-way house" is possible as a permanent solution of the issue between Ireland and England. There were and are only two alternatives: an enslaved Ireland and a free Ireland.'[73] The stark choice available suggested by Pearse rejected any thought of compromise between the two positions. It was all or nothing. It is an attitude which has become a prevalent feature of the republican tradition. The movement does not see itself in business to gain improvements which merely rehabilitate the status quo. Sean MacStiofain, the first Chief of Staff of the Provisional IRA, stated clearly the root antipathy towards concessions when he claimed that 'the sacrifices and sufferings of revolutionary war can never be justified by mere reform'.[74] The implication that concessions cannot compensate for past sacrifices makes the concept of absolute obedience to republican objectives a highly symbolic principle. Any relaxation in the demand for independence is seen as a betrayal of the republican ideal. In Pearse's words:

The man who, in the name of Ireland, accepts as a 'final settlement' anything less by one fraction of an iota than separation from England . . . is guilty of so immense an infidelity, so immense a crime against the Irish nation, that one can only say of him that it were better for that man (as it were certainly better for his country) that he had not been born.[75]

The concept of absolutism compounds republican suspicions about the constitutional process. Not only has political participation been regarded as ineffective but also as ideologically corrupting. This has led to the movement's abstinence from direct involvement in the political institutions of Ireland. The reasons for political abstention were spelled out succinctly in 1976:

At no time will they [republicans] give substance to the shadow of democracy by participation in partitionist politics. To do so would be to acknowledge not only the existence of two states in Ireland but also by contesting elections and taking their seats they would be acknowledging the rights of those two states to legislate for and on behalf of their respective areas and would spell the end of republicanism as we know it today.[76]

The sense of threat felt by the movement of being seen to confer any degree of legitimacy on British rule in Ireland has been a major republican concern through many generations. Lalor disapproved of any participation within a constitutional arrangement, which he believed had its boundaries of action artificially restricted by the British.[77] Neither were the Fenians especially interested in politics. Indeed, the Fenians in some respects were born out of disillusionment with parliamentary politics after the failure in the 1850s of the Tenants Rights League to make any headway on the land reform issue. One leading Fenian, Charles Kickham, argued that the experience of the period had demonstrated that parliamentary action was 'a demoralising sham'.[78] Later in the century, the IRB gave limited backing to the Home Rule party which was co-operating with the Land League to secure land reforms. Despite its initial sympathy, the IRB withdrew its support in August 1876 on the grounds that land rights were really a distraction from the principal goal of seeking independence.[79] Fundamentally, republican misgivings over political activity have for a long time been rooted in the perception that the political process is the domain of the unprincipled where the purity of the ideology could be entrapped and undermined in the murky world of compromise, careerism and expediency. It is this sort of feeling which has often offended the ascetism of republican certainties; the belief that it is simply dishonest for the movement to enter into a political system which it has been pledged to destroy for so many years. As one republican writer remarked:

To put it bluntly: We cannot live the lie of false oaths and declarations; we cannot swallow the lie of participating in – and thereby perpetuating – parliamentary assemblies which have their being in Britain's alleged right to decide what kind of administration Ireland is to have and how far she will be permitted to conduct her own affairs. We cannot break our covenant of truth with either the living or the dead.[80]

(emphasis in original)

The uncompromising stance of the republican movement has a distinctive influence on the process of strategic formulation. It provides the movement with a clear sense of direction in life, ensuring that it will not be shaken from the primary function of confronting British rule in Ireland. For example, Pearse asserted that no national leader should involve himself in any issue other than the struggle for independence 'except with the object of strengthening his forces for the main fight – the fight for nationhood'.[81] The stubborn refusal to be deflected from the central task has done much to consolidate the republican tradition, which has made the movement resistant to short-term setbacks and enabled it to withstand a long-term challenge to British power.

For the most part, however, republican absolutism brings with it prospective adverse effects, largely because it robs the movement of political flexibility. Speaking in the early years of the conflict in Northern Ireland, Daithi O Conaill declared:

> Today the central issue in the war is one of conflict between Ireland's right to freedom and England's determination to keep us in subjection. All other issues are subordinate to this basic point. There can be no compromise on the fundamental issue as to who should rule Ireland – the parliament or the Irish people.[82]

O Conaill's opinions heavily paralleled those of Pearse and the rest, but they were also a strong indication that the republican movement had little or no conception that ends in war could be modified to take into account the varying abilities of political actors to coerce each other. Such a view tends to refute the idea that in low intensity warfare the weaker side should wield the military instrument in order to maximise its power and then endeavour to reach a political settlement which reflects this optimal position. In other words, republicans have often viewed war as a straight attempt to win all of the objectives being pursued, regardless of the actual capacity to achieve them through violent means. This places the republican movement in something of a rhetorical bind as its deficiency in coercive power relative to that of Britain occasionally leads it to employ tendentious arguments to sustain the advocacy of physical force. The problem lies in the duality in republican thinking over the issue of concessions. From the Anglo-Irish Treaty of 1921 to the Anglo-Irish Agreement of 1985, republicans portray all key political reforms as the fruit of their struggle, but nonetheless, at the same time, they also see reforms as a mere palliative, as a counter-revolutionary plan designed specifically to undermine their struggle. Republican proponents claim that: 'Only physical force has succeeded in winning any reforms or concessions.' But they are quick to add that 'concessions can never be accepted at the price of perpetuating greater injustices than those they alleviate'.[83] This is a non-sequitur. As those like Pearse and MacStiofain have argued, there can be no half-way house on the demand for independence. Reforms are unacceptable to republicans precisely because they promote half-way house solutions which perpetuate injustices by maintaining the status quo. Republicans cannot, therefore, plausibly contend that reforms and concessions validate the use of violence if reforms and concessions are actually considered to be good for nothing because they merely entrench the existing political order without bringing the movement any nearer to its objectives. The element of sophistry evident in some republican rhetoric appears as an implicit admission that the movement has been strained in constructing a viable strategy which centres around the employment of armed force. This is an important point, because it suggests that the movement has great difficulty in countenancing the use of force to move towards its goals through intermediate stages. The movement can, therefore, feel inhibited from taking advantage of any political opportunities created by a military campaign out of fear that interim positions will become permanent.

One reason for republican inflexibility stems from the concept of the nationalist vanguard which excludes any requirement for prior popular support as an aid to revolt. Historically, the absence of the desire to cultivate a political constituency has meant that the movement has seen little need to produce social, political and economic policies which would encourage a wide following. For most of the twentieth century, though, republicans have felt it necessary to enunciate vague socialistic ideals, but they have also been careful to stress where the priorities of the struggle lay, as Jack Bennett made clear:

> it may be considered valid in today's conditions to set some form of socialism as an ultimate objective – so long as 'socialism' is not made a pre-condition for achieving national freedom, and so long as the attainment first of the necessary democratic, national framework is kept to the forefront as the central and most important objective.[84]

Without the articulation of a clear vision of a post-independence society, the movement has frequently had to base its appeal on the hazy image of an indivisible nation which provides powerful inspiration for the committed few but often lacks broader appeal. This can prove detrimental for any national liberation group because it bypasses sources of latent power which might be tapped by a more politically and socially conscious movement. Some theorists like Connolly recognised the potential in trying to couple political issues to the republican cause. In Connolly's words:

> the linking together of our national aspirations with the hopes of the men and women who have raised the standard of revolt against that system of capitalism and landlordism . . . would serve to place us in touch with fresh reservoirs of moral and physical strength.[85]

However, the dismay at the Irish workers' enthusiasm for the British cause in the First World War, which finally drove Connolly into the 1916 uprising,[86] ensured that his legacy became firmly rooted in the vanguard tradition. According to one republican tract of the early 1970s: 'Apathy forced him to countenance the one shock method that could not be ignored – armed resistance to alien rule.'[87]

The mix of ideological absolutism with military vanguardism can leave organisations like the republican movement politically desensitised with the result that they find it difficult to alternate between political and military tactics. Peace can literally become a pause in between a period of fighting as all energies will be directed towards preparing for the next military exploit. This problem has been reflected in the Irish republican experience. The question of the relationship between force and politics in republican strategy has proved a recurring source of dispute for much of the twentieth century. Before his conversion to the precepts of insurrection, James Connolly castigated those republicans who idolised physical force. He believed that for many, physical force was the only principle upon which they could agree. This precluded discussion of all other topics relating to the nature of the ends to be attained. 'Nationalists of our day', Connolly exclaimed, 'are utterly regardless of principle and only attach importance to methods – an instance of putting the cart before the horse, absolutely unique in its imbecility and unparalleled in the history of the world.'[88] Within the militarily top heavy political organisation to which Connolly alluded, it is going to be difficult to identify any source of authority beyond the military realm capable of influencing the organisation's conduct. In this respect, the paucity of political thought can negate the idea that policy should be able to shape the military instrument for the purpose of achieving specific goals. Yet if one is not precise about the extent of the political aims to be sought, then how can one gauge with any accuracy the military objectives necessary to realise one's political demands? The risk of employing armed force without having clearly defined policy objectives is that a group such as the republican movement will end up as a permanent military conspiracy where the use of violence becomes internally legitimised as an end in itself rather than as a means to achieve anything politically tangible.

RHETORICAL SECULARISM VERSUS CRYPTO-SECTARIANISM

The republican movement maintains an explicit commitment to the establishment of a secular society in Ireland. The aim is 'to limit the control of the Churches to things spiritual and to treat everyone equal before God'.[89] Along with this undertaking the movement promotes the idea of a common national identity to which all groups in Ireland can subscribe. The rejection of sectarianism was made plain by Wolfe Tone when he stated that his means of undermining the connection with England were to 'unite the whole people of Ireland, to abolish the memory of all past dissensions and to substitute the common name of Irishman in place of the denominations of Protestant, Catholic and Dissenter'.[90] Tone believed that both Catholics and Dissenters (Presbyterians) were excluded from power by the perpetuation of the ruling aristocratic Anglo-Irish ascendancy. He concluded that it was in Protestant interests to combine forces with Catholics against the common enemy. 'Thus', as one republican reflected, 'were two groups drawn together by injustices perpetrated on both of them and this mutual bond was soon to be reinforced by the most dynamic political ideology in the history of this island – that of Republicanism.'[91] So it was that many of the leading figures in the United Irishmen and Young Irelanders were Protestants, including Tone himself, as well as Davis and Mitchel. Protestants were also prominent in the sphere of constitutional nationalism, with people such as Isaac

Butt, the founder of the Home Rule party and the outstanding parliamentary leader, Charles Stewart Parnell. Invariably republicans invoke the tradition of Protestant involvement with the nationalist cause to appeal to Protestants, in Daithi O Conaill's terms to 'work with us for the creation of a new Ireland worthy of the memory of Wolfe Tone'.[92] While republican ideology sees the Protestant community as integral to the Irish nation, this conception sets clear boundaries to the Protestants' room for political manoeuvre. These limits were signalled by Patrick Pearse, who insisted 'that the nation is more important than any part of the nation'.[93] Accordingly, as Protestants are deemed to be a national minority they can have no independent existence outside the nation as a collective whole. It is this attitude, combined with the analysis of Ireland as a problem of colonialism, which has governed the way republicans have interpreted developments in Irish political history since the 1790s. As they see it, after the rebellion of the United Irishmen there emerged not two nations but two traditions. Sean O Riain has described one tradition as that which has transcended religious differences and dedicated itself to the cause of independence. The other, he has alleged, 'was prepared to subjugate nationality to economic, sectarian and social expediency'.[94] The main republican contention here is that, after the British relinquished formal control over the twenty-six counties of the Irish Free State in 1922, they continued to exert a form of colonial control over Ireland by carefully nurturing these anti-nationalist elements. Eamon de Valera expressed republican concerns thus: 'England cannot continue ruling us, and cheating us alike equally North and South, unless she can find here a section of our own people prepared to play her game for her.'[95]

Republicans disclaim the view that the collaborationist tendency in Irish politics has any intrinsic foundation in the Protestant religion,[96] but they do recognise that the 'political alignment of the people in the six counties approximates to the differences in their religious beliefs'.[97]

This factor has been of inestimable value to England in pursuing her policy of 'divide and conquer', because of it she has been enabled to give the struggle for Irish freedom, in so far as it pertains to Ulster, a religious complexion. By playing on religious fears and beliefs of Protestants she has built up a garrison of natives prepared to serve her purpose and what she has taught them to believe are their own interests.[98]

Normally republicans have been more hesitant than the passage above implies to specifically name the Protestant community as the sole agents of unionism. Rather, they have preferred to see Protestants as part of a wider 'ruling class . . . determined to hold onto the privileges they enjoy under British rule; privileges that to some extent at least, would be denied to them in a "free" Ireland'.[99] As a result, republicans believe that, along with the 'majority of the Protestant population', Britain's native allies since the late eighteenth century have included 'middle-class . . . Roman Catholic business people and the Catholic Church hierarchy'.[100]

Not surprisingly, the depiction of loyalists as mere ciphers in the British imperial system hardly endears the majority of Protestants to the republican cause. To most Protestants, Irish republicanism appears a sectarian doctrine geared towards the defence, and triumph, of Irish Catholic nationalism. Conversely, republican suspicion of loyalism can shade off into crypto-sectarianism and, on occasions, barely disguised anti-Protestant prejudice. Gerry Adams, for instance, asserts that 'loyalists have a desperate identity crisis . . . over whether they are Ulster-Scotch, Picts, English or British'. Rather than participate in a common Irish heritage, he argues, 'they waste their time trying to work out some kind of obscure notion of Ulster Protestant culture'.[101] Regardless of whether Protestants embrace Irish culture as a whole either inside or outside the framework of a unitary state, it is not unreasonable to expect that Northern Protestants, with their own distinctive traditions, should wish to cultivate a regional identity. The denigration of this aspiration by the republican movement's foremost contemporary theoretician, and his implicit association of Protestants with what he calls loyalism's 'bigoted and irrational hatred of Catholics'[102] registers a sectarian dimension to republican thinking. The movement's sectarian affiliations have been most discernible in Northern Ireland, where the IRA has traditionally been regarded as a Catholic defence force. In 1987 the prominent Catholic churchman, Father Denis Faul, affirmed that for many Catholics the Provisional IRA provides 'the last insurance card against the madmen of extreme Protestantism'.[103]

A glance beneath the secular rhetoric reveals republican attitudes towards the Protestant community to be just as confused as republicans believe loyalists are over their own identity. In one pronouncement on the issue, Adams sought to emphasise 'that "Brits Out" is not a call as is often mischievously suggested, for the forced banishment of those in the north who presently consider themselves to be British subjects'.[104] Despite this apparent statement of good intent, it has been republicans as much as anyone else who have helped fuel speculation as to whether Northern Protestants would have much of a future in a republican Ireland. The analyst, Padraig O'Malley, has pointed out that in the republican mind Protestants exist in a kind of limbo where regard for the loyalist community can veer with rapidity from conciliation to animosity.[105] On occasions, republicans claim the loyalists to be an intrinsic element of the Irish nation, or that the 'Protestant working class are our brothers and sisters'.[106] At other times, loyalists have been variously described as 'Williamite adventurers, planters and settlers . . . their outlook as hopelessly anti-Irish as their ancestors',[107] or as 'neo-fascists, anti-nationalist and anti-democratic'.[108] As late as 1986 loyalists were being stigmatised as *'colonisers who will always wage terror against the colonised as a form of blackmail against the imperial power when it threatens to upset their hegemony'* (emphasis in original).[109] It is the ambivalence in the republican position, stemming from the movement's own uncertainty over the identity of loyalists, which can seem threatening to many Protestants. Moreover, the blurred republican distinction between Protestants and a so-called ideology of loyalism can make the sectarian threat appear all too real when IRA actions are directed against local security forces in Northern Ireland drawn largely from the Protestant population.

Perhaps the most curious aspect of the republican movement's position over the sectarian issue is its relationship to the philosophy of Wolfe Tone. During the PSF–SDLP talks in 1988, the SDLP team claimed that when Tone wrote of his intention to '"substitute the name of Irishmen in place of the denominations of Protestant, Catholic and Dissenter" he was stating with great clarity that his means or method of breaking the link with England was to unite the people of Ireland first'.[110] In other words, Tone was not advocating a simple 'Brits Out' policy but appealing for conciliation between the communities in Ireland before moves towards independence could be contemplated. The SDLP pressed PSF by asking whether the:

> republican vision is being advanced and whether the Tone goal 'to abolish past dissensions' is being furthered in any way by an IRA campaign which is directed largely against indigenous people seen by the Protestant people as the defenders and protectors of their heritage?[111]

PSF did not respond to the SDLP line of questioning but, in fact, previous republican statements do supply an answer. In 1981, during the speech delivered to the annual Wolfe Tone commemoration ceremony at Bodenstown, Co. Kildare, Danny Morrison of PSF admitted that Tone's original aim had been to unify Catholics and Protestants against Britain. Morrison argued that British instigated sectarianism was stronger than Tone had realised. Consequently, the scale of rural Catholic discontent at the time of 1798 was such that it gave way 'to an almost Catholic peasant rebellion in parts of the South'. 'And how else could it have been', he continued, 'given the power of the British in Ireland and the sectarianism which they had deliberately sown and continued to sow to this day?' There was a clear lesson for the republican movement to draw:

> While the British remain in the North propping up partition, they feed sectarianism and overwhelmingly determine the behaviour pattern of the Protestant people. There can never be real unity between the people of the North while the British remain because they distort the picture. But with the British out and Ireland one national unit, all will savour equally the fruits of freedom, justice, prosperity and peace.[112]

Morrison's analysis, partial though it was, did contain a degree of logic. It was true that during the 1798 rebellion the uprising around Wexford drifted into sectarian conflict with atrocities being committed against local Protestants.[113] Partly out of fear at the sectarian passions aroused in the rebellion, but also for a variety of social and economic reasons, Protestants turned away from nationalism and embraced the union with Great Britain, leaving the mass of aggrieved Catholics standing for self-determination.[114] The alternatives facing republicans in the wake of Protestant estrangement from the nationalist cause were limited. Either they could try to reach an accommodation between Catholic and Protestant interests, which risked being both divisive and ineffectual, or attempt to travel with the majority of disaffected Catholics. There was no real choice in the matter. By the mid-nineteenth century and the rise of the Fenians, the republican movement was representative of a constituency overwhelmingly Catholic in composition. The development of republicanism towards the late nineteenth and early twentieth centuries, with its promotion of a distinctive Gaelic cultural vision, became a doctrine with which Protestants found it increasingly difficult to identify.[115] Although republicans may not have preferred it this way, the logic, and irony, of their position was that the practical mechanics of Irish republican nationalism since the mid-nineteenth century were never fully national.

The intention here is not to pass moral judgement on the republican movement's stand over the sectarian question, but to point out that it does raise a number of issues within the strategic ambit. In the republican view, because the phenomenon of loyalism is a product of a British imperial power play, it does not have a great deal of innate power. According to one PSF discussion paper, 'loyalism derives an artificial strength from the British presence'.[116] Correspondingly, loyalism cannot be expected to have any independent life outside the configuration of a British presence in Ireland and it will collapse once British support is withdrawn. In the words of the republican sympathiser, journalist Jack Bennett:

> ultimately, whether they remain British or not is entirely up to Britain to decide. And should Britain decide otherwise, it is difficult to imagine what degree of determination would enable them to remain British in any realistic sense, unless that determination included the ability to row a boat [presumably to Great Britain].[117]

The assumption contained in this interpretation is that no power other than Britain can act to prevent Irish unification, thus eliminating loyalism from the republicans' strategic calculations. Therefore, from the republican perspective, as Jack Bennett has claimed, there is nothing to stop Britain from legislating the loyalists in Northern Ireland, against their will, 'into a new situation in which they could quickly adapt themselves to the idea of equal citizenship and claim for themselves an effective democratic voice in the running of their own country'.[118] The implication here is that because loyalists cannot influence British policy towards Northern Ireland one way or the other, republicans can use the military instrument to disrupt the British connection without any regard for the political repercussions this may have inside the loyalist community.

Because republicans assume that loyalism has no status in the eyes of the British, they believe that with Britain removed from the picture, the loyalists can be enticed into seeing the virtue of obtaining a real degree of influence within an all Ireland context. Gerry Adams thinks that loyalists will continue to fight for their own sectarian interests so long as the British connection remains. Once Britain is out of the way, the loyalists would eventually work out where their real future lay. 'Loyalists', Adams declared, 'can have no significant say under British rule . . . but they can have and should have a very big say in the future shape of an independent Irish constitution and in the shape of an independent Irish society.'[119]

Republican prophecies are highly speculative. There can be no foolproof guide to future loyalist actions. For that reason one can ponder the nature of possible loyalist responses to changes in the political climate. Conceivably, it might be true, as Bennett has suggested, that there would be little the loyalists could do if the British government decided to legislate them out of the United Kingdom. But could they be legislated into a united Ireland? If Adams' proposition is right, that the loyalists would be able to have a 'big say' in the future shape of a new post-British Ireland, then what would happen if the loyalists used their 'big say' to say 'no' to the political union of Ireland? Could they then be coerced? This raises the question about the extent to which any so-called British withdrawal would actually change the existing power relationship in Ireland between the forces of unionism and the forces of nationalism. These questions provide the opportunity of contemplating how much of a real barrier the lack of loyalist consent poses to the unification of Ireland, and whether the effects of republican military operations on Protestant opinion detracts significantly from the movement's prospects of attaining its objectives.

THEMES IN IRISH REPUBLICAN STRATEGIC THINKING

The purpose of this chapter has been to map out the parameters of republican strategic formulation. It has sought to do this by exploring the characteristics of, and lines of continuity within, republican thought. Many of the characteristics alluded to are central to both republican ideology and identity. As a consequence, they are likely to affect the way the movement relates to the military instrument.

The features which have been analysed in this chapter have not exerted a uniform influence on republican strategy. Certain themes have been more domin-ant at different times. For example, the extent to which the republican movement could adhere in practice to a non-sectarian stance became a crucial issue from the early to mid-1970s. The question as to how far the military instrument could be manipulated to achieve the movement's political goals was pertinent to the period between 1919 and 1923. The relationship between force and politics in republican strategy was to become an object of fundamental contention in the late 1960s and early 1980s. The analysis has also ventured to set down some of the potential drawbacks, as well as advantages, in the republican approach. No political actor can be expected to be entirely rational or intellectually coherent. If this was the case, then political actors would always be able to exploit the military instrument with absolute efficiency and maximise their interests to the optimum. In the real world this never happens. Political actors have to endeavour to carve out a strategy through a mire of complexity, always with limited resources, deficient information and often with divergent requirements. In the process of trying to fashion a clear-sighted strategy actors are likely to confront tensions within their own thinking. Mentioning some of the theoretical difficulties with the republican viewpoint is not to suggest that the movement will inevitably become tangled in a web of its own contradictions. Rather, the intention is to describe the possible lines along which the application of force may develop in order to provide a guide to work through aspects of republican strategic thinking to their logical conclusions.

Through these means, it is possible to evaluate how republicans seek to construct their strategy, utilise the military instrument and reconcile doctrinal contradictions – in other words, all those elements which make the Irish republican movement a genuinely interesting case study in low intensity warfare.

2 Transitions in Irish republican strategy

The development of the military instrument from the Easter rising to the civil war

For many republicans the apotheosis of the tradition of rebellion was reached in the Easter of 1916 when a small group of rebels seized the centre of Dublin and proclaimed the creation of an Irish republic. The event has mesmerised the movement ever since. The rising is celebrated annually and the memory of its leaders intoned regularly to validate republican actions in the present. In 1986 the movement's Easter declarations insisted that the modern day members of the IRA 'are the inheritors of 1916 because they have the same spirit of freedom which motivated the 1916 rebels'.[1] Ruairi O Bradaigh identified the influence of the 1916 rising as the central feature of the modern republican persona: 'a republican today is one who rejects the partition statelets and gives his allegiance to and seeks to restore the 32 county republic of Easter Week.'[2]

In the chronicles of Irish revolt, the rising of 1916 was a large military encounter. The rebels held out for five days before surrendering. The end of the rising left some 500 people dead, 2,500 injured and a large area of the centre of Dublin devastated. The significance of 1916 lies not in the relative merits of the rising as a military operation, but in how the event was subsequently interpreted by the republican movement in relation to the changing political climate in Ireland between 1916 and 1918 that would culminate in the outbreak of the Anglo-Irish war, 1919-1921, followed by the Irish civil war, 1922-1923.

The reason why the Easter rebellion occupies such a reverential position in the republican mind can be explained not only with reference to the succeeding years, but because the rising crystallised so many of the movement's emotional drives in one single event. These primary motivations were encompassed in the proclamation issued by the rebels at the start of the rising:

> In every generation the Irish people have asserted their right to national freedom and sovereignty: six times during the past three hundred years they have asserted it in arms. Standing on that fundamental right and again asserting it in arms in the face of the world, we hereby proclaim the Irish Republic as a sovereign independent state, and we pledge our lives and the lives of our comrades-in-arms to the cause of its freedom, of its welfare, and of its exaltation among the nations.[3]

Here we have the fulfilment of the republican imperative – a desire to express a commitment to a concept of Irish freedom and nationality by using exemplary military action to maintain continuity with a history of nationalist rebellion. In particular, the twin influences of the apostolic succession and the nationalist vanguard are clearly perceptible. The theme of generational revolt was an idea which weighed heavily with Patrick Pearse. He feared that his countrymen would commit an act of national betrayal by allowing an era to pass without some symbolic rejection of British rule. He scorned the previous generation, and its preoccupation with home rule, for failing even to attempt any demonstration against the British: 'the failure of the last generation has been mean and shameful, and no man has arisen from it to do or say a splendid thing, in virtue of which it shall be forgiven.'[4]

Pearse and his colleagues felt it their duty to shake the Irish people out of their passivity. For this reason the rising was an archetypal elitist intrigue, evident in the way the IRB's secret Military Council manipulated the Irish Volunteers into an insurrection behind the back of the organisation's leader, Eoin MacNeill. The rebels' faith in the ability of a devout few to regenerate the republican cause was made plain by James Connolly at his court martial:

> Believing that the British Government has no right in Ireland, never had any right in Ireland, and never can have any right in Ireland, the presence, in any one generation of Irishmen, of even a respectable minority ready to die to affirm that truth, makes that Government for ever a usurpation and a crime against human progress.[5]

It was not so much the violent act itself which caused the greatest political repercussions, but the execution of fifteen of the rebel leaders in the weeks after the rising (there were ninety-seven executions in all) and the internment of 2,000 other Volunteers. The rebellion had been deeply unpopular in Ireland, but the executions and the subsequent enforcement of martial law were greatly resented. The deaths of the rebels, Pearse and Connolly amongst them, sealed the 1916 rising in the image of sacrificial martyrdom, thereby providing the means by which the movement had always hoped it could reawaken the nationalist spirit in the masses. On this occasion the figure of the patriot-martyr did strike an emotional chord. Ernie O'Malley, later a renowned guerrilla leader in the Anglo-Irish war, wrote that in the atmosphere immediately after the executions 'a strange love was born that for some was never to die till they lay stiff on the hillside or in quicklime near a barrack wall'.[6]

The public reaction to the executions was a major factor in consolidating opposition to British rule. Even so, one should be careful not to overestimate the contemporaneous impact of the 1916 executions. They were not the only factor. The frustration caused by the failure to implement home rule, discontent with the First World War and, in particular, the prospect of the extension of conscription to Ireland also aroused much ill-feeling.[7] Disaffection had swelled to an extent that, when the general election of December 1918 was held, Sinn Fein, an avowedly separatist party, won seventy-three out of the 105 Irish seats in the Westminster Parliament.[8] Sinn Fein's manifesto committed the party to the establishment of a republic and declared that it would stand by the Proclamation of the Provisional Government of 1916. Although Sinn Fein contained republican elements, it was not an overtly physical force party.[9] In spite of its broad pledge to make 'use of any and every means available to render impotent the power of England to hold Ireland',[10] the party primarily advocated withdrawing from Westminster and appealing to the Paris Peace Conference for recognition of Ireland's right to statehood. Sinn Fein's first major act after the election on 21 January 1919 was to set up its own assembly, the Dail Eireann, and declare independence. The rise of Sinn Fein quantified the widespread antagonism to British rule and lent substance to the republican claim that Ireland was a colony held in subjection against its will. For the first time, political conditions offered republicans the opportunity of developing a strategy with demonstrable evidence that the majority of the Irish population shared their fundamental objective – to get rid of the British once and for all.

TRANSITIONS IN IRISH REPUBLICAN STRATEGY – THE EMPLOYMENT OF THE MILITARY INSTRUMENT IN THE ANGLO-IRISH WAR

The question facing members of Sinn Fein in the few weeks after the 1918 election was how to give effect to their desire for separation, as the British government appeared content to ignore the moves to set up the Dail. In one of the first statements issued after the declaration of independence, the Dail proclaimed that the 'existing state of war, between Ireland and England, can never be ended until Ireland is definitely evacuated by the armed forces of England'.[11] The reference to a pre-existing state of hostilities may have been a rhetorical flourish, but it intimated that the Dail accepted the need for armed resistance to British rule. Whatever the exact meaning, it was the closest the Dail ever came to a formal declaration of war.

The challenge confronting republicans was how best to employ their military resources to force out the British. Traditionally, republican-nationalists had tended to view war in the conventional terms of brigades and battalions, fixed positions, decisive battles and so on. According to one republican military commentator, this thinking had held sway amongst the Irish Volunteers, and consequently the 1916 rising 'was the logical outcome of the outlook and training of the Volunteers during the two preceding years. It was a blunt, straightforward opposing of Irish military force to English military force.'[12] But given the disparity in military strength between Britain, which could draw on tens of thousands of well-equipped troops, and the few thousand ill-trained forces the republicans could muster, the outcome of head-on clashes, as past rebellions up to 1916 had demonstrated, could never be in real doubt.

In fact, the realities of the military situation prior to 1916 were not lost in all nationalist circles. A group centred around the leadership of the Irish Volunteers under Eoin MacNeill, including people such as J.J. O'Connell, Eimar O'Duffy and Bulmer Hobson, was sensitive to the likely nature of a future conflict with

Britain. They frowned on the legends of romantic rebellion. MacNeill, especially, was strongly against committing the Volunteers to any hasty venture of the type that the 1916 conspirators had in mind.[13] Hobson had for some years seen the impossibility of openly defying British military power and had developed alternative ideas of passive resistance and nonco-operation which he believed could 'offer an even, steady, invulnerable resistance to all government'.[14] Both Hobson and O'Connell drew up innovatory ideas on tactical doctrine that argued for a move away from large-scale confrontations, and towards more mobile forms of warfare using smaller military formations and minimising losses in combat.[15]

Possibly the most significant shift in the process of republican strategic thought was due not to any formal reassessments of military technique, but to a broader, less specific change in attitude amongst the Volunteers who returned home after their release from internment. The stimulus for change had been summed up by John MacBride, a rebel deputy commander in the Easter rising, who, in a valedictory statement before he surrendered, told his comrades never again to allow themselves 'to be cooped up inside the walls of a building again'.[16] During their internment some of the Volunteers, such as Michael Collins and Cathal Brugha, had time to reflect on the essence of MacBride's words. They emerged from the camps with serious reservations about the conduct of the Easter rising. Collins, for instance, considered the rising to have been disorganised, while some like Brugha, felt that a secretive conspiratorial group like the IRB could no longer provide a viable basis for a military challenge.[17] Upon their return to Ireland at the end of 1916, the ex-internees set about reorganising the Volunteers. A better regional network was established and plans were once more formulated to resist the introduction of conscription.[18] Yet there was still no real comprehension of the need for a switch in tactical emphasis towards a more guerrilla-orientated approach. Most were still inclined to view a future war in the conventional terms of static positions.[19] What had changed with the new wave of republican leaders was the recognition that, if the military instrument was to be employed effectively, a very different style of warfare would have to be waged compared to what had gone before. Romanticised visions of gallantly futile stands in the face of British military might would have to be banished. Instead, a future conflict would call for a more surreptitious and ruthless attitude. An indication of what republican leaders envisaged was given by Richard Mulcahy, later to become Chief of Staff of the Volunteers, while he was interned:

> Freedom will never come without a revolution, but I fear the Irish people are too soft for that. To have a real revolution, you must have bloody fierce-minded men who do not care a scrap for death or bloodshed. A real revolution is not a job for children or for saints or scholars. In the course of revolution, any man, woman or child who is not with you is against you. Shoot them and be damned to them.[20]

Although by 1918 republican strategy was still not defined to any great degree, Mulcahy's remarks did suggest the lines along which the movement's thinking would progress. The core of the evolving strategy centred not simply on the search for the technical means to achieve a margin of military advantage in combat, but on confronting Britain on a psychological plane. If republicans could synthesise the military instrument with perhaps their most formidable asset, namely, the unflinching single-mindedness in pursuit of their objectives, they could begin to pressurise perceived weaknesses in the British position. By exchanging decisive battles for the prospect of more stubborn and ferocious forms of warfare, republicans could hope to demonstrate a more aggressive commitment to removing the British vis-à-vis Britain's comparable resolve to maintain its interests in Ireland. This represents only the bare mental frame of republican strategic thinking as it appeared to be taking shape towards the beginning of 1919. It would be, primarily, the hard-edge of practical experience and necessity rather than pre-planned conceptions that would do most to mould the republican movement into an effective guerrilla force. However, the more realistic and tractable attitudes that prevailed in the republican leadership after the 1916 rising enabled the evolution of new military methods to be absorbed easily into republican strategic doctrine.

In the months following the beginning of 1919 the military instrument developed in a rather ad hoc fashion from Volunteer raids on police stations which were carried out in order to steal weapons. It was from these small-scale attacks that Ireland slid into the conflict now known as the Anglo-Irish war. The killing of two policemen guarding a load of gelignite at Soloheadbeg, Co. Tipperary, on 21 January 1919 is often taken as the start of the war, though in fact sporadic Volunteer attacks had been going on since 1918. It was not just the brutality of the Soloheadbeg incident which marked it out as the starting point, so much as its timing, occurring as it did on the same day that the Dail met to declare independence. Taking its cue from the 'state of war' said to exist by the Dail, the Volunteer journal, *An t-Oglach* announced on 31 January that, 'as the principle means at the command of the Irish people', the Volunteers would be entitled to 'use all legitimate methods of warfare against the soldiers and policemen of the English usurper, and to slay them if it is necessary to do so in order to overcome their resistance'.[21]

The raids against police barracks broadened into a more concerted campaign of violence and intimidation against the Royal Irish Constabulary (RIC). Many barracks, especially in country areas, were abandoned. Between January 1919 to October 1920 some 492 vacated barracks were destroyed, a further twenty-one occupied barracks had also been destroyed and 117 RIC men had been killed.[22] By July 1921 there had been 2,000 resignations from the force and recruitment was badly hit.[23] The RIC's retreat from the countryside ceded partial control to the IRA. In some areas the Dail attempted to substitute its own legal and administrative structures, like republican law courts and police, in order to legitimise their claim to the governance of Ireland.[24] In tandem with the overt conflict against the RIC, the Volunteers, now increasingly referred to as the IRA, established an effective network of informers which extended into G Division of the Dublin Metropolitan Police, the department responsible for dealing with subversive activities, and even reached as far as the centre of government in

Ireland, Dublin Castle. In addition, the IRA's Director of Intelligence, Michael Collins, set up an assassination squad to eliminate British agents. The most renowned enterprise undertaken by Collins' men was the killing of eleven suspected agents on 20 November 1920. Taken together, these measures effectively neutralised the RIC as a counter-insurgency force. The destruction of the British intelligence network also shut off the flow of information to the RIC and further eroded Britain's ability to strike at the IRA. Indeed, towards the end of 1920 more audacious operations were carried out against army and police patrols. Many of these attacks were undertaken by what became known as flying columns, full-time mobile units which engaged in fast offensive operations from concealed bases.[25] Although flying column attacks were rarely very destructive, they did succeed in keeping the countryside in turmoil, which necessitated the strengthening of armed escorts, thereby adding to the strain imposed on the British.[26]

The important point is that IRA actions, particularly against the RIC, damaged Britain's capacity to govern Ireland through established administrative structures. The attacks did not eliminate or neutralise British power so much as undermine civil authority to an extent where Britain was forced to rely on the crudest expression of that power, namely coercion. This turn of events was most noticeable in relation to the behaviour of the auxiliary forces which were introduced in spring 1920 in order to reinforce the police. Elements of these forces, the most notorious of which were the so-called 'Black and Tans', were often undisciplined and easily provoked into reprisals. In spite of the apparent inability of British forces to deal with IRA attacks with anything other than heavy handed repression, the general military situation remained the same. If anything, the arrival of the auxiliary forces substantially increased the military odds against the IRA. The combined strength of crown forces during the conflict, including police, soldiers and auxiliary units, amounted to some 80,000 men. Against this number, the IRA, according to Michael Collins, could muster 3,000 ill-equipped activists.[27]

The crucial aspect of the conflict for those like Collins was never the military numbers game, but the fact that the improprieties committed by the crown forces demonstrated the breakdown of civil control which, in turn, hardened Irish opinion against British rule. Collins signified the importance of this point in a newspaper interview in April 1921: 'The terror the British wanted to instil in this country has completely broken down. . . . The people of this country are with us and they do not give a damn what the English do.'[28]

The strategy which the IRA practised attempted to deny Britain the opportunity of waging a war of annihilation for which its forces were most suited. The British always had the capacity to absorb the relatively small losses imposed by IRA attacks. At no time, therefore, did the IRA attempt to defend territory through positional warfare. Instead, in the words of *An t-Oglach*:

> We will strike in our own way, in our own time. If we cannot, by force of arms, drive the enemy out of our country at the present moment, we can help to make his position impossible and his military activities futile.[29]

The central point about the strategy of denial was specified by Tom Barry, one of the IRA's best commanders, who said that the 'paramount objective' of his forces 'should not be to fight but to continue to exist'. He continued:

> The very existence of such a Column of armed men, even if it never struck a blow, was a continuous challenge to the enemy and forced him to maintain large garrisons to meet the threatened onslaught on his military forces and the security of his civil administration.[30]

If the IRA could avoid destruction and maintain its ability to strike at British forces, it could prevent any military conclusion from being reached in the short term. It was in these circumstances that the republicans believed their greatest opportunity lay. The following piece, written in 1927, reflected on the IRA's experience in the war thus:

> guerrilla tactics can never achieve against a regularly organised army a military decision. What they can do is to create what is really a political situation whereby government by the big battalions becomes impossible: a situation that may be dragged out to an indefinite length and that may ultimately achieve for the side adopting these methods, the same result as might be achieved by a decisive military victory.[31]

The efficacy of the republican strategy rested on the political effects of the IRA's campaign. The cumulative political impact, both of a steady level of IRA operations and of the British response to those operations, could be interpreted in a way which was suggestive of a number of things; first, that Britain's inability to restore civil control implied the lack of popular legitimacy in Ireland for British rule; second, that, correspondingly, the republican cause enjoyed greater support; and third, that as a result of both of these implications Britain would continue to face a long, drawn out conflict.

Republicans did their best to refine these perceptions in the public mind with an efficient propaganda campaign. The Dail's Publicity Department set up its own newsletter, the *Irish Bulletin*, which was circulated to newspapers and politicians both in Britain and abroad.[32] The reprisals of the auxiliary forces, such as those in Balbriggan, Trim and Cork, received widespread publicity throughout Britain and America.[33] Elements of the British press, such as *The Daily News*, *The Manchester Guardian* and *The Daily Herald*, had been critical of the use of force in Ireland at the outset. After the sacking of Balbriggan on 20 September 1920, the first major reprisal of its kind, some papers, such as *The Times* and *The Daily Express*, which had previously supported the restoration of order in Ireland, began to question the wisdom of the British government's Irish policy.[34] Other sections of British society, like churchmen, opposition leaders and trade unionists, also campaigned against the war.[35] The truth was that for many, the British position in Ireland had become morally indefensible.

The destabilisation of British opinion represented the apex of the republican strategy. The British government was faced with a major political embarrassment. Republicans could hope that the threat of further domestic and international censure, and the prospect of a long and costly war, would form the conditions in which Britain would seek to re-evaluate its interests in Ireland. The fact that by June 1921 the British government felt obliged to seek a truce and an end to the conflict was the firmest indication of the effectiveness of this strategy.

STRATEGY AND BARGAINING – THE FORMATION OF THE ANGLO-IRISH TREATY

A truce arranged between the British and Eamon de Valera, President of the Dail, came into effect on 11 July 1921. Full negotiations between the British and Irish delegations were scheduled for October. Although the truce was technically only a temporary cessation of hostilities, it did in fact mark the end of the Anglo-Irish war. The war had been about the degree of autonomy Ireland should be granted. Britain was not fighting to defend the status quo. Home rule, albeit with the separation of Northern Ireland under the terms of the Government of Ireland Act of 1920, had already been conceded. For republicans, the role of the military instrument in the war had been about the establishment of a strong negotiating position in order to extract the further concessions necessary to accord with their political objectives. In the few months preceding the truce, Collins had spelled out what the republican movement would expect to obtain from its exertions. He told a reporter that the British Prime Minister, David Lloyd George, should recognise the Irish republic. Collins confirmed it was his belief 'that the same effort which would get us Dominion Home Rule would get us a Republic'. He also reiterated Sinn Fein's opposition to the partition of Ireland: 'We do not intend to have Lloyd George put a little red spot on the map of one corner of Ireland and call it part of England, as he does Gibraltar. We want a united Ireland.'[36] It was a sentiment echoed by de Valera, who stated: 'Sinn Fein will conduct no peace negotiations that do not provide for the full recognition of the Irish Republic and complete separation of Ireland from England.'[37]

The main problem in trying to realise the objectives set out by Collins was that the republican movement lacked the means to seize anything tangible from the British with which it could transact in negotiations. The republican movement's limited capacity to hold territory was illustrated in the Anglo-Irish war. Despite the Dail's attempts to establish its own administrative zones to give the otherwise symbolic republic some substance, republican government was effective only in remote parts of the south west of Ireland. The rest of the region was held firmly under martial law.[38] The success of the IRA's strategy rested precisely on the skill with which the military instrument was manipulated to demonstrate to the British that their civil writ had broken down in many parts of Ireland and that a high political, as well as financial, price would be exacted for the continuation of their rule. The IRA had been able to raise the level of violence to a point where existing tensions in British society over Irish policy were further sharpened. IRA actions also helped convince the British government that its measures were not having the desired impact on the level of IRA operations. Towards the end of spring 1921 the number of IRA attacks had risen from a previous average of about thirty a week to fifty-five.[39] Moreover, it was calculated that the pacification of Ireland would require a commitment of Boer War proportions: a raising of troop levels to 100,000 men, the establishment of security zones, massive ground sweeps, and so on, at a probable cost of around £100 million per annum.[40] Overall, the British came to terms with the republican movement, not because the physical costs of maintaining a form of control underpinned by a substantial military presence was necessarily intolerable, but because the estimate of the future costs of suppression appeared unreasonable in the light of possibly more amenable ways to preserve their interests in Ireland through the re-definition of political relations between the two countries. This is an essential point, because although the treaty settlement of December 1921 reflected the extent of the IRA's success, it was also a reflection of the underlying power relationships in Ireland and not the ideals of the republican vision.

The main British concession under the terms of the Anglo-Irish Treaty was the provision for the legislative independence of the newly created Irish Free State. The province of Northern Ireland was given the right to remain separate from the Free State. The sensibilities of the delegates over the issue of Irish unity was partially assuaged by the promise of a boundary commission which would review the borders of Northern Ireland. The assumption on the Irish side was, in Collins' words, that 'Ulster cannot live without the South of Ireland'.[41] The monarchy was to remain the head of the Free State and an oath of allegiance was to be sworn by all those who wished to participate in constitutional politics. The Treaty also allowed Britain to retain control of a number of naval installations. In total, though, the Treaty fell some way short of Collins' and de Valera's confident expectations of a fully united and independent republic. This was because the Treaty was an expression of altered political circumstances and not any basic shift in the relative strengths of the two belligerents. Regardless of the optimistic rhetoric about the attainment of a republic, the Irish delegation in the negotiations, of which Collins was a prominent member, were aware both of the reality of British power and the comparative weakness of the Irish military position. It was Collins, above all, who proved the arch-pragmatist, as his review of the war revealed:

> We took as much of the government of Ireland out of the hands of the enemy as we could, but we could not grasp all of it because he used the whole of his forces to prevent us doing so, and we were unable to beat him out of the country by force of arms. But neither had he beaten us. We had made Ireland too uncomfortable for him. . . . The British had not surrendered and had no need to agree to humiliating terms any more than we would have done. It was time for a settlement that would secure for us their withdrawal and evacuation. There was duress, of course. On their side, the pressure of world opinion to conform their practice to their professions. On our side, the duress the weaker nation suffers against the stronger, the duress to accept really substantial terms.[42]

Collins' analysis provides an accurate impression of the pressures with which he and his colleagues in the Irish delegation had to contend. For the Irish plenipotentiaries, the IRA's military campaign had established a very particular negotiating advantage. It derived not from the literal inability of the British to apply their superior strength, but from the fact that, because of the way in which the IRA had fought, the British government had been placed in a decidedly awkward political position. The guerrilla tactics employed by the IRA, and the effectiveness with which British intelligence in Ireland had been neutralised, had made it difficult for the police and army to detect and destroy the IRA's military capacity. The only way that the republican insurgency could have been extinguished would have been through the wholesale subjugation of Ireland, which would have starkly identified Britain in the role of the colonial oppressor.

Theoretically, though, there were few military–technical barriers to obstruct the British from imposing an even harsher security regime. Indeed, throughout the war, the British military commander, General Macready, had pressed for the full introduction of martial law all over the country.[43] The British government refused as it was anxious to avoid any measure that would appear to confer belligerent status on the IRA. Such moves, it was believed, would indicate Britain's inability to contain the situation, while also suggesting that the IRA was an authentic expression of Irish national will.[44] Furthermore, it seems that the British were genuinely expecting a fairly short policing operation against a gang of hoodlums.[45] Once it became clear that the degree of support for the IRA had been underestimated and the resultant security measures implemented inadequate, the government felt unable to embrace stronger methods through fear of alienating British public opinion.[46] Consequently, the British response to the protraction of the conflict was both half-hearted and counterproductive.

The decision to accept the Treaty was reinforced by Collins' pessimistic assessment of the IRA's prospects should the war have been resumed. In the months before the truce the IRA had begun to come under severe pressure. Civilian morale had been affected by the reprisals of the crown forces, and, as a result, citizens were more wary of co-operating with the IRA.[47] Also, the IRA became more vulnerable as the British intelligence system recovered from its initial setbacks. Of greatest immediate concern was the acute shortage of arms. For example, one commander, Liam Lynch, told Collins that the shortage in the Cork area had become critical.[48] Collins is even said to have remarked that the British had been mad to offer a truce when they did, as the IRA would not have lasted another three weeks.[49]

Collins' appraisal was probably coloured by the condition of the IRA in Dublin, which was close to breaking point, whereas the situation in the rest of the country varied from area to area. In the south west, for instance, Tom Barry felt that the IRA 'was a stronger and more effective striking force than at any time in its history'.[50] None of this detracted from the decision to negotiate. The IRA did not have the power to force its terms on the British. Therefore, talks with the British were a necessity if republicans wished to advance towards their objectives. However, the timing of the truce was crucial. The point was that the IRA had survived long enough for Britain's will to falter first. This gave the republicans an important psychological edge in the negotiations which they could exploit to gain concessions. To have continued the war for the sake of it, especially as the IRA had reached, and arguably already passed, its optimum operational capacity,[51] would have been futile as it would merely have weakened the republican negotiating position. This assessment is reinforced if we look at the impact of the truce on the IRA itself. Initially, many IRA personnel believed the truce would be only a temporary affair; a time to rest and re-equip. At most it was expected to last a few weeks before hostilities recommenced.[52] In truth, this belief was probably subverted the moment the fighting stopped. With the beginning of the truce tensions eased and discipline slackened. IRA members now moved openly among the population, thereby losing much of the anonymity upon which a guerrilla force relies for its efficacy. Tom Barry sensed the corrosive effects of the truce on the organisation. Its members were not professional soldiers. In peacetime there was no-one to look after them: 'They couldn't afford to stay around training and maintaining a state of readiness.' As a consequence Barry estimated 'that by the time the Treaty was signed there was at least a 30 per cent deterioration in our effectiveness and our structure and our morale'.[53] To have restarted the war from the truce would possibly have fatally disadvantaged the IRA campaign. All things considered, Collins concluded that: 'We had reached the high-water mark of what we could do in the way of economic and military resistance.'[54] The Irish delegation was prepared to reach an agreement on this basis. Essentially, what Michael Collins and his pragmatic associates understood was that at the political level the type of war in which they had been engaged was essentially a bargaining process where threats and counter threats could be traded. Some of Collins' more purist compatriots found themselves unable to relate to this conception of warfare.

THE TREATY SETTLEMENT AND THE CLASH OF STRATEGIC PERSPECTIVES

On 7 January 1922 the Dail ratified the Treaty by sixty-four votes to fifty-seven. A Provisional government was set up under the terms of the Treaty as an interim administration to pave the way for elections to the Free State Parliament. For those who supported the Treaty settlement the period from 1916 to 1921 counted as a solid success. Republicans had shown that, by adapting their military methods to harness their traditional strengths of tenacity and fortitude, they could fight a prolonged war against a vastly more powerful opponent and, in so doing, achieve positive political results. The pro-Treatyites regretted that their efforts in the Anglo-Irish war had been unable to secure the republic they desired. However, they tried to place the settlement into some sort of historical perspective. The view of those like Collins was that the tradition of nationalist struggle had not been a remorseless march towards the unfettered independence of a united republic, more a case of sporadic resistance to the slow but inexorable absorption of Irish national identity into British culture. The Treaty halted this process of Anglicisation.[55] It provided for the evacuation of British forces, the creation of a national army, as well as for full internal autonomy over fiscal and social policy. To the pragmatists, all this was far too important to be endangered by some pedantic debate over republican emblems. It was substance which mattered. This did not mean that the pragmatists had abandoned their commitment to a republic. The Treaty was simply a means of stopping the rot. Above all, they saw the Treaty as a device which Ireland could use to extricate itself from British domination in all its manifestations. According to one pro-Treaty newspaper:

> The shortest way to the full Republic is not through barren wrangles over unrealities, but through the path opened by the Treaty. The Republic will not be conjured out of the vasty deep by an incantation: in a world of might and the use of might it will take shape when a consolidated and united people have evolved the power to assert it.[56]

However, as the vote in the Dail indicated, there was a large dissenting minority who remained unconvinced by the pro-Treaty case. For them, the Treaty was no reward for the years of sacrifice. The Free State was not the united, independent republic for which they had been fighting, but merely a partitioned, quasi-autonomous dominion. The anti-Treaty faction were unable to reconcile themselves to the idea that the settlement could be used as a stepping stone to a republic. They regarded the Treaty with dismay, suspicion and bitter hostility. How was it, then, that a Treaty negotiated by appointees of the Dail could prove so unacceptable to such a sizeable part of the republican movement? The answer discloses not simply shades of disagreement over nuance, timing and direction, but the presence within the same movement of two entirely different modes of thinking and strategic approach.

For the anti-Treatyites the concept of the republic held great meaning. In their view, the republic was an actuality. It had been proclaimed in 1916 and estab-lished by the elected representatives of the Dail in 1919. Further, all of those involved with the movement during the Anglo-Irish war had formally sworn to 'defend the Irish Republic and the Government of the Irish Republic, which is Dail Eireann, against all enemies, foreign and domestic'.[57] Anything which interfered with the notion of the republic was deemed to be an illegal trans-gression against the lawfully constituted authority in Ireland. The existence of the republic was considered an unalterable fact:

> There is only one legitimate Government in Ireland – the Government of the Irish Republic. Even the most extreme of the Slave State [pro-Treaty] party admit that the Dail Eireann is the supreme authority in the country. The Irish Republic is the Republic of all Ireland, not twenty-six counties merely, and to it every citizen of Ireland owes allegiance.[58]

From the point of view of the doctrinaire republicans, the Anglo-Irish war had never been about fighting *for* something – concessions, negotiating positions, compromises, etc. – but about safeguarding a pre-existing entity. As a conse-quence, any subsequent political arrangement that failed to sustain the republic would be seen as a humiliation because it would mean the actual loss of something to which they had been supremely committed. For example, speaking in 1925, Eamon de Valera, who led the opposition to the Treaty, stated that he had rejected the settlement because it meant the 'disestablishment of the Republic – the State established on the will of the people – the State which I had been elected to uphold and defend', and because it entailed 'the surrender of the sovereignty of this nation to an outside power'.[59]

The explanation for the anti-Treatyites' attitude can be traced initially to the monochrome view of Britain's guilt which seemed to prevent republicans from making any allowance for the change in political circumstances brought about by the Anglo-Irish war. Their complete aversion to any form of British influence meant that they found it difficult to distinguish qualitative differences in political relationships between Britain and Ireland. Therefore, a loose connection with Britain was almost as bad as an all-engulfing British presence. Of particular concern in this respect was the requirement under the Treaty of an oath of allegiance to the British monarch. This was felt to be especially demeaning, not only because it violated their oath to the republic, but also because it meant accepting a lingering affinity with the evil British empire. What had been the point of two and a half years of war if at the end of it republicans had to swear allegiance to the very enemy they had been fighting to rid from Ireland? 'Are they', the anti-Treatyites enquired of the pragmatists, 'ready to avow that there is a common citizenship, a community of race, of language, of ideas, of ideals, of aspirations, between them and, for instance, the British Black and Tans?'[60] Nor were the anti-Treatyites persuaded by the pragmatists' argument that the oath of allegiance was simply a meaningless formality. 'Mr. Collins . . . says the Oath is only symbolical. Just so. But the symbol to which he swore fidelity and wants the Irish people to cry "Amen", is the symbol of England's sovereignty in Ireland.'[61]

The conviction of the doctrinaire republicans that clauses in the Treaty, like the oath of allegiance, were not simply trivial affectations to satisfy Britain's pretence at imperial control, but were absolute and binding, ruled out any thought that the Treaty could be built on in the future. One anti-Treaty publication declared:

> The people who talk of the Free State being a step towards the Republic do not realise the almost utter impossibility of raising Ireland from the status of a partly contented country whose highest and noblest rights and interests are denied, to the full status of sovereign independence.[62]

Exhibited here are various overtones which indicate that the doctrinaires' stand over the Treaty arose from a mixture of nationalist-elitism, suspicion of Britain and unwavering loyalty to the republican vision. The 'no-half-way-house' attitude of many republicans suggested that the extension of the Treaty would be hopeless because it had been specifically designed to preserve British interests by staving off full Irish independence. As a result, the Treaty was not an advance but a step back because once British concessions had defused the nationalist threat, the Irish people would lose the inclination to seek the real republic. In the doctrinaires' highly polarised view, the Treaty was nothing more than a dead-end which undermined all the principles of republicanism.

To the pro-Treaty faction all this was incomprehensible. They were sceptical of the contention that the Treaty would somehow legally oblige Ireland in perpetuity to relinquish any claim to greater independence. Would those anti-Treatyites who propounded this view, the pragmatists asked, feel duty bound themselves to abide by such an obligation? Not even the most rigid republican was reckoned to be that naive. The pragmatists sensed that the argument was merely a scare story to dissuade people from voting for pro-Treaty candidates in the parliamentary elections due in June 1922. Supporters of the Treaty predicted, accurately as it turned out, that the 'very men who assert now that the Treaty will bind Ireland in honour for ever will assert the contrary as soon as the elections are over'.[63]

More consequentially, the pragmatists saw in the anti-Treatyite position an obsessive concern for 'theories and abstractions which for the sake of appearing to preserve a sham is ready to enter into a covenant of eternal association with England'.[64] How could anyone, they wondered, be so preoccupied with something which did not exist except in the symbolic form of proclamations, declarations and a few gestures at republican government during the Anglo-Irish war? The republic was an aspiration. It was never a power-reality. 'The enemy were pushed back from the unchallenged usurpation of the functions of civil government into standing on naked military strength,' said an article in *The Free State*, 'But they had the military strength and they stood on it. There was no town in Ireland where our flag could fly with impunity for a day.'[65] To profess blind adherence to a mythical republic was not regarded as a quaint act of loyalty to an inspiring dream but a dangerous inability to separate the ideal from reality: the failure to discriminate what were essentially propaganda moves intended to influence world opinion from the fact that a functioning, sovereign republic had not been established as a power political reality.

The pragmatists refuted any suggestion that their arguments were based on the lame acceptance of Irish impotence in the face of British strength and the foreswearing of any right to pursue republican goals. Their reasoning was that as the republic never physically existed then the ideal could not have been betrayed. Nor could the Treaty kill it as an aspiration. Their position over the Treaty was outlined thus: 'The continuance of the struggle for independence is a question of tactics. It is not a question of principle. . . . All tactics must be judged by their success, and the key to success is adaptability.'[66] This statement indicated that the debate over the rather distractive issues of the oath and the materiality of the republic masked a more serious dispute over differing perceptions of power and the extent of the utility of violence in the political process. As time went on, it became clear that the clash was so fundamental that it would not be resolved without further conflict. Therein lay the path which would lead Ireland to civil war.

The doctrinaire faction also believed firmly that the success of the IRA's military campaign should have enabled the movement to have gained its full demands. They assumed it was only the actions of the weak-willed Irish delegation that threw away this opportunity. One republican writer claimed that guerrilla methods had 'brought victory within our grasp and placed the nation in the same position that a victory in the field would have done'. He continued: 'The methods did not fail, the men who should have reaped the harvest sown by these same methods did.'[67] This allegation represents the crux of the anti-Treatyites' critique. So what is the validity of the claim that the Treaty supporters threw away the elements of victory? Merely because the IRA was successful at fighting the British to a stalemate did not equate to a victory on the field of battle. The British capacity for physical resistance had not been eliminated, therefore the republicans could not be expected to prescribe the terms of a settlement. If no outright victory was achieved then any overall settlement was always likely to be an expression of a politico-military situation in which neither side has been able to prevail over the other.

It seems plain that the anti-Treaty republicans identified military indecision with total victory in war. We can see this connection in the following anti-Treaty pronouncement: 'The English can never come back. Ireland beat the Tyrant to a standstill last year. England only made a truce because she could not fight on. England will never come back.'[68] The association of a military standstill with the idea that the enemy *could* not fight on infers that, as far as the doctrinaire republicans were concerned, the truce had been offered, not out of any British reluctance to further embroil themselves in a small but politically damaging conflict, but because Britain had been physically compelled to discontinue the fight. The supposition seemed to gel in the minds of many republicans that the truce signified Britain's defeat and willingness to give in. From a hardline republican angle, it is easy to understand how such a perception might have arisen. After years of prevarication and obstruction over the issue of Irish self-government, the IRA's military campaign had forced the British to relinquish the greater part of their control over Irish affairs. By any standard this was a major accomplishment. It cannot be surprising that many republicans felt it their right to dictate terms. That any thought of reneging on the demand for full independence was so repugnant to republican hardliners can be attributed, in part, to the belief that it would be impossible to sell-out an overwhelmingly advantageous military position. In reality, of course, circumstances were far more ambiguous. One can surmise that the successful execution of most IRA operations in the Anglo-Irish war may well have led many republicans to overstate the impact of their military campaign. Since the IRA's actions had not diminished British military power to any significant degree, it was improbable that Britain would have conceded in peace what had not been won in war. So it was to be expected that Britain would use the fact of its continuing military might in Ireland to bargain down any demand for a full republic. As a consequence, during the tough negotiations in London between October and December 1921, the British threatened the resumption of full-scale hostilities unless the Irish delegation came to terms; thereby reminding the Irish delegation of the limited scale of the IRA's military achievement, which, as Richard Mulcahy reiterated to his colleagues in the Dail, had been no more than to chase the British out of a few 'fairly good sized police barracks'.[69]

The anti-Treatyites' inflated impression of republican power sprang from the apparent conviction that the communication of threat flowed only in one direction – from the IRA to the British. This seemed to inform the rather curious notion that while republicans were entitled to exert the maximum leverage earned by their military efforts to demand what they liked, the British should somehow not be similarly permitted to use their superior strength on the ground to protect their own interests. The effect was to render hardline republican elements oblivious to any idea that the British could themselves pressurise the Irish delegates to reach a political settlement which fell short of a republic. This was demonstrated by remarks made by Austin Stack, an opponent of the Treaty, who recalled that at the Dail Cabinet's first meeting after the signing of the Treaty, 'Mr. [Arthur] Griffith [the leader of the Irish delegation], if I remember aright, would not admit duress by the British. Mr. Collins said if there was duress it was only the "duress of facts", whatever he meant by that.'[70]

When it became clear to the anti-Treatyites that Britain had indeed used the 'duress of facts' to force the Irish delegation to sign the Treaty, they came up with the exotic allegation that the Treaty was invalid because it did not represent the true aspirations of the Irish people. In 1926 de Valera restated the basis of the argument: 'We again challenge those who proclaim that this State has been established by the will of the Irish people, to allow a plebiscite to be taken with the threat of force removed.' De Valera believed that 'even those who accepted the Treaty had only done so under the threat of "immediate and terrible war"'.[71] It was this kind of simplistic attitude towards the political process which so exasperated the pragmatists. The doctrinaire view was treated with scorn. How could popular opinion be gauged, they asked, without regard to outside factors?

> The national will, according to this theory, must not be based on a consider-ation of existing facts but must be interpreted as being what the people might be expected to wish if these unpleasant facts were non-existent, and if the national will were functioning *in vacuo*, free from all external influence or pressure.[72]

It was erroneous, therefore, to assert that political decisions could be decided in the context of a 'national vacuum'. Such a context, if it had any basis in reality at all, could only come about through the wholesale defeat of the enemy. Plainly, since the republican movement had not performed such a military feat, then public approval for the Treaty could not be measured against some abstract ideal. In these circumstances, the pragmatists reasoned, 'the will of the people re-cognises perforce, as does the will of an individual, the limitations of physical conditions'.[73] The hard truth, as the pragmatists saw it, was that there was no option but to accept the fact of Ireland's comparative weakness. 'There is no doubt', said *The Free State*, 'as to where the preponderance of power lay when the Dail decided to go to London to talk about a settlement.'[74] Accordingly, the pragmatists acknowledged that the Irish plenipotentiaries were sent to London 'to get the best terms possible but with practically no hope of bringing back an ideal Republic'.[75]

The basic inconsistency in the doctrinaire republican position was to consent to talks in the first place. If a republic was the minimum guarantee acceptable to the republican movement, nothing being negotiable up to that point, then logic demanded that the war should have been continued until this principle had been conceded. Yet the very act of agreeing to the truce and to the peace talks signalled that both sides were willing to retreat from their previous rhetorical positions. The pragmatists called attention to the fact that de Valera 'did not stipulate recognition of the Irish Republic as a basis for the Peace parleys'.[76] The farthest de Valera went in setting pre-conditions was to tell Lloyd George that there could be no satisfactory outcome to the talks if the British denied 'Ireland's essential unity and set aside the principle of national self-determination'.[77] In the end, de Valera accepted the British invitation to negotiate on the even vaguer proposition of 'ascertaining how the association of Ireland with the community of Nations known as the British Empire may be best reconciled with Irish national aspirations'.[78]

The anti-Treaty followers were not simply confused over the approach to the negotiations, but appeared to have *no* concept of negotiations. This outlook extended back to the apparent inability of the doctrinaires to comprehend that, in the type of conflict in which they were involved, war was essentially a political bargaining process where threat and counter-threat are exchanged to induce conciliation and concession. The hardliners' antagonism towards the Treaty was seemingly predicated on the outright mistrust of the nature of the political process itself; the belief that the Irish delegation had been undercut less by the frailty in the republican military position so much as the artful perfidy of British diplomacy and the gullibility of the delegates themselves. The politicians in the British delegation, de Valera once declared, 'treated their pledges and their promises as scraps of paper to be flung to the wind'.[79] The disillusion in republican ranks, the feeling that they had been tricked out of their advantageous position, was certainly a factor which reinforced the traditional view of the political environment as one of improbity and duplicity. The ideological root of the misgivings concerning peaceful political discourse can be traced back to the unconditional nature of republican ideology. The doctrinaire view of the political arena was that it lay in the orbit of absolutes which demanded the complete fulfilment of all political objectives in one go. The Treaty offended against republican shibboleths as it adulterated the doctrinaire ideal by compromising with the vile British enemy. Overall, the controversy surrounding the negotiations and settlement of 1921 provides an illuminating contrast between a strategic interpretation of the Anglo-Irish Treaty, as represented by the pragmatists, and the doctrinaire approach which was unable to address how to get around British power, as it excluded any thought of tactical compromise, no matter how small or temporary, because anything short of the absolute was considered an irredeemable defeat.

Maybe the main point of contention regarding the period from 1919 to 1921 is not of a strategic nature at all but boils down to one question, to which there can be no conclusive answer: this is quite simply, was the Anglo-Irish Treaty worth the Anglo-Irish war? Did the concessions justify the sacrifices? Did the republicans of 1921 really get much more than the home rulers were promised before the First World War? The IRA leader, Tom Barry, once contemptuously remarked: 'It wasn't a treaty at all, it was an imposition on the Irish people. . . . Redmond could probably have got that for us without a drop of blood being spilt.'[80]

THE EXPOSURE OF THE WEAKNESSES IN IRA STRATEGY IN THE CIVIL WAR

It would be unfair to caricature all those who opposed the Anglo-Irish Treaty as leaden hardliners. There were more moderate elements represented by those like de Valera who were, to a degree, prepared to be more flexible. The basis of their opposition to the Treaty was not that all republican objectives could have been met but that a better bargain could have been struck. But it was never made clear by any of the anti-Treaty republicans exactly how they proposed to extract better terms from the British. Instead, the anti-Treatyites sustained their opposition with nebulous appeals such as that contained in *The Nation* which promised that 'if the Republicans win out' then the 'rottenness of British imperialism will no longer corrupt the hearts of the weak people here'. *The Nation* went on: 'Think what a rapid growth of our great nation MUST follow the break with England. Is this not worth any temporary sacrifice?'[81] The pragmatists suspected that 'temporary sacrifice' meant plunging Ireland back into war with Britain without any defined purpose. These suspicions were confirmed by the reported remarks of Eamon de Valera at a meeting in Cork in February 1922, when he had declared that Ireland should be prepared 'to go another round in the race'.[82] The pro-Treatyites attacked any such intimations of further conflict as an 'insane gamble' that would jeopardise the gains already made under the Treaty 'on the remote chance of our being able to worst England in a physical struggle, in which England this time will not be hampered in her *modus operandi* by any considerations as to what the rest of the world may think'.[83] Later in March, de Valera was even more explicit when he warned that 'in order to achieve freedom' the anti-Treaty IRA would have 'to march over the dead bodies of their own brothers'.[84]

The probability of civil strife suggested by de Valera was really the inevitable result of the intractable divisions over the Treaty, as one anti-Treaty tract, reflecting on the outbreak of the fratricide, explained:

For five terrible years the nation had remained united on three great principles: 1) The existence of the Republic founded in Easter Week and confirmed by national plebiscite in 1918; 2) The sanctity of our national independence declared by the Sovereign National Assembly in January 1919; and 3) The territorial integrity of Ireland, which had outlasted history itself. . . . The Treaty violated those fundamental principles, destroying the Republic, surrendering our national independence, partitioning our ancient nation. . . . Sooner or later nothing but war could have followed from so overwhelming a surrender of national rights.[85]

In March 1922 the split between the two republican factions was formalised when a General Convention of the IRA, attended mainly by anti-Treatyites, repudiated the authority of the Dail and elected its own executive. The anti-Treaty IRA, or 'Irregulars' as they were called, set up their headquarters in the centre of Dublin, in an area known as the Four Courts, in defiance of the Free State government. Pressed by the British to deal with the Irregulars, Free State forces besieged the Four Courts on 28 June 1922. This signalled the beginning of the Irish civil war which lasted until May 1923. There is no precise record of the human cost of the war. Estimates vary between 800 and 4,000 killed.

The Irregulars were quickly driven out of Dublin and back to their strongholds in the south and west, where they reverted to the same type of guerrilla tactics used in the Anglo-Irish war. Yet the outbreak of hostilities exposed the insubstantial nature of the IRA's strategic thinking. There is no conspicuous evidence to indicate that the IRA had any distinct ideas about how to apply the military instrument to achieve its political objectives. As far as Ernie O'Malley could discern, the IRA had no military plans:

> It looked as if we would be worn down piecemeal, but men seemed to think that we could carry out much the same tactics as we used against the British. During the first month no definite operations orders had been issued and in many instances Republicans awaited attack.[86]

The most plausible explanation of the IRA's conduct was that it was attempting to draw Britain back into Ireland. This might have brought the republican factions together to resist the common enemy.[87] O'Malley confirmed that before the outbreak of the war some members of the anti-Treaty IRA Executive had advocated attacking the remaining British forces in Ireland in the belief that 'A fight would probably unite the Staters and Republicans; some of the Staters would want to fight with us'.[88] Certainly, the general tenor of anti-Treaty propaganda during the civil war seemed to imply that this may have been the intention:

> War with united forces against England is preferable to civil war – so the people thought; but [William] Cosgrave [the Free State Prime Minister] does not think so. He who was so timid against the English is most fierce against his fellow countrymen. He who was unwilling to spend the economic resources of war against England cannot bring himself to make peace to save the resources of Ireland, resources which will be wasted in a war against his fellow countrymen, whom he can never beat.[89]

It is difficult to envisage how any plan to reinvolve Britain could have been tenable. The pragmatists had always felt that further conflict with Britain could only end in 'a new parley with the enemy under infinitely worse conditions'.[90] The Free Staters thought that the Irregulars' objective in the civil war was to 'compel the country, thus shattered and disorganised, to take up arms once more against the ordered and disciplined power of the British Empire'.[91] The prospect of fighting a double war, one to unite the republican movement and another against the British, was regarded with horror, as the pro-Treaty newspaper, *The*

Irish People, emphasised: 'The leaders – the inventors of this policy – can hardly be considered sane. The astonishing thing is that they have succeeded in inducing any sane man to follow them.'[92] The Free State's room for manoeuvre was very limited. With the British unlikely to tolerate any accommodation between the two republican factions which broke the terms of the Treaty, it was unclear how Irregular resistance could have inspired a change in attitude by the Free State. Besides, the very basis of the pragmatists' case rested on the argument that the Treaty gave Ireland the substance of independence and protected the people from armed British reintervention.[93] With their principal objectives satisfied, the pragmatists could not realistically be expected to acquiesce to the return of the British. Such a prospect, it was feared, would not only inflict more suffering and hardship, but under such circumstances the British might even be welcomed back as peace keepers by the bulk of the Irish population.[94]

In actuality, the doctrinaires' alternative to the Treaty did not encompass any concrete design to lead Ireland from the Treaty to something tangibly better. Rather, they were holding out the profoundly metaphysical reward of maintaining the purity of the republican ideal. Appealing to the Irish people to reject the Treaty, the doctrinaire republicans issued the following entreaty:

> you are asked, asked simply, by the historic nation speaking through its protagonists in our time to remain true to the spiritual inheritance of Nationality that has been handed down to you through the ages, and preserve it, and pass it on to your children, pure, unsullied and uncompromised, as you receive it from the men who fought and fell in Easter Week and as they received it from the freedom fighting generations that preceded them.[95]

Similarly, right at the start of the civil war the Irregulars tried to rally support by invoking the devotional mysticism of republican ideology: 'The sacred spirits of the Illustrious Dead are with us in this great struggle. "Death before Dishonour", being an unchanging principle of our national faith as it was theirs, still inspires us to emulate their glorious effort.'[96]

One can gather from the appeals to the tradition of heroic martyrdom that the military instrument, as practised by the IRA in the civil war, was not wielded as a functional tool to make political headway on the Treaty, but as a means of preserving historical continuity in order to make another violent stand to ensure the apostolic succession. This understanding is important as it helps us to comprehend a possible strategic rationale for the doctrinaires' conduct in the civil war. In particular, it helps to answer the question as to why the anti-Treaty IRA continued to prosecute the war for a further ten months in the face of overt public hostility. After all, the Treaty settlement had been ratified by the Dail and approved by the people in the elections of June 1922 which returned a large majority of pro-Treaty representatives. If the doctrinaires were interested purely in making a token stand against the Treaty as a marker for future republican generations, then they could just as well have retired, honour satisfied, after the initial fighting in Dublin. The reason for the IRA's persistence can be discovered with reference to the ideological underpinnings of the republican strategic tradition.

Of special relevance in this respect were the concepts of absolutism and the nationalist vanguard. It has been mentioned above that any solution which did not provide for the absolute fulfilment of republican goals was unacceptable in the minds of many doctrinaires. The Treaty was rejected out of hand. It did not matter how public opinion regarded the settlement. Their loyalty was to the republican vision, not to the Irish people. The doctrinaire outlook simply did not admit the possibility that changes in popular attitudes could affect their strategic calculus. So they felt no need to moderate or adapt their views to take account of changing political conditions, because no individual or group had the right to place restrictions on Irish independence, as de Valera stated plainly: 'The majority have no right to do wrong.'[97] In this sense, the civil war meant very different things to each side. For the Free State, the central issue of the war was the 'defence of the rights and liberties of the Irish people . . . against the attempt by an armed band to rule by virtue of their revolvers'.[98] For the anti-Treatyites, the war was the continuation of the eternal struggle between those who wanted the unalloyed republic and those who would traitorously oppose it.

Although many republicans saw their actions as an expression of private morality rather than as an outgrowth of popular feeling, they did believe that a violent stimulus administered to the body politic could also serve a direct strategic purpose by drawing out the latent republican sympathies of the Irish people. The precedent for this was the 1916 rising which had succeeded in overcoming public hostility to help galvanise the national effort in the Anglo-Irish war. It was the doctrinaires' belief that the 1916 Rising had 'washed the scales from the eyes of the Irish people and enabled them again to see, and to follow the path, the only path, that leads to liberty and Independence'.[99] Similarly, the anti-Treatyites hoped that exemplary violence, combined with republican mysticism, would prove as effective in crystallising public support in the civil war as it had been in the Anglo-Irish war. This belief is reflected in the anti-Treatyites' literature during the civil war which was full of 1916 metaphors: 'the Republic consecrated by Pearse and Connolly, and the dearest and noblest of our patriots', proclaimed one anti-Treaty paper, 'is once more fighting for its life. Citizens, defend your Republic.'[100] In the same way, the Irregulars attempted to appeal to the nationalistic feelings of the Free State Army by comparing its role to that of the RIC in the Anglo-Irish war:

> The RIC were Irishmen to whom England gave arms and orders. Are you any better? You know in your hearts Pearse did not die for the British Empire. . . . Are you going to murder those who carry on their work and the holy cause for which they gave their lives?[101]

By evoking the imagery of republican martyrology, the anti-Treatyites felt they could wean popular sentiment away from the Free State. So the doctrinaire republican perspective did contain a certain strategic logic, though not one which the Free Staters found especially impressive. They heavily criticised the emphasis placed on the role of the republican vanguard in doctrinaire thinking. They argued that most people would reject the false analogies with 1916 and the Anglo-Irish war:

In all developments that have taken place since the approval of the Treaty, the Irregulars have shown a singular incapacity to see their own position.... They were convinced that they had only to imitate one or two details [of the] tactics of the leaders of 1916 in order to induce an indiscriminating public to accept unquestioningly the theory that they were re-doing the work of the heroic men to whose courage and foresight the success of the past six years is due. They will not get the support and co-operation of the people, they will never be looked upon as the successors of the flying columns which harried the British last year and the year before.[102]

The events of the civil war bore out the pragmatists' analysis by revealing the doctrinaires' flawed assumptions about violence as a mobilising factor. Moreover, the war corroborated the pragmatists' argument about the fragility of the republican military position in the Anglo-Irish war and the constraints which that imposed on the ability to achieve political objectives. It is somewhat paradoxical that while the doctrinaires were readily identifiable as the most bellicose of the two factions, it was the pragmatists' willingness to accept the limitations of the republican capacity for armed conflict with the British which betrayed the far more hard-headed appreciation of the function of the military instrument in the political process. The pragmatists saw themselves as heirs to the old Fenians, who they asserted 'recognised clearly the influence of force', and who were 'out to beat the enemy and were held back by no unsoldierly scruples'.[103] The Fenians, it was said, cared little for the fantasies of a mythical republic. They were acute realists who were easily reconciled to the harsh world of power politics: 'They knew that in international affairs it is the military position which rules the issue. They did not waste time and eloquence standing oratorically on the Rock of Right.'[104] In the civil war, the Free State applied this philosophy with ruthless efficiency. On 2 October 1922 the Free State instituted special Military Courts to deal with those charged with attacking, or conspiring to attack, the forces of the state. Such offences were to be punishable by death, penal servitude, imprisonment, deportation, internment or fines.[105]

The doctrinaires accused the Provisional Free State government of being 'a military Junta set up and armed by England' in order to wage a 'war of aggression against the forces of the Irish Republic'.[106] The Free State, they said, was 'in exactly the same position as the British Enemy were before the truce.... The machinery is the same; the lying propaganda; the midnight terrorism; the murder of prisoners of war: These are England's methods.'[107] Although there were certain similarities, the direct comparison of the Free State's conduct with that of the British in the Anglo-Irish war was inaccurate. For a start, the emergency laws enacted by the Free State were far more repressive and systematically applied than anything introduced by the British. The Free State's policy towards the IRA was ferocious. By the end of the war seventy-seven IRA men had been executed, three times the number executed by the British between 1919 and 1921.[108] Yet the Irregulars' analogy with the repression of the British illustrated the misapprehensions under which their campaign laboured. The crucial point was that the implementation of the Treaty had altered the political climate in Ireland and this permitted the Free State to adopt sweeping counter-insurgency measures without incurring the same negative political consequences experienced by the British in the previous two years of fighting. During the Anglo-Irish war, the IRA's greatest asset was the solid backing, or at least toleration, it received from the majority of the Irish people who identified themselves with the IRA's central aim of getting rid of the British. After 1922, with the British gone from most of the country, the IRA found it difficult to sustain the popularity of its cause, as O'Malley came to recognise: 'Now the people, on the whole were against us. . . . We now had to face ourselves and not the English.'[109] With the endorsement of the Treaty at the polls, the Free State leader, William Cosgrave, was prepared to use his mandate to force the IRA to comply with the popular will. He had made his intentions plain at the opening of the Irish parliament on 11 September 1922:

> The Nation which has struggled so long against the most powerful foreign aggression will not submit to an armed minority which makes war upon its liberties. . . . The National Army is prepared to pay the price, and so are we. . . . There is now no reason why blame should be shifted on the British or any other Government blamed if we do not succeed. This Parliament and this Government is of the People and expects to get that support which is essential to a Government and a Parliament.[110]

In effect, the new political atmosphere which the Treaty ushered in stripped the IRA's strategy of its utility. Bolstered by domestic opinion and by external support from the British, the Free State did not feel constrained in seeking a decisive military victory against the Irregulars. In this context, the IRA's strategy, which aimed to disrupt the popular base of the Free State through low level military actions, became all but meaningless. Such a strategy could only be successfully employed, as in the Anglo-Irish war, as a result of some degree of forbearance on the part of the stronger belligerent which would allow the weaker side to endure and eventually break the opponent's political will. But if the stronger side attaches few self-imposed restraints to its conduct then the conflict will not be presented in these terms as there will be little or no moral dimension for the weaker side to exploit. The war will simply become a contest over who has the ability to commit the greatest military resources to the conflict. If the stronger belligerent is prepared to use its resources in a brutal and probably, to some extent, indiscriminate fashion, then all the advantages a guerrilla organisation might have enjoyed will disappear as small-scale raids will make little impression on a well armed and determined adversary. This is what happened in the Irish civil war. The anti-Treatyites 'asked the nation to endure that it might be free'.[111] Yet the fierce suppression of the Irregulars and their sympathisers denied them the opportunity to make political capital out of a protracted conflict as they simply could not *endure* the overwhelming onslaught of the state.

THE DEVELOPMENT OF IRISH REPUBLICAN STRATEGIC THOUGHT, 1916–1923 – THE UNFINISHED REVOLUTION AND THE INCOMPLETE STRATEGY

By early 1923, having been subjected to the unrelenting assault of the Free State, the IRA reached the point of exhaustion. The conflict continued until late April when the IRA finally succumbed to the inevitable and suspended offensive operations. De Valera, the nominal leader of the anti-Treatyites, told his companions that further resistance would be useless. 'Military victory', he said, 'must be allowed to rest for the moment with those who have destroyed the Republic.'[112]

The end of the Irish civil war brought to a close one of the most impassioned periods in the history of the republican movement. In the first instance, the 1916 rising solidified republican strategic culture, reinforcing the conviction that the actions of a nationalist elite standing in line as the successors of past republican generations could, through their sacrifices, enthuse the bulk of the Irish people to unite around a broad appeal for freedom. The events from 1916 to 1919 still resonate through the republican movement to this day as it is from this epoch that later republicans would draw the inspiration to continue the fight to complete the unfinished task of national liberation. As one republican tract of the mid-1970s put it, the IRA 'owes its allegiance . . . to the 32-county independent Irish Republic as proclaimed in 1916 and endorsed by the Dail in 1919. This is not the Free State; it has yet to be achieved.'[113]

The years between 1916 and 1921 also fortified the belief in armed force as the primary means to achieve the republic. For many republicans, the success of the IRA's campaign in the Anglo-Irish war in dislodging the British from most of Ireland served to authenticate Pearse's maxim that 'Ireland armed will attain ultimately as much freedom as she wants'.[114] Faith in the military instrument was strengthened as a result of the enormous innovations which took place at the tactical level. The younger, more practical, generation of republican leaders who emerged in the aftermath of the 1916 rising were, in the early months of 1919, able to weld the largely extemporaneous violence of bands of Irish Volunteers into a coherent campaign of action. The conduct of the Anglo-Irish war shifted the entire focus of the republican military outlook. Conventional ideas of massed confrontations and decisive victories were discarded in favour of much smaller military encounters which allowed the movement to fight a war of extended duration. In consequence, the guerrilla tactics of the Anglo-Irish war, the killing of policemen and soldiers, attacks on military, government and economic targets, and so on, became enshrined in republican military methodology.

Ultimately, though, the development of republican strategy in this period can only be described as partial because innovations in military techniques were not accompanied by any new thinking at the political level. It was this point that caused the internal divisions over republican strategy and which led Ireland into civil war. The pragmatists in the movement were able to accept that the new guerrilla-orientated strategy could only be used as a limited pressurising tool to extract concessions from the British. In their view, to make advances towards political objectives, republicans would have to show flexibility in their dealings with the British. To the doctrinaires this was heterodoxy. For them, the entrenchment of republican ideology in the wake of the 1916 rising reinforced their antagonism to compromise. Concessions from the British were taken as a sign of the efficacy of violent methods, not as a means of reaching some half-baked deal with their sworn enemy. The failure of the Treaty to live up to the idealism of Pearse, Connolly and all the other republican sages merely hardened their resolve to carry on.

For that section of the movement calling itself the IRA, which would continue the struggle into the civil war, the period from 1916 to 1921 left it dogmatic, inflexible and unable to detect the limits of its capacity to achieve its objectives with its chosen methods. For example, as late as February 1923, when it was evident that the IRA was near to defeat, its Chief of Staff, Liam Lynch, was still promising that 'victory is within our grasp if we stand unitedly and firmly'.[115] Florence O'Donoghue was prompted to comment that Lynch's 'appreciation of the military situation was more optimistic than the facts warranted. . . . He could not and would not face the thought of defeat and collapse of Republican resistance to the imposition of the Treaty.'[116]

What the civil war illustrated above all was the inability of the IRA to appraise critically the utility of armed force in the context in which it sought to practise it. The IRA's campaign appeared to be governed, not with reference to what was realistically attainable through violence, but by ideological imperatives which suggested that the true republic could be achieved through immediate resort to arms with hardly any thought to the consequences, chances of success, or of more effective alternatives. Thus, the IRA ignored one of the most basic strategic principles, that political circumstances will, almost inevitably, affix limits to what is obtainable with the military instrument. This stood in contrast to the IRA's campaign in the Anglo-Irish war. Pragmatic leaders like Michael Collins and Richard Mulcahy were able to appreciate the confines of their strategy. The proficiency of the IRA's campaign between 1919 and 1921 rested on the premise that the more powerful enemy would in some way feel restrained, for political or moral reasons, from bringing the full force of its superiority to bear on its weaker opponent. The skill of the IRA's conduct depended on the manipulation of military engagements to affect political perceptions in Britain to an extent that caused influential sections of British opinion to question the wisdom of Britain's policy in Ireland. Therein lay the main weakness of this type of low intensity strategy, a weakness that the IRA failed to heed in the civil war, which was that the strategy relied exclusively on the exploitation of the psychological, rather than the destructive effects, of armed action, thereby rendering such strategies vulnerable to those who were willing to view the resolution of clashes of interest purely in terms of the tangibles of military power. As the philosopher of war Carl von Clausewitz accurately prophesied:

If the political aims [in war] are small, the motives slight and tensions low, a prudent general may look for any way to avoid major crises and decisive actions, exploit any weaknesses in the opponent's military and political strategy, and reach a peaceful settlement. If his assumptions are sound and promise success we are not entitled to criticise him. But he must never forget he is moving on a devious path where the god of war may catch him unawares.[117]

3 Political control versus the autonomous military instrument

Irish republican strategy from the civil war to the 1970s

From the IRA's initial pronouncements at the outset of the Anglo-Irish war the organisation's status within the republican struggle appeared, at first glance, to be quite obvious. In August 1918, the newspaper *An t-Oglach* said that the Irish Volunteers were a 'military body pure and simple', mere 'agents of the national will'.[1] Similarly, in January 1919 the paper stated that if the Volunteers 'are called on to shed their blood in defence of the new-born Republic, they will not shrink from the sacrifice. For the authority of the nation is behind them, embodied in a lawfully constituted authority.'[2] The implication of such announcements is that the 'lawfully constituted authority' resided in the elected representatives of the 'national will', namely, the Dail. In reality, the situation was more complicated. Far from a harmonious symbiosis, the relationship between the Dail and the IRA was ill-defined and tense because for all practical purposes the two were separate organisations following complementary, but unco-ordinated, policies. There was no better illustration of this position than the outbreak of hostilities in early 1919, which took place without approval from the Dail. The Volunteers believed that the election of the Dail and its declaration of independence had given them the right to pursue the republic in the manner they saw fit.[3] This was indicated in the *An t-Oglach* article of January 1919, which declared that the 'state of war' said to exist between Ireland and England in the Dail's first official address was 'a fact which has been recognised and acted on by the Volunteers almost from their inception'.[4]

As IRA raids grew, which in turn stimulated British repression, so the Dail was presented with a fait accompli. Increasingly, the members of the Dail felt compelled to align themselves with the IRA's campaign. De Valera admitted there was no formal connection between the Dail and the IRA when in April 1919 he announced that the Dail's Minister of Defence, Cathal Brugha, was only in 'close association with the voluntary military forces'.[5] The oath of allegiance to the Dail of August 1919 was administered to the IRA in order to give the impression that the military campaign was politically accountable. In practice, military operations continued unhindered by any political strictures from the Dail. It was only towards the end of the war that the Dail unreservedly accepted responsibility for the IRA's actions. In an interview on 30 March 1921 de Valera stated:

The Army of the Republic is a recognised state force under civil control of elected representatives of the people, with an organisation and discipline imposed by these representatives. . . . The Government is, therefore, responsible for the actions of this army. These are not acts of irresponsible individual groups therefore, nor is the IRA, as the enemy would have one believe, a praetorian guard. It is the national army of defence.[6]

The statement was a complete exaggeration of the Dail's influence over the IRA. It was made for propaganda reasons. Without sanction from the Dail, the IRA's campaign would be seen by the outside world as an uncontrolled series of sporadic murders rather than the actions of an authentic national-liberation movement. Therefore, by openly endorsing the IRA, the Dail could strengthen its bargaining position, as the image of a unified political and military organisation would make it more difficult for the British to use the negotiating process to drive wedges through the movement (though this was exactly what the British were eventually able to do).

Although the moves to establish the Dail's seniority were only paper resolutions to put a veneer of political respectability on the military campaign, they were still resisted by many in the IRA. Even the politically astute Michael Collins was hesitant over the introduction of the Dail's oath of allegiance, fearing it would allow civilian control of military policy.[7] He was later to refer to those in the Dail, such as de Valera, as 'irresponsible meddlers'[8] who he felt were more concerned with criticising the IRA than with defeating the British. Many IRA members felt it was they who were the leading edge of the struggle. It was they who were taking on the British, suffering the hardship and making the sacrifices. They did not feel the need to cede control of the struggle to anyone outside the IRA, even if it was in name only. The essence of the IRA's attitude was captured by Liam Lynch, who was later to become the organisations' Chief of Staff in the civil war, who remarked that: 'The Army has to hew the way for politics to follow.'[9]

The poor state of intra-republican civil–military relations was sharpened in the months preceding the civil war. In early 1922 de Valera was still sounding optimistic that the IRA would adhere to the authority of the Dail over the question of whether to accept or reject the Treaty. Circumstances belied such confidence. Restlessness in IRA ranks over the terms of the Treaty had become swiftly apparent. The unrest was compounded by the disparate command structure which gave IRA units in the localities a large measure of autonomy. The IRA factions most resistant to the Treaty, notably those in the south west, were those which had seen the most fighting. These units were especially difficult to control as they had always been wary of attempts to impose central authority of any kind, be it military or political.[10] It was the firm belief of Rory O'Connor, the leader of the anti-Treaty IRA, that 'the army should be kept apart from politics under separate control'.[11] Indeed, with the repudiation of the Dail in March 1922, and the introduction of a new IRA constitution in April 1922, the IRA arrogated to itself the prerogative to act unilaterally 'to protect the rights and liberties common to the people of Ireland'.[12] The IRA Executive declared that: 'Their opposition to the Treaty is not a matter of interference in politics, but a fulfilment of the object for which they voluntarily banded together, surrendered their personal liberty and offered their lives.'[13]

During the civil war a republican government was set up in October 1922 to present a political face to the Irish people. In spite of de Valera's initial scepticism that a republican government would have any authority, he did agree that it was necessary to 'provide a rallying point and a centre of direction to co-ordinate various efforts in various fields to maintain the Republic'.[14] Such a government was considered essential to try to win back the support of the people which de Valera recognised was 'by far the greatest weakness of our cause at the moment'.[15]

The republican government was a wholly cosmetic exercise and formed too late to have any effect on the anti-Treatyites' position. In any case, de Valera's civilian role in the civil war aroused just as much suspicion within the ranks of the IRA as it had done in the Anglo-Irish war. Rory O'Connor had even remarked that he was 'no more prepared to stand for de Valera than for the Treaty'.[16] In fact, the formation of the republican government made relations between the civil and military wings worse as de Valera resented having to accept public responsibility for the IRA while being denied any influence over its actions.[17]

The IRA's conduct during the civil war was a prime demonstration of how the absence of overt political counsel could affect a military organisation's strategy. There is no evidence that the IRA had thought much about how to use its military resources to proceed from the Ireland of the Treaty to the full independence of the true republic. 'Men did not know what they were fighting for,' opined the veteran republican, Peadar O'Donnell, about the IRA's campaign in the civil war.[18] He observed that there was no IRA strategy worth speaking of, only a simple faith that the republic needed to be protected. The 'devout men' of the IRA, as O'Donnell called them, 'were just not capable of coming down from the high ground of the Treaty. On the simple ground of their allegiance to the Republic, such men would have taken their stand and accepted martyrdom.'[19] What O'Donnell was suggesting was that the IRA's actions did not reflect a coherent plan of action but rather a pre-conditioned ideological reflex to use violence to defend the mythical republic. This was certainly borne out by the IRA's conduct in the war which was bereft of proper planning. The IRA's general headquarters itself had little control over day-to-day operations which were largely determined by local units. Yet the IRA's confidence in the efficacy of force led it to believe that the simple exertion of military pressure, no matter how unco-ordinated, would enable it to dictate terms.[20]

The lack of political steering destroyed any real hope for the IRA in the civil war, as the vague commitment to expunge British influence and unite Ireland did not inform any readily attainable military objectives. If there are no specific objectives in war then the terms of military success cannot be defined, nor can a basis for compromise or negotiations be established. In all wars, individual tactical engagements provide the means to reach intermediate military aims, which are themselves the means to obtain the ultimate objective in war. The enunciation of clear and realistic political goals are vital to establish the relationship between the final object in war and the intermediate stages. In this respect, the poor quality of political guidance in the civil war unhinged the IRA's campaign as it was never spelled out how tactical engagements related to the achievement of the overall strategic goal.

THE DECLINE OF POLITICAL CONTROL OVER THE MILITARY INSTRUMENT IN THE 1920s AND 1930s

Irish republican strategy from the Anglo-Irish war to the civil war evolved, in the main, independently from either internal or external political control. Despite the disaster of the civil war, the experience was to reinforce, rather than dilute, republican idealism in the following years. This reinvigorated commitment was exhibited in the movement's analysis of its failure in the civil war, which focused on narrow problems of tactics and organisation rather than reflecting on whether insufficient political support or the unrealistic expectations of its strategy also played their part. For example, one IRA commander criticised the movement for its use of guerrilla tactics and for not exploiting its superiority in the initial weeks of the war by launching an offensive against Free State forces. In his view, the IRA failed because it 'continued to use the methods adopted by the British to meet an entirely changed situation', and because it lacked the 'unifying machinery', such as a general staff, which could coordinate 'resources as they should have been used'.[21] So what were the elements which made the republican movement so politically unresponsive, with all the negative effects this implied for the IRA's strategic development over the next twenty years?

The course that the republican movement had charted after the civil war appeared set. Its publicity reaffirmed the belief that it was in 'the armed citizens of the broken nation that the deepest hope of the people rests', and that the movement's duty was to build up the IRA in order 'to pick up again the unfinished task of breaking the British connection'.[22] However, there were more politically minded elements, mainly within the anti-Treaty faction of Sinn Fein under de Valera, who looked for other ways to advance the republican cause. De Valera persuaded the movement to contest the 1923 general election in which Sinn Fein did surprisingly well, winning forty-four seats. But the absolutist nature of republican ideology meant that the movement was unable to scan other available options, which in itself was a manifest expression of the lack of political leadership. Unity and sovereignty could only be obtained through armed force. Therefore, the notion of constitutional participation was foreclosed from the start, a fact which inhibited the general fertilisation of political ideas within the movement.

Although Sinn Fein's performance in the 1923 election revealed considerable sympathy for a more nationalistic alternative to the pro-Treaty government of the Cumann na nGaedheal party, abstention from electoral politics held out little prospect of progress within a functioning democracy like the Free State. Many Sinn Fein pragmatists were frustrated by the ideological rigidities of republican doctrine. It had been evident, even after the split over the Treaty, that sections of the anti-Treatyites were unhappy at the IRA's inability to square its absolute demands for a republic with its actual military capabilities. Dissatisfaction was expressed by de Valera when he wrote during the civil war, in late 1922, that: 'What guerrilla warfare leads to is a desire on our opponents' part to come to terms with us, provided these terms do not mean complete surrender by him to us, which is unfortunately what we require.'[23] The subsequent years in the political wilderness convinced many Sinn Fein members that the opportunities for accomplishing republican goals through the constitutional process were sufficiently substantial to warrant a tactical reassessment. Fundamentally, they believed that force could no longer serve a useful purpose within the structure of the Free State. De Valera argued in 1926 that 'a nation within itself ought to be able to settle its polity so that all occasions of civil conflict between its members may be obviated'.[24]

The Sinn Fein pragmatists' view implied ditching the policy of abstention and accepting that political flexibility would be necessary to gain popular support for constitutional changes. Clearly, such an advocacy meant traversing the quagmire of traditional republican philosophy which specifically rejected any move that would give recognition to what was regarded as the illegal Southern parliament. At the IRA Convention of November 1925, the merest hint that de Valera and his colleagues were thinking about the possibility of entering the Irish parliament was enough to prompt the IRA to sever its links with Sinn Fein, because, in the words of the resolution:

> the Government [Sinn Fein] has developed into a mere political party and has apparently lost sight of the fact that all our energies should be devoted to the all-important work of making the Army efficient so that the renegades who, through a coup d'etat, assumed governmental powers in this country be dealt with at the earliest possible opportunity.[25]

The convention consolidated control in the hands of the IRA Executive which further reduced the level of political influence within the movement. The split was formalised at the Sinn Fein Ard Fheis in March 1926 when a proposal put forward by de Valera to contest the next general election was defeated. It was inconceivable that the Sinn Fein pragmatists could prosper in surroundings which were so antagonistic to peaceful political involvement. A day after his resolution failed de Valera and his followers withdrew from Sinn Fein to form a new party, Fianna Fail, which entered the Irish parliament on 12 August 1927. Fianna Fail maintained that, although force was justified, 'There are times, as we all know when, because the odds are too enormous, or because the opportunity for swift blows for liberty do not exist, the use of force does not further the cause of national independence.' The 'kernel of Fianna Fail policy', the party claimed, 'is to keep open for the people a constitutional way of winning their freedom', but emphasised that the goal remained the same as the IRA's, 'namely, the wresting of the whole of Ireland from foreign control and the establishment there of the full sovereignty of the Irish people'.[26]

The IRA's attitude to Fianna Fail was initially favourable. For a while it seemed that the movement would recognise the party as its de facto electoral arm. In mid-1927 the republican movement put forward proposals which would enable the two organisations to co-operate in elections. The IRA demanded Fianna Fail members pledge 'that they will not enter any foreign controlled Parliament as a minority or a majority'.[27] Instead, the IRA argued that if Fianna Fail won a majority of seats, a new assembly should be convened which would repudiate the 1921 Treaty. In effect, this meant a continuation of the abstentionist policy. Fianna Fail spurned the IRA plan. In response, the IRA chose to restate its principal belief that the goal of the republic could 'more surely be achieved by the means set forth in the Constitution, namely: 1 "Force of Arms." 2 "Organising, training and equipping the manhood of Ireland as an effective military force" '. In addition, it was reiterated that 'the creation of a revolutionary situation favourable for military action should be supported actively by all Volunteers'.[28] Later, in the early 1930s, the IRA openly backed Fianna Fail in the hope that a Fianna Fail government would be more tolerant of the movement's activities than the Cumman na nGaedheal government.[29] In actuality, though, there was little love lost between the two. Once in office, Fianna Fail called for a fusion of republican forces; in effect a call for the IRA to disband. The IRA refused, rejecting 'sentimental and meaningless pleas for unity' on the grounds that 'the ultimate aim upon which the Fianna Fail party was founded – the restoration of the Republic of Ireland – seems to have been lost sight of'.[30]

The rising popularity of Fianna Fail began to erode the republican movement's support. In 1926 the movement was thought to have a membership of around 20,000–25,000. By 1929 it had fallen to some 5,000.[31] The spectre of impending political obscurity encouraged left-wing republicans, like Peadar O'Donnell and George Gilmore, to try to broaden the appeal of the movement by hitching the nationalist standard to social policies which addressed popular grievances. Socialist-republicans initially looked back for inspiration to the writings of Liam Mellows, an IRA member executed by the Free State in the civil war, who had argued for the 'Republican political and military outlooks to be co-ordinated'.[32] To that end he suggested that the Dail's Democratic Programme of 1919, which declared the 'right of the people of Ireland to the ownership of Ireland',[33] be 'translated into something definite' to ensure that the 'great body of the workers are kept on the side of independence'.[34] By the mid-1920s socialist-republicans were becoming increasingly prominent. The break with Sinn Fein in late 1925 was engineered in part by O'Donnell who believed that the party was a traditionalist deadweight which would obstruct moves to radicalise the IRA.[35] In 1931, to facilitate his plans, O'Donnell set up a party of 'Workers and Working Farmers' called Saor Eire, which aimed at the 'mobilisation of the mass of the Irish people behind a Revolutionary Government, for the overthrow of British Imperialism and its allies in Ireland'.[36] Later in 1934 O'Donnell and Gilmore tried to fashion a broader 'anti-imperialist' coalition called the Republican Congress.[37] These developments necessitated some revision in the role of the military instrument. By 1927 commentaries in *An Phoblacht*, of which Peadar

O'Donnell was editor, were beginning to question traditional assumptions about the utility of physical force and to indicate the need for a more politically responsive organisation. One article asserted that the 'superficial knowledge which most Irishmen have of their native country has led to our boundless faith in the efficacy of guerrilla warfare as a means of freeing this country'.[38] The article continued:

> It is no uncommon thing to meet a patriotic Irishman, who, placing all of our past heroes who fought against England in the same category, jumps to the conclusion that as the cause for which they fought and the principles which they held were, broadly speaking, the same, therefore the methods of warfare which they used cannot be improved upon. The utter absurdity of this proposition will be evident to everyone who realises that all warfare and strategy must be placed on the living conditions of a people.[39]

The socialist-republican critique expanded into a fully-fledged advocacy to 'undo the British conquest' in all its forms which entailed the dismantling of native Irish capitalism and the return of all 'wealth producing sources' to the people.[40] All the same, the proponents of this programme were anxious to retain the support of the conservative elements within the movement by stressing that the nationalist and socio-economic struggles were complementary, not exclusive, as George Gilmore sought to elucidate:

> In answer to certain people who are suggesting that we are 'sullying the flag' by introducing 'bread-and-butter politics' and that we should keep our movement on a higher and spiritual plane. I say that the spiritual life of a nation is not a thing apart from its material welfare but that it can be compared to a blossom growing from its own roots.[41]

By 1936 the republican movement's socialist initiatives had collapsed in a welter of internal bickering and public indifference.[42] Both Saor Eire and the Republican Congress were attempts to stem the flow of support towards Fianna Fail, which was becoming increasingly unsympathetic towards the IRA. Following a resurgence in IRA activity in the south between March and April 1936, which resulted in the killing of a retired Royal Navy Vice-Admiral and a Garda (police) officer, the organisation was declared illegal and its leaders arrested. Disillusionment with de Valera's Fianna Fail, and with the failure of the movement's socialist excursions, hardened the perception that the political road was a profitless one to travel. This feeling was reflected among grass roots IRA members, who were fed up with their leaders' contorted and ineffective political manoeuvrings. In fact by the late 1930s many of the leftist radicals had gone off to fight with the International Brigade in the Spanish Civil War. Their departure further concentrated power in the hands of the militants. It was not surprising that the leadership passed to Sean Russell, an ardent militarist, who advocated a bombing campaign against England. The election of Russell as Chief of Staff at the IRA Convention of April 1938 caused the defection of people such as Sean MacBride and other politically dextrous minds still left in the movement. Even some of the more thoughtful military elements, like Tom Barry, who disagreed with the idea of a bombing campaign, left the movement for good.

Russell's plans came to fruition on 12 January 1939 when the IRA, claiming the authority of the 'Government of the Irish Republic', delivered an ultimatum to the British government which warned that unless its forces were withdrawn from Ireland in four days, the IRA would 'reserve the right of appropriate action without further notice'.[43] The ultimatum was ignored and on 16 January the bombings began. By the end of 1939 there had been 291 explosions which had resulted in seven deaths and ninety-six injuries.[44] The campaign was based loosely on a document known as the S-Plan, drawn up by Seamus O'Donovan, a former IRA Director of Chemicals, which proposed launching a widespread series of attacks on a range of industrial, transport and symbolic targets with the aim of disrupting the economic and social life of the country. The extensive and detailed nature of the S-Plan always made its successful implementation problematic. The IRA units in Britain were not equipped to maintain the constant level of military activity needed to fulfil the Plan's ambitions. As late as spring 1938, IRA officials who went to Britain to assess the movement's strength reported that: 'In general it can be said that the state of the organisation in the units which exist is poor and loose, and militarily should be described as almost elementary.'[45]

The bombing campaign was a graphic illustration of the paucity of strategic planning induced by the loss of internal political guidance. Had there been firm guidance then the campaign might have at least identified some specific military and political goals to be achieved by the bombings. As it was, there was no co-ordinated targeting policy nor any attempt to engage in a sustained propaganda dialogue with the British to continually remind them of IRA demands. There is little to suggest that the IRA had any clear idea of how its disparate bomb attacks would coalesce into an effective instrument of pressure with which to achieve republican objectives. Presumably the bombings were designed to cause sufficient panic and fear within British society to force the government to open negotiations on the ending of partition. Press reports at the time noted that the campaign did not produce panic but merely aroused anti-Irish feeling in Britain. The poisoned political atmosphere enabled the British government to usher in the Prevention of Violence Act of July 1939 which permitted the deportation of IRA suspects.[46] In the seven months after the Act's introduction there were 145 expulsions.[47] British preoccupation with the far more threatening spectre of the German conquest of Europe in the Second World War further diminished the effect of the campaign, as was demonstrated by the muted response, both in Britain and abroad, to the execution of two IRA men who had been convicted of taking part in a bomb attack in Coventry which had killed five people.[48] Neither did the bombings generate much support in Ireland. De Valera was concerned to preserve Ireland's neutrality in the war and did not want reports of the IRA's intrigues with the Germans to give the British a pretext to reoccupy the country.[49] In a speech in Co. Cavan, in February 1940, de Valera denounced the IRA campaign by warning: 'These people may get the country into a mess that the whole Irish people might not be able to get out of. We sympathise with their ambitions, but we cannot allow that to blind us to the consequences of their deeds.'[50] In January 1940, the Irish government passed the Emergency Powers Act and immediately began interning IRA members.[51] By mid-1940 the bombing campaign had petered out under pressure from special police and judicial measures in both Britain and Ireland.

The absence of any real planning or direction in the bombing campaign was displayed when the IRA fell back on slogans as a strategic rationale. With the start of the Second World War Russell declared, in October 1939, that 'England's difficulty–Ireland's opportunity has ever been the watchword of the Gael . . . Now is the time for Irishmen to take up arms and strike a blow for the Ulster people.'[52] The notion of striking against Britain while she was distracted by foreign entanglements had been elevated by the 1916 rising. It was felt that Britain's commitments during the First World War had weakened its forces in Ireland and contributed to the rising's military effectiveness. As a consequence, this aphorism was repeatedly promulgated during the inter-war years as a standard for republican action:

> the simple fact that Ireland's right to freedom imposes a duty to attempt to seize freedom when the occasion offers. . . . To let an opportunity to break the British connection go by default would be a crime . . . we are not free to dodge such action when opportunity presents.[53]

Beneath the superficial catchcrys, the entire 1939 bombing enterprise exposed the dominant influences which had come to exert themselves upon the republican movement's thinking. Recourse to violence was evaluated not as a method to achieve political objectives but almost as an impulse to satisfy the ideological needs of the republican tradition. Despite the political dabblings of the 1930s, the pressure for military action had always been there, and had been building up ever since the end of the civil war. Indeed, in many respects, the republican tradition held little meaning without its militarily confrontational bearing. The movement affirmed in 1928: 'The position today is that a state of war exists between England and the Irish Republic. . . . Until peace is made . . . Republicans will continue to work everywhere against England and English interests.'[54] This type of statement was buttressed by constant exhortations which emphasised 'the right of the armed manhood of Ireland to free the country'[55] and that: 'It is not the bargainers of relief but the soldiers of freedom that represent the wisdom of the Irish people.'[56]

The process by which the pressure for military action was allowed to be vented untutored by rigorous strategic analysis can be traced back to the concept of republican absolutism which insisted that the 'Sovereignty and Unity of the Irish Nation are inalienable and non-judicable, and the Irish Republican Army cannot relinquish or surrender these fundamental national principles, which are a sacred trust.'[57] The IRA's unfaltering devotion to these principles ruled out compromise on any aspect of the republican agenda and precluded involvement in the parliamentary institutions of Ireland for fear of contaminating its ideological commitment to the republican struggle. The republican world of doctrinal absolutes proved an inhospitable environment for those of a pragmatic disposition. The essence of the republican experience from the 1920s to the late 1930s therefore reflected the gradual paring away of all the layers of political influence, as those pragmatic elements which sought to challenge the movement's ideological parameters in search of more effective ways of facilitating republican goals eventually felt compelled to dissociate themselves from the movement. Beginning with the original division over the 1921 Treaty, the process was followed later by the break with Sinn Fein and the Fianna Fail split, with the final haemorrhage taking place after the IRA Convention of 1938. Each successive defection enhanced the deference to republican orthodoxy of those who remained and further compressed the movement's strategic thinking into a narrow framework from which it was increasingly hard to deviate. The systematic diminution of political influence over the IRA allowed ideological pressures to override dispassionate calculations of the organisation's actual military potential. Arguably, the key event in this regard was the break with Sinn Fein in 1925, which cut off the IRA from its only link with a tangible political constituency. With all control over IRA policy centred within its own Army Council, the steady slide towards the 1939 campaign proceeded unchecked by any non-military source which, theoretically at least, might have been able to align the IRA's military capabilities with more limited, but attainable, political goals.

Besides the internal ideological dynamic which spurred the IRA to military action, the 1939 bombing campaign can also be seen as a symptom of the movement's desperation to break out of the political isolation imposed by the rising popularity of Fianna Fail. By gearing up to mount a military campaign, the IRA hoped to out-manoeuvre Fianna Fail on the question of Irish unification where the party's commitment seemed least convincing.[58] It is possible that for this reason the republican movement was at pains to deny that it was simply an armed clique hankering after a piece of the action. According to a statement issued by the Army Council in 1933:

> The Irish Republican Army is not a militarist caste. It springs from the people and arises out of their natural desire for national freedom, and out of their intense need to be relieved from Imperial exploitation. The Army is the leadership and the vanguard of the historic struggle for national freedom and for economic liberation.[59]

Yet this statement went on to confuse the IRA's pretensions to represent the people with its adherence to its own private morality when it added 'that the Irish Republican Army exists to serve the interests of the Irish Nation and to free the people from political subjection and economic exploitation'.[60] The fact that the IRA's concept of the 'Irish Nation' patently did not enjoy demonstrable mass support merely emphasised how much of a loose cannon the organisation had become within Irish politics. As the Army Council statement implied, the IRA claimed the right to employ violence in any way it chose to achieve its objectives. Yet by defining its role so narrowly as a military organisation dedicated to the nationalist cause, the IRA undermined its ability to attract the necessary public support and resources to sustain a prolonged military campaign, so reducing its power to reach its objectives. In this sense, the 1939 bombing campaign can be seen not as a serious attempt to advance the nationalist cause, but as a sign of the movement reverting to type, as a vehicle for preserving the doctrinal purity of the republican vision. The bombing campaign underscored that a 'militarist caste' was exactly what the IRA had become.

TOWARDS A SELF-PERPETUATING MILITARY TRADITION – THE 1956–1962 BORDER WAR

The quality of republican strategic thinking would never again prove quite so barren as it was in the 1939 campaign. Even so, the IRA's next military venture in the 1950s verified that the inwardly generated pressures which gave rise to the bombing campaign were not unique to the time but endemic to the process of republican strategic formulation. During the 1940s and 1950s the same impetus to initiate hostilities against Britain was established. This time the accent was placed on tackling the problem of unification at source, Northern Ireland.

The origins of the IRA's Northern campaign had very specific historical antecedents. The idea had first been raised by Tom Barry during the latter part of the Anglo-Irish war in June 1921. Later, in 1934, Joseph McGarrity of the Clan-na-Gael in America suggested that the bulk of the IRA's efforts should be channelled towards British forces in the North.[61] In general the IRA was shifting inexorably in this direction. In fact the organisation had been planning to launch attacks in Northern Ireland during the mid-1930s. Plans were shelved in 1936 because the prospective campaign had been compromised by poor security which alerted the authorities on both sides of the border to the possibility of an IRA offensive.[62]

The political background which influenced the switch from the IRA's over-riding goal of creating the 'real republic' to the winning back of the six counties is important. During the 1930s there was a growing sense within republican ranks that the movement should take into account the differences between the two prevailing systems of government in Ireland. There was no disagreement as to the intended purpose of both the Northern and Southern regimes: 'Indubitably both areas are ruled by partition governments whose functions in maintaining a sundered and divided Nation are identical.'[63] Although the function of both governments may have been the same in the republican view, it was felt that there was a qualitative distinction to be made. Britain was seen to be maintaining direct control over Northern Ireland, whereas the people of the twenty-six counties were able to enjoy some measure of autonomy. One Sinn Fein pamphlet (undated, but probably produced in the late 1920s/early 1930s) summed up the nature of the debate:

> The difference in the existing situations [between the Northern and Southern governments] . . . makes the problem with which Republicans are confronted more complicated and in many respects more difficult to solve. It presents them with the immediate problem of deciding whether a single line of policy

can be formulated suitable to general application over all Ireland, or whether a different line will be necessary in respect of the two areas of existing government.[64]

In particular, it was felt that the reforms carried through by de Valera had taken much of the ideological steam out of the republican movement in the South. The abolition of the oath of allegiance, the 1937 Constitution and the Anglo-Irish Agreement of 1938, which handed back the Treaty ports and settled many of the other outstanding sources of dispute between the two countries, had to most people's satisfaction given the twenty-six counties the substance of a republic. The issue of Irish unity appeared to be the sole remaining nationalist grievance.

Actual planning for the next campaign began in 1950, and the six years that elapsed before hostilities opened in 1956 did ensure that as a technical undertaking it was a better organised affair. Between 1951 and 1955 the IRA raided the ammunition stores of a number of army barracks in Northern Ireland and England and netted a considerable quantity of arms. Promising auguries were also offered by the large measure of popular steam built-up behind the nationalist cause, which had arisen as a result of the Free State's declaration of a republic in 1948. Sinn Fein had been reactivated as the IRA's political arm in 1948 and during the mid-1950s it campaigned vigorously in Northern Ireland. In the Westminster elections of May 1955 the party received 152,310 votes, almost the entire nationalist electorate in the North, and in the process won two seats for abstentionist candidates. In fact, the Sinn Fein vote was inflated by the non-participation of the Nationalist Party of Northern Ireland, which gave Sinn Fein's candidates a free run.[65] Sinn Fein hailed the vote as a landmark in its 'campaign to organise all Irishmen into one united people to end forever British occupation and influence in Ireland'.[66] For these reasons the movement was able to strike an up-beat note in its first pronouncement after the campaign had begun on 11 December 1956. 'This fight', the movement confidently predicted, 'will be won when the united strength of our people is thrown in the scales against British imperialism. . . . The enemy's bridgehead is weakening. We hope that in the months to come it will crumble completely.'[67] From these reasonably auspicious beginnings the IRA's border war slowly, but remorselessly over a period of five years, ran into the ground.

The military objectives of the border war were stated in an IRA document which was captured by police in the Irish Republic on 8 January 1957:

Our mission is to maintain and strengthen our Resistance centres throughout the Occupied area. To break down the enemy's administration until he is forced to withdraw his forces. Our method of doing this is the use of guerrilla warfare within the Occupied area and propaganda directed at the inhabitants. In time, as we build up our forces, we hope to be in a position to liberate large areas and tie these in with other liberated areas – that is areas where the enemy's writ no longer runs.[68]

The IRA's secret training manual issued to its volunteers asserted confidently that there was only one method to achieve these objectives:

A small nation fighting for freedom can only hope to defeat an oppressor or occupying power by means of guerrilla warfare. The enemy's superiority in manpower, resources, materials and everything else that goes into the waging of a successful war can only be overcome by guerrilla methods. . . . In regular warfare the tactical objective is to destroy the enemy in battle by concentrating superior numbers at a decisive time and place. The guerrilla strikes not one large blow but many little ones; he hits suddenly, gnaws at the enemy's strength, achieves surprise, disengages himself, withdraws, disperses and hits again.[69]

The IRA's military stipulations were in fact a neat demonstration of the immediate shortcomings of the organisation's approach. Its tracts on guerrilla warfare were long on theory and short on realistic advice. Much of the theory itself seemed heavily indebted to Maoist strategic thought and was therefore of dubious applicability to the Irish context. The emphasis in the movement's military literature on the creation of secure, independent base areas from which to launch operations could have been lifted straight from Mao's texts.[70] The very notion of guerrilla bases was suitable only to the rough, inaccessible terrain and quasi-anarchic political conditions pertaining to China in the 1930s and 1940s. The idea that this might have borne any resemblance to the Ireland of the 1950s and 1960s was unreal.

In a similar fashion, the IRA made much of the need to bolster popular resistance by utilising a campaign of 'clever propaganda on top of guerrilla successes' because: 'From the point of view of guerrilla warfare, the co-operation of the people is essential. If this is lost – or never received – the guerrillas cannot win.'[71] Republican military writings of the period were festooned with earnest reminders that 'support for the aims of the guerrillas must come from the population'[72] and of the necessity of becoming a 'People's Army in the real sense of the term . . . recruited from the people . . . aided and sheltered by the people' and which 'fight[s] in the interests of the people'.[73] The IRA was content to ape Maoist rhetoric in this way without acting on it. For a start, the movement had to acknowledge that it could not even hope to obtain the support of the majority Protestant population of Northern Ireland: 'a guerrilla force will be unable to operate in an area where the people are hostile to its aims. And it must be remembered always that it is the people who will bear the brunt of the enemy's retaliatory measures.'[74] It was for this reason that the republican movement decided not to try to mobilise support or mount attacks in urban areas for fear of provoking reprisals against the Catholic population in the towns and cities of the province.

The point is, though, that republicans did not really try to mobilise the nationalists in the rural areas either. In fact, the tendency to elitism in republican ideology rose to the fore in the campaign. It was the major factor that dulled the movement's political senses and which helped contrive to fritter away the nationalist sympathy established in the two years preceding the outbreak of the conflict. The first symptom of this elitism was that it was never made plain at the start of the war, either to the nationalist population or the wider public, exactly what the violence was meant to achieve politically. Only a very generalised and somewhat incoherent explanation was provided some three months into the campaign in an interview with an IRA officer who stated that the purpose of the attacks were threefold: '(1) To spotlight . . . [that a] part . . . [of] Ireland is still occupied by British troops, (2) that [the] occupation is bitterly resented by 80% of the whole Irish people and by almost 40% of the people in the six occupied counties', and finally, '(3) We aim to rally our people in their resistance to the occupation forces and to make the occupation difficult, costly and impossible.'[75] It was a characteristic exposition of the republican attitude towards the role of force in politics. Violence was seen as an agitationary instrument that would solidify public support into a cohesive expression of mass opposition to British involvement in Ireland. This, in turn, would be reflected through increased republican military activity, with either the tacit or open backing of the Southern government, and so further embroil the British in a general conflagration in the North. As in the Anglo-Irish war, the combination of financial and domestic political pressure would, it was believed, eventually force Britain out.

The movement's self-image as the trail-blazer of Irish nationalism governed the way it viewed the large Sinn Fein vote of 1955. Rather than regarding it as a manifestation of broad Catholic discontent in Northern Ireland – a popular base to be developed and fashioned towards specific republican objectives – it was seen, instead, as a straight licence for military action. Once the campaign was underway, no effort was made to retain and nurture nationalist confidence through an effective propaganda offensive in order to explain the motives of the IRA's strategy, or through the formulation of economic and social programmes to appeal to the population at large. Admittedly, the banning of Sinn Fein in the North in the first days of the conflict would have undoubtedly hindered any such attempts had they been made, but the movement's basic reluctance to build up a more solid political profile was apparent in the public pronouncements of its members, as evinced in the following comments made by Sinn Fein President, Padraig MacLogain, in his address to the party's annual Ard Fheis in 1957:

> Quite frequently Sinn Fein is bitterly attacked because of an alleged failure to put its policy and programme before the people and abide [by] their decision. Such attacks are but a further example of the quibbling indulged in by the opponents of our movement. In point of fact Sinn Fein as a national organisation puts its policy before the people on both sides of the Border and gives them the opportunity of signifying their attitude towards the restoration of the unity and independence of Ireland.[76]

The tone of these remarks implied that not only did the movement take the large vote for Sinn Fein as approval for a military campaign, but also as an endorsement of the general leitmotiv of the republican tradition which itself legitimised violence without popular consent. This assessment can be cross-referenced with other republican statements during the campaign which explicitly linked the two subjects. For example, the IRA's Easter message of 1957 declared:

> We base our claim for the support of the Irish people throughout the world on the proclamation of 1916. This is our declaration of Independence and charter of liberty. . . . Nothing less can claim our allegiance and we will accept nothing less. . . . We are uplifted and encouraged in our fight when we see the return to the old allegiance and how brightly the torch of freedom glows. The magnificent success of the Sinn Fein candidates in the recent election gives us new strength, after being abandoned so long.[77]

It is not surprising that a movement with a long heritage of revolt should seek to vindicate its actions in the present by relating them to the events of the past. What is interesting in the above statement, though, was how the 'allegiance' to the 'proclamation of 1916' was taken as the ultimate source of authority for the movement's conduct. It was as if the backing shown for Sinn Fein in 1955 was perceived not as a direct mandate for armed struggle so much as a recognition of the validity – a 'return to the old allegiance' – of the republican approach. Again, this can be seen as the product of nationalist elitism as it clearly established loyalty to the republican tradition above popular consent for IRA actions. What this suggests is that, as in the 1939 bombing campaign, republican strategic thinking was being driven by ideological symbolism without any real idea as to what could actually be achieved through a military campaign. Perhaps the closest the movement came to acknowledging that the military instrument was being governed by internal impulsion free from any consideration for the limits of public tolerance for its violence came in 1958 when the journal the *United Irishman* testified that: 'The policy of the Resistance movement is made by the Movement itself. It is dictated by principle and one aim: *the freedom of our country*. It takes help from no-one but the Irish people *in carrying out this mandate of history*' (emphasis in original).[78]

The practical effect of the IRA's behaviour was to make its violence appear politically worthless. The movement again had to deflect criticism that it was simply glorifying a tradition of violence. 'Members of the Movement', Padraig MacLogain averred, 'do not face death or imprisonment and hardships just to maintain a tradition of militarism or self-sacrifice. The struggle today is striving to accomplish the task of achieving full freedom.'[79] However, the point was that, although the IRA's *own* strategic calculations suggested armed force as a perfectly suitable means to achieve its political objectives within its own narrow, elitist understanding of the function of violence, to many others outside the movement its strategy was incomprehensible. As the campaign progressed, the IRA increasingly tended to wallow in the mythical language of republican imagery. For example, in mid-1958 the movement pronounced that those fighting for the IRA 'are in direct succession to the freedom fighters of all other generations of Irishmen who followed the same proud road', and who would enjoy entry into 'the great brotherhood of heroes and martyrs that mark 700 years of struggle to drive British forces out of Ireland'.[80] Such lofty rhetoric merely added weight to the perception that the entire campaign had become an irrelevant self-indulgence. The lack of political mobilisation and evident lack of success cooled Northern Catholic opinion towards the IRA's border war. The growing unpopularity of the campaign was reflected in the general election of October 1959, when Sinn Fein received only 73,415 votes. The collapse in Sinn Fein's vote, down by over half from its 1955 performance, owed much to the reintervention of the Nationalist Party which decided to contest the election.

The IRA's prospects for success in the border war had really melted away within the first year of the campaign. One of the most crucial blows came in July 1957 when the government in the Irish Republic introduced internment. For the IRA this was a heavy blow. By the end of 1958 nearly all the Army Council, GHQ staff and Sinn Fein executive were in gaol. The loss of the limited sanctuary offered by the South badly affected IRA operations. By 1960 the level of IRA attacks had fallen to just twenty-six, down from a peak of 341 in 1957.[81] Despite the declining effectiveness of the campaign, throughout 1958 and 1959 the movement was still optimistically assuring that 'Resistance is growing stronger'[82] and pledging itself 'to intensify the Campaign, to press home the fight, and never to desist in its efforts until British Occupation Forces are withdrawn from Ireland'.[83] There was no truth in these avowals; they simply underlined that the IRA had become an inflexible, militarily autonomous organisation, its violence being wholly unregulated by any meaningful political authority.

The inherent dynamic within republican ideology, with its fervent commitment to the nationalist vision wedded to an ardent belief in the efficacy of violence, seemed to be dictating the course of the IRA's military activity unhindered by any need to reach a favourable political conclusion. The tone established within the movement's rhetoric by the latter half of the border war bears out this assessment. Even before the verdict of the 1959 elections was delivered upon the IRA's campaign, the movement was making no pretence to justify the continuation of the war with reference to anything else except to the elitist themes of its ideology. According to one republican commentary of mid-1959:

> When Pearse went forth to wage his struggle, the authority he heeded was not that of the effete Parliamentary party – which might well term itself then the representative of the people. No! The authority Pearse heeded was the authority of history, the authority of armed resistance to foreign rule, the authority of the Republican tradition. . . . There can no longer be a debate about how best to liberate the six counties of our country held by foreign rule. The constitutional way has been rejected. The way of struggle has been accepted. The path of resistance has been trod and must continue to be trod until either our people's will for freedom prevails or our enemy destroys that will. There is no other way.[84]

Nearly all organisations, especially political groupings, are bound together by a series of principles which give them their meaning and purpose and, doubtless, the adherence to a particular set of beliefs will to some degree affect the external behaviour of organisations in the pursuit of their objectives. What appears so unusual in the IRA's case is the extent to which violence itself had become an integral component of republican belief, seemingly employed less as a rationalinstrument of policy but more to maintain the ideological identity of the movement. This goes to the heart of the matter concerning the lack of political regulation of the military instrument, as the conviction that 'There is no other way' explicitly rejected the thought of any internal political dialogue capable of continuously evaluating the effectiveness of the military option. In this respect, the movement was not strategically engaged at all. There was no ends–means analysis. The movement had become a self-perpetuating military tradition.

The difficulties imposed on republican strategic formulation by the lack of political control were systemic. The elitist attachment to violence, combined with doctrinal inflexibility, excluded all potential for either the consideration of alternative non-military options or the modification of political goals to accommodate actual military capabilities. As such, republican strategic thought was confined largely to a few simplistic precepts. The ideology defined the political object – a united independent republic. It defined the enemy – Britain. And it defined the means to challenge the enemy in order to attain the object – military action. Yet, as five and a half years of wasted effort testified, it also defined the most likely outcome – isolation and defeat.

THE IRA REFLECTS – THE STRATEGIC REAPPRAISAL OF THE 1960s

The IRA called off its campaign in February 1962. The ideologically elitist prism through which the IRA viewed the world was displayed in its final campaign communiqué of 26 February. It blamed the movement's defeat on the 'attitude of the general public whose minds have been deliberately distracted from the supreme issue facing the Irish people – the unity and freedom of Ireland'. And, in renewing its pledge of 'eternal hostility to the British Forces of Occupation', it called on the Irish people to show greater support in its preparations for the 'final and victorious phase of the struggle for the full freedom of Ireland'.[85] Beneath the pugnacious language, far from drawing up the battlelines for the next confrontation, the collapse of the border war had caused the IRA to slip into a mood of despondency. The task of reviving the movement fell to Cathal Goulding who was made Chief of Staff in 1962. Goulding was a veteran IRA activist but was unassociated with the failure of the border campaign as he had spent the early years of the conflict in prison for his part in an arms raid in England in 1953. Under his direction, the IRA instituted an extensive reappraisal of the republican tradition to discover why the movement had been, in Goulding's words, 'unable to succeed in spite of the fact that the people engaged in its revolutionary activities were willing to make any sacrifice for it'.[86] The basic conclusion reached by the internal debate, said Goulding, was that the 'people had no real knowledge of our objectives', largely because the movement did not really have any:

> The fight for freedom had become an end in itself to us. Instead of a means, it became an end. We hadn't planned to achieve the freedom of Ireland. We

simply planned *to fight* for the freedom of Ireland. We could never hope to succeed because we never planned to succeed.[87]

(emphasis in original)

Goulding was admitting, in a very candid fashion, that for most of the twentieth century the republican movement had been strategically redundant.

The analysis of the failure of republican strategy developed from the thesis that the nature of British imperialism in Ireland had been refined in the face of nationalist resistance in the Anglo-Irish war. British control, it was believed, no longer rested on the primitive imposition of foreign institutions backed up by military might, but on a more subtle system of 'neo-colonialism', a concept defined by Roy Johnston, the IRA's leading political theorist, as 'a means of retaining the substance of imperial rule while giving the shadow of independence'.[88] So, in this way, the Treaty of 1921 ceded most of the paraphernalia of political autonomy but did not grant real independence that would have allowed full control over Irish resources. Instead, these remained in the hands of British financial concerns. 'Failure to understand this', Johnston argued, 'led the Republicans to concentrate on the outward trappings of alien rule in the North, ignoring the economic domination of the whole country.'[89] Therefore, the first extrapolation derived from the analysis, as Goulding explained, was that if the republican leadership wanted to maintain a revolutionary organisation then it 'would need to have a policy for the next phase of the fight against British Imperialism in Ireland'.[90]

The spirit of republican thinking of the time was summed up by Deasun Breatnach, who contended that 'freedom is not something to be flaunted at the national level, in the council of the nations; it must go down to all the people'.[91] The challenge for the movement in this respect was to devise a policy that could win popular support by promising social and political emancipation to the ordinary citizens of Ireland. 'This is what we were fighting for', Goulding argued, 'and we had to make it plain to the people. To do this we had to involve ourselves in their everyday struggles for existence.'[92] In 1964 the IRA gave approval to the movement's involvement in a programme of political agitation and endorsed a plan to build up a leftist coalition – a 'national liberation front' – which would campaign on a broad social and economic agenda (though one recommendation to abolish the policy of abstention was rejected).[93] By the mid-1960s ideas were being circulated concerning possible republican involvement in areas such as campaigns to combat unemployment and emigration through active participation in farming and industrial co-operatives, trade unions and so on.[94] At the rhetorical level, too, the movement's language was increasingly using the discourse of class confrontation by talking about the unity of the 'urban and rural dweller' versus 'the class of exploitation, the class of gombeenism [term meaning usury: pejorative description of Irish business interests], the class of slavery'.[95]

Although the leadership's diagnosis was couched in the terms of social revolution, the notion that the whole rethink represented an enormous Marxist digression – a fundamental transformation in republican thinking – can be overstated. In fact, the changes advocated by those like Goulding were contiguous with the tradition of socialist-republicanism which went back to Lalor and Connolly, whose inspiration the modern leadership frequently cited.[96] More particularly, the revisionists' arguments paralleled those made in the 1920s and 1930s by people like Peadar O'Donnell and George Gilmore. For example, it was Gilmore who wrote in 1932 that only when:

> the system of exploitation has been destroyed and a system based upon the recognition of the fact that the lands and other wealth-producing resources of Ireland are the property of the people of Ireland and not of the exploiting class – until that has been accomplished we will not be in a position to say the [British] Conquest has been undone.[97]

The language used in the 1930s may have been similar to that of the 1960s, but, more importantly, so was the analysis which underpinned it. Gilmore believed that, although republicans were motivated by the highest ideals of service to the nationalist cause, in practice 'the IRA often bewilders the Ireland it would serve and so loses the mass backing which alone could make it effective'. He continued:

> The Republican Movement is rich in principle but disastrously short in policy. It is poor leadership that rests itself entirely on principles and neglects sorting out, in all their concreteness, the conditions within which its struggle must develop, for it is only on this sorting out that policy can be properly based.[98]

These were exactly the type of criticisms Goulding and his kind were making of the contemporary IRA. But it should be noted that although the social–republican critique, both in the 1930s and the 1960s, led the movement in a politically leftward direction, it did not countenance that republicans should be tied to any formal political doctrine. Rather, it advocated that the movement should get away from the belief that it could operate in a vacuum, where idealised images of the republic would have a timeless attraction, and should become more attuned to the ever-changing political climate. In a phrase, the struggle needed to be seen to be relevant to modern Ireland. Undoubtedly, the IRA in the 1960s was influenced by aspects of Marxist thinking, and also, in part, by the radicalism of the age with its anti-authority ethos and emphasis on agitationary politics. Gerry Adams has written tangentially of the influence of 1960s radicalism as an era animated not by rigid ideologies but by 'the whole undefined movement of ideas and changes of style', which 'produced a sense of impatience with the *status quo*, allied to a young, enthusiastic and euphoric confidence'.[99] The most radical move undertaken by the IRA's leadership at this time was to consult political thinkers from outside the movement, people like Roy Johnston, who later joined the IRA, and Anthony Coughlan, both of whom had contacts with communist groups and radical factions. However, as Henry Patterson, who has charted the history of republican–socialism, has pointed out, Goulding's motive for bringing in outsiders was essentially to re-import the tradition of radical thinking which, through some three decades of neglect, had been all but eradicated from the movement as a whole.[100] Avid admirer of the radical left though Goulding was, nevertheless, he was not a slave to a Marxist ideological obsession.

Though the radicalisation of the IRA was influenced by various external factors, overall the process can be seen as largely internal to the republican tradition. Indeed, the nationalist question remained to the fore of the movement's thinking. In enunciating his theories of neo-colonialism and the crisis in the Irish economic system, Johnston expressly stated that all these problems 'are in fact connected: they add up to the Irish National Question of the Sixties'. Johnston went on: 'For it will be found that the major obstacles to the satisfaction of the people's needs is the reality of alien rule over the whole of Ireland.'[101] The remedy, of course, was the creation of a fully united and independent state which would have total control over Ireland's economic surplus.[102] The change from the IRA's previous position was simply that the movement felt that it could derive a greater level of support across the whole of Ireland by basing its appeal on a platform which went wider than the concentration on the political unification of the country.

Overall, the neo-colonial argument provided the IRA with a comforting view of its situation. In the first instance, it explained why the IRA had become isolated and had gone down to continuous military defeat since the civil war, as the failure to participate in the labour struggle had caused the movement to detach itself from the everyday needs of the people. Second, the theory painted an optimistic picture of a huge potential republican constituency; an image of the Irish masses who subconsciously yearned to be unburdened from the manacles of imperialism and whose revolutionary awareness could be stimulated provided they were given the necessary organisational leadership. In other words, the neo-colonial analysis reassured republicans of their continuing relevance while skirting around less savory explanations for their predicament, such as the possibility that they, and the cause they represented, had simply come to be regarded as an anachronism in the modern era. And finally, it provided a useful hook upon which to hang the nationalist cause. Altogether, a highly convenient explanation.

Nonetheless, the leadership's rethink did challenge aspects of conventional republican wisdom, especially by opening up the question of peaceful political participation which confronted the traditional refusal to engage in 'partitionist' politics. Putting the reassessment of the 1960s into perspective, it can be said that the revisionist process stemmed from a psychological change, as opposed to structural changes in terms of, say, the age or education of the IRA's membership. The IRA's low ebb after the demoralisation of the border war was such that socialist republicans were able to hold sway within the leadership and assert their agenda more forcefully than before. An agitationary socialist manifesto was embraced, not out of the whole-hearted conviction of the movement, but out of a prevailing sense of apathy because it looked like the only way the IRA could preserve its raison d'être.

All this is not to suggest that there was no hostility to the leadership's new programme. Initially, opposition was muted, but it grew as the implications of the strategic review, in particular how they would affect the military instrument, were thought through. Concern at the leadership's policies was aired in the pages of *An Phoblacht*. The journal had been revived under the aegis of a group established in 1965 calling itself the Committee for Revolutionary Action (CRA) with the specific intention of 'combating deviationism and revisionism within the ranks of organised republicanism'.[103] The immediate cause for discontent was the suspicion that the movement was being controlled by a left-wing cabal based in Dublin which was attempting to shut out all other ranks from the decision-making process. *An Phoblacht* argued that the debate over the movement's future should be conducted openly amongst the membership as a whole. Instead, *An Phoblacht* complained, the 'business of the Irish Revolution *is but* the exclusive domain of the few who are organisationally engaged in the functioning of Irish Republicanism' (emphasis in original).[104] The CRA's real bête noire was the 'foreign directed clique' made up of those, like Johnston and Coughlan who, it was felt, were out to manipulate the movement 'along the lines advantageous to the interests of a foreign power', namely 'the British Communist Party, and its Irish sections, which are in turn directed from Moscow'.[105] Whether or not the idea of a communist ploy to subvert the movement had substance, such allegations were symptomatic of the resentment felt by the more traditionalist faction against the influence of those deemed to be outsiders who had been brought in to advise the leadership. Sean MacStiofain, one of the few dissenters remaining on the Army Council, believed that the leadership's leftward drift into radical politics was depriving the movement of a proper sense of direction. Rather than focusing the movement's attention on the need to confront the crucial issue of British rule in Ireland, the Army Council was getting bogged down in what he saw as meaningless nit-picking over policy resolutions and discussion documents that had no practical value. Meanwhile, the movement's military assets were being wasted. MacStiofain believed that if the situation went on 'the IRA would end up as a paper army'.[106] The deep-seated fear was that neglect of the military side in favour of developing an agitationary organisation would eat away at the movement's moral fibre, causing it to lose its strength, cohesion and, ultimately, its very identity. *An Phoblacht* was apoplectic at the very thought:

> But in addition to it being incapable of effecting what our people want, parliamentary agitation is in a thousand ways demoralising. Even if it could win our independence, independence so won would do no good; for freedom to do good, must be gained with difficulty and heroic sacrifice, in the face of perils and death. . . . Platform movements are necessarily unmilitary, and, consequently, bad for a nation that wants to free herself from a foreign yoke. . . . In short, *no more insane and wicked idea could enter the brain of fools and knaves, than the notion of reviving the system of agitation.*[107]
>
> (emphasis in original)

The continued presence of such hardline traditionalist views, which saw the use of violence as virtuous for its own sake, was something of which Goulding was well aware. He understood that unless a specific role for the armed struggle was guaranteed, the potential existed for the hardliners to become a law unto themselves in the worst traditions of Irish republican militarism. As Goulding reflected: 'we had on our hands trained physical force revolutionaries who were, to some extent, still armed. They would decide for themselves what would happen next, if we didn't decide for them. . . . It was essential to stop any premature action by these people.'[108] The priority for Goulding was to hold the movement together during a period of transition, which meant averting any outright hardline–revisionist cleavage. This returned the leadership to the fundamental problem concerning the imposition of greater control over the military instrument; how to carve out a definitive role for the physical forcers while trying to subordinate the IRA to more general policy objectives, without, at the same time, either raising the ire of hardliners or encouraging those tendencies to military autonomy.

The dual process of mollifying traditionalist elements while attempting to shift the focus of republican military thinking took place at three levels. The first was at the rhetorical level to reassure hardliners of the continuing need for a military dimension to republican strategy by quashing rumours that the revisionist programme would entail the abandonment of the armed struggle:

> There is no thought of relinquishing the use of force. No-one who has thought at all about the nature of the division of this country is willing to rule out the necessity for using the gun to bring about the realisation of the aspirations of the Irish people.[109]

Yet these assurances were also carefully qualified by placing the military instrument within a broader context as just one facet among a range of options that the movement could pursue, as Goulding signified when he declared: 'We have only to look around us to see that we will have to fight on the military front, the social front, the economic front and the cultural front.'[110] These sorts of pronouncements conveyed the feeling that the armed struggle would be retained as a matter of absolute necessity, while in fact it was being de-prioritised within the overall course of republican strategic formulation. This impression was maintained at the second level – the military planning level. To convince the traditionalists that the commitment to armed force was not just idle rhetoric, the leadership authorised a degree of military planning. According to interviews carried out by the analyst Henry Patterson with Cathal Goulding and Sean Garland, another prominent IRA revisionist, the movement had, since the mid-1960s, been drawing up plans for another guerrilla campaign in Northern Ireland.[111] Further evidence to support the belief that some degree of military planning was occurring was provided by a confidential IRA document seized by Irish police in May 1966. Recognising that 'our campaign will be fought in the Six County area', the document went on to set out in some detail the training and organisation for a potential military campaign. For example, the document outlined the need for 'Large stunt-type operations' which 'should and must be of a purely "killing nature" designed to inflict as many fatal casualties on the British as possible'.[112] Apparently trying to learn some of the lessons of the failure of the border war, the IRA admitted that because of the 'limited area of operation, the density and hostility of population, the vast array of police and other parliamentary and military forces . . . that classic guerrilla operations cannot be successful'. Therefore the military object would be to 'engage in terror tactics only'. 'Assuming that terror is to be our weapon', the document stated, 'we must create an organisation capable of seeing it through.'[113] Although the IRA later argued that the document was 'never in fact more than a draft for discussion' and did not represent official IRA policy, it can nevertheless be taken to represent an accurate indication of the lines upon which the republican leadership was moving.[114] In addition to planning in the abstract, a limited number of small-scale operations were sanctioned, or at least tolerated, to placate the more restive military elements. For instance, in summer 1965 the IRA fired shots at a British naval vessel in Waterford harbour and in May 1968 the organisation burned a number of company buses in furtherance of an industrial dispute.

In fact, however, neither the occasional attacks nor the formal military planning itself heralded any full-scale campaign. Goulding and his followers had no real intention of launching a new military offensive. Goulding acknowledged 'that our whole future as a political and revolutionary force should be geared to keeping our people out of gaol, and leading a revolution'.[115] It was this primary consideration which formed the basis of the third level – the actual conditions upon which the leadership believed military action could be sustained. In a seminal article setting out the movement's attitude towards the armed struggle, a republican writer, Tony Meade, identified 'a new element in the willingness to use force, namely that this force will be defensive'.[116] The leadership visualised a time when violence would have to be used against the forces of reaction, they being the Stormont and Leinster House governments in the North and South respectively, which would inevitably attempt to crush the republican revolution once it looked like gaining popular momentum. 'When that day comes', Meade argued, 'it is hoped that the defensive measures adopted by the Movement will ensure that victory will be ours.'[117] The declaration was vague but significant as it reversed the traditional premise of republican strategy. No longer would the movement be a military spearhead. It would remain an elitist outfit but only in the sense of being political organisers and agitators. In Garland's words:

> The Republican Army, north and south, must become the Army of the People, in fact as well as in name. It must be the vanguard of all militant and radical revolutionary groups in this country and as the vanguard be ready to move in defence of those struggling for their rights.[118]

The emphasis was now on using republican resources and energies to build up mass support. Tony Meade asserted that: 'Only in this way will we arrive at the day when the use of force will succeed.'[119] So the probability of a final military showdown with the forces of counter-revolution was something for which the movement had to be prepared. As Goulding proclaimed: 'I am not naive enough to think that we don't have to use guns. An armed proletariat is the only assurance that they can have the rule of the proletariat.'[120] It should be stressed that such a scenario was envisioned only *after* the IRA had obtained widespread popular support. In the meantime, that support would have to be won through hard political campaigning. As if to underline the changes in outlook that this would necessitate, Meade sought to remind his colleagues that: 'Before that day comes we must be prepared to work in a way in which many of us are unaccustomed.'[121]

Meade's implicit appeal to IRA members to move away from the militarist ways of the past hinted at the scope of the changes being contemplated by the leadership. Adopting a social revolutionary posture towards the whole concept of Irish nationalism altered the entire substratum of republican strategic analysis. The stress 'placed on arms and battle tactics' would now be downgraded 'to a secondary position', so said the IRA's 1966 discussion document, 'and be replaced by an emphasis on Social and Economic objectives. . . . Under no circumstance should the Army recruit . . . on the basis of the emotional appeal of arms.'[122] For a movement that had been bred on the belief of violence as a first resort, the new accent upon reviewing the value of armed force, both as just one component of the republican struggle and with specific reference to the suitability of such means to the political circumstances prevailing at any particular time, represented a radical transformation in the movement's approach to military matters.

One of the most important features of the reassessment was the plan to assert political control over the military instrument by gradually removing the General Army Convention, the supreme authority of the IRA, from the policy-making process. For a number of years Goulding was circumscribed about what he could say in public on this issue for fear of alienating the hardliners, but according to the IRA's 1966 document it was clear where the intentions of the leadership lay. The document revealed that, in the long term, decision-making power would be transferred to a 'National Conference', while the IRA Convention would contract to a 'specialist conference of certain people in the Movement for examining technical problems connected to the military aspect of the revolution'.[123]

What these restructuring proposals demonstrated was that, in the end, the revisionist and hardline perspectives were irreconcilable. Notwithstanding Goulding's efforts to bring as many hardliners as he could along the socialist–republican road, the plans to reduce the IRA's influence, the stress on gaining public confidence as the first priority of republican policy, the rejection of military vanguardism and the willingness to be open-minded about the mix of methods to achieve the movement's objectives, all repelled traditionalist assumptions concerning the pre-eminence of military means. Primarily, the leadership was interested in obtaining real political power based on popular consent. This meant disposing of the encumbrance of the apostolic succession. The revisionists did not want a movement that was merely capable of sustaining itself through myths and martyrs. Sean Garland, in his Bodenstown oration in June 1968, was adamant that the republican movement was not sacrosanct but simply a vehicle to achieve tangible political goals:

Let no mealy-mouthed sentimentalist tell us that we must preserve the movement as traditionally constituted if this proves impractical and hand on these impracticalities to the next generation. The struggle for the emancipation of the Irish people is inevitable and by saddling the next generation with useless tools and tactics we are not helping them but destroying their chances of success by binding them to a line of thought and action that was a failure with one generation and must just as surely be a failure with the next.[124]

Such forthright language displayed the strength of feeling amongst the leadership. Although the 1960s' reassessment by no means surveyed all of the options and the strategies open to the movement at the time, there is little reason to suspect that the republican leaders simply and cynically latched on to the nearest passing political fad to save the movement from what might otherwise have been its inevitable demise. Their conversion to the socialist path was genuine and they reflected carefully on how this would shape the movement's future organisation and strategic doctrine. The commitment to the socialist approach was underlined by Tomas MacGiolla, the President of Sinn Fein, who in 1969 declared: 'We do not regard socialism as a fashionable cloak to be worn or discarded as popular tastes dictate. I think we can say that no-one is today in any doubt where a Republican stands ideologically.'[125] Of course, whether social revolutionary maxims had any real relevance in a country with an established democratic tradition like Ireland is debatable. What we can say, though, is that the outcome of the IRA's self-examination did help to contain the military instrument within a more satisfactory theoretical framework. Yet the main problem is precisely that we only have *theory* to pronounce upon, chiefly because, although the way the leadership *thought* about the relationship between ends and means certainly underwent a transformation, in practice very little was done in this period to implement the recommended changes. For most of the decade the movement hardly participated in any sustained agitationary activity. In fact, it barely had any political profile. Sean MacStiofain's allegation that the IRA was being allowed to atrophy while the leadership debated abstract policy positions was substantially correct. Moreover, Goulding admitted it:

> By 1967 the Movement had become dormant. It wasn't active in any political sense or even in any revolutionary sense. Membership was falling off. People had gone away. Units of the IRA and the Cumainn [local branches] of Sinn Fein had become almost non-existent.[126]

When an IRA conference was called in August 1967 to evaluate the movement's overall strength, the republican leaders 'suddenly realised that they had no Movement at all'.[127] The conference recommended that the IRA should 'openly declare for a socialist republic'.[128] This was the first time that the movement had decided to act on the proposals endorsed by the IRA's rethink begun in 1964. The leadership was to pay for this laxity as events in Northern Ireland in the late 1960s reopened the whole debate on the future role of the armed struggle in republican strategy.

TENSION AND DIVISION OVER REPUBLICAN STRATEGY IN NORTHERN IRELAND – THE ROAD TO RUPTURE

During the early years of the IRA's introspection the rise of the civil rights movement in Northern Ireland largely passed it by. The original civil rights organisation, the Campaign for Social Justice, was founded by a Dungannon couple, Conn and Patricia McCluskey, in 1964 to campaign against anti-Catholic discrimination in the province. Later in January 1967 the Campaign for Social Justice was superseded by the Northern Ireland Civil Rights Association (NICRA), which brought together a number of civil rights groups under one umbrella organisation. NICRA was composed mainly of a loose affiliation of liberal-minded professionals, trade unionists, left-wing activists and students. Our knowledge of the civil rights movement – its derivation and subsequent progression – is still hazy, though thanks to research in recent years we have a much clearer picture than we once did. The picture which emerges is that, although the IRA were not involved in civil rights agitation at its inception, there were collections of left-wing republican sympathisers who, from the early 1960s, had been formulating a civil rights strategy aimed at undermining partition. C. Desmond Greaves of the London-based Connolly Association (an organisation with close ties to the Communist Party of Great Britain) was probably the first to suggest that forcing concessions on civil rights could help subvert unionist power in Northern Ireland by eroding sectarian divisions.[129] These ideas were refined by the Wolfe Tone Society, a republican gingergroup, of which both Roy Johnston and Anthony Coughlan were prominent members, and who themselves, as we know, enjoyed a direct line of communication with the IRA leadership. What is still less than clear is whether a programme of civil rights agitation had always been integral to the whole socialist–republican agenda, or whether the IRA behaved more opportunistically, simply latching on to the civil rights bandwagon once it started to gather pace after 1964.

What has become increasingly transparent in recent times as the years slowly yield new information is that once the IRA's interest in civil rights had been engaged, its members did take a leading part. Republicans were instrumental in setting up NICRA itself, though they did not control the Association and remained a minority faction within it.[130] The republican leadership believed that NICRA could be used as a vehicle to 'help get the Protestants involved, and get away from the old divisions'.[131] Republican thinking held that, in order for the unionist political establishment to maintain power, behind which lay its British imperial sponsor, it was necessary 'to divide the Protestant people from their Catholic fellow-countrymen and "protect" them behind a sectarian border'.[132] It was reasoned that the introduction of civil rights reforms and the establishment of political equality in the North would break down sectarian barriers, thereby undermining the basis of unionist government. Released from their sectarian blinkers, Protestant workers would combine with their Catholic brethren collectively to resist British colonial rule. The 'North is imperialism's strongest bastion in Ireland,' claimed the *United Irishman*. 'Weaken imperialism there and the winning of civil liberties would be such a weakening – and its hold on Ireland is weakened all over.'[133]

Because the aim was to build a cross-community movement capable of uniting Catholics and Protestants, the principle of non-sectarianism was considered paramount. As a consequence, republican leaders were keen to play the civil rights issue with caution. They were particularly anxious to avoid the impression that NICRA was a stalking horse for the IRA to revitalise the nationalist cause. Any such impression, it was felt, would antagonise and repel Protestants. The emphasis was to be on peaceful political participation to win the confidence of Protestants by proving that republicans 'were the best champions of the needs of the ordinary people'.[134] For this reason, when the large-scale civil rights marches got under way, individual republicans were allowed to act as stewards but not to adopt any corporate IRA profile. The role of the stewards was to try to steer the marchers away from any trouble with the police. The Goulding/Johnston leadership had become increasingly concerned at the participation of a number of extreme left-wing activists, with no connections to the republican movement, who were placing themselves at the head of the marches in order to manufacture violent confrontations with the police in the belief that this would expose the elemental brutality of unionist power. According to one of these activists, Eamonn McCann, the intention was 'to provoke the police into over reaction and thus spark off mass reaction against the authorities'.[135] After the first march from Coalisland to Dungannon in August 1968, the movement voiced criticism that 'some marchers should have tried to break through the cordons of police', arguing that 'this was just what [William] Craig [Stormont Home Affairs Minister], and the police would have liked, for then they could have represented the whole thing as a sectarian riot'.[136]

As the civil rights marches progressed, so the Goulding faction's fears were borne out, as the number of clashes with the police increased. One march in January 1969 from Belfast to Derry, led by the student-based People's Democracy party, gained particular notoriety. When the marchers reached the village of Burntollet Bridge, Co. Londonderry, they were attacked by a loyalist gang. The police stood aside and it later emerged that some of the attackers were off-duty members of the police auxiliary force, the B Specials. However, those like Roy Johnston were annoyed with the march organisers whom he called an 'immature ultra-leftist element'. The march itself he described as 'ill-advised and provocative'. 'Burntollet need not have happened,' Johnston said, 'It achieved nothing except to inflame sectarian hatred.'[137] From the beginning of 1969 Northern Ireland imploded. The disruption which accompanied civil rights marches developed into riots and running street battles between the police and Catholic and Protestant mobs. Events culminated in August 1969 when British Army units were sent onto the streets of Derry and Belfast to restore law and order.

Northern Ireland's plunge into violent chaos severely damaged the IRA leadership's design to transform the civil rights campaign peacefully into a broad non-sectarian movement. Where the republican leadership had been mistaken was in assuming that sectarian conflict could, in the long run, ever have been avoided. The depth of communal hostility was always likely to transcend any latent feelings of cross-community working-class solidarity, if such a thing ever existed in the first place. The Goulding faction tacitly admitted that the violent reactions of the authorities to the civil rights marches had dented its faith in the ability of the Stormont administration to reform itself when it called on the British government to impose civil rights reforms on Ulster.[138] In fact, by late 1969 the IRA's entire strategic construct had unravelled. The prospect of Catholic–Protestant working class unity had disappeared. Furthermore, in the process of trying to preserve its non-sectarian stance, many republicans felt that the IRA had abrogated its traditional role in the North as the defenders of the Catholic population, so leaving nationalist areas at the mercy of Protestant rioters. The sight of Catholics in the Bogside area of Derry welcoming the arrival of the British Army as protectors was especially galling. Responsibility for this humiliation was laid at the door of the Dublin leadership, with the result that Goulding and his cohorts presided over an increasingly divided movement.

Such was the background to the split in the IRA's ranks which occurred towards the end of 1969. The rift was sparked by the decision to resurrect the proposal to end the policy of abstention in order to allow republican candidates to take their seats if elected. The leadership claimed that it was a necessary move to stop 'political opportunists' from capitalising on the IRA's agitationary activities and to enable the movement to 'use the tactics best suited to the occasion to smash the power of the establishment, North and South'.[139] An extra-ordinary Army Convention, meeting in December 1969, agreed to the lifting of the restraints on electoral participation and also to the formation of the so-called national liberation front. For the opponents of the leadership, these ideas were a fanciful distraction and the final straw for those like MacStiofain.[140] After the Convention, MacStiofain and his followers met under the banner of a new body, the Provisional Army Council, to repudiate the IRA resolutions and to pledge 'allegiance to the 32-County Irish Republic proclaimed at Easter 1916, established by the first Dail Eireann in 1919, overthrown by force of arms in 1922 and suppressed to this day by the existing British imposed Six-County and 26-County partition states'.[141] The break was formalised at the Sinn Fein Ard Fheis held on 11 January 1970. When the resolution to abolish abstentionism was pushed through about one-third of the delegates walked out. There were now two Irish Republican Armies – one under Goulding, referred to as the Official IRA (OIRA), and the other led by MacStiofain – the Provisional IRA (PIRA).

Because the rupture occurred over the issue of abstention, the events from late 1969 onwards can appear as a straight traditionalist–revisionist split.[142] This is too simple. While abstention was certainly the immediate cause for contention, the roots of the division went deeper and concerned the whole course of the 1960s reassessment, the nature of the IRA leadership's policy towards developments in the North and the movement's non-performance in the riots of August 1969. Those who broke from OIRA were not members of one single faction, more a coalition of forces who for one reason or another opposed the IRA leadership. This coalition can be categorised into three groups. By looking at the motives of each group it is possible to see the centrality of the argument concerning the role of the military instrument in the whole controversy.

The first group can certainly be described as a traditionalist faction. They were by no means the largest group, but they were predominant within the Provisionals' leadership. They were people mainly from the South, often veterans of the 1956–62 border war. They had been hostile to Goulding's new thinking from the outset, hence they were the most organised of the three groups. As has been mentioned above, opposition during the 1960s centred on the Committee for Revolutionary Action. Although the Committee remained a shadowy and indistinct contingent, it is plausible to suggest that its members were those who comprised the Provisionals' first echelon, people like Daithi O Conaill, Ruairi O Bradaigh and his brother Sean, and possibly MacStiofain as well. The fact that the CRA's newsheet, *An Phoblacht*, became the Provisionals' chief mouthpiece in the South lends weight to this supposition. As self-proclaimed guardians of the republican heritage, the CRA saw Goulding and his cronies as reformists and compromisers who were diluting the IRA's struggle with their fangled ideas of political campaigning. The CRA asserted that 'the traditional programme of Republicanism is revolutionary, and therefore can only be realised through unqualified revolutionary action'.[143] In case there was any doubt over what was meant by the term 'revolutionary action' the CRA spelled out that: 'Force is the mailed fist of revolutionary principles.'[144]

What differentiates the traditionalists above all from the rest, was the probability that they would have broken away irrespective of whether the Northern situation had erupted or not. Over two years before the actual break took place, *An Phoblacht* had openly canvassed the possibility of a split if and when the 'Sinn Fein "Progressives"', as they were labelled, made their 'final move to integrate with Free State politics' by ending abstentionism.[145] The CRA counselled against any premature action which could shatter the movement into a diffusion of splinter groups, but warned that 'real revolutionary Republicans' should be in a 'position to swiftly regroup Republican activists in a new organisation when events dictate that this is essential to the perpetuation of Republican objects'.[146] For the traditionalists, abstentionism was an emotive subject and its proposed abolition represented the crowning betrayal of republican orthodoxy. MacStiofain declared that the choice was 'between accepting the institutions of partition or upholding the basic Republican principle of Ireland's right to national unity'.[147] Developments in the North added a new element to the traditionalists' case. They believed that the civil rights campaign could be manipulated to allow the IRA to undertake 'offensive action . . . on the main national objective of ending British rule'.[148] Frustrated both ideologically and practically by the IRA leadership, the traditionalists decided that their ambitions could be best served in a separate organisation.

The second group, and almost certainly the largest component within the Provisionals, can be classified as the Northern republicans. Many were young enthusiasts who were to provide the majority of PIRA's footsoldiers. At their head were a group of older, mainly Belfast-based republicans such as Joe Cahill,

Francis Card and Billy McKee. Although the Northerners undoubtedly shared many of the traditionalists' aspirations, they were less political in the sense that their paramount concern was not national unity but to obtain guns to secure the defence of Catholic districts. The older republicans especially had been deeply depressed by the IRA's failure to safeguard Catholic areas in August 1969, for which they blamed Goulding's leadership. Commenting on the welcome accorded by Catholics to the British Army, Joe Cahill said, 'people were glad to see them because the IRA had betrayed them'.[149] In particular, anger was directed at a statement from Goulding which claimed that IRA units had been sent to the North and had played 'their part in defensive operations in Bogside, Derry'.[150] This was a fabrication. There had been virtually no centrally coordinated IRA activity during the August riots.[151] According to MacStiofain, the statement had been concocted by the Dublin GHQ to pre-empt the British government from stepping in to abolish Stormont by giving credence to unionist claims that the riots had been fomented by the IRA.[152] The reasoning was that, as Stormont was an Irish parliament, it could be democratically reformed and would evolve into an anti-imperialist body. If direct British rule was imposed any such prospect would be lost.

By this time, many republicans felt that the leadership's thinking had slipped into the realms of absurdity and that the non-sectarian approach had become incredible. Goulding and his followers had believed that the rise of the civil rights movement signalled the success of the initial stage of their Northern design – 'the first effective political weapon which has been forged by the anti-unionist forces', as Tomas MacGiolla called it[153] – when in reality it was the prelude to Northern Ireland's political disintegration. For many Northerners, the Dublin leadership's vision of inter-communal harmony rang hollow while loyalist mobs were on the rampage through Catholic neighbourhoods. The IRA leaders themselves were caught in a vice. If they stuck to their policy of doing as little as possible to antagonise the Protestants, they would lose much Catholic backing. Conversely, by moving to the defence of Catholic areas, they would undermine their anti-sectarian image which had been one of the main pillars of their thinking since the mid-1960s. Within the ranks of the Belfast IRA, disillusionment was so strong that in September 1969 they made up their own minds about the quality of the leadership they had been receiving by withdrawing their allegiance to the Dublin GHQ.[154] This pre-existing split set the tone in the months after the formal break had occurred with many Northern IRA units and new recruits flocking to PIRA's side. Yet for OIRA, although the Northern tumult had provided an unwanted catalyst for the split, the logical endgame of its socialist–republican philosophy *was* the eventual eradication of the Catholic-defender tradition from its doctrine. Ultimately, the Officials were probably glad to see the backs of their erstwhile colleagues in the belief that they had got rid of a conservative–militarist millstone. But the price for this was the forfeiting of the support of many in the North who wanted protection, not some distant illusion of a workers' paradise. Cahill summed up the basic nature of PIRA's appeal: 'We receive our support from the Nationalist people and it is our job to defend them.'[155]

The third group were those, like the young Gerry Adams, who were sympathetic to many of the ideas contained in the 1960s rethink, but who fundamentally disagreed with the IRA leadership's analysis of events in the North. Adams has written approvingly of the 'small, politically conscious organisation' that was beginning to emerge from the 1960s review and of the need for agitationary work to 'enlist mass support'.[156] Adams has also claimed that the depiction of the 1970 rift as a traditionalist–revisionist split resulted in the 'simplistic projection of the "Stickies" [Provisional slang for the Officials] as politically conscious radicals with the "provisionals" as nationalist militarists'.[157] This group of mainly Northern radicals felt that the leadership had gravely underestimated the reactionary nature of the Northern Irish state. Since sectarianism, they argued, was a phenomenon deliberately cultivated to pit Irish people against each other in order to maintain British rule, then the unionist establishment could always manipulate the sectarian issue to keep the Protestants on side. Ipso facto, the Northern state was inherently irreformable. The implication of this interpretation was that as long as the British connection lasted, so the notion of cross-community working-class solidarity would be unattainable. Therefore, the Dublin leadership's faith in the reform process was felt to be misplaced and merely constituted 'temporising in front of the Orange ascendancy' which could only lead 'to a total dilution of Republicanism'.[158] The radicals felt that their assessment had been confirmed by the authorities' violent reaction to the civil rights marches and, consequently, shared the same resentment at the leadership's complacency during the August disturbances. The radicals were undoubtedly the smallest and least important faction at the time of the split, but being highly motivated politically they were to move swiftly through the Provisionals' ranks to positions of influence in the years ahead.

When the Provisionals issued their first statement detailing the reasons why they had broken with OIRA, the areas of overlap between the various shades of opinion within PIRA were defined more precisely. The statement listed five areas of disagreement: 1) the ending of abstention and the recognition that this was deemed to confer on the Westminster, Stormont and Leinster House parliaments; 2) the failure to offer adequate protection to 'our people in the North' during August 1969; 3) the controversy over the leadership's insistence that Stormont should be preserved; 4) the movement's tendency to 'an extreme form of Socialism'; and finally 5) the methods used by the leadership to counter dissent through the expulsion of members who objected to the politicisation process.[159] There were slight incongruities here and there. For instance, the reference to extreme socialism and the description of PIRA's own brand of socialism as being based on 'Christian values' may well have jarred with the more secular minded radicals. In this sense, the statement reflected a largely traditionalist perspective. Though the movement strenuously resisted the militarist–traditionalist tag, there is little doubt that the belief in the value of armed force, both to sever the British connection and to protect Catholic areas, was the central unifying thread which bound the factions together. There was no outward expression of the willingness to open up a military campaign, though it was conveyed by inference, for example, by stating the preference for a 'direct confrontation with the British Government on Irish soil'.[160] There were, naturally, different qualities of commitment to the use of force. The traditionalist faction, with the Catholic defenders in tow, were the most instinctively affiliated to the armed struggle, whereas the radicals were probably inclined to view military action in more functional terms, though they were no less convinced of its necessity at the time.

What emerges about the OIRA/PIRA split was that it was not the result of a violent spasm in August 1969, but was a process that had a long lead time extending back to the very early stages of the strategic review in the mid-1960s. Nevertheless, it is perhaps somewhat ironic to note that, hitherto, the only consistent attempt in republican history to develop a more politically conscious strategy which sought to separate the military instrument from, and subordinate it to, policy requirements should have come undone so quickly when it was placed under strain for the first time during the August riots. The organisation which had done all the talking about the obligation to be responsive to popular needs manifestly failed to react to the calls for help from the people who were its natural supporters in the North. As a result, Catholics turned increasingly to the Provisionals who were willing to offer them the practical assistance which OIRA leaders seemed intent on denying. For many Northern Catholic 'workers', OIRA's new model strategy was not simply doctrinally inflexible, it was irrelevant.

Meanwhile, on the flipside, hardly any Protestants trusted the Officials either. The sincerity of OIRA's commitment to build a mass movement that could genuinely span the sectarian divide cannot be disputed. But the process by which it was believed this could be achieved was presumptuously mechanistic. The assumption, which to varying degrees the Provisionals also shared, that Protestants would discover their true national consciousness once the 'terrorising political conformity forced upon them'[161] by the imperialist tool of unionism had been lifted, was certainly a condescending argument, if not an actual sectarian view in itself. Occasionally, when socialist–republicans of the 1960s inveighed against what was termed 'the Scotch–Irish nonsense',[162] meaning a separate Protestant–Irish identity, they sometimes seemed to blur even further the line between criticism of a specific philosophy of loyalism and the more atavistic responses generated by inter-communal suspicion and hostility.

THE THEORY AND PRACTICE OF POLITICAL CONTROL – THE OFFICIALS TAME THE MILITARY TIGER

From the early 1920s until the end of the border war in 1962, the military instrument in republican strategy had become an independent dynamic, almost entirely disconnected from any serious consideration as to whether such means were appropriate to the attainment of the movement's political goals. The employment of force was based less on realistic calculations of its utility, given the resources at the IRA's disposal, and more by the inclination to fulfil the doctrinal imperative to engage in military action. This restraint on the proper application of violence to aid the achievement of political objectives made the republican movement an impossible place for the more politically sighted elements, like Eamon de Valera and his followers. In effect, republican military thinking defied the very concept of strategic rationality, as the military instrument ended up serving the ends of ideology, not the ends of policy.

The abject failure of the 1956-62 border campaign brought home the futility of IRA militarism to its leaders who resolved to try to restore some semblance of political authority over the use of violence. To a casual observer looking on events from the 1970 split it is easy to assume that republican strategic thinking was entrenched and immobile. The 1960s reassessment disproves this, showing that the movement was neither impervious to self-criticism nor unable to challenge key republican tenets, like abstentionism and the primacy of the armed struggle, though admittedly only under the threat of extinction, as Garland accepted: 'It was only when we were beaten to the wall and almost annihilated as a political force that the true meaning of revolution began to dawn on us.'[163] We can question the validity of the leadership's ideas about social revolution, but the reassessment did attempt to examine critically the correlation of ends and means in republican strategy. In this way, the social revolutionary concept set out the theoretical context in which the military instrument could be subjected to greater political control by redefining it as a single tactical component within a far wider political framework aimed at winning popular support.

The fly in the ointment for the IRA's leadership was the outbreak of the Northern conflagration in the late 1960s. It is possible to speculate about the course of the social revolutionary approach had events not flared up when they did. As it happened, the situation in the North provided another compelling reason for the anti-leadership coalition to break away. However, what the early years of conflict demonstrated was the tension between the theory and practice of OIRA's new strategy. It was one thing to devise a mechanism to control the military instrument in the abstract, quite another to implement it in the midst of the violent turmoil that had engulfed Northern Ireland. In particular, these years illustrated the difficulty that the Officials had in trying to escape their militarist past. OIRA was trapped between its formal non-sectarian, gradualist policies and the highly charged atmosphere of the times which seemed to call for a more traditional military response. In mid-1971 Garland warned the movement against allowing itself to be swept up by the gathering momentum of PIRA's violence: 'Unfortunately, because of our history as a movement committed to force, we are liable to be brought down along with these elements.'[164] At the beginning of 1972 OIRA reaffirmed its position towards Northern Ireland:

It has never been and is not now our intention to launch a purely military campaign against British forces in the North. We have seen the failures of past campaigns based on military action only and have set our faces against such campaigns which are doomed to failure. We do not see, nor do we want a repetition of the fifties.[165]

Such sentiments seemed discordant when matched with OIRA's actions both in late 1971 and early 1972. Disregarding Garland's warnings, the Officials were sounding increasingly bombastic. In a speech in mid-1971 Goulding had declared that the only answer to the repressive actions of the 'forces of imperialism and exploitation' must be 'in the language that brings these vultures to their senses most effectively, the language of the bomb and the bullet'.[166] This belligerence was later to manifest itself in a series of actions which put its non-sectarian credentials at risk with the killing of the unionist politician, Senator Jack Barnhill, in December 1971, followed by an assassination attempt on another unionist, John Taylor MP, in February 1972. The worst incident also happened in February when an OIRA bomb planted at the Aldershot headquarters of the Parachute Regiment killed seven people, including five women canteen workers and a Catholic priest. The Officials justified the Aldershot bombing as retaliation for the 'Bloody Sunday' shootings, which occurred in Derry, 31 January 1972, when thirteen people were killed by paratroopers during a civil rights demonstration.[167] Overall, the bombings and shootings left OIRA's image severely tarnished. All the innovatory ideas of a non-sectarian, non-militarist, all-Ireland agitationary movement appeared to have fallen by the wayside in favour of a violent pre-occupation with the Northern conflict.

It is inconceivable that OIRA's descent into a frenzy of destruction reflected the true wishes of Goulding and his partners. In truth, OIRA's violent spree represented less of an ideological reversion to full-scale militarism and more a desperate attempt to curb the flow of support to the Provisionals. Viewed in this light, we can see how important military symbolism was to the republican tradition in general and how crucial the Officials believed to be the preservation of a military role, not so much for its political instrumentality, but as a means to sustain their legitimacy. In this battle for the moral high ground of republicanism, OIRA's attempts to 'out-militarise' the Provisionals were never likely to succeed. By 1972 Goulding was prepared to concede this point. 'What helps the Provos most in the North', he claimed, 'was that every Catholic youth is a Provo at heart.'[168]

Throughout March and April 1972 the Official IRA's campaign continued at full-swing. On 21 May, OIRA shot dead William Best, an off-duty British Army soldier on home leave in Derry. The killing produced widespread anger against the Officials and led the OIRA Army Council to reconsider its campaign in Northern Ireland. On 29 May 1972, OIRA announced a ceasefire, though it reserved the right to act in self-defence and undertake defensive operations. The announcement was made only after much acrimonious debate inside the organisation. Opposition to any cessation of hostilities came from a militant ultra-leftist faction led by Seamus Costello and from OIRA representatives in Belfast and Derry who feared that a ceasefire would be both difficult to enforce on local activists and would allow the Provisionals to extend their influence at OIRA's expense.[169] At the practical level, the ceasefire appeared to have little effect. After all, the reservation of the right to take defensive action had been OIRA's officially stated position all along. The organisation had never formally declared an offensive. OIRA operations simply persisted on through 1972 and 1973. The true significance of the 29 May announcement was that it marked the start of Goulding's push to put theory into practice by once and for all reining in OIRA's military elements under his own authority. The problem, as leading Officials in the North had already identified, was that OIRA's violence was being driven along more by the fervour of local operatives than official sanction. In this respect, the ceasefire order was a clever balance between the reality of local autonomy on the ground and the longer term intentions of the leadership. Allowing local units to continue their operations under the defensive clause provided a theoretical justification for OIRA's violence, while in the longer term giving Goulding the scope to disengage the organisation from the military struggle. The ceasefire announcement served the first stage in this process as a rhetorical cut-off point, beyond which the leadership ceased to openly back military initiatives. Further attacks were sanctioned by the Dublin GHQ after the ceasefire, but from May onwards permission for operations was gently scaled down while front line units in the North were slowly deprived of the resources and equipment necessary to keep the campaign going.[170] Through shrewd bureaucratic manipulation, Goulding was able to apply a steadily more stringent interpretation of the terms of the ceasefire. In effect, by the end of 1973, OIRA's military campaign had been defused by stealth, finally fulfilling the essential desideratum of the 1960s' strategic reappraisal.

The gradual winding down of OIRA's military activities did not pass without imposing further strain on the organisation. The militants under Costello remained implacably opposed to the ceasefire. This faction eventually broke away to form the Irish Republican Socialist Party (IRSP) in December 1974. Along with its military arm, the Irish National Liberation Army, the IRSP went on to enjoy an extremely violent history (INLA's most notable exploit was the killing of the Conservative Northern Ireland spokesman, Airey Neave, in March 1979), but its influence waned when INLA descended into bitter factionalism in the mid-1980s. Any other objectors either drifted off to join PIRA or simply dropped out of republican politics altogether. Once the IRSP faction had removed itself, the Officials had no real internal military constituency to answer to, freeing them to develop their political programme by directing the movement's efforts ostensibly towards the South where its prospects seemed brightest. During the 1970s the Officials were to become embroiled in a number of violent feuds both with PIRA and INLA (OIRA assassinated Seamus Costello in 1977), but the military instrument was never employed as the main arm of policy, and by the end of the decade OIRA had largely faded from the scene. There were periodic reports in the 1980s of the Official IRA's continued military activities,[171] but by this time the crown of physical force republicanism had long since passed to the Provisionals.

4 The military ascendancy

The Provisional IRA on the offensive, 1970–1972

The fracturing of the republican movement in early 1970 left the Provisionals in a distinct minority in Northern Ireland. Although PIRA more or less cleaned up in Belfast, obtaining the allegiance of nine of the thirteen IRA units in the city,[1] elsewhere in the province its membership was patchy. In the country areas the Officials tended to hold sway. The division of 1970 had caused much confusion inside republican ranks, and units untouched by the turbulent events of 1969 on the whole remained cautious and stayed with the Officials, even though their sympathies may have lain with PIRA. Initial reports submitted to the first meeting of the Provisional Committee of Sinn Fein indicated that support for the new breakaway grouping was forthcoming from many areas in the South. However, the committee acknowledged that the 'situation in the 6 counties was not very clear but their [sic] is definate [sic] support in Derry, Belfast, Nth [sic] and Sth [sic] Armagh and Sth [sic] Down and Fermanagh'.[2] Whatever the organisational and numerical weaknesses in Northern Ireland, the Provisionals were determined to go their separate way. There was no prospect of accommodation with the Officials. PSF's first committee meeting concluded with a proposal 'that no such reconciliation should take place. This was passed unanimously.'[3]

In spite of being a 'one-town' organisation, PIRA's position at the beginning of 1970 was fortuitous. It was Belfast which was the focus of attention because it was there that sectarian tensions were most inflamed. In the months of inter-sectarian rioting ahead, it was the Provisionals who were to gain most in publicity terms. In the space of a year the Provisionals had effectively superseded the Officials as the main republican driving force in Northern Ireland. From these origins, the Provisional IRA was to embark on a systematic campaign of military confrontation. The years between 1970 and 1972 were to see PIRA's military activity reach a scale of intensity that has never since been matched. The Provisional IRA Army Council met in January 1970 to decide on the outline of the movement's strategy. The Council agreed that its first priority was to devote the movement's resources to establishing an adequate defensive force. Ensuring that PIRA was equipped to protect Catholic neighbourhoods was to be only the first step in the gradual build-up to an offensive. It was Sean MacStiofain's intention that: 'As soon as it became feasible and practical, the IRA would move from a purely defensive position into a phase of combined defence and retaliation.'[4]

During the first few months of 1970 the Provisionals remained very much in the shadows. Catholics were not drawn automatically towards the organisation. Most were content to place their faith in the ability of the British Army to protect them from the visitations of loyalist rioters. Committed republicans saw the army not as benign guardians but as the enemy whose job it was to underwrite unionist rule. MacStiofain felt that 'with its imperial mentality'[5] the army would be unable to retain Catholic confidence for long.

As the inter-communal strife continued to boil over onto the streets of Belfast, the army increasingly resorted to heavy-handed methods to suppress the disturbances. The use of CS riot gas and baton charges became commonplace and all helped to fulfil the predictions of those like MacStiofain by eroding Catholic support for the army. Two incidents in particular helped swing Catholic opinion. The first happened in late March when troops tried to disperse a crowd of young Catholics on the Ballymurphy estate in West Belfast. Soldiers used CS gas and then charged the crowd causing mayhem all over the estate. This event was followed by further large-scale clashes in the area over the next few days as the army battled it out with Catholic and Protestant rioters. It was during this time that barricades started proliferating, both in Ballymurphy and in other Catholic districts. The barricades, some of which had been up in the Creggan and Bogside areas of Derry since the riots of August 1969, were largely an instinctive response by Catholic residents to prevent incursions by loyalist mobs. The army allowed the barricades to remain in place and tried to co-operate with the local citizen defence committees which manned them in the belief that this would help defuse the tension.[6] Because these districts were left alone by the army they became so-called 'no go' areas for the security forces. This permitted the Provisionals to take root behind the barricades and eventually to control the areas. From these areas they were able to recruit and build up their organisation. The second major incident of 1970 came in early July when the army imposed a curfew on the Lower Falls district of West Belfast in order to search the area for weapons. The curfew, which was in fact illegal, was carried out with particular severity. Four men were shot dead by the army during the operation. In both instances, the army's harsh reaction cemented nationalist solidarity and boosted support for the Provisionals, providing them with their first big influx of recruits.[7] The Lower Falls curfew was an especially notable blunder as the district was a stronghold of the Officials who had been following a policy of non-confrontation with the army.

There was a widespread feeling in the early 1970s that the rioting and general street disturbances of this period had been orchestrated by the Provisionals as part of a deliberate strategy to weaken the relationship between the army and the Catholic community.[8] PIRA was certainly hoping for such a breakdown in nationalist–British Army relations. On occasions there had been PIRA agent provocateurs involved in the riots, but there is little to suggest that confrontations with the army had been intentionally provoked from the start. Usually, the army was sucked into the violence by inter-sectarian feuding. For example, in the Ballymurphy disturbances the army had intervened to prevent Catholic youths from ambushing an Orange parade which the authorities had allowed to march through the area.[9] If anything, PIRA's role was often one of trying to restrain the rioters. There is evidence that on at least two occasions, on 12 and 17 January 1970, PIRA attempted to subdue riots in the Ballymurphy district of Belfast.[10] Riots, it was felt, disrupted PIRA's recruitment and training and risked a premature 'confrontation with the British army being forced on the IRA'[11] for which it was still unprepared. Evidence indicates that, generally speaking, the Provisionals discouraged rioting, certainly of the sporadic, uncontrolled kind. They did not wish to cause hardship to the residents from whom they derived their support and who they aspired to protect.[12]

Overall, the civil disturbances of 1970, and the British Army's response to them, did have a visible impact on Catholic attitudes. Although the army's rough treatment was handed out to both Catholics and Protestants in equal measure, it had an especially alienating effect on Catholics, who grew to share the Provisionals' perception of a force trying to protect, not the Catholic population, but the repressive Unionist Party government at Stormont. PIRA's stock within the Catholic community rose in proportion to the decline of the army's popularity as the movement increasingly made its name as an energetic defence force. Understanding PIRA's defensive role helps to explain how it was able to mount such a formidable politico–military challenge in the years to come. The Provisionals derived genuine popular kudos from fulfilling such a practical function. For example, in June 1970 PIRA units were able to repel an invasion of the Catholic enclave of the Short Strand in East Belfast by thousands of loyalists while the army was seemingly nowhere in sight. Conor Cruise O'Brien has remarked that PIRA's most potent asset 'was its simple relevance to the situation'.[13] PIRA was not advocating stoic pacifism, as the civil rights movement and the Catholic Church were both tending to do, nor waiting around for the Officials' non-sectarian conditions to materialise, but offering to resist any transgressions against the nationalist community. PIRA's popularity, in the main, was not forced but rested on the legitimacy acquired from its protective role.[14] Accordingly, one newspaper reported that in some ghetto areas of Belfast, PIRA 'enjoys almost total support from ordinary people and is not as isolated as the Government believes'.[15] Although its popular base was often conditional on the continuing perception of the Provisionals as a defensive force, PIRA had nevertheless succeeded in establishing a firm wedge inside the Catholic community on which it could work to expand its struggle.[16]

To understand the resilience of PIRA both as a social and a military phenomenon, it is essential to appreciate the sometimes tense but often mutually supportive relationship between the Provisionals and the nationalist population of Northern Ireland. By and large nationalist paramilitaries have enjoyed widespread toleration in Catholic inner-city districts, not solely as a consequence of their perceived role as community defenders but also because, in the absence of locally acceptable law enforcement agencies in such districts, they are seen as necessary to police these areas, to control crime and anti-social behaviour. Indeed, in this sense, the Provisional IRA was quite different from its progenitors of the

Anglo-Irish war and the 1950s border campaign. PIRA's perspective, as Ian McAllister observes, was shaped specifically by 'the sectarian environment of post-1969 Ulster'. It was now much more an urban movement, drawing its support largely from the inner-city areas of Belfast and Derry; the 'organisation was now almost indistinguishable from its habitat'.[17]

PIRA was different, but not that different. It was far more rooted in the North. It was more community based. It did offer a form of defence to the beleaguered Catholic populations in the city areas. But, as one commentator has observed, 'the IRA was never a reflex of oppression – it was an army of an alternative state, which derived its right and legitimacy to take up arms from . . . Nationalist ideology'.[18] The Provisional IRA was never conceived solely as a defensive organisation. The Provisionals regarded themselves as the rightful heirs to republican historical tradition and ardently maintained the idea of the incomplete national revolution. As Ruairi O Bradaigh stated:

> Our Movement bases itself on Ireland's National rights, and the right of the Irish people to the ownership of Ireland. . . . That is the main basis on which we rest our case. We also rest it on the natural and historic right of resistance to British rule.[19]

Yet, in public at least, the Provisionals were coy about what form the resistance would take. The only action to which they had openly committed themselves was the vague proposition to 'support all efforts to defend our people in the Six Counties'.[20] They were prepared to hint at possible violent consequences, but only in the context of British Army provocation, as, for instance, when Daithi O Conaill warned the British that: 'The more your troops impose their will, the nearer you bring the day of open confrontation.'[21] The plans for proactive military operations were, for the time being, kept firmly under wraps. Even so, the Provisionals' adherence to republican orthodoxy, with its stress on the colonial interpretation of Ireland's relationship with Britain, predisposed them to see the route to Irish unity as lying through military action.

The belief that Northern Ireland was a product of British imperialism influenced the way PIRA saw the Protestant population. The Provisionals subscribed wholeheartedly to the view that the Protestants were simply being used as collaborators to maintain Britain's control of Ireland. It was assumed that once Britain had withdrawn from the North, the Protestants, being 'hard-headed, sensible' and 'very realistic' (though not apparently hard-headed or sensible enough to realise that they were the witless dupes of the British), would soon come to terms with the situation and accept 'that the best thing to do would be to participate in the building of the new Ireland'.[22] Ever since 1969 there had been speculation about an overwhelming Protestant backlash against the Catholic community.[23] Apart from the loyalist riots, there was no all-engulfing onslaught. Consequently, the Provisionals were content to play down the prospect of mass Protestant resistance, describing the possibility of a backlash as 'over-rated'.[24] The Provisionals paid lip-service to secular adages about how the 'movement must be based on the common working people of Ireland, North and South, Protestant, Catholic and Dissenter',[25] but in practice the notion that the Protestants should be conciliated, at least in the terms envisaged by the Officials, was resolutely squashed. In MacStiofain's words: 'You've got to have military victory first and then politicise the people afterwards. To say you've got to unite the Catholic and Protestant working class is just utter rubbish.'[26]

So, although for the greater part of 1970 PIRA kept a low profile by avoiding direct military contact with the British Army, the movement was gearing itself up for the opening of hostilities. Feelings amongst PIRA's ranks had been running high for some time. 'I would dearly love to have a go at the British troops,' said one activist, but added with caution, 'We will go on the offensive at the right time. Our policy at present is not to take the initiative.'[27] By October, the movement felt sufficiently prepared to begin the third phase of MacStiofain's strategy – the launching of 'all-out offensive action against the British occupation system'.[28]

THE SHIFT TO THE OFFENSIVE – THE THEORY AND PRACTICE OF PSYCHOLOGICAL ATTRITION

In October 1970, PIRA began a systematic bombing campaign, directed primarily at commercial targets. By the end of the year there had been 153 explosions. At the beginning of 1971 the Army Council authorised attacks against the British Army,[29] and on 6 February the first British soldier committed for duty in the province, Gunner Robert Curtis, was killed by PIRA. The attacks increased, though a Provisional spokesman, Leo Martin, insisted that operations were 'still confined to acts of retaliation against the British Army'.[30] It was only in October 1971 that MacStiofain formally announced that PIRA's fight had shifted to an 'offensive campaign of resistance in all parts of the occupied area'.[31] During 1971 there were 1,756 shootings, 1,515 bombing incidents and 174 deaths. The violence rose dramatically the following year to 10,628 shootings and 1,853 bombings, which left 467 dead, 208 of which were the result of known PIRA activity.[32]

PIRA's political objective was, for a relatively small, minority-based movement, a formidable task. To achieve the complete removal of the British presence and the integration of Northern Ireland into a wholly new unitary political entity would require a highly potent strategy. Propaganda exhortations aside, the Provisionals were realistic enough to accept that, given the disparity of resources between themselves and the British, they would be unable to defeat the British Army in any conventional military sense. However, they did believe it would be possible to wage a limited form of war 'until Britain is forced to sit at the conference table' to negotiate on PIRA's terms.[33] To this end, the Provisionals utilised a multi-layered strategy which was composed of a series of distinct intermediate and long-term political and military goals which would enable them to attain progressively their overall objective. This is expressed diagrammatically in Figure 4.1.

The Provisionals' strategy was premised on the assumption that individual

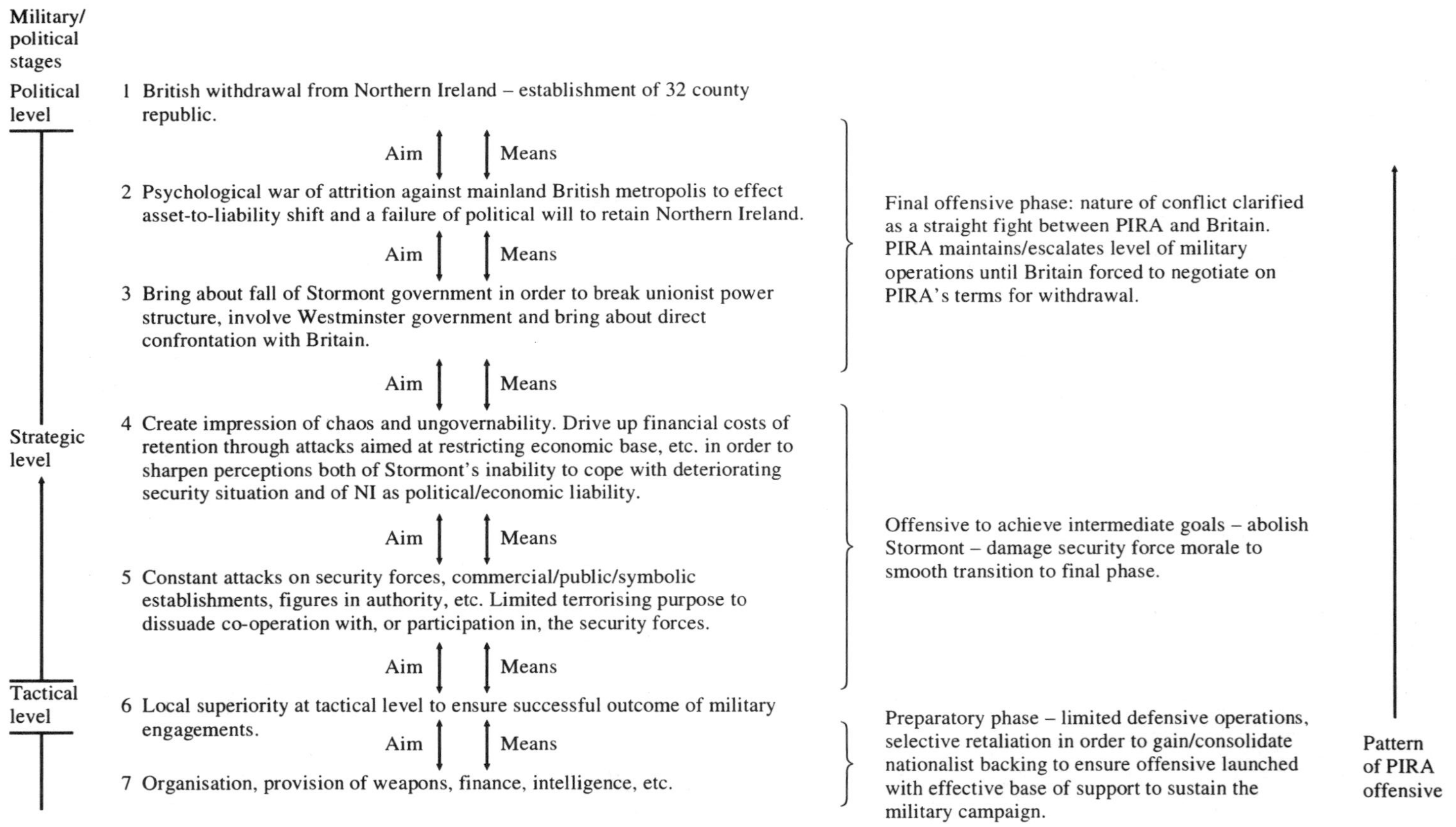

Military/political stages

Political level

1 British withdrawal from Northern Ireland – establishment of 32 county republic.

   Aim ↔ Means

2 Psychological war of attrition against mainland British metropolis to effect asset-to-liability shift and a failure of political will to retain Northern Ireland.

   Aim ↔ Means

3 Bring about fall of Stormont government in order to break unionist power structure, involve Westminster government and bring about direct confrontation with Britain.

   Aim ↔ Means

Strategic level

4 Create impression of chaos and ungovernability. Drive up financial costs of retention through attacks aimed at restricting economic base, etc. in order to sharpen perceptions both of Stormont's inability to cope with deteriorating security situation and of NI as political/economic liability.

   Aim ↔ Means

5 Constant attacks on security forces, commercial/public/symbolic establishments, figures in authority, etc. Limited terrorising purpose to dissuade co-operation with, or participation in, the security forces.

   Aim ↔ Means

Tactical level

6 Local superiority at tactical level to ensure successful outcome of military engagements.

   Aim ↔ Means

7 Organisation, provision of weapons, finance, intelligence, etc.

Final offensive phase: nature of conflict clarified as a straight fight between PIRA and Britain. PIRA maintains/escalates level of military operations until Britain forced to negotiate on PIRA's terms for withdrawal.

Offensive to achieve intermediate goals – abolish Stormont – damage security force morale to smooth transition to final phase.

Preparatory phase – limited defensive operations, selective retaliation in order to gain/consolidate nationalist backing to ensure offensive launched with effective base of support to sustain the military campaign.

Pattern of PIRA offensive

Figure 4.1 Provisional IRA strategy 1970–72

military engagements could generate a degree of coercive psychological pressure out of proportion to their destructive consequences. A sustained rate of small-scale military operations would help engender a high level of duress, which would lead the British to pull out of Northern Ireland as a result of the inordinately high economic and political price incurred in trying to retain control.

The Provisionals' thinking reflected the experiences of many minor wars during the era of decolonisation after the Second World War. Rebel campaigns succeeded in altering perceptions in the colonial metropolis, forcing the imperial powers to forsake their possessions in order to minimise public opprobrium on the international stage as well as to avoid the escalating costs of retention. To this extent, the basic theoretical mechanics of PIRA's strategy were little different from the IRA's campaign in the Anglo-Irish war fifty years previously, itself in many ways the prototype anti-colonial campaign of the twentieth century. It was entirely consonant with PIRA's outlook, with its image of Britain as the foreign oppressor, that it should seek to construct its strategy along the lines of the classical anti-colonial wars of the past. According to Maria McGuire, who was close to Army Council circles in the early 1970s, the Provisionals had keenly studied recent conflicts such as those in Palestine, Cyprus and Aden, where guerrilla campaigns had resulted in a British evacuation.[34] She also claimed that the Army Council set an initial target to kill thirty-six British soldiers because it was thought that this figure matched the number of troops killed in Aden and would supposedly impose enough pressure on the British to oblige them to negotiate.[35]

PIRA's strategic construct was not simply a replaying of the Anglo-Irish war. There were three important differences which influenced the particular context of PIRA's campaign. First, PIRA's military operations were wholly confined to Northern Ireland. Second, PIRA had secured a strong political foothold amongst the Catholic populace, something that it had failed to achieve during the 1956–62 border war, which it could use to sustain a prolonged campaign. Finally, Northern Irish unionism was in crisis. The ruling Unionist Party at Stormont, which had been in power since Northern Ireland's creation, had proved incapable of dealing with the civil rights issue when it blew up in 1968 and was now in the grip of a paralysing split between reformists and hardliners. The Unionist Party and government was teetering on the brink of disintegration and appeared highly vulnerable to further destabilisation. All of these factors helped map out the direction of PIRA's strategy as they presented the movement with a prime opportunity to exploit the Northern crisis in order to engage the attention of the politicians and public in Great Britain – the key actors who, it was felt, had the real power to affect the political destiny of the province. In summary, the Provisional IRA was attempting to use its limited resources to wage a war of psychological attrition against the British. A constant level of military activity would transmit the political message that PIRA would continue operations until the British authorities acceded to its demands. The impression of chaos and instability in Northern Ireland would eventually exasperate public opinion which would in turn demand to be extricated from the morass. Eventually, the British government's resolve would fail, causing it to finally relinquish political control of Northern Ireland.

PIRA'S STRATEGY AND THE FALL OF STORMONT

The Provisionals believed that they could only embark on the final phase of their struggle to end British rule in Northern Ireland by getting the British government to intervene directly in the administration of the province. From PIRA's stand-point, so long as the Stormont government remained, the British could look on at a distance without involving itself on any significant scale. Moreover, in PIRA's view, Stormont's existence obfuscated the nature of its campaign. Many in the Provisionals' ranks believed that because PIRA's attacks, particularly those against the security forces, often resulted in the deaths of Protestants, they were at war with the Protestant community. One Provisional admitted that many new recruits 'joined because they hated Protestants'.[36] PIRA spokesmen, though, were anxious to deny the sectarian label and to stress the real nature of their fight as they saw it: 'We have no fight with the Protestants, in fact we detest these terms "Protestant" and "Catholic". . . . Our fight is with the English for our God-given right to nationhood.'[37] The Provisionals argued that to bring about such a face-to-face fight with the English it was necessary, as an 'intermediate objective', to aim for the 'suspension of Stormont'.[38] This would open the way to the final offensive, because with Stormont gone, the 'British forces of occupation could then be clearly seen as forces of invasion on Irish soil'.[39] In other words, abolition would break the unionist power structure, and unambiguously expose the colonial relationship between Britain and Northern Ireland. The loyalists would then be able to see their true position as mere cogs in the British imperial system. Abolition would, as a consequence, 'establish the lines of demarcation . . . between those whose wish would be to sell their birthright and nationality and those who would strive to maintain it and defend it'.[40] Direct rule would turn the conflict into a straightforward confrontation between PIRA and the British, along with any remaining native collaborators. In turn, this would render the Westminster government susceptible to the pressure of public opinion at home over its policies in Northern Ireland.

To bring down Stormont PIRA needed to cause sufficient instability in Northern Ireland in order to create the perception of chaos and ungovernability. If Stormont was seen to be unable to deal with the political crisis, then the pressure on the British government to intervene would be great. Concurrently, the image of a province in perpetual strife, paralysed by PIRA's operations, would help wear down mainland opinion.[41] Therefore, PIRA's initial political goal was, in O Bradaigh's words, to 'rock Stormont and to keep it rocking until Stormont comes down'.[42]

The cutting edge of PIRA's strategy was its bombing campaign. PIRA's most potent weapon was, in fact, its own invention, the car-bomb. It was introduced into PIRA's arsenal in early 1972. The capacity of a mobile platform to transfer large bomb loads over a wide area had a devastating impact on the province. 'The strategic aim' of the car-bombings, MacStiofain said, 'was to make the government and administration of the occupied North as difficult as possible, simultaneously striking at its colonial infrastructure'.[43] The rationale was to restrict the province's economic base by hitting commercial and business premises to drive away investment and force the British to pay compensation.[44] This would drive up the financial costs of holding Northern Ireland and reinforce the impression of an ungovernable liability and accentuate, in the British public's mind, the relief to be had from a withdrawal.

In tandem with the economic war, the bombings served a number of tactical objectives. The Provisionals believed that the bombing threat could divert the security forces from counter-insurgency operations by tying down large numbers of troops in static positions guarding potential targets. In addition, by 'stretching the British Army to the limits of its resources', the Provisionals felt they could 'keep pressures off the nationalist areas'.[45] By reducing the army's presence in Catholic areas, the Provisionals could hope to enhance their credibility as defenders. In practice, such a proposition was untenable. Lieutenant-General Sir Harry Tuzo, the British Army's commanding officer in Northern Ireland, pointed out in late 1971 that the mere fact of PIRA's existence caused the security forces to concentrate their efforts on the Catholic community.[46] At times PIRA's bombings may well have deflected the security forces' attention, but such distractions were always likely to prove temporary. In due course, the security forces were bound to resume their activities in Catholic areas – patrols, house searches, round-ups, interrogations, etc. Some Catholics suspected that the Provisionals were not really aiming to keep away the security forces at all, but more interested, instead, in drawing them into Catholic areas so that PIRA could mount attacks, using the population as a shield, while benefiting politically from the army's excesses which the Provisionals themselves had partially provoked.[47] There is no direct evidence to suggest that this is what PIRA had intended, though it was a natural consequence of its actions. As the sociologist, Frank Burton, has argued, this problem turned on the definition of what was meant by defence. Since the Provisionals believed that ultimately only in the framework of a united Ireland could Northern Catholics be properly protected, then they may have seen little contradiction in the provocation of the security forces in this manner.[48]

Although the heart of PIRA's strategy was directed at an audience in Great Britain, it was also the case that its campaign was, to an important degree, directed towards affecting political and military conditions in Northern Ireland. In this sense, PIRA was able to practise a limited policy of terrorism aimed at demoralising the unionists, in effect making them more pliable to its demands. By 'terrorism' one refers to the deliberate creation of fear, through the use, or threat of use, of individual acts of physical violence for political and military ends. The constant attacks on Royal Ulster Constabulary (RUC) and the Ulster Defence Regiment (UDR) personnel were an attempt to deter local people from joining the security forces. Between 1970 and 1972, fifty-eight RUC and UDR men were killed and over 1,000 injured.[49] Success in this sphere would have improved tactical conditions for the Provisionals but their campaign, then and since, has had no discernible impact on the level of recruitment into the local security forces. Figures for RUC recruitment show that on average applications for places have been some eleven times oversubscribed.[50] More significantly in this regard, PIRA's violence was also aimed at sustaining a high level of public anxiety among the populace in Northern Ireland in general. Maria McGuire claimed that although it was no part of PIRA's strategy to deliberately cause civilian casualties, the creation of a feeling of terror as a by-product of the bombing campaign was intentional.

> By causing such terror we demonstrated that whatever steps the army took, the Provisionals could continue the military campaign; half a million people in Belfast would be kept wondering where the Provisionals would strike next and would be forced to tell the British to make peace with us.[51]

There is no indication at all whether the fear of bombs had the desired effect of cowering the population into submission. However, the Protestant community as a whole remained surprisingly subdued in the face of PIRA's onslaught. Although loyalist counter-violence was on the rise, groups like the Ulster Volunteer Force (UVF) had been relatively quiet, particularly at the outset of PIRA's campaign in 1970. The Provisionals were in no doubt that their campaign was responsible in large measure for Protestant quiescence, and made no secret of their contempt for loyalist fighting abilities. According to a senior PIRA spokesman:

> You would get a large number [of Protestants] who would attack a defenceless nationalist community as in August, 1969. But I think only a small minority would fight now. We took on the UVF in June 1970 and we taught them a lesson in hard defensive fighting. You'll notice there has been no sectarian fighting since then.[52]

In other areas, the effects of PIRA's campaign were more easily quantifiable. Inevitably the violence had an impact on the Northern Irish economy. Economic growth in the first half of 1971 was only 1 per cent, down from a projected 10 per cent, while the fear of bombs had depressed inner-city trade by as much as 30 per cent.[53] Even so, the effect on employment appears to have been marginal. From 1966 to 1971 unemployment increased by 2 per cent which was slightly lower than the rise in Great Britain (2.1 per cent) over the same period.[54] There is no doubt that the financial cost to the central exchequer of maintaining the high level of security and economic support was considerable. Up to 1979 the average cost arising directly from the violence was put at £182 million per year, while the total annual bill for financial assistance to the province was running at approximately £1 billion.[55] Therefore, along with the general confusion and violence (between 1971 and 1972 there averaged seventeen shooting incidents and nearly four bombings per day), we can assume that PIRA was successful in attaining its intermediate military goal of creating and sustaining the impression of Northern Ireland as an unfathomable political and economic burden. This was reflected in opinion poll evidence which gave PIRA cause to believe that its campaign had convinced people that withdrawal was the only realistic option. The Provisionals made much of a *Daily Mail* poll in September 1971 which indicated that over 60 per cent of the British public favoured the withdrawal of the British Army:

> It is refreshing to hear the sweet voice of reason and common sense expressed by the ordinary people after all the inane prattle and inconsequential ramblings of the politicians. . . . The effects [of the military campaign] are becoming apparent on all sides. Economically the Six Counties is [sic] tottering. Politically Stormont is about to collapse and now we are seeing the first chink in the enemy's armour.[56]

Towards the end of 1971 these initial political gains convinced the Provisionals that their campaign was dictating the course of events.[57] They were sufficiently buoyed up for *Republican News* to proclaim 1972 'The Year of Victory'.[58] The year was certainly to prove crucial for PIRA. The most significant sign that its strategy was proceeding to plan was the suspension of Stormont on 24 March 1972. The imposition of direct rule from Westminster was a major political success for the Provisionals who claimed full credit for the fall of 'the puppet parliament in Belfast'.[59] MacStiofain maintained, not all that surprisingly, that he had 'yet to meet a single person who ever thought that Stormont fell for any other reason than the armed struggle of the Republican movement'.[60] More objectively, it can be said that PIRA's campaign pushed Stormont over the edge by high-lighting its inability to cope with the deteriorating security situation or to respond to the need for substantive political reforms. But the Stormont regime had already been fatally weakened by the civil rights movement back in 1968 and 1969. In the meantime, the Stormont administration, with its own internal divisions, was proving adept at destabilising itself. The best illustration of this was the botched introduction of internment without trial on 9 August 1971, which dealt a great blow to Stormont's credibility. The initial swoop was based on inaccurate and out-dated intelligence and 105 of the 342 arrested had to be released within forty-eight hours. Most PIRA operatives had been forewarned and had gone into hiding. Only in Derry were the Provisionals badly hit by the arrests. The intro-duction of internment instantaneously united all shades of Catholic opinion against the authorities.[61] Far from stemming the violence, internment provided PIRA with an enormous propaganda victory which boosted recruitment. In the four months preceding internment there had been a combined total of eight civilian and military deaths. The four months after the introduction of internment saw the deaths of thirty soldiers, eleven RUC officers and seventy-three civilians.[62]

Overall, it would be true to say that PIRA's violence applied the stimulus which opened up the tensions and contradictions that existed between Stormont and Westminster. The British government was placed in an invidious position. It was reluctant to prorogue Stormont because of a general disinclination to become em-broiled in the complexity of the province's affairs and also because the dissolution of an elected assembly, no matter what its many imperfections were, was basically an anti-democratic step. Yet in trying to defend Stormont, the world saw the British government propping up a discredited sectarian regime that did not command any degree of support among Northern Ireland's substantial Catholic population.

In no small measure, PIRA's strategy up to early 1972 had proven highly successful. PIRA had skilfully implanted itself within the Catholic community. From there it was able to launch a military campaign that turned what had originally been a quest for protection and the redress of social and economic grievances into a far wider political debate concerning, not just the competence of the Stormont regime, but the legitimacy of the Northern state as a whole. This was a major political victory for the Provisionals. PIRA had demonstrated the potency of a campaign comprising small-scale military actions designed to pressurise a more powerful opponent. On the other hand, the attainment of PIRA's main intermediate objective emphasised the delicate nature of its strategy. PIRA had not 'bombed down' Stormont. It had been the British who had actually dismantled the Stormont edifice and, to this extent, it was with the British that the political initiative continued to reside. PIRA's military operations had been able to elicit a response which was amenable to its long-term objectives, but this did not mean that PIRA was now in the political driving seat. For the Provisionals to achieve their final goal of a British withdrawal they would have to convert their military position into political influence. This called for the formulation of a coherent political programme and definite negotiating proposals with which to tempt the British. To establish a firm bargaining position required close political and military coordination and it was in this regard that the real test of PIRA's strategy was yet to come.

THE POLITICS OF PIRA'S OFFENSIVE

In any conflict the tactical efficiency with which military operations are executed will be meaningless unless they form part of a coordinated plan to achieve political ends, because the success of a strategy can only be judged with reference to the attainment of the overall political objective. By 1972, few could doubt the technical ability of PIRA to mount limited military engagements against both the security forces and the institutional and economic infrastructure of the Northern Irish state. For PIRA's strategy to be truly effective, though, these engagements had to be converted into the means to fulfil political ends. The problem for the Provisionals was the correlation between the nature of the goal sought and the resources available with which to achieve it.

The objective of the Provisionals' strategy required a complete change in the status of the territory of Northern Ireland through the removal of any kind of British presence. The only way such a change in political control could be guaranteed was through the physical destruction of the resources that Britain was prepared to commit in order to keep Northern Ireland within the United Kingdom. Yet the total strength of the Provisionals in Northern Ireland just after the introduction of internment in August 1971 was estimated at a little over 1,000.[63] Opposing them were a regular British Army presence of 14,000 troops, the RUC at 6,000 and an expanding UDR with over 8,000 members.[64] PIRA's clearly limited capacity to inflict damage on the British meant that the efficacy of its strategy could only be assessed at any point in the conflict by the political effects generated by its military campaign. The physical consequences of PIRA's tactical engagements could never be decisive in altering the ratio of forces in their favour. So, the challenge for PIRA was to exploit what could only be positions of temporary military and psychological advantage for maximum political gain. The logic of PIRA's position meant that if it was to stand any chance of achieving its political objectives, the movement would have to confront Britain, not in the field of battle, but over the negotiating table. Irrespective of the success of its military actions, eventually the Provisionals would have to persuade the British that they were a serious political force with substantive and realistic proposals for the future of Ireland.

The initial problem for the Provisionals was to surmount the traditional republican reluctance to get involved in politics. The nature of the 1969/70 split dictated that PIRA was primarily a military organisation with little concern for the political machinations of the Official IRA. In any case, the Provisionals already enjoyed widespread backing from the Catholic community. There seemed little overwhelming reason to draw up a precise political manifesto. Nevertheless, there was general acceptance, even among the most hardline elements of PIRA's leadership, that if the movement was to establish a firm negotiating agenda then it would have to clarify its political ideas. According to Maria McGuire's testimony:

> The Military campaign was vital; and we knew as we achieved success after success that the British would have to talk to us. But when MacStiofain came into the Kevin Street office [Dublin HQ of PSF] and announced, 'We've got to have a policy', it was for him a change of emphasis indeed.[65]

The first tangible sign of the Provisionals' intent to give its campaign a political dimension came with the issuing of the *Eire Nua* (New Ireland) programme in June 1971. The programme set out PSF's thoughts on the creation of a federal administration in a post-united Ireland. The plan envisaged an Ulster parliament (*Dail Uladh*) comprising of the original nine counties of the province. The federal solution was PSF's way of trying to soothe Protestant animosity towards Irish unity by guaranteeing them a major role within a regional assembly.[66] This was supplemented in September 1971 when PIRA announced a five-point plan for the suspension of hostilities: the end to the violence of the British forces, abolition of Stormont, free elections to a new Ulster assembly, the release of political prisoners and compensation to victims of British violence. Given the scale of the demands, and the fact that PIRA's offensive was barely a year old, there was little prospect of the plan being accepted. However, it could be seen as the opening gambit in an implicit bargaining process which was attempting to set a negotiating agenda with the British. The plan was coupled with an explicit threat to intensify the campaign if the British did not comply within four days.[67]

PIRA's next political initiative came on 10 March 1972, with the declaration of a seventy-two hour truce. This was accompanied by a moderated ceasefire plan which called for the withdrawal of the British Army from the streets, an acknowledgement of the right of the Irish people to determine their own future, the abolition of Stormont and an amnesty for political prisoners. This move was a further attempt by PIRA to gain political credibility and to pre-empt the impending British proposals for the province, which were widely expected to include the abolition of Stormont.[68] 'We were by now sure', McGuire said of the 10 March proposals, 'that the British government would be compelled to ask where we stood politically, such was the success of our military campaign.'[69] To increase the pressure on the British government, the expiry of the truce was followed by the resumption of widespread bomb attacks all over the province.

Stormont's demise later in March posed the first real problem for PIRA. Abolition had rectified one of the major Catholic grievances. As a result, there was some pressure on PIRA from within the Catholic community to call a ceasefire. Many were tired of the hardships imposed by the conflict. There was also a growing concern at PIRA's increasingly casual regard for civilian casualties.[70] Incidents like the killing of two people in the bombing of the Abercorn restaurant on 4 March, which PIRA has always denied but widely suspected to have been the work of PIRA's 1st Battalion, and the killing of six people in a car bombing in Belfast, were seen as especially reckless.[71]

PIRA ignored the calls for a ceasefire and decided to continue with its campaign. The reasons for the decision were broadly ideological and strategic. The tradition of the nationalist vanguard never inclined hardliners to take more than a passing interest in popular opinion. For MacStiofain, any peace now, with or without Stormont, would still be peace under colonial rule. It would not end the suffering of the nationalist people. It would merely result in a loss of military momentum and allow the initiative to pass to the constitutional politicians. He scorned the demands for an immediate ceasefire:

> Laying down arms with no guarantee would amount to surrender, leaving Republicans wide open to arrest and wholesale round-ups by the military . . . [the] struggle was not to play politics or to grab momentary praise from the media and the middle class. It was to liberate the country and get the British out of it once and for all.[72]

As if to indicate that the much greater goal of British withdrawal was now in sight, as well as to allay Catholic opinion, the Provisionals assured their supporters that they were 'now entering the final phase of the struggle'.[73] MacStiofain was certain that:

> If we could continue to inflict high British casualties and step up the sabotage campaign it would be difficult for them to bear the strain and the drain on their economy, and no government could be prepared to continue indefinitely in such a situation. They were really in no position to sneer at a truce.[74]

Two months later PIRA's calculations seemed to pay off. PIRA announced that a ceasefire would take effect from 26 June. In response, the Northern Ireland Secretary, William Whitelaw, agreed to meet a PIRA delegation in London. The major medium-term objective of PIRA's military campaign had been achieved. Through a blend of coercive military pressure and limited political manoeuvre,

PIRA had been able to lever itself into a position where it had the chance to shape future British policy towards Northern Ireland. As an example of a strategy aimed at asserting influence over a more powerful adversary, PIRA's conduct had been a model of its kind. Anxious to maintain the tacit bargaining process to keep the pressure on the British, MacStiofain ordered the continuation of operations up to the last minute before the ceasefire. MacStiofain concluded that

> Irish Republican resistance had demonstrated to the British, the Unionists, to our own rank and file and to the whole world that after three years in battle against imperialism the movement was as tough a fighting force as ever and was speaking from strength.[75]

Now that the military instrument had fulfilled its political task it was up to the Provisionals to use their political technique to extract the concessions that would help them realise their overall objectives. On 7 July a delegation representing the Provisionals consisting of Sean MacStiofain, Daithi O Conaill, Seamus Twomey, Ivor Bell, Gerry Adams, Martin McGuinness and Myles Shevlin was flown to London to meet William Whitelaw.

THE PIRA–WHITELAW TALKS

Notwithstanding the impeccable strategic logic and the undoubted operational skill of the military campaign which had placed the Provisionals at the negotiating table, a number of questions about PIRA's strategy still lingered. Was, for instance, PIRA's strategy designed to suit the prevailing political circumstances, or did the circumstances happen to suit its campaign? Did it really take all that much planning to make Northern Ireland appear ungovernable? After all, in the age of world-wide telecommunications violence of all kinds tended to be amplified. A few selectively covered incidents could easily convey the televisual impression of a mass killing ground. Horrible though the suffering was, the violence between 1969 and 1972 still claimed only half the lives lost in road accidents in the province over the same period.[76] And Stormont, for all its bastion-like facade, was really an anachronism waiting for its own downfall. Therefore, the collapse of the unionist power structure cannot be regarded as having provided the supreme test of PIRA's strategy. PIRA's campaign was certainly not inconsequential. No government agrees lightly to talk with those it has branded terrorists. However, the point is that, by placing themselves within the tradition of militant republicanism, the Provisionals were conditioned to respond to the status quo in a pre-determined way. As Bishop and Mallie have argued, by initiating their offensive the Provisionals 'were simply resuming hostilities against anyone in the Queen's uniform in a war they had never declared over'.[77] As evinced by all the disastrous campaigns since the end of the Anglo-Irish war, careful evaluation of the utility of armed force had just not been a historical prerequisite for IRA action.

Nonetheless, whatever doubts over the quality of PIRA's political and military analysis, the talks with Whitelaw would provide an ideal opportunity for the

Provisionals to show how far their strategic thinking had advanced. To reach the final goal of a British disengagement would require a high degree of political sophistication and negotiating skill. For it would be in the political arena that the real test of PIRA's abilities would lie. What was to make negotiations with the Provisionals problematical was the unaccommodating nature of republican ideology – the absolute demand for the realisation of an independent, united republic. As the Provisionals saw it, any compromise would be a betrayal, as MacStiofain declared in April 1971, 'concessions be damned we want our freedom'.[78]

The uncompromising commitment to the republican ideal meant that the Provisionals, like their predecessors who resisted the Anglo-Irish Treaty, held a different conception of the term 'negotiation' from the British. Although the Provisionals may have had a basic grasp of the notion of bargaining through military pressure, it is clear that they had little comprehension of political bargaining. To them, negotiation was not about the lengthy process of teasing out common ground through proposal, counter-proposal, tactical concessions and so on. As demonstrated by the controversy over the 1921 Treaty, the concept of negotiation was, in many respects, alien to the republican tradition. How could there be any common ground with the never failing source of all Ireland's political evils? Instead, 'negotiation' was about demand, threat and coercion – in other words, a complete British surrender. This image of the political process was evident in the months preceding the truce. In April 1972, *Republican News* argued: 'It is the British, not we, who still refuse to negotiate. We have made very few, very simple and very reasonable demands, the granting of which would lead to an immediate truce.'[79] Yet these 'reasonable demands' referred to PIRA's unconditional terms as contained in the plan announced during the seventy-two hour truce on 10 March, namely a wholesale British withdrawal. Likewise, when the Provisionals put forward their truce proposals of June 1972 they demanded that the meeting with Whitelaw should take place soon after the implementation of the truce:

> in order to discuss *and secure acceptance of the IRA peace plan* [italics mine] viz: (i) A declaration acknowledging the right of the Irish people to self-determination; (ii) A commitment to withdraw from Ireland by a specific date; (iii) A general amnesty for all political prisoners in Britain and Ireland.[80]

Being so bold as to pre-judge the outcome of the talks suggests the Provisionals believed that, simply because Whitelaw had agreed to a meeting, Britain was willing to acquiesce to their basic demands. When MacStiofain put these demands to Whitelaw he made it plain that the Provisionals were not prepared to compromise on the substance of their plan. They were willing only to discuss issues such as the announcement of further meetings and the timing of a British withdrawal.[81] According to Gerry Adams' biographer, Whitelaw made no promises of substance other than to place the Provisionals' demands before the Cabinet and to give a formal reply within one week, provided the truce remained intact.[82]

Having presented their terms, the Provisionals were unimpressed by Whitelaw's equivocal attitude. Whitelaw was not looking for a way to withdraw from Northern Ireland. Whitelaw himself claims he was persuaded that a refusal to meet PIRA during the ceasefire might have left the Provisionals with a propaganda victory. If the talks failed, then at least he could justify an increase in security measures, particularly to those in the Catholic community such as the SDLP who had been pressing him to meet PIRA so that no opportunity for ending the violence would be missed.[83] The pretension of the Provisionals' demands was obvious since they plainly had no idea of the legal constraints under which the British were compelled to operate. For example, PIRA expected the British government to brush aside the constitutional obligations under the Ireland Act of 1949 which guaranteed the position of Northern Ireland within the UK with the consent of the population. In addition, PIRA's proposals appeared to assume that the British government could override the sovereignty of the Republic of Ireland. It was quite erroneous to think that the British could agree off-the-cuff to Irish unity, which would have entailed the disbandment of the Southern state, or to the release of political prisoners in Irish jails. The British simply had no legal authority in either matter. As Whitelaw recalls dismissively:

> The meeting was a non-event. The IRA leaders simply made impossible demands which I told them the British Government would never concede. They were in fact still in a mood of defiance and determination to carry on until their absurd ultimatums were met.[84]

What is more, the talks seemed to reveal that the Provisionals still had only the most rudimentary understanding of the relationship between politics and violence. In particular, they appeared unaffected by any notion that their own restricted military potential might have some impact on their ability to attain their extensive political demands. The inconsistency in PIRA's thinking was exhibited in a speech by Joe Cahill in 1971 in which he agreed with the view that the conflict would eventually be settled through a political solution, rather than any outright military victory by either side, but went on to say:

> If there is to be a political settlement in Ireland, there must never be another sell-out. We must ensure that the politicians who have betrayed the cause of Ireland for the past 50 years are not allowed to sit on any conference table [sic]. It is our duty to ensure that Republicanism is a felt force and that when a settlement is arrived at, that the last vestige of British Imperialism is driven from our shores.[85]

By arguing that the only acceptable terms for a political settlement could be those that granted PIRA exclusive negotiating rights, and by seeking the total extirpation of British influence, the Provisionals were, in effect, demanding all those things which could only be obtained as a function of military victory – a probability that they had already discounted.

The jumbled signals put out by PIRA's leaders suggested that while they appreciated that they could never physically eliminate Britain's military capabilities, they could still, somehow, induce the British to capitulate. In actuality, what these signals added up to was customary republican zero-sum thinking, which precluded the possibility of a settlement based on mutual compromise and blinded the movement to the realities of the political and military circumstances. Martin McGuinness, one of the PIRA delegates to the talks, claimed some years afterwards: 'I learned in two hours what Irish politicians still haven't learned: that the British don't give easily.'[86] Yet a brief reconnoitre of the prevailing political situation would have shown that the British had little spellbinding reason to give anything at all. The conflict in Northern Ireland was unpopular in Great Britain but it was sufficiently removed from most people's lives for any discontent not to be translated into a significant political issue in mainstream British politics. Also, British politicians made it clear that the situation, in the words of Reginald Maudling, the Home Secretary, could be tolerated so long as the violence could be held at 'an acceptable level'.[87] So far as the British Army's attrition rate was concerned, MacStiofain himself recounts that British officials let it be known to the PIRA delegates that the level of casualties was not especially worrisome.[88]

PIRA's strategic position raised the question about how far a strategy of low intensity attritional warfare could be employed in pursuit of designated ends. Was there a time to recognise the limits of the military instrument and pursue the ends through other, non-violent means? The trouble was that the persistence of ideological absolutism within the movement's thinking inhibited any serious understanding of these sorts of questions. The essence of the Provisionals position was summed up in an article in *An Phoblacht* in 1970, entitled 'The Republican Ethic'. It stated that the movement's primary concern should not be with politics, which was described as the 'the science of the possible', but with the preservation of the purity of republican principles.

> The truth, the entire truth: that is what we mean by a republican ethic, a republican code. As long as republicanism lives, there will be people prepared to live by that code and, if necessary, to die in its defence. So long will the nation survive.[89]

This tract exemplified the nature of the internal dynamic contained within republican ideology, which dictated that any solution which failed to live up to the absolute truth of the 'republican code' would be a violation of the movement's birthright. Given this belief, the fate of the June 1972 talks were more or less preordained, as McGuinness explained:

> The only interest that we had in going to meet Whitelaw wasn't to talk about side issues, this element or that element. Our aim was – and it would be a failure if we didn't get it – to secure a binding agreement from the British declaring their intention to leave Ireland at some date in the future. That was the only interest. The attitude of republicans to the ceasefire was that it was going to be short-term. At the meeting we were going to identify very quickly whether or not we were being played along. We had a single-minded approach to it. If the British weren't going to come up with a declaration of intent to withdraw, then the truce was over.[90]

The resumption of PIRA's campaign took place two days after the talks on 9 July, after PIRA accused the British Army of contravening the truce following a relatively minor conflagration on the Lenadoon housing estate in West Belfast.[91] Although the timing of the breakdown was not altogether to the Provisional leadership's liking, it was, given the basic nature of PIRA's ideological perspective, an inevitable eventuality.

It was the unyielding character of republican maxims that was responsible for the incoherence of PIRA's strategic thought. The main damage this caused to the Provisionals' prospects was that the movement was rendered incapable of exploiting the potential political benefits that its military campaign had created. PIRA's willingness to continue the fight for the absolute republican ideal, regardless of whether the circumstances were propitious for its attainment, was both a symptom and a cause of what was perhaps the most fundamental problem which afflicted, not just the strategy of the Provisionals, but those of generations of physical force nationalists before them as well – the inability to come to terms with the reality of British power and unionist opposition. PIRA's subsequent actions in the days ahead would prove the point.

UNLIMITED IDEOLOGY IN LIMITED WAR

Following the breakdown of the truce, PIRA decided to escalate its campaign. MacStiofain declared that the renewed offensive would be 'of the utmost ferocity and ruthlessness'.[92] Only three days after the resumption of hostilities PIRA actions had claimed the lives of eight soldiers and a policeman. By the end of July the monthly death toll had reached ninety-five, the highest monthly figure recorded in the conflict. PIRA believed that while the British may have been willing to reach an agreement, they had begun backsliding because of growing loyalist unrest. Protestants were worried and resentful at the truce; even more so when news broke of PIRA's meeting with Whitelaw. The main loyalist paramilitary organisation, the Ulster Defence Association (UDA), took to the streets and put up its own barricades to match the 'no go' areas controlled by PIRA in the nationalist districts of Belfast and Derry. Senior UDA leaders were quoted as saying that they would now 'take steps to eliminate the gunmen'.[93] The random assassination of Catholics increased. The reasoning behind the renewed offensive, MacStiofain said, was:

> to re-establish a strong IRA presence throughout the North. This pulled the attention of the British back from the Unionist blackmail move with the UDA, reminding them that the IRA remained the hard central factor in the whole Northern situation. The feeling was that if the offensive could be maintained in sufficient strength it could lead to renewed contact regarding a solution.[94]

'On Friday, July 21', MacStiofain explained, 'a concerted sabotage offensive was carried out.' The Provisionals planted twenty-two bombs in Belfast city centre. All were timed to explode in the space of an hour. The purpose was to 'impose a sudden and severe load on the British–Unionist system'.[95] In all, nine people were killed in the explosions (initial reports put the figure at 11 because of the difficulty of counting the shattered remains of bodies). The atmosphere in the city that afternoon was described in press reports: 'It was impossible for anyone to feel perfectly safe. As each bomb exploded there were cries of terror from people who thought they had found sanctuary, but were in fact just as exposed as before.'[96] Public opinion was outraged. One woman at the scene said: 'This is the end. Mr. Whitelaw should take his coat off and mop up the blood.'[97] 'Bloody Friday', as it became known, was a turning point for PIRA's strategy. Whitelaw had been planning an army operation to regain control of the 'no go' areas since the breakdown of the ceasefire. 'Bloody Friday' provided the final impetus. Hitherto, the 'no go' areas had been tolerated for fear that any move against them would alienate Catholic opinion at a sensitive time when their support was crucial to sustain any new political initiative.[98]

On 31 July, under the code name of 'Operation Motorman', the British Army reoccupied the areas of the Creggan and Bogside known as 'Free Derry' and the barricaded districts of Belfast. There was little resistance. The Provisionals decided not to try to take on the army during the operation, which involved thousands of troops. Motorman represented a decisive blow against PIRA. Not only did the Provisionals lose the propaganda value of the 'no go' areas, which often took on the appearance of PIRA mini-states, but, more importantly, the movement's operational capacity was severely reduced. These areas were a considerable military asset. They provided the Provisionals with safe havens from where they could mount operations and remain effectively immune from the security forces. The 'no go' districts were also the crucible of a great deal of low level violence; casual shootings, stonings, riots and so on, which did much to keep the city areas in a state of turmoil. Motorman also broke up the hard core of PIRA operatives in Belfast and Derry, most of whom were dispersed into the countryside or over the border. The rate of attacks fell sharply. In comparison with the three week periods before and after Motorman, the statistics show a decline in explosions from 180 to seventy-three, shooting incidents declined from 2,595 to 380 and the number of soldiers killed fell from eighteen to eleven.[99] Thereafter, the rate of violence continued to decline in absolute terms slowly over the next few years. The loss of military momentum devastated the military bargaining strategy that the Provisionals had striven to maintain. A high level of military activity had been the key to maximise the psychological pressure on the British to respond to the violence in a manner advantageous to PIRA.

One of the grave weaknesses in PIRA's approach was that its exclusivist apolitical outlook ensured that it was unable to contemplate the necessity of coalition building, tacit or otherwise, with other nationalists. Moreover, after 'Bloody Friday', the Provisionals were politically untouchable. There was no way back to the negotiating process. Whitelaw publicly vowed that he would never again meet with the Provisionals and promised to toughen up security measures by increasing troop levels and expanding the UDR and police.[100] Primarily though, 'Bloody Friday' had given the British Army the pretext it needed to remove the 'no go' areas – perhaps the most significant military factor which had made PIRA a potent threat. Reflecting on the period, Whitelaw believes that in a political sense he was 'extremely fortunate' over the ceasefire episode:

> If as a result of deciding in favour of a secret exploratory meeting, I had become involved in further discussions with IRA leaders, I would eventually have landed myself in great difficulties. Clearly, those ought to have been the IRA tactics. As it turned out, by returning to violence almost at once, they presented me with a considerable advantage. They proved that they were intransigent and that it was the British Government who really wanted an end to violence.[101]

By refusing to play the kind of diplomatic game to which Whitelaw was alluding, that is using the meeting with him to manoeuvre the British into substantive negotiations, the Provisionals undid much of the potential advantage created by their military efforts. Above all, by refusing to accept limited goals in a limited war scenario, the Provisionals had, thanks to the absolutist nature of republican ideology, torpedoed their own strategy, thus providing a clear case of over-escalation in a low intensity conflict.

It is clear from MacStiofain's account that the renewal of PIRA's offensive after the collapse of the truce was intended to increase the pressure on the British to re-open negotiations in the belief that one final push would assure victory. The Provisionals could have learnt from the history of the Irish civil war that a strategy which rests on attaining political goals through psychological pressure is invariably premised on a degree of self-restraint on the part of the more powerful combatant. Similarly, PIRA's strategy was inherently risky because the British always had the power to re-contain, or if sufficiently provoked, to extinguish, the Provisional IRA threat.

Most Provisionals recognised that the military odds were heavily in favour of the British. Myles Shevlin, a member of the PIRA delegation that met Whitelaw, admitted: 'They [the Provisionals] can, of course, be beaten. If the British Army puts the boot in they could be flattened. But will they do it?'[102] PIRA's strategy was premised on the belief that the British would restrict the full employment of their military resources because, in the long run, the aim of holding Northern Ireland within the UK would not be considered worth defending. As Shevlin, again, put it:

> But to me its the mentality of the thing that's incomprehensible. A people that would put up with this sort of thing night after night. Knowing that there were four British soldiers killed last night – all of whom, I'm sure, if you met on your local darts team, would be 'the boys'. What sort of people will accept that? And for a useless cause? That's my answer to 'is it worth it?' Is it worth it to them – the British?[103]

So if it was believed that the British people would not consent to a full-scale commitment to a 'useless cause', then the Provisionals could assume that an escalation in their military actions would increase the desire for a withdrawal from Northern Ireland, rather than provoke a counter-strike. In this regard, the

Provisionals seriously misinterpreted official British perceptions of the conflict. The British government ultimately saw PIRA as an anti-democratic challenge to a freely consenting part of the realm. The escalation of PIRA's campaign merely convinced the British that the Provisionals constituted a sufficient threat to warrant the physical denial of certain operational assets which, until Motorman, it had enjoyed without hindrance. It illustrated PIRA's ignorance of how the British would react to an increase in military activity. These issues needed to be addressed within PIRA's strategy in order that it could build up a realistic picture of its own strategic position relative to that of the British. Only through an appreciation of its own strategy could PIRA have defined what constituted a position of political advantage and begin to identify the areas of opportunity that it could exploit. Above all, it displayed PIRA's failure to realise that its military/political strength reflected a relative, not an absolute, position at any particular point in time, and that simply upping the ante would prove counter-productive. In other words, the logic of military realities meant that PIRA would have to accept more limited political goals commensurate with its military potential and pursue any further objectives through other, non-violent, means.

There is little evidence, in MacStiofain's memoirs or elsewhere, to suggest that the Provisionals gave any serious thought as to how the British might react to the escalation of their campaign following the collapse of the truce. We can infer that the Provisional IRA fell victim to the escalation fallacy in limited war because of an inaccurate assessment of the dimensions of the conflict in which it was fighting. This caused it to over-estimate the power of its own strategy vis-à-vis a militarily superior opponent. But why did such a fundamental misjudgment occur? More intriguingly, why did the Provisionals choose to persist with their campaign even though, after 'Bloody Friday' and Motorman, they had lost their premier negotiating opportunity? Surely, it must have been obvious to the Provisionals that, with the declining impetus of their campaign, it would be virtually impossible to regain the political initiative? The explanation that emerges reveals a darker side to PIRA's internal machinations regarding the military instrument which were seemingly untouched by any real strategic rationale.

PIRA'S MILITARY RECIDIVISM – MARIA MCGUIRE VERSUS SEAN MACSTIOFAIN

One indirect consequence of the carnage of the summer of 1972 was that it led to the revelations of Maria McGuire. She had been a member of the movement (probably of PSF) and had become a confidant of a number of Army Council members. She left the movement in disgust after the 'Bloody Friday' episode. The recollections of her experiences, first in a series of articles in *The Observer* in September 1972 and later in her book, *To Take Arms*, published the following year, threw light onto the debates within the leadership over strategic policy. Her memoirs also provide a useful foil to MacStiofain's autobiography, *Memoirs of a Revolutionary*, which appeared in 1975.

McGuire's *To Take Arms* is a racy account of her involvement with the movement between 1971 and 1972. The book contains a number of defects and her testimony must be treated with caution. The title itself is misleading since it is evident that McGuire never saw any combat with PIRA. Further, her status within the movement was obscure. It is unclear whether she was a member of PIRA or PSF, as is the extent to which she was privy to top level PIRA decision-making. Also, a large part of her statement is taken up with the retelling of her travails during a bungled arms smuggling operation in Amsterdam – an insignificant episode if ever there was one. Fundamentally, though, McGuire was not typical of IRA personnel. She was a young graduate from a well-to-do background, rather naively attracted into the movement by what she believed at the time was its radical chic. Nevertheless, McGuire's account is lucidly written and she is strong in the latter part of the book where she describes the internal manoeuvring that eventually caused her to defect from the movement.

By contrast, Sean MacStiofain's *Memoirs of a Revolutionary* is the somewhat dour testimony of PIRA's first Chief of Staff. MacStiofain concentrates on the bare historical mechanics. Utterly unreflective, with no hint of any kind of introspection that would have allowed him to probe his own motivations for the general edification of the reader, they are the memoirs of someone convinced of the righteousness of his cause. Little is said about strategic or policy debates or any sort of policy discussions within PIRA's Army Council, and, on the whole, he does not say much beyond which was already known. Even so, MacStiofain does enlighten some of the significant phases in republican history. For all their deficiencies, both MacStiofain and McGuire are highly instructive. Both works are flawed. But both are important precisely because they are the only detailed accounts we have of life in PIRA circles during this period, or any other period for that matter.

The crux of McGuire's testimony, so far as it dealt with strategically related matters, was that the main issue of contention within the leadership was the extent to which the armed struggle could continue to be exploited for political benefit. In other words, at what point should the Army Council accept that it had secured the maximum advantage from the military campaign? McGuire says that the argument was split two ways, between hawks and doves. The dovish faction, led by Ruairi O Bradaigh and Daithi O Conaill, with whom McGuire most sympathised, argued that armed force should be complemented by a strong political campaign. This faction, McGuire said, 'saw that ultimately the struggle would have to be translated into political terms, and that how successfully to do this depended on the size of the movement they built up and the basis for unity it had'.[104] Set against such a course were those like MacStiofain, the Chief of Staff, and the commander of the Belfast Brigade, Seamus Twomey, who conceived the struggle almost wholly in military terms.

The first outward sign of tension between the two factions came after the fall of Stormont, when O Bradaigh hinted publicly that the movement might be prepared to call a truce.[105] Any such thought, though, was quashed by MacStiofain, who quickly declared that the military campaign would go on.[106] McGuire paints a grim picture of MacStiofain: an imperious, self-obsessed, politically inarticulate power-seeker, virulently anti-Protestant and constantly mistrustful of the politicos around him, especially O Conaill, who he feared was out to replace him as Chief of Staff.[107] As it was, having subsequently fought his way to a meeting with Whitelaw, MacStiofain could feel vindicated by his decision in April 1972 not to bow to his political doves. However, once at the negotiating table, the Provisionals were flummoxed when Whitelaw was not tempted to submit to their demands. What the July ceasefire revealed was that, once the fighting stopped, the Provisionals lost any kind of power to control events. Without a solid political machine capable of exploiting the opportunities opened up by a period of peace, PIRA found itself unable to extract even the most modest political advantage from its military efforts. After the debacle of the meeting with Whitelaw, the Provisionals were left to drift around rather meaninglessly in the wake of their own political emptiness.

The key players in the aftermath of the Whitelaw talks were the Belfast Provisionals under Twomey. For them, even agreeing to the July truce was a wrench. They were anxious not to lose military momentum and regarded truces with suspicion, especially since the unilateral ceasefire of September 1971 had given the security forces an opportunity to arrest PIRA activists.[108] More fundamentally, most of the Belfast members had joined in the whirlwind years of 1969 and 1970 when the emphasis had been on building up a Catholic defence force. Consequently, the level of political refinement among the grass roots was low, as one member remarked: 'Volunteers were reacting to their hatred of the Brits and the RUC and the feeling that they stood between us and a united Ireland. We never thought of politics.'[109] In deciding what should be done after the Whitelaw meeting, McGuire says that the 'poverty of thought within the Belfast command' largely dictated the future course of events:

> All along they believed – as I had – that by terrorising the civilian population you increased their desire for peace and blackmailed the British government into negotiating. But now it seemed Belfast [PIRA's Belfast Brigade] could not deviate from its course. A political judgement was needed which would determine the nature of the Provisionals' selective response; but all the Provisionals knew was to bomb.[110]

McGuire also alleges that MacStiofain himself was getting agitated at the continuation of the truce because the longer it went on, the more he feared politically minded elements would gain the upper hand in the Army Council.[111] The breakdown of the truce gave him the chance to reassert his authority by throwing his weight behind the Belfast Brigade and the reopening of hostilities. This was one of the main reasons McGuire claims she lost heart in the Provisionals. In her words: 'I saw the power play itself was having a decisive effect on the campaign as MacStiofain sought to confirm his position by using those very methods of which his rivals disapproved.'[112]

So there were a multitude of forces that caused the Provisionals to resume their offensive: ideological pressure which prevented the bulk of the movement from entertaining compromise, MacStiofain's internal power-struggle against

O Conaill and O Bradaigh, the ebbing away of the political initiative to the SDLP and the UDA,[113] but above all, the simple fact that, without the armed struggle, the Provisionals were deprived of any purpose in life. Denied the opportunity to practise violence, the movement looked like it was disintegrating or being eclipsed completely as any kind of political force. Maria McGuire summed up the near-pathetic desperation of the Provisionals' dilemma: 'With the end of the truce we were almost relieved to be getting back to what we understood: but we also knew that the breakdown of the truce was likely to be tragic for all of us.'[114]

All this made the return to the military offensive more disquieting. 'Bloody Friday' was only the worst in a line of atrocities in the following six weeks after the breakdown of the truce, as PIRA gave full vent to its fury. Some twenty-five civilians were killed, mostly by crossfire in gun battles with troops. There was also a renewed car-bombing campaign which devastated town centres all over the province. In one car-bomb attack on the village of Claudy, Co. Londonderry, on 31 July, eight people were killed. Even in the months after Operation Motorman, when it was clear that PIRA's political fortunes were receding, MacStiofain was still indulging in loud, threatening histrionics. 'Let it be placed on record', he said, 'that the Army Council is determined to continue the armed struggle until total victory, regardless of the cost to ourselves or others,' and adding 'that there will not be another truce until our demands have been met'.[115]

There appeared little real strategic reasoning behind the havoc. Even if the resumption of the military campaign was just a rash piece of escalation rather than undertaken to satiate internal organisational pressures, there was little it could have achieved, certainly nothing on the grandiose scale MacStiofain still envisaged. The fact remained that PIRA had blown its best political opportunity. The resumption could only have had a most marginal impact on PIRA's overall bargaining position. In any case, the British government, which had already taken a political gamble by meeting the Provisionals, was in no mood to be led back into direct negotiations. The conclusion we come to is that PIRA was simply out of control. McGuire commented when the movement exploded back onto the military scene: 'Soon we were becoming prisoners of a new situation. We were being carried along by a series of senseless killings that only MacStiofain and Twomey could stop: but they had no idea what else to do.'[116] Years later, one Provisional confessed that he was still at a loss to explain the psychosis which gripped the movement in those few months in 1972: 'It just seemed that something snapped. There was death everywhere in the North in those days. I guess it just rubbed off on the lads.'[117]

By the end of the summer of 1972, PIRA could barely be described as a coherent political organisation with clearly attainable goals based on the cultivation of popular support and possessed of the flexibility of means and outlook to advance towards its objectives in measured steps. The level of tactical skill it had exhibited was indisputable, and the thinking governing how these small military engagements could be manipulated to entice the British into a negotiating position was initially sound. Yet, because of a powerful mixture of ideological pressure to resist compromise and unflinching reliance, not to say dependence, on armed force, the Provisionals, or at least those who held sway like

MacStiofain and his cohorts, were unable to recognise that their expansive objectives could not be achieved by military means alone. The outcome was that PIRA was not psychologically equipped to convert its military campaign into any kind of political currency. Instead, the movement slipped back into a form of violent recidivism which merely concentrated on the narrow search to preserve the military modality of its struggle, regardless of how its ability to achieve its objectives was affected. Overall, the unpoliticised nature of the Provisionals left the movement incapable of observing restraints on the use of force and, therefore, prone to ill-considered acts of escalation. One newspaper article of mid-1972 encapsulated the fundamental character of PIRA's strategic pre-disposition: 'too few ideas chasing too many guns'.[118]

5 The erosion of Provisional IRA strategy, 1972–1977

Despite the setbacks during the summer of 1972, the Provisional IRA still looked a formidable organisation. The continuing destabilisation generated by PIRA's violence over the preceding two years still left it in a position to influence the political atmosphere in Northern Ireland. Over the longer term, however, PIRA's persistence with its campaign was to prove calamitous for the organisation. By 1976, following a prolonged ceasefire, PIRA had exhausted its military options and been brought to the brink of defeat, not just by the improvements in the efficiency of the security forces, but by the faulty assumptions of its own strategy.

THE PROVISIONALS' DILEMMA IN THE SECTARIAN WAR

If there was one decisive phase in the conflict which destroyed much of the credibility of PIRA's strategy it was the sectarian war which gripped Northern Ireland for most of the mid-1970s. From the spring of 1972 onwards, the rise in the murder of Catholic civilians marked the beginning of the much talked about Protestant backlash. The backlash was the product of fear and despair at what Protestants saw as PIRA's relentless assault on their people, towns, businesses and way of life. The height of loyalist disillusionment was reached in mid-1972 following the imposition of direct rule and later the British government's truce with the Provisionals. Tommy Herron of the UDA explained the sense of frustration:

> Remember, we waited three and a half years. All that time we just didn't believe the security forces would let us down – would leave us so exposed. But when they started, literally sheltering them and harbouring them in the ghetto areas . . . and at the same time arranged a ceasefire. . . . I think that was the point that broke the back of some and put heart into others. . . . Don't forget we didn't ask for the violence. The mistake the loyalist population made was to show too much restraint and compassion in the beginning. It was taken for apathy and cowardice. . . . From now on, we'll do whatever's necessary.[1]

In 1972 loyalists were responsible for 102 deaths, mainly through shootings and bombings. By 1977, total loyalist killings reached 531.[2] The two main agencies behind the backlash were the UDA's military wing, the Ulster Freedom Fighters

(UFF), and the Ulster Volunteer Force (UVF). From the outset, the loyalist paramilitaries tended to regard all Catholics as potential rebels.[3] Consequently, most of the loyalists' victims were Catholics who had nothing to do with the republican movement. The intention of the killings was to choke-off support for the Provisionals by terrorising the nationalist population.[4] The killings did generate great fear and anxiety within the Catholic community. Martin Dillon and Denis Lehane, who studied the early years of the sectarian war, have suggested that the 'profound sense of shock' in the Catholic community resulted from:

> the change in a position where Catholics had been led to believe they were 'winning' to one where their vulnerability had become apparent. The Catholics had been vulnerable all of the time, but while the initiative was held by, and all the running made by, Catholic groups, many Catholics failed to realise this.[5]

Whether the Protestant paramilitaries had planned it or not, their campaign of sectarian attacks challenged the whole basis of PIRA's strategic thought. The Provisionals were placed in a dilemma. Loyalist killings were undermining PIRA's claim to be the defenders of the Catholic population. If PIRA failed to react to stop the attacks it risked losing much of its credibility amongst nationalists. Realistically, all PIRA could do was to retaliate equally randomly against Protestants. Yet to respond in kind would confute the republican principle of non-sectarianism, which the movement had sought to observe in principle. The Provisionals believed that beneath the artificially induced veil of sectarianism the Protestants were just as Irish as the Catholics.[6] The notion that the Protestants could be reconciled to the Irish nation caused the Provisionals to take a relaxed attitude to future loyalist intentions. A typical view was expressed in one Provisional publication:

> If the average Protestant knew that Britain was withdrawing on a certain date and if such a withdrawal would cause him no financial loss (through social services etc.) and no loss of civil liberties, he would not strenuously object to some form of united or federally united Ireland.[7]

In consequence, when the murders of Catholics reached a more worrying scale, the Provisionals found it incomprehensible why any Protestant 'would want to murder their fellow Ulstermen at this stage of the conflict.'[8] Instead, the killings were ascribed to British Army death squads:

> The Brits then took the only course they know [sic]. They had to attempt to lower, the by now sky-high morale of the people. They had to try and discredit the freedom fighters and protectors of the people. They did this, not by trying to 'flush' out the IRA nor by 'hot pursuit', but by the lowest of Black and Tan terror tactics. After making sure that a couple of areas, were 'cleared' of any form of protection, they sent in their mobile murder squads. With orders, not just to shoot anyone, but instead, to shoot, the youngest people that they could find, and so strike fear into the hearts of the fathers and mothers in all areas.[9]

According to Dillon and Lehane's investigations, only two of the 200 deaths they examined could be blamed on the army.[10] The army's role in the assassinations, they concluded, was 'statistically insignificant'.[11]

Protestants remained sceptical of PIRA's non-sectarian incantations. In their view, PIRA's attacks, particularly those against the RUC and UDR, had always been sectarian in form. PIRA strongly denied the charge: 'It never mattered whether it was RUC, BA or UDR. Once they donned those uniforms they became symbols of repression. . . . The fact that they were Catholic, Protestant or Hindu didn't matter, we never allowed religion or personalities to deter us from the task in front of us.'[12] The image of non-sectarianism was necessary to sustain the theory of the single nation and to reassure Protestants that they would not be discriminated against in a future united Ireland. But the nature of the emotional drives that powered the Provisionals clashed with the commitment to the non-sectarian ideal of republicanism and revealed the tangle of contradictions which underlay PIRA's strategic thinking.

In spite of what PIRA's leadership said, it was clear that, from mid-1972 onwards, Provisional units were killing Protestants in the same indiscriminate fashion. Dillon and Lehane conclude that during the fourteen days of the 1972 summer truce, ten Protestants were killed, of which six deaths were almost certainly the work of PIRA units.[13] The leadership formally denied any PIRA involvement in the killing of Protestants and would only go so far to accept the existence of what they termed 'freelance' elements.[14] The reality was that at local level there was considerable anti-Protestant sentiment. One volunteer in Belfast remarked: 'Maybe you can't bomb a million Protestants into a united Ireland but you could have good fun trying.'[15] Such antagonism was symptomatic of more elementary sectarian feelings which often extended to the highest levels of the movement. For example, Maria McGuire alleged that at one particularly fraught meeting of the Army Council, Sean MacStiofain blurted out: 'What does it matter if Protestants get killed. They are all bigots aren't they?'[16] Usually, though, sectarian threats were communicated more euphemistically. The Provisionals' would speak of their aim being the 'Withdrawal of the British way of life from this island',[17] or argue that: 'The Anglophiles must be removed from power and the Ulster-British prevented from frustrating – as they have done hitherto – the self-determination of the Irish nation.'[18] Even O Bradaigh, one of the more conciliatory figures in the Provisional leadership, occasioned to warn Protestants, somewhat ominously, that: 'If you do not want to liberate yourselves then we will liberate you.'[19]

One of the most intriguing pieces of evidence of inherent sectarian bias within PIRA came in May 1974 when a number of PIRA documents were seized during a raid on the safe-house of the organisation's commander in Belfast, Brendan Hughes. According to British government officials, the documents purportedly revealed PIRA's intentions to foment huge civil disorder through indiscriminate violence. The idea was to provoke so much inter-sectarian anarchy throughout the province that PIRA would be able to pose as the only true protectors of the Catholic population.[20] The Provisionals admitted the authenticity of the documents but denied the interpretation put on them by the British,[21] arguing that it was purely a contingency plan 'in the event of civil conflict occurring'.[22] Even so, the documents stated that in such an event 'the IRA has no alternative but to employ its full resources to the defence of its people in the face of the armed offensive against the Catholic working class'.[23] The reference to 'its people' being the 'Catholic working class' clearly identified the sectarian inclinations of the Provisionals' thinking. This seemed to be reinforced further by the plan's specific instructions to place car-bombs in 'P. areas', presumably Protestant districts.[24]

The contradiction between PIRA's theoretical adherence to non-sectarianism and the anti-Protestant prejudice of many of its members stemmed from PIRA's role as a Catholic defence force, which was still a primary motivation for many members. Consequently, sectarian assassinations were publicly rejected but implicitly accepted. For this reason PIRA never acknowledged responsibility for any sectarian killing of Protestants. They were either left unclaimed or claimed under cover names. For example, in the autumn of 1974, PIRA's third Belfast battalion, based in the Ardoyne and New Lodge areas of the city, claimed a series of sectarian murders under the name of the Red Flag Avengers.[25]

Within PIRA's rank and file, sectarian feeling could be an all-consuming force, satiating a certain need to indulge in violence largely for its own sake. In the very early years of the conflict all civilian killings had to be authorised by brigade commanders after a full report had been carried out. Following the introduction of internment, and with the general improvements in the intelligence apparatus of the security forces, which netted the more senior PIRA operatives, such rules governing civilian assassinations tended to be overlooked.[26] This produced a movement that was often volatile and unmanageable. Reflecting on her own experience in the movement, Maria McGuire recounted:

> Once we could say this brigade was doing this and this brigade was doing that, but we could not at the end. We were saying, 'My God, is this one of ours', because in May and June [1972] we lost control completely. . . . All the real IRA men are in jail now. Who's left? Eighteen-year olds control the battalions with a few fanatics. That is the organisation. In fact it broke down when the IRA men were pulled in. Command had to be given to people who would normally never have a command.[27]

Itchy trigger fingers proved especially difficult to restrain during ceasefires. The frustration at being unable to attack the security forces meant that the aggression of the volunteers was often re-channelled onto the Protestant community. During the 1972 ceasefire, the involvement of PIRA units in sectarian attacks rose dramatically, while the 1975 truce saw the worst period of inter-communal warfare the province had known. The most notorious of PIRA's renegade groups was the South Armagh Republican Action Force (SARAF), a flag of convenience for PIRA's units in the border areas of counties Armagh and Down. These units never accepted the 1975 truce and were responsible for a spate of sectarian murders in the area, including the worst single incident of its kind. Ten Protestant workmen were shot dead by SARAF units near the village of Kingsmills on 5 January 1976, in apparent retaliation for the killing of five Catholics in two shooting incidents near the village of Whitecross in the same area a day earlier.

The participation of PIRA units in the sectarian war confirmed many Protestant fears about their future in a united Ireland, making them more determined to resist such a prospect. An editorial in the Belfast journal *Fortnight* noted that in the early days of the troubles that PIRA's activities merely fuelled Protestant suspicion: 'They don't even bother to make any attempt to persuade Protestants that they are really wanted in the new Republic. . . . Virtually everything they do is directly geared to increase rather than decrease Protestant separation.'[28] This comment went to the heart of the conflict in PIRA's thinking between the explicit acceptance of the Protestant tradition as part of the Irish nation and the assumption that unionists were tools of British imperialism whose will to defend their position would collapse once colonial patronage was removed. In effect, the Provisionals ruled out Protestant opinion as a factor which had any significant bearing on their strategic position. The efficacy of PIRA's strategy therefore rested on the presumption of Protestant passivity. PIRA believed that because it was fighting a colonial occupier it could reach an agreement with the British over the heads of the Protestants, who would then simply accept what Britain told them.

The problem for PIRA was that the closer it came to achieving success, the more restless the loyalist paramilitaries became. Once the loyalist paramilitaries initiated their campaign against Catholics, PIRA's strategy was fatally exposed as 'the talk shifted from "fear of the backlash" to "the danger of civil war"'.[29] For the loyalists, this ensured that the simple, cheap option of a quick deal to get rid of Northern Ireland was unavailable to the British government. The political implications of the rise in sectarian killings during the summer truce of 1972 produced alarm in PIRA's leadership, as McGuire made evident:

> It was of course in their [the loyalists] interests to destroy the accommodation the British government had come to with the Provisionals, to demonstrate that any attempt at reaching agreement with us was bound to fail. . . . But clearly, too, some members of the Republican movement were retaliating in the same senseless way, and the slide into outright sectarian warfare seemed to be continuing. This could wreck the position we had reached.[30]

By late 1972, even MacStiofain was forced to admit that it was difficult to dismiss the loyalist paramilitaries, claiming: 'Only a fool would do so.'[31] Yet this was exactly what he had been doing a few months previously. In early 1972 MacStiofain said of the unionists: 'I can't see these people preparing themselves for a protracted guerrilla war. It's just not in them.'[32] It was symptomatic of PIRA's superficial understanding of the loyalist perspective that it ignored potential Protestant power. The Protestants had proven, ever since 1912 and the home rule issue, that they had sufficient cohesion to mount a credible threat against inclusion in an all-Ireland political framework. The Provisionals chose to glide over this point because their ideology had difficulty entertaining the idea that many of their compatriots did not want to be 'liberated' from British rule.

The sectarian war confronted the Provisionals with this historical fact. It was, and remains, one of the most deep-seated inconsistencies in PIRA's strategic thinking. Far from the Protestants having to reconcile themselves to the inevitability of a united Ireland, it was the Provisionals who had to face up to the reality that Protestant opposition could sabotage their plans.

Some evidence also suggests that once the Provisionals had become used to the fact of the loyalist killings, they themselves sought to exploit the conflict for political gain. At certain times it does appear that PIRA was trying to stoke up sectarian violence. For example, by mid-September 1974 the scale of UFF and UVF attacks had tapered off, if only temporarily. Yet on the 16 September, PIRA touched off another round of sectarian killings by assassinating two magistrates. Within a month there had been over a dozen sectarian killings, with the Provisionals implicated in the deaths of at least two Protestants.[33] Potentially, the fostering of sectarian tension could assist PIRA in two ways. First, by provoking loyalist attacks, Catholics would continue to seek PIRA's protection and second, communal hostility polarised society and eroded the political middle ground which destroyed any hope for an internal settlement within Northern Ireland.[34] It was a low risk option for the Provisionals. They could hope that political sterility and the threat of civil war would encourage exasperation in Great Britain and raise calls for withdrawal, while being assured of sufficient political instability to give the movement sustenance.[35] There was little doubt that PIRA could be a beneficiary of the distress created within the nationalist community. For instance, in early 1973 journalistic sources reported that: 'The terror of the local people increased by every murder and its inevitable reprisal has given the Provisionals a new authority.'[36]

One of the most substantive indications that PIRA at least contrived to turn a blind eye to sectarian attacks carried out by its own members can be seen by looking at the relationship between PIRA and the SARAF during the 1975 ceasefire. This period illustrates the complexity and ambiguity that surrounded PIRA's involvement in the sectarian war and the quandary in which the leadership found itself when confronted with rogue elements that would not obey Army Council directives. On 5 June 1975, Francis Jordan, a local Provisional commander in South Armagh, was shot dead by the British Army while planting a bomb outside a Protestant pub in Bessbrook. PIRA's leaders were embarrassed at such a clear cut affirmation that its members had been engaging in blatantly sectarian attacks. They could not deny that he was a member of their organisation as it might have encouraged the border units to break away completely. Neither could PIRA attempt to crush these units without admitting that it had lost control over sections of the movement. Even if the movement did dissipate its energies trying to put down an internal rebellion, there was no surety that PIRA forces would have been able to deal with such tough border units. According to one apparently informed source writing under the pseudonym of 'MacMoney' in *Fortnight*, the leadership reached a quid pro quo with its border units. So long as the name of the SARAF was used to claim for the more brutal sectarian assaults, then the leadership would condone the autonomy of its units in the area. In return, the leadership would publicly claim on behalf of PIRA any other SARAF operations which could be justified either as legitimate retaliation against the UDR and regular army, or as measures against loyalist paramilitaries in defence of the local Catholic population. Thus, the *Fortnight* article concluded: 'It is a case of the Provo dog being waved by the [SA]RAF tail into civil war, which many of the Provos in fact believe is the only realistic way to a united Ireland.'[37]

There is no absolute proof that PIRA intentionally triggered sectarian killings as a matter of official policy. Unofficially, though, it is a different matter. The bulk of the circumstantial evidence suggests that some Provisionals were deeply involved in the sectarian war. Attacks against the Protestant community can be seen as a natural consequence of the underlying sectarian motivations of many members of the movement. The loss of PIRA's military ascendancy caused by the appearance of the loyalist paramilitaries undermined its strategy. No longer could it expect to reach a decision in Northern Ireland through force of arms without the compliance of the Protestants. Although the leadership did not openly approve of retaliation against Protestants, it did, at least, seem adept at fishing in the troubled waters of inter-communal strife. In this sense, the sectarian conflict did help revive PIRA's flagging fortunes as it renewed its defensive mandate with the Catholics, even though the unofficial reprisals meant admitting, de facto, that there could be no rapprochement with the Protestants. Victory for PIRA appeared even less certain once the loyalist paramilitaries arrived on the scene, but at least the Provisionals could ensure a protracted stalemate in Northern Ireland by working the cycle of sectarian violence to block any political moves in which they were not involved. By participating in the sectarian war PIRA condemned its strategy but saved itself.

EXTENDING THE WAR – PIRA'S BOMBING CAMPAIGN IN ENGLAND

The sectarian war was one of the main factors which stalemated the Provisionals' campaign in Northern Ireland. Of course, PIRA's limited capacity for military manoeuvre had already been revealed after the 'Bloody Friday' and Operation Motorman episodes. Now, PIRA could not even begin to make the military running without being immediately checked by loyalist counter-violence. Additionally, the growing efficiency of the security forces was succeeding in confining PIRA's activities largely to certain areas of Belfast, Derry and the border regions. By late 1972, the constraints on PIRA's ability to retain the political initiative by increasing the rate of military operations was glaringly obvious. So far as PIRA's strategy was concerned, the violent crucible of Northern Ireland could no longer be regarded as the only, nor even the decisive, area of operations.

The nature of PIRA's analysis did, however, provide a route out of the impasse in the North. The Provisionals saw no need to alter the basic tenor of their strategy because loyalist resistance was regarded as a function of colonial rule which would collapse when the British prop was withdrawn. At most, the loyalists were seen as a tactical inconvenience because the theory of British imperialism eliminated them as a strategic barrier. There was certainly no reason, therefore, why PIRA should have wished to defer to loyalist violence by reaching some sort of internal accommodation with the Protestants. This would just be a British inspired ruse to maintain imperial control: 'The subtle use of the phrase "Settle their differences" is an attempt to shift the onus of responsibility from her own shoulders where it rightly belongs, on to the shoulders of the Northern Gaels and Planters.'[38]

Ultimately, then, it did not matter to the Provisionals if the Protestants could fight them to a standstill in the North because their strategy had always assumed that the power to change the political status of Northern Ireland did not lie in the province, but in the hands of British politicians in London. The pivotal element in PIRA's thinking had been, first and foremost, directed at using the military instrument to affect British opinion as a lever on the politicians. As Gerry Adams put it: 'the English people have a responsibility for Ireland's British problem. They have the power to persuade their Government to withdraw.'[39] In this respect the attempt to hold the military initiative by mounting a campaign in England represented an extension of PIRA's strategy, not a complete change in direction, by shifting the focus of the conflict to another theatre.

As the Fenian and 1939 bombing campaigns demonstrated, the idea of taking the struggle to English soil exercised a powerful allure for republicans. In the Provisionals' view, the British people were ignorant and apathetic about Ulster because they were untouched by the violence and because they:

> were informed by the British propaganda machine that the Ulster problem was simply one of religious conflict, that the British Government (by some miracle) were really no part of the conflict, that it was simply the mad Paddies killing each other and it would soon cool down with the help of the British army.[40]

'English people should be interested in what their country's army is doing in Ireland,' Adams opined, 'Sadly this interest had only come when the problem had involved them directly.'[41] By 'involving them directly', Adams was referring to a campaign in Great Britain which, it was believed, would knock the English out of their complacency. 'England has to waken up and realise that the sooner she removes her troops from Ireland, the better it will be for everyone concerned.'[42] It was in propaganda terms that an English campaign was considered most valuable because actions in Great Britain would gain far greater publicity – the idea that one bomb in Britain was worth ten in Belfast. The effects of such publicity would ensure that the population in England could never feel immune from the conflict in Northern Ireland.[43] It was assumed that the feelings of insecurity would translate into political pressure for withdrawal because people would start 'to question the role of the British army in Ireland and whether continued British rule in NI helped the continuation of the conflict'.[44]

In other words, the main theoretical thrust of PIRA's campaign in Great Britain was an advocacy of terrorism, in its strictest descriptive sense, as the intention was to manipulate violent incidents to create a disproportionate sense of fear relative to the actual damage caused. The pronouncements of PIRA leaders also indicated that this was the motive. Seamus Twomey, for instance, one of the main proponents of extending PIRA's campaign to Great Britain, said: 'But every war has a psychological side. We must be careful the people don't get used to war. We increase the fear of war, when we think it is right, and we reduce it for the same reason.'[45] The character both of Twomey's remarks and of the earliest phase of PIRA's campaign in England, with its attacks on civilian premises such as tourist sites, pubs, stations, etc., certainly seemed to accord a terrorist intent which holds that it is the indeterminate nature of the threat that can make a political actor more compliant to the demands of its adversary. So, a measure of indiscrimination in targeting policy will be essential to maintain the sense of unpredictability in order to heighten the feelings of insecurity and fright.[46]

Beyond a straight terrorist motive, PIRA's attacks could also be used in a more precise way to manipulate the political agenda. Indeed, it was a clearly stated aim to use the military instrument to intervene in the political process so that 'at every stage of every British political initiative, of every British political failure in the background and often in the foreground will be that predictable, consistent act of IRA violence'.[47] The Provisionals acknowledged that their first attack in Great Britain, on 8 March 1973, when three car-bombs exploded outside the Old Bailey, killing one person and injuring 147 others, was timed to coincide with the border referendum in Northern Ireland, held on the same day.[48] The referendum antagonised many nationalists as there could be little question that the outcome would be a conclusive vote in favour of retaining the union. For that reason, the Army Council determined on a show of strength in Great Britain both to undermine the impact of the poll and regain nationalist support.[49] In similar fashion, the Provisionals said they bombed a London hotel in September 1973 to correspond with the negotiations between the constitutional parties in Northern Ireland to form a power sharing government.[50] These examples were indicative of the Provisionals' attempts to underscore the psychological attrition strategy by demonstrating at each turn of events the irrelevance of any proposed solution which sought to exclude them.

Later, in 1975, a new twist was added to PIRA's campaign with a spate of attacks on exclusive hotels and restaurants in the West End of London, as well as on prominent individuals. Two people were killed by an explosion at the Hilton Hotel on 6 December. This was followed by attacks on banks and London underground stations. Between October and November, four people were killed in restaurant blasts, while Professor Gordon Hamilton Fairley was killed in a car-bomb intended for Conservative MP, Hugh Fraser, and Ross McWhirter, co-editor of the *Guinness Book of Records*, was shot dead on the doorstep of his home. These attacks were designed to intimidate wealthy and influential members of society in the belief that if these people were affected by the violence PIRA's message would be sure to get through to the highest establishment circles.[51] In 1977 Twomey confirmed the thinking behind these attacks: 'By hitting Mayfair restaurants, we were hitting the type of person that could bring pressure to bear on the British Government.'[52]

In certain respects, the targeting of supposedly select, 'establishment' figures was a measure of the anxiety which had crept into PIRA's campaign by the latter part of 1975, as it became increasingly evident that its previous attempts to intimidate the general population were not producing the intended effects. The bombing campaign in England illustrated many of the false premises upon which PIRA based its calculations of the efficacy of the military instrument within the context of low intensity warfare. The bombings did raise public apprehension, especially when they were directed against overtly civilian targets.[53] However, the success of the campaign in England was contingent on the fear and publicity generated by the attacks initiating a specific set of responses from the British population that would advance PIRA's cause. PIRA's thinking began from the hypothesis that, having created a general level of fear through a systematic campaign of violence, the public's reactions would proceed from cause-to-effect in a very exact manner: first, people would detect the source of their fear which they would trace to the political situation in Northern Ireland; second, this would cause the British role in the conflict to come under scrutiny; third, the people would recognise the justness of PIRA's cause, or simply want to remove the source of fear; and fourth, this would lead to popular pressure for withdrawal from Northern Ireland.

All told, this was a highly presumptuous strategy based on a series of wholly unproven suppositions about human behaviour under stress. Simply creating a sense of fear through a certain level of military activity could not guarantee triggering such a precise chain reaction. The Provisionals had only to look at the effects of their campaign on the Protestants in Ulster and the rise of the loyalist paramilitaries to see that a community's will to resist could be fortified when placed under threat. It is probably true to say that societies, like individuals, have some psychological breaking point when subjected to enough hardship. But thresholds of tolerance can be enormously high. In fact the strategy of psychological attrition which the Provisionals sought to practise was something of a contradiction in terms. The strategy aimed to administer an unacceptable level of violence sufficient to disrupt civil society in order to force the British to concede PIRA's demands. The strategy is an inexact instrument of war and succeptible to a law of diminishing returns. The ability to sustain high levels of fear in the public mind will tend to decrease the longer the conflict goes on. Therefore, a campaign of psychological attrition is not a timeless strategy as the term implies. Far from sustaining a climate of terror, a campaign can, instead, simply give rise to a climate of indifference because the continual exposure to low levels of military action may mentally anaesthetise the public to a point where they are prepared to tolerate an extra degree of violence just as they may tolerate a degree of crime, deaths through road accidents, etc. The moment terrorism loses its unpredictability the strategy becomes meaningless as it is deprived of the very component which makes it terrifying.

The ambiguity of strategies which rely on the evocation of various psychological responses to circumvent the power of a superior opponent illustrated the main difficulty which afflicted PIRA's campaign both in England and Northern Ireland. The fact that PIRA's attacks often resulted in the deaths of security force personnel or the destruction of buildings and so on did not mean that such attacks automatically related to the attainment of the strategic goal because individual operations were not aimed at the equalisation of power with Britain. The killing of individual soldiers and policemen was immaterial to the military balance. Instead, PIRA's operations sought to stimulate certain reactions amongst the population at large – fear, alarm, agitation – in the belief that the cumulative impact would wear down Britain's resolve. But trying to gauge the effectiveness of military actions with reference to elusive psychological factors is itself an unpredictable business. The truth was that the Provisionals had no idea of 'how much' would prove unacceptable to the British, so they just had to kill more soldiers and plant more bombs in the hope that this was having the desired effect of grinding down the will of the public. In reality, it seemed that the culminating point of public stress caused by PIRA violence had passed relatively quickly, both in Great Britain and Northern Ireland. Thereafter, the continuation of PIRA's campaign merely further desensitised popular opinion to the effects of violence. This was the very opposite of what was intended because a lack of interest made the public potentially less receptive to PIRA's political message.

The Provisionals were aware of the extent of public indifference to their campaign, and it was a source of frustration and bewilderment to them that their attacks could, in the words of one republican spokesman, be 'Front page news one day and forgotten the next'.[54] The conclusion that the Provisionals reached, however, was not that the premises of their campaign had been incorrect, but that they had failed to turn the military screw hard enough. A good example of the impulsive desire to step-up the violence produced by the 'frustration factor' was provided by Daithi O Conaill in this excerpt from an interview with the journalist Mary Holland for the Weekend World programme, broadcast on 17 November 1974:

> *O Conaill*:   What have we got from British public, what have we got from the British people? Total indifference. They can't wash their hands. We said last week in a statement that the British Government and the British people must realise that because of the terror they wage in Ireland they must suffer the consequences.
> *Holland*:   Will you escalate that campaign?
> *O Conaill*:   We will.[55]

Four days later, the Birmingham pub bombings occurred, killing twenty-one people. The bombings were widely seen as the Provisionals acting upon O Conaill's warning.[56]

Whether or not the Birmingham bombings represented an intentional piece of escalation, they did show how public reactions could diverge from what was required by the Provisionals to help them move towards their objectives. The anger and revulsion engendered by the bombings found expression not in demands for withdrawal from Northern Ireland, but in calls for sterner security measures.[57] A few days after the bombings a package of security measures, the Prevention of Terrorism Act (PTA), was rushed into law. Among other things, the

Act extended the powers of arrest and detention and placed strict controls on the movement of terrorist suspects between Great Britain and Ireland. The Home Secretary, Roy Jenkins, summed up the reasoning for introducing what he admitted was 'the most draconian programme of security measures we've ever had' thus:

> During my visit to the Birmingham hospitals on Friday and before that to Guildford in October and to the victims of the Tower of London explosions in July, I saw injuries I had hardly dreamt of since the war and I abandoned any attempt to understand the minds of people who can do this.[58]

Jenkins expressed the popular perception of the Provisionals by emphasising incomprehension at something that was seen as psychopathic. The immediate public reaction, therefore, was to seek protection from these outrages, not to empathise with the cause of the people who perpetrated them. The bombings had merely provoked the British into more counter-measures which further hampered the Provisionals' ability to carry out their operations. The Provisionals found out that the fickle nature of public opinion meant that while PIRA's attacks might just about be tolerable at a 'nuisance' level, the moment the violence looked like becoming a real menace to society then the extent to which the public was prepared to indulge the Provisionals' licence for action could be very limited.

PIRA never admitted any part in the Birmingham bombings, though there can be little doubt that its units were responsible for the attacks.[59] At the time, there was a widespread assumption that the indiscriminate 'bombing of the English public into a new level of terrorist reality' was an entirely deliberate course of action.[60] According to the republican sources of the journalist Peter Chippindale, there were many PIRA recruits who were 'quite prepared to try to force a solution to the Irish problem by deliberately and without warning killing large numbers of people in England'.[61] In the aftermath of the Birmingham pub bombings O Conaill was quick to reiterate 'that it is not, and never has been the policy of the IRA to bomb targets without warning to ensure the safety of civilians'.[62] Nevertheless, by the end of 1974, with the possibility of a ceasefire being raised, the Provisionals might have had some reason to believe that their English campaign, atrocities and all, was making the British position more pliable. It was a feeling that PIRA did little to dispel. Despite O Conaill's prevaricatory attitude over the Birmingham bombings, his faith that the campaign was making its mark remained unstinting as he promised to uphold PIRA's policy of 'taking the war to the mainland of Britain'.[63]

THE CEASEFIRE AND THE RECURRING THEMES OF REPUBLICAN STRATEGIC THOUGHT

At the end of 1974 the possibility of a PIRA ceasefire was being aired. There is no firm evidence to show that PIRA's bombing campaign in England had any impact on the timing of the 1975 truce, but it is conceivable that, in the minds of the Provisionals at least, their bombing campaign could be seen as one of the factors to have placed added pressure on the British to agree to a truce.

The actual process that led to the truce of 1975 came quite suddenly following a meeting between a group of Protestant clergymen and top Provisionals in the village of Feakle, Co. Clare, on 10 December 1974. The churchmen provided an informal line of communication between the PIRA and the British government. The Army Council declared a Christmas ceasefire on 22 December while contact continued. After a brief resumption of hostilities from 16 January 1975, PIRA suspended its operations against the security forces on 10 February. The terms of the truce were never formally agreed, but in return for a halt to PIRA's operations the British undertook to phase out internment and to reduce the army's presence in Catholic areas. In addition, a number of incident centres staffed by members of PSF were established to monitor the truce and liaise with the Northern Ireland Office (NIO).[64]

From the British point of view the truce offered a breathing space to concentrate on the latest political initiative, the setting up of a Constitutional Convention to work out a devolved form of government for the province (this followed the collapse of the Power Sharing Executive earlier in 1974). Furthermore, in January 1975, the Gardiner Committee, set up to examine the legal issues involved in the suppression of violence in Northern Ireland, recommended the abolition of internment and the ending of special category status for prisoners which had been in place since June 1972. This formed a key part of the government's overall aim to return the province to a sense of normality. According to the then Secretary of State, Merlyn Rees, the ceasefire could help this process by creating the conditions which could weaken the Provisional's military organisation and possibly draw them into peaceful political action.[65]

PIRA's motives are more difficult to decipher. It seems that there was agreement between hardliners and moderates on the advantages of a ceasefire, though for divergent reasons. The peace-feelers via the Feakle intermediaries came at an opportune moment for PIRA, just when its stock within the Catholic community had been diminished by the Birmingham bombings. The background to the truce had also seen PIRA's military campaign continue to lose momentum in Northern Ireland. In 1974, fifty members of the security forces had been killed compared with seventy-nine in the previous year. Shooting incidents declined from 5,018 to 3,206 and explosions from 978 to 685.[66] The hardliners on the Army Council led by Twomey, who had replaced Sean MacStiofain as Chief of Staff following the latter's arrest in the Irish Republic in November 1972, remained convinced of the necessity to raise the military tempo, but recognised the value of a ceasefire to replenish reserves prior to the relaunching of hostilities. On the other hand, the moderates under O Conaill felt that a truce could offer a chance to test the political waters by getting the British involved in negotiations.[67] Either way, the two factions could at least agree that a truce gave PIRA the chance both to extract further concessions from the British over issues like internment and to re-establish its popularity amongst Northern Ireland's Catholics.[68] Even so, PIRA's shilly-shallying over the Christmas and New Year periods did indicate that a vigorous internal debate was going on. Initially, the movement extended its Christmas ceasefire 'to enable the British Government to establish proper communications with the Republican leadership and thus begin negotiations which will lead to the removal of the English way of life from this island'.[69] The Army Council then called off the ceasefire because the British failed to respond to PIRA's terms,[70] but still left the door open by publicly regretting the breakdown and saying that they were 'sincere about negotiating for a just and lasting peace'.[71]

PIRA's eventual acceptance of the February ceasefire was the clearest sign that O Conaill's moderates were now in some sort of ascendancy. The concessions PIRA obtained from the ceasefire also strengthened O Conaill's hand. The release of internees and the reduction in the army's presence on the streets, for which PIRA could claim credit, were popular with nationalists. Moreover, the immunity of PIRA members from arrest and the establishment of the incident centres conferred a degree of official British recognition on the Provisionals' position. Beyond this lay the prospect of full-scale negotiations with the British. Presented with these opportunities, however, PIRA failed to consolidate its political ground as the recurring themes of the republican tradition were once again to demonstrate the movement's inability to cope with a period of peace. The paucity of political thinking, the refusal to conceive republican objectives in anything other than black and white terms, and the indiscipline of many PIRA units, were all features of the movement's conduct during the truce.

For the Provisionals to capitalise on their positive image engendered by the ceasefire agreement required them to demonstrate the extent of their support to the British through the electoral process. Since the British government had lifted the ban on PSF in 1974, it had been hoped that the Provisionals might be tempted to stand in the Convention elections due in May 1975.[72] This was a vain hope. As in previous elections, the Provisionals were resolute in their opposition to the ballot box:

> Anyone who stands in this convention election, who works in polling stations or votes, is giving assent to intimidation and accepting that the orange fascists have a right to lay down the terms under which the six counties can be governed – any vote is a vote for a return to the old loyalist sectarian domination.[73]

By ignoring the elections, PIRA simply allowed their constitutional rivals in the SDLP a free run. The SDLP captured 23.7 per cent of the vote on a 64 per cent turn-out, which underlined the failure of PIRA's boycott campaign.

PIRA's objective in the ceasefire was not to participate in what was seen as the phoney internal politics of the province but, as O Bradaigh spelled out at the end of 1974, to get the British to pull out. 'This requires firstly', said O Bradaigh, 'talks with the British Government for a phased withdrawal, and then talks with Loyalists would have to follow to discuss the sort of political arrangement that would come afterwards.'[74] It was the same old list of PIRA demands. Like the summer truce of 1972, the Provisionals fell into the trap of believing that they had forced Britain into the ceasefire, and were, consequently, in a position to exact everything they wanted:

It must be remembered that the Republican Leadership did not agree to the Truce for the sake of limited peace but for the cause of progress so necessary at the time . . . the English must declare their intention to withdraw and have the final solution among Irishmen of all political creeds and religious denominations. . . . Republicans have faced some thirty thousand Crown troops and police and were not only successful but stronger militarily than ever before and fully prepared for all future contingencies.[75]

This sort of exaggerated view of PIRA's military prowess was to prove highly detrimental to the psychological fabric of the organisation. The strident calls for the complete fulfilment of republican demands while being so obviously deprived of the power to achieve them was a recipe for humiliation. The British, who had no intention of being drawn into direct negotiations,[76] were quite happy to ignore the Provisionals' diatribes, with the result that the movement slid into disarray.

The problems began when O Conaill was arrested in the spring of 1975 in the Irish Republic and jailed for a year for IRA membership. His loss was critical for the movement. He had been the prime mover behind the ceasefire on the republican side and was the one leader with sufficient stature to be able to steer the Provisionals in a more flexible direction. O Conaill's departure clearly affected the make-up of the Army Council. The hardline and moderate factions were now deadlocked, each cancelling out the influence of the other. The hardliners were always wary of O Conaill's political leanings. 'If they stand for elections they will get well and truly bloody hammered,' one hardliner warned.[77] With the main politico gone, the hardliners seemed satisfied to sit out the truce, assured that they could block any political move from within the organisation which might either degrade the military structure or endanger republican orthodoxy. Meanwhile, the leadership of the moderates fell to O Bradaigh, the President of PSF. He was an uninspiring figure who appeared to carry little weight within the movement and so was poorly placed to offer any imaginative political leadership in the face of the strengthened position of the hardliners. The upshot was that the Provisionals subsided into a state of insipid listlessness, seemingly content to peddle sterile propaganda to which few outside the movement paid much attention.

Militarily, the Provisionals also had their problems. In July 1975, *Republican News* claimed: 'As for the IRA, the Truce has shown their military strength and discipline unique, in the world of guerrilla war and revolution.'[78] Since the beginning of the ceasefire PIRA had shown some restraint against the security forces. In other areas, the claims of self-control were less convincing. The ceasefire had immediately raised the suspicions of the loyalist paramilitaries which sparked another outbreak of vicious sectarian murders. Most of the 216 civilians killed in 1975 were Catholics but PIRA units also engaged in tit-for-tat killings throughout the ceasefire. The lack of respite for the Catholic community was compounded in February when a bitter feud broke out between OIRA and the newly-formed Irish Republican Socialist Party. Although the IRSP criticised PIRA's lack of commitment to the 'Socialist Republic', both organisations agreed on the principal point of a British withdrawal. 'To the extent that the Provisional policy runs parallel to ours', said IRSP leader Seamus Costello, 'we are prepared to co-operate with them.'[79] The co-operation took the form of a few Provisionals joining in with the IRSP to defeat OIRA's attempt to destroy the breakaway group.[80] The Officials came off worst, losing three men, including their respected Belfast commander, Billy McMillen. Yet this was only a prelude to an even bloodier feud between OIRA and PIRA in October, which left eleven dead. The origins of the feud resided in a host of territorial and personal resentments stretching back to the split of 1970.[81] According to the authoritative journalist, Jack Holland, the Provisionals saw the truce as an opportunity after four years of fighting the British both to settle some old scores with the Officials and to assert their ghetto supremacy.[82]

The point about PIRA's participation, both in the quarrels with OIRA and the sectarian war, is that it demonstrated yet again how the apolitical nature of the republican tradition could give rise to a self-sustaining military dynamic. For many volunteers the ceasefire was an irrelevance. Having been promised constantly over the years that 'victory was staring [them] in the face',[83] they were certainly not going to give up their struggle for the sake of a few incident centres. Indeed, the incident centre in Newry, South Down, was closed after a few months because of the lack of interest from PIRA units in the area. The ceasefire became increasingly ductile the longer it went on. Some thirty members of the security forces were killed during 1975, mainly by the rogue units near the border. Even discounting the sectarian killings and ghetto feuds, the Belfast Brigade stretched the truce to its limits by continuing to attack buildings and police stations. The rhetorical justifications for such attacks, that they constituted retaliation 'against breaches of the truce by the British, i.e. Cold Blooded murder of innocent civilians, harassment of the community and indeed torture',[84] were a thin disguise for the basic frustrations of many PIRA members. To illustrate the point, as early as April 1975 PIRA bombs destroyed £500,000 worth of offices in Belfast in retaliation for an allegedly violent British Army raid on two houses in North and West Belfast. An independent assessment put the repair bill for both the homes at £20.[85]

At the end of 1975 the Provisionals restated their belief that 'the only way to bring peace in Ireland is the full acceptance by the British Government of the demands made by the Leadership of the Republican movement', and added:

> We still honour the truce, fragile though it may be, but if it becomes apparent that our basic demands are to be rejected, then we have no alternative but to renew the armed struggle with an ever greater resolve, ferocity and intensity than ever before.[86]

In fact the truce was already dead, having petered out with the growing indiscipline of PIRA units. The lack of firm leadership from the Army Council meant that many PIRA members had taken matters into their own hands, believing that the reactivation of military operations was the only way they could claw back any political relevance.[87] In a sense, no one could blame them. The absence of peaceful political tactics to absorb the efforts of PIRA's activists during the truce meant that the ceasefire, certainly in the minds of many grass-roots volunteers, was nonsensical. To this degree, PIRA's descent into the welter of sporadic and uncontrolled sectarian violence and factional feuds was merely the logical expression of the movement's basically militaristic ideological drives.

PIRA's predicament was compounded by its growing unpopularity within the nationalist community. PIRA's heavy-handed policing of the ghetto areas and its violent vendetta against OIRA, along with the threat from loyalist killers, created a mood of despondency from which PIRA's political immobilism gave no foreseeable prospect of relief. The extent to which many ordinary Catholics, especially the women, blamed PIRA for the depressing situation was revealed the following year with the rise of the cross-community Peace People. In the meantime, the ceasefire outlived its usefulness to the British. On 11 November, Rees announced the closure of the incident centres and broke off all contacts with PSF in early 1976. To cap a period of almost complete disaster for the Provisionals, when they resumed full-scale hostilities they discovered that many of their operations had been blown by informers. The British had used the truce to increase their surveillance and infiltrate PIRA's ranks, and in the first five months of 1975 over 400 people were charged with violent offences.[88]

The ceasefire trauma was to have a marked effect on the movement. In 1981 a member of PIRA's GHQ staff declared:

> There is no foreseeable prospect of another truce or of any cessation along the lines that obtained in the last two bilateral truces. . . . Because the British were not serious, honest or in any way forthright about their intentions, and because they were just trying to divert the IRA into a demoralising and damaging ceasefire situation, I cannot foresee any circumstances in which the army will get involved in that situation again.[89]

Although the ceasefire revealed the effects of PIRA's political vacuity on its conduct during the truce, it still begs the question, why did the Provisionals, both moderates and hardliners alike, allow themselves to be ensnared in a 'demoralising' and 'damaging' truce for so long? Theoretically, they could have called off the ceasefire at an hour's notice, yet they persisted even after it was clear, in the first few months of 1975, that the British were not interested in talking to PIRA and were busily pursuing their own political agenda with the Constitutional Convention. There are few conclusive answers, but some sort of insight can be gained by looking at the relationship between PIRA's strategy and propaganda, and the impact this had on the movement's self-perception.

Although the Provisionals admitted they could never overcome British military strength, they did believe they could fight in such a way as to force Britain to the conference table. The role of force in this process, as an article in *Republican News* explained in 1974, was to 'bring about suitable conditions to enable political persuasion to operate under more favourable conditions than those prior to the commencement of hostilities'. This was a sound statement of strategic principle but the article proceeded to confuse the issue by adding: 'The aims of the IRA are clear cut and decidedly straight forward. They seek not to defeat the English, but to *compel them* [italics mine], through their political leaders, to disengage so as to have the way for their eventual withdrawal.'[90] Persuasion and compulsion are diametric opposites. One cannot persuade an adversary to feel compelled. He is either compelled or he is not; that is, when he is forced under extreme duress to take the only available option. In other words, compulsion is a function of defeat. A stronger belligerent is unlikely to give into a full set of demands under the limited military duress of a less powerful opponent. PIRA's strategy could *entice* compliance but it could not *enforce* it. There existed a fundamental misapprehension in republican strategic thinking which seemed to blur the relationship between military power and political demands, so that minor British concessions were equated with an admission by Britain of defeat. In the run up to the truce, for example, the Provisionals believed that the British were ready to negotiate a withdrawal. The impression was reinforced because the Provisionals had openly stated in the days beforehand that a British pull out was 'our first pre-requisite for a permanent truce'.[91] So when the truce ended, the Provisionals had felt that the British, in the words of the 1981 PIRA statement, had been neither 'honest' nor 'forthright about their intentions'. As there was never any written ceasefire agreement, there is no way PIRA's claims can be verified. One likely explanation of the situation was that the Provisionals managed to convince themselves that Britain was withdrawing while the British government remained studiously ambiguous over the issue of face-to-face talks in order to keep the ceasefire going.[92] The important aspect here is how the Provisionals perceived their own position at this time. The incident centres, contacts with British officials, the release of internees, the acceptance of PIRA's quasi-policing role in the nationalist areas, all might have given the Provisionals sufficient evidence to confirm their own opinion that they were close to victory. As a result, PIRA could confidently proclaim in March 1975: 'Our military action had the desired effect. The British Government indicated a willingness to give serious consideration to the three basic demands of the Republican Movement for a lasting peace in our land.'[93] The fact that PIRA seemed entranced by the prospect of talks with the British can help explain why it held to the truce for as long as it did in the absence of any negotiations. The paraphernalia of the truce appeared to endow the Provisionals with a powerful self-image which over-rode any previous caution they had concerning the ability of their strategy to score an outright military victory. The idea that British rule was on its last legs filled the Provisionals with a belief that they had literally beaten the British in battle which could now enable them to hammer home their advantage. *An Phoblacht* drew this parallel, and this moral:

> If we look back half a century we will see that Republicans having brought England to her knees on the fighting front, were not able to follow through on the political front – consequently what was won in the military field was lost on the Conference Table . . . no-one can prevent us achieving the ultimate aim but ourselves.[94]

The statement was symptomatic of the Provisionals' misreading of their own position. They were tailoring their demands, not in relation to what could be feasibly achieved given the prevailing balance of forces, but in accordance with their own exaggerated sense of power. This raises a more fundamental question. Was the inflated self-image just a by-product of the ideology, mere propaganda bravado, or was it also an intrinsic element of PIRA's strategic thought, indicative of a more systematic process of self-deception which affected the movement's military thinking?

THE PROCESS OF PIRA'S STRATEGIC ANALYSIS – STILL LOOKING FOR THE YEAR OF VICTORY

The Provisionals proclaimed 1972 to be 'The year of victory'.[95] Two years later the banners read, 'Victory to the IRA 1974',[96] and in early 1977 PIRA's leadership declared: 'We are now confident of victory as we face the final phase of the war with England.'[97] For sure these statements, and many others like them which adorned the republican press throughout the period, were intended as rousing propaganda, but there is no reason to suppose that the movement did not take seriously its own confident assurances of victory. Such confidence was understandable up until 1972, but from then onwards the predictions of victory became less credible for external observers, though seemingly not for the Provisionals themselves. Why did they choose to deceive themselves by continuing to assert unfounded expectations of triumph? The explanation provides a link between all the problems experienced in the sectarian war, the bombing campaign in Great Britain, the 1975 ceasefire, and the overall process of the movement's strategic formulation.

In any war, the particular conditions which affect the conflict scenario are going to have a major bearing on how the instrument of violence will be employed. Against whom? For how long? To achieve what? In essence, this is a contextual issue which concerns the quality of analysis. Incumbent upon any combatant is an accurate appreciation of the circumstances in which it chooses to fight, and on that basis, it can select the most appropriate strategic option. The Provisionals' own assessment of the context in which they fought can be summarised concisely along the following lines: 1) Ireland has a right to self-determination and it is PIRA's aim to bring this about; 2) the aspiration to self-determination is denied by the British who seek to maintain their rule through the artificial division of the island; 3) while this situation prevails there can be no prospect of peace and justice in Ireland; 4) the constitutional arena has shown itself to be an ineffective environment in which to pursue British withdrawal; 5) force, practised within a guerrilla war framework, as in the Anglo-Irish war, has proven the only method guaranteed to shift the British; 6) therefore, force should be concentrated on what has always been the weakest link in the British design, namely, the relationship between the colony (Northern Ireland) and those who underpin the position of the colonial policy-makers (the British public). These were the terms of reference in which the Provisionals sought to construct their strategy, evaluate the military instrument and develop their tactics. This was PIRA's strategic paradigm.

Leaving aside the debate on the desirability of republican objectives or the validity of PIRA's mandate to act in the manner it did, neither of which are the concern of this analysis, how cogent was PIRA's strategic paradigm as a model upon which to devise a realistic military policy? It has always been possible to challenge the pivotal element which held the paradigm together – the notion of Northern Ireland as the artificial product of British imperialism. The central justification to sustain the charge of imperialism, an economic motive, is missing. Although it is true that the most prosperous and industrialised part of Ireland was retained in the Union in 1920, this on its own is not convincing. Historically, Northern Ireland has had the highest percentage unemployment of any part of the United Kingdom. For most of the twentieth century it has had a declining industrial sector and an impoverished agricultural sector. It has no mineral sources in abundance and is a net drain on the central exchequer. Beyond the economic motive, the argument that Britain has security interests in retaining Northern Ireland is also unpersuasive. The only conceivable advantage of the province is as a naval asset, but at best this is marginal since the Northern Irish seaboard faces the wrong way to guard the Atlantic approaches. PIRA's campaign in the 1970s merely went to underline the fact that Northern Ireland detracted from rather than enhanced the UK's overall security position.

Apart from the intellectual case against the colonial interpretation, more empirical evidence in the form of attitude surveys conducted in the late 1970s and early 1980 also negated PIRA's analysis. The findings revealed the extent to which Catholic opinion appeared to diverge from traditional republican perceptions of Britain, with majorities often indicating that they found British influence to be a neutral and, to some degree, even a positive element. In a series of polls 67 per cent of Catholics thought that the British did not care what happened to the province, 69.9 per cent believed that the British treated Protestants and Catholics equally, while 60 per cent agreed with the proposition: 'Were it not for the British Government, the situation in Northern Ireland would be worse than it is.'[98]

The most significant piece of empirical refutation, as PIRA's parlous state in the mid-1970s provided adequate testament, was that the movement's strategy had completely failed to secure its objective. Even so, when the prolonged truce officially expired in early 1976, the Provisionals reiterated their demands for a wholesale British withdrawal, and affirmed:

> Until these demands are met in full, the Irish Republican Army will continue to resist British rule with sustained military pressure. . . . We pledge ourselves to strike at all variants of imperialism in Ireland in the struggle for a Socialist Democratic Republic. . . . The capability of the Irish Republican Army to develop the war of liberation is unquestionable.[99]

Yet in renewing the armed struggle, all the Provisionals were doing was persisting with something which had, after five years, demonstrably not worked, and with little prospect that it would be any more successful in the next five years.

Could it be that PIRA's faith in its ability to 'strike against all variants of imperialism' remained undaunted because the colonial analysis conspired to bolster the perceived potency of its strategy? For a start, the advantage of forming the problem of Northern Ireland within a colonial context was that it fed an image of an inwardly flawed opponent; the notion that although outwardly stronger than republican forces, the British were psychologically weak, without the stomach for a fight, and unable to withstand the continuous assault on the inherently brittle colonial link with Northern Ireland. The following extract from *Republican News* exemplifies the point:

> The Brits are beaten . . . and final victory is within our grasp . . . Britain is the sick man of Europe. Her economy is virtually bankrupt, her Tory Prime Minister tries to encourage his unfortunate citizens not to see themselves as the fifth rate power they are. . . . Britain cannot afford the money, the humiliation and the public shame she is perpetrating here . . . SHE CAN GET OUT NOW ON OUR TERMS AND THAT MEANS UNCONDITIONAL SURRENDER ON HER PART BECAUSE SHE CANNOT MAINTAIN THIS POLICE STATE FOREVER . . . the whole point is that we have proved we can go it alone and bring her to her knees. Britain is a paper tiger.[100]

The paper tiger syndrome juxtaposed a clapped-out imperial edifice against a confident and vigorous protagonist, thereby transforming a campaign of small-scale guerrilla raids into a potentially decisive weapon of victory. The belief that the British were an eminently beatable enemy was pressed relentlessly in the republican media with cries of 'English withdrawal any week now' (1974),[101] 'British disengagement now inevitable' (1975),[102] 'Brits about to withdraw' (1976),[103] and '1977 onward to victory'.[104] The extent to which the Provisionals believed in the potential of their strategy to surmount superior odds can be seen in the following passage from PIRA's 1977 Easter Message. The passage is replete with ringing declarations of imminent victory. What is especially notable is how the movement used the lexicon of conventional war, wholly inappropriate to a guerrilla scenario, to rub in the supposed power of its strategy:

> IRA successes which have routed the enemy on many fronts are Victory signs. . . . We Are Winning! We are fighting courageously, with determination and with great success on all fronts against British Occupation of Ireland. That the risen Irish People have withstood such a long struggle, that the People continue to go forward and not retreat, that the People not only resist but HIT BACK, and continue to do so, has stunned, frightened and demoralised the enemy.[105]

As the excerpt above implies, the corollary of the Provisionals' conviction that their strategy was capable of smashing Britain's rule in Northern Ireland was that their superior inner-moral strength must also make them a formidable and revered opponent in the eyes of the British and general observers alike. This was reflected in the Provisionals' own self-laudatory prose: 'The world recognises that the Provisionals are the greatest guerrilla fighters the world has ever seen,'[106] or, slightly more modestly: 'The People have the strongest, most admired and most respected guerrilla force in Europe.'[107] Another intriguing facet in this respect was the way the Provisionals used the term 'the People' to suggest that its strength and fortitude derived from mass public backing. Again, this contributed to PIRA's inflated self-image as it allowed the movement to justify its actions without recourse to any quantifiable source of public support. After all, if a political actor is apparently so close to its objectives, having all but vanquished the enemy, then by implication it *must* have 'the People's' support: 'The British military withdrawal . . . is a complete victory for the heroic determination and resistance shown by the anti-imperialist people and their army, the Provisional IRA.'[108]

Perhaps most importantly from PIRA's own standpoint was that the colonial analysis upheld the principal republican aspiration that once the British were expelled, the main burden preventing Ireland from fulfilling her potential would have been lifted:

> Things will never be right, can never be right, while this ultimate source of hatred and division continues. Britain has never brought freedom, never brought peace, never brought justice or respect for humanity to Ireland. Everybody knows that what British power has brought has been war and strife, slavery and servility, shame and disgrace and cruelty.[109]

There was a discrepancy here. How can one have a paper tiger opponent who was prepared to inflict all manner of 'strife', 'servility' and 'cruelty'? A regime which imposes a rule of repression 'more vicious than any seen in Budapest or Prague'[110] was not exactly the stereotype of a crumbling and irresolute adversary. This paradox was one which PIRA's literature did not enlighten. We can postulate, though, that having an enemy to which one can subscribe every kind of malicious intent automatically endows one with a morally virtuous self-image. In PIRA's case, the delineation of a malevolent antagonist could also boost its self-perception, enabling it to portray itself as a bold, determined force capable of facing down the massive repressive efforts of its foes. Such a postulation is lent weight by assertions like those of Daithi O Conaill, who told the 1973 Ard Fheis that: 'Despite the naked military terror in the North and the vicious Free State oppression in the South, the Movement has held its own and forges ahead in the struggle for freedom.'[111] In effect, the Provisionals wanted it both ways. They wanted the image of a weak opponent to show that their strategy could prevail over the British. Yet they also wanted the image of stronger, more dangerous opponents to explain why they still had not won.

All this seemed to amount to a self-deluding basis upon which to define a coherent strategy. PIRA's strategic paradigm appeared less a means to analyse objectively the value of the military instrument, more a way of mentally framing the conflict to its own advantage by building in a process which ran from unfounded assumption to unfounded assumption, like so: 1) PIRA's strategy has proved effective which means it is going to win; 2) this means it is a powerful entity; 3) this means it has the support of the people against a common enemy; 4) this means it does not have to pay much attention to other potential obstacles (like the prospect of mass Protestant opposition) in its way. In this respect, the theory of colonialism reflected not so much a dispassionate assessment of Northern Ireland's political status, but rather an attempt to divert PIRA away from hard strategic realities. The fact was that howsoever Great Britain's relationship with Northern Ireland was defined, the British were not a structurally flawed enemy and were prepared for some sort of long-term political and military commitment to the province.

The colonial theory was also vital to circumvent the question of Protestant hostility as a barrier to PIRA's objectives by linking the severance of the British connection to the collapse of unionism. 'We believe when the time comes, the Protestant people will accept a united Ireland for peace sake [sic],' was PIRA's considered opinion, 'We know a lot of Protestants who would privately agree to a united Ireland.'[112] Aside from the improbability that the Provisionals did know that many Protestants, there is no substantive evidence to suggest that loyalist resistance would disintegrate after a British withdrawal.[113] This perception is also backed up by some survey findings which indicated that a majority of people in the Irish Republic (59.4 per cent) and in Northern Ireland, both Protestants (87.5 per cent) and Catholics (67.4 per cent), felt that a British withdrawal would lead to a large increase in violence.[114] Indeed, the bulk of evidence points to the fact that loyalism has been largely independent of British policy and predicated on the suspicion of, rather than reliance on, the British government. In the mid-1970s Protestant opposition to the concept of Irish unity in general, and PIRA in particular, had been exhibited in the border poll in 1973, the Ulster Workers Council strike in 1974, which brought down the Power Sharing Executive, and, in its most violent form, in the activities of the loyalist paramilitaries. All this made little impression on the Provisionals. Peter Arnlis, a republican theorist, was moved to say: 'I ignore Loyalist violence because it is pathological and parochial and unlike IRA revolutionary violence is devoid of major political considerations.'[115]

The fact that the Provisionals were so nonchalantly unconcerned at the capacity of both the Protestants and the British government to obstruct the attainment of republican goals suggests that PIRA's strategic paradigm was no more than a self-rationalising mechanism which existed to screen out information which clashed with key assumptions. Discrepant information was not allowed to enter the paradigm to challenge or modify the parameters of PIRA's strategic thought because these parameters, so it seemed, had become as sacrosanct as the ideology itself.

That ideology and self-image influence perception and behaviour is axiomatic. PIRA remains no different in this respect than any other political actor. Nevertheless, PIRA's calculations of the efficacy of armed force did appear to represent an inversion of the process of strategic formulation which one might expect within a rational actor model of political activity. The rational actor model can be depicted in the following way:

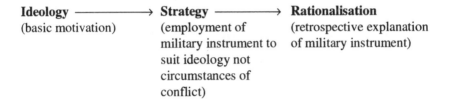

Ideology ⟶ **Analysis** ⟶ **Strategy**
(basic motivation and the (evaluation of military (employment of military
definition of objectives) instrument within instrument in policy to
context but inevitably achieve ends)
affected by normative
influences and values
of ideology)

In PIRA's case, either at the point of departure, or at some point during its campaign, this process appeared to have become inverted, like so:

Ideology ⟶ **Strategy** ⟶ **Rationalisation**
(basic motivation) (employment of (retrospective explanation
military instrument to of military instrument)
suit ideology not
circumstances of
conflict)

Under the inverted model, the strategy becomes dictated directly by the ideology and the 'analysis' merely a form of ex post facto explanation of pre-conceived ideas about the role of the military instrument. The Provisionals described their armed struggle as 'a war not of their choosing, it is a war because there is no alternative method of winning Irish freedom'.[116] Also, they have said: 'Republicanism . . . clearly gave us the method to use against the British.'[117] Pronouncements like these indicated the involuntary submission of the military instrument to the ideology, and is reflected also in the rationalising techniques of disparaging the enemy – 'The morale of British soldiers has never been lower'[118] – and the vocabulary of imminent victory – 'The Provisionals are proving that military victory is inevitable.'[119] Expressions such as these strongly implied that the employment of the military instrument was already a pre-chosen path, this is to say, that the concept of violence as the means to republican goals was as much enshrined in the ideology as republican goals themselves.

It should be emphasised that PIRA was not unique in having its policies formed and rationalised by ideological principles rather than serious contextual analysis. Arguably, this phenomenon affects every political actor to some degree.[120] It is also difficult to prove conclusively that PIRA's violence between 1972 and 1977 was governed by a process similar to that described in the inverted model because it takes place at an unconscious level. Rarely will any political actor set out deliberately to misapply the military instrument, still less admit it. When the Provisionals discussed the armed struggle in their publications they usually described its instrumentality, not its emotional appeal. Neither is it clear whether the inverted process of strategic formulation was present at the outset of PIRA's attempts to fashion its strategy in 1970 or whether it developed over time. It is sometimes the case that a strategy properly formulated at the start can, over time, become internalised in an organisation's belief structure.[121] In PIRA's case, it did seem in the early years of its struggle that its strategy had been well-judged. The successful destabilisation of Northern Ireland made it seem plausible that PIRA might just accomplish its objectives. As time wore on, its strategy became less convincing, particularly in the light of extensive loyalist antagonism to PIRA's aims and methods. Yet the rigidities of PIRA's strategic doctrine prevented it from modifying its campaign to take account of the changing nature of the conflict. Moreover, PIRA's persistence in practising armed force with reference to an anti-colonial warfare model resulted in its campaign becoming not only increasingly ineffective, but actually *regressive* in relation to its stated goals. For example, although the bombing campaign in Great Britain had the potential to sway public opinion in the short run, the ephemeral nature of its impact in terms of its ability to sustain high levels of fear meant that over the longer term it could have only a marginal impact on British attitudes and policy. PIRA's only real hope was to pursue political change in Northern Ireland itself by prevailing upon the population to conform to its views either by peaceful persuasion or through coercion. Since the Provisionals did not believe in the value of the former, they ended up with the worst of both worlds. On the one hand, PIRA's energies continued to be misdirected to a bombing campaign in England which was just not successful in its aim of wearing down public tolerance to a point where the question of a British withdrawal became a serious political issue. On the other hand, PIRA's violence in Northern Ireland was not widespread enough to bulldoze the Protestants into submission, yet quite sufficient to alienate and embitter them, and to stimulate the rise of the loyalist paramilitaries. Similarly, PIRA's unofficial, though nonetheless quite obvious, participation in the sectarian war merely confirmed Protestant suspicions, making the question of loyalist compliance even more problematic.

The tone of PIRA's headline rhetoric became more clamorous and bombastic through the mid-1970s. However, towards the latter part of the mid-1970s it was increasingly possible to detect more subdued remarks in the republican press, such as 'The basic strategy of the guerrilla fighter is to stay alive and keep fighting',[122] and 'the Provos have fought hard and long and their survival alone is a political victory'.[123] Remarks like these hinted at the beginnings of a shift in nuance, suggestive of the first, tentative admission that the overblown claims of victory by vanquishing the enemy in battle were inappropriate and unobtainable. But stressing that somehow 'survival alone' was a 'political victory' was also symptomatic of defective strategic thinking. While it is true in the tautological sense that surviving is a necessary requirement to achieve one's objectives, PIRA's idea that surviving meant winning provided the clearest indication that the basis of its strategic formulation amounted to a set of contrived rationalisations aimed at preserving the purity of republican ideology simply by permitting the movement to endure through military expression. It was this state of affairs that allowed the movement to languish in the 1975 ceasefire which, once again, proved that PIRA was incapable of making political capital out of its military campaign.

This brings us to the central puzzle of PIRA's strategic position during this period. The Provisionals' perception of British colonial interference in Ireland provided them with an argument to legitimise their campaign of violence free from any political dimension, because in their view there could not, literally, be any politics so long as the colonial relationship lasted. As O Bradaigh stated, there could be 'no Ulster government, no partnership and no reconciliation while British rule remained'.[124] The problem here was that while this provided an internal intellectual mechanism to justify PIRA's existence, externally, in the real world, PIRA's existence was being threatened, as shown by continued decline on the military level. Between 1976 and 1977 the number of shootings fell from 1,908 to 1,181 and bombings halved from 766 to 366.[125] Ironically, the very mechanism which rationalised PIRA's survival was directly responsible for its existence being jeopardised. The continuing use of violence without any political consideration was detaching PIRA from the roots of its support in the Catholic community and so making it far more vulnerable to the security forces.

A good strategy is underpinned by a rigorous and dispassionate assessment of the conflict scenario. Proper contextual analysis enables the selection of the strategic option most likely to maximise political interests. It appears that PIRA forewent such an assessment seemingly to avoid confronting some of the more difficult obstacles which stood in its way. The Provisionals constructed an inflexible interpretation of the Northern Ireland conflict as a colonial war. It was an idealised mental image which justified their existence and assured them of the probability of victory, despite the odds ranged against them. While the Provisionals may have found comfort in this escapist illusion, the stagnating military campaign and declining nationalist sympathy testified that in practice it had condemned them to fighting their own brutal flight of fancy.

6   The evolution of PIRA's total strategy, 1977–1983

The despondency experienced by the Provisional IRA as a result of the 1975 ceasefire coincided with a shift in British security policy towards Northern Ireland. This policy, referred to as Ulsterisation, involved reductions in the overt presence of the regular British Army and turning over greater responsibility for security to the locally recruited forces of the RUC and UDR. The purpose was to restore an atmosphere of normality to the province. The Provisionals viewed the reductions of regular army personnel as a 'withdrawal, forced upon them by the IRA's success', but emphasised that it was a 'pragmatic withdrawal with no gains intended for the IRA'. They believed that because the 'Brits' will to beat the Irish Republican Army by military means had diminished', so they had 'resorted to political strategy as a means of weakening resistance'.[1]

Ulsterisation bestowed a number of benefits on the British position. The policy aimed to contain the conflict in Northern Ireland and minimise its impact on the wider British body politic. Accelerating police primacy over the army and pushing more locally recruited forces into an up-front role against the Provisional IRA enabled the conflict to be characterised as a problem of internal civil disorder. The withdrawal of regular British Army units from most areas, except inner-city troublespots and border districts, lowered the overt profile of central government involvement in the province, thereby lessening any negative impressions of external British interference.

In military terms the reduction of the regular army's presence gave the Provisionals fewer visible symbols of British rule to attack. Instead, the Provisionals were to feel ever more compelled to target RUC and UDR forces, which began to bear the brunt of PIRA's campaign.[2] The greater toll exacted on the UDR and RUC helped to reinforce the picture of an internalised conflict: to put it coarsely, a picture of locals killing locals, as opposed to locals killing British soldiers. All this aided British policy in two other ways. First, the decreasing proportion of regular army casualties diminished the prospect of public disquiet arising in Great Britain from the violence in Northern Ireland. Second, the increased number of attacks on local security forces drawn overwhelmingly from the Protestant population facilitated the charge that the Provisionals were narrowly sectarian in outlook.[3] It should be remembered that PIRA's aim was not to see the conflict localised, with the British government taking a back seat and promoting itself as the neutral arbiter between two warring communities. The plan was to embroil the British government in as direct a manner as possible in order to represent the conflict as a struggle for national liberation against an imperial oppressor. Ulsterisation was intended to work against this perception.

Part of the Ulsterisation policy involved the criminalisation of PIRA by the phasing out of internment and ending Special Category Status for all prisoners convicted of paramilitary offences after March 1976. This struck deep at PIRA's strategy and moral self-image as the policy sought to portray the troubles as a conflict of the forces of law and order versus a purely sectarian, self-serving criminal gang that lacked popular legitimacy. The extent to which the Provisional IRA had become vulnerable to this indictment was revealed in 1976 and 1977 at the hands of the Peace People, a cross-community movement which called for an end to paramilitary activity. The rate at which the Peace People gained support from the traditionally hardline nationalist areas jolted the Provisionals. It under-lined the exhaustion of many in the community and, though the influence of the Peace People was short lived, its rise signified the final demise of all the early hopes invested in PIRA's campaign.

With the demoralisation of the ceasefire, PIRA's strategy came under close scrutiny from those identified in Chapter 3 as the younger group of Northern radicals within the Provisionals. This group, composed of those such as Gerry Adams, Joe Austin, Danny Morrison and Tom Hartley, were increasingly critical of the Southern-based leadership. They believed that the leadership had been hoodwinked by the British, who had used the bilateral truce to speed up the Ulsterisation process and to end political status in the prisons. The Northern radicals were determined that PIRA's campaign would not be allowed to drift into history as just another republican stand which burned itself out through unthink-ing military zeal. They planned to reshape the movement and to construct a more viable basis upon which to develop their strategy. By 1976 the Northerners were rapidly gaining prominence and by 1977 were able to establish a commanding influence within the movement.

During 1975 and 1976 letters began to surface in the republican press, some genuine, others possibly orchestrated by the Northern faction, condemning PIRA's disproportionate dependence on the armed struggle and the lack of involvement in working-class politics. One correspondent in *Republican News*, T. Ennis, wrote: 'Left wingers are often accused of being automatically stickies by the Provos who feel the ultimatum of "Britain must go" is politics enough to sustain an anti-imperialist struggle in its fullest sense.'[4] Even further back in 1974, an internal PSF document warned that 'the "closed circuit" mind which develops from moving in a narrow circle is a danger to the effectiveness of republican propaganda' and urged greater participation in community politics in order to expand the base of PIRA's support.[5] These precursors of the sea-change in PIRA's thinking show that sections within the organisation were conscious of the political hole in the move-ment's campaign. It is even possible to speculate that, with or without the disastrous 1975 ceasefire, whenever the Northern radicals moved into positions of authority they would have embarked on the road of politicisation.

REORGANISATION AND POLITICISATION

The first significant changes in the structure of the movement came in late 1976 when a separate Northern Command was created to coordinate operations across Northern Ireland. The Northern Command was largely autonomous of the Army Council, which was a sign of the increasing influence of the young Northern leaders who had been pressing for a greater say in the running of the movement. The arrest of leading PIRA commanders allowed the Northerners to move into vacant positions. Martin McGuinness, the first commanding officer of the Northern Command, became Chief of Staff following Seamus Twomey's arrest in December 1977 and was himself probably succeeded by Gerry Adams in 1979.[6]

The most urgent task facing PIRA's leaders during the mid-1970s was to stem the number of arrests caused by the security forces' infiltration of PIRA's ranks and by intensive interrogation methods. In 1977 PIRA's GHQ staff commissioned a report to examine both the structure and long-term military plans of the movement. The *Staff Report*, as it was known, possibly written by Adams, was found in the possession of Seamus Twomey when he was arrested. The document recommended a 'reorganisation and remotivation' of the IRA, emphasising that it should 'return to secrecy and strict discipline'.[7] To that end, tougher anti-interrogation training was recommended along with the dissolution of the old system of battalions and companies to be replaced by a network of cells, or active service units (ASUs), which would operate independently from each other and receive information through an anonymous hierarchy. This would limit the scope for infiltration and restrict the damage that could be done by informers or interrogations. The cell system idea was not new. A variant had been in operation with some of PIRA's Belfast units since mid-1973,[8] but as a matter of necessity the system had to be extended across the entire organisation. The system was successful in stopping the haemorrhage of arrests. In 1978, there were 465 fewer charges for paramilitary offences than the previous year. As part of the restructuring process, the organisation was slimmed down to a core of 300 or so activists. PIRA's increasing efficiency was noted by a secret British Army assessment in 1978 compiled by Brigadier James Glover and subsequently either captured or leaked to the Provisionals, which claimed that the ASUs were:

> for the most part, manned by terrorists tempered by up to ten years of operational experience. . . . They are continually learning from mistakes and developing their expertise. We can therefore expect to see increased professionalism and greater exploitation of modern technology for terrorist purposes.[9]

By itself the reorganisation of PIRA ensured merely that the military arm could continue to function with less manpower and less dependence on public support. As such, it was an admission of weakness. The main preoccupation of the Northern leaders was how to develop their campaign so that the movement could become a real political force, not just a small, violent entity. Much of the impetus to address this issue came from the republican prisoners. Away from the heady mixture of action and conspiracy they were able to reflect on the problems now afflicting the movement. In Danny Morrison's words:

> We had to work out why the struggle was not all over and done with as quickly as we thought it would be. The jail experience, the lengthy debates which I suppose could be defined as politicisation, and the experience on the streets all went into the melting pot.[10]

The basis of the radicals' critique was that the Provisionals lacked the necessary political consciousness to exploit the momentum created by the military campaign. With no clear idea of how the progression of republican politics related to the armed struggle, few political advances could be made. As a consequence, the Provisionals ceded ground to their political rivals such as those in the SDLP.[11] So under these circumstances, sole reliance on the armed struggle was not only ineffective but highly damaging. Fundamentally, the Northerners felt that the primacy accorded to the armed struggle was a distraction from the task of mobilising political support behind republican goals. In his assessment of the 1975 ceasefire, Gerry Adams declared: 'When the struggle was limited to the armed struggle the prolongation of the truce meant that there was no struggle at all. There was nothing but confusion, frustration and demoralisation resulting from what I call spectator politics.'[12]

The price for PIRA's increasing political irrelevance was a contracting political and operational base. The excessive dependence on the military instrument meant that the attraction for many recruits had been the cosmetic appeal of action and adventure. As one Provisional leader admitted: 'People were joining for all the wrong reasons, hundreds simply because they wanted a gun to defend their immediate area.'[13] When they ended up 'behind the wire' their self-doubt and lack of commitment to the republican cause was exposed. This was exhibited in the low levels of reinvolvement. PSF estimated that only about 12 per cent of those released from internment became reinvolved in violence.[14] What these figures meant was that PIRA was running into the sand both politically and militarily. In any guerrilla conflict, the declining effectiveness of the military campaign and consequent receding prospects of success is unlikely to inspire others to support, let alone join, the insurgency. The result for the Provisionals was that they ended up, in the words of one revolutionary theorist, 'Fighting to survive rather than surviving to fight!'[15]

The Northerners concluded that the military campaign could not bear the sole burden of the Irish republican struggle. This may seem a straightforward deduction, but, given the weight of traditional republican thinking about the primacy of the military instrument, it was a significant landmark. For example, in 1977, even though the problems facing the Provisionals over Ulsterisation and criminalisation were accepted by republican commentators, some still asserted the old solutions. 'Sheer revolutionary determination is what is needed to defeat the latest British phase,' said Peter Arnlis. 'The military struggle must be intensified: The Brits must withdraw *under pressure*' (emphasis in original).[16] The conclusions reached by the Northerners put an end to such barren advocacies. The *Staff Report* was explicit about the necessary alternative: 'Sinn Fein should come under Army organisers at all levels. . . . Sinn Fein should be radicalised (under Army direction) and should agitate about social and economic issues which attack the welfare of the people.'[17] In many ways this was a corollary of the adoption of the cell system, which reduced contact with the nationalist community, so an attempt to cultivate a broad republican constituency was deemed essential if PIRA was to remain a potent force. This formed the core belief of the new thinking and was developed in a series of articles in *Republican News* by Gerry Adams under the pseudonym of 'Brownie', many of which he wrote while inside the Maze prison during the mid-1970s. He argued that there was a need for republicans not only to spell out their vision but actively to involve themselves in local issues which affected day-to-day life in the community. Only by these means could PIRA's campaign have any relevance for the people on whose behalf it was meant to be waged. Adams criticised conventional republican thinking on the issue: 'Who are we fighting for? There is a lot of talk about "The People" as if they are a thing. As if the people we fight for are, as yet, unborn, as if they will fit into the new order of things in our new Ireland.'[18] In later articles he continued to expand this theme: 'Without the people we are nothing; we must be prepared to listen to their ideas, their visions and to structure our struggle so that it satisfies their needs and overcomes their oppressions.'[19]

The first act of politicisation, as enunciated by the *Staff Report*, to allow PSF to emerge as a distinct identity, represented the first real attempt to restore a sense of balance within the Provisionals. PSF's new role was to inject political meaning into PIRA's campaign in order to depict the violence as a direct outgrowth of public discontent, rather than being independent, or merely a cursory reflection of it: 'IRA Volunteers, because they live with the people and among the people, are directly responsible to the people for their actions. Their level of support and shelter is dependent upon public approval for their actions.'[20]

By building up a strong political machine, the Provisionals believed they could capitalise on the impact generated by PIRA's violence in order to establish a separate political dynamic which could embrace all republican sympathisers. According to Adams, support for PIRA tended to fluctuate, rising in periods of tension over issues like internment, or else people were part-time republicans who supported PIRA's campaign but voted for the SDLP.[21] By welding a political movement onto the military campaign, the Provisionals aimed to capture and hold those who otherwise might have hovered on the fringes of the movement without actually joining it. This would enable the Provisionals to both survive and grow. The British had shown that they could isolate and nearly destroy a military conspiracy. If PIRA was part of a wider, popularly based movement then, Adams said, 'the Brit must remove everyone connected, from school-children to customers in the co-ops, from paper sellers to street committees, before he can defeat us'.[22]

THE IMPACT OF POLITICISATION ON REPUBLICAN STRATEGIC THINKING

Becoming a more politically relevant organisation presented the Provisionals with many difficulties. In particular, the radicals had to resolve the tension between what revolutionary theory sometimes describes as 'theory and praxis'. How does one develop a practical political programme without compromising deeply held ideological principles? Too much concentration on the everyday problems of the masses can lead to the neglect of revolutionary goals. Too much ideological theory can turn a movement into a remote, ineffective clique. Too much emphasis on a programme of revolutionary action can lead to a pre-occupation with military technique.[23] The Northern radicals were aware of these difficulties and anxious to stress that the theory and practice of politicisation should be a unified process, each helping to inform and temper the other, because 'Political theory is something that should expand as practical experience is gained'.[24] An essential pre-requisite to the building of a new, viable republican strategy, free from the structural weaknesses of the past, entailed a revolution in the way the Provisionals evaluated the various components of their struggle. This meant developing a more flexible attitude towards the process of strategic formulation and, as such, an end to elitism and ideological exclusivity.

The first sign of a transformation in PIRA's thinking came in June 1977 when the veteran republican, Jimmy Drumm, delivered the Wolfe Tone commemoration speech at Bodenstown. Drumm argued that the British were not about to withdraw. They were 'committed to stabilising the Six Counties' by large financial support. It was admitted that the decline in the province's industrial base was due mainly to economic recession but had been wrongly attributed to PIRA's campaign and, therefore, could not be treated as a symptom of British withdrawal. Part of Drumm's conclusion was that 'a successful war of liberation' could not revolve 'around the physical presence of the British Army. Hatred and resentment of the army cannot sustain the war.'[25] The speech, no doubt written for Drumm by the Northern radicals, catalogued a series of flawed assumptions and strategic failure. It was all the more remarkable given PIRA's previous sense of self-belief. It contained an implicit recognition that military acts were not intrinsically politicising and to rely on them as such could produce the sorts of alienating effects which the Provisionals had already discovered could endanger a movement's survival. Most significantly, the speech represented a rejection of the view, held by many republicans, that the campaign could be sustained simply through ideological assertion. No longer could the people be harangued in the manner of Maire Drumm in 1973 who branded all those who did not support the Provisionals as 'moral cowards' who 'should be haunted by the ghosts of the Irish dead'.[26] Nor could there be any more bland pronouncements by PIRA spokesmen who claimed that the movement enjoyed 'the full support of the people'.[27] The aim now, as proclaimed in Drumm's speech, was to create 'an irrepressible mass movement' through active participation in 'the everyday struggles of the people'.

If the efficacy of PIRA's strategy could no longer be justified with automatic reference to the old republican dogmas borne of the nationalist-vanguard mentality, then the movement required an entirely new framework to define and construct a campaign of action. For the more pragmatic Northerners, this meant taking a more functional attitude towards strategic formulation which rejected any notion that the means of PIRA's campaign should be elevated to a point of principle, as had been the case in the past. In the main, the constituent elements of any strategy were to be viewed as tactics and assessed by their capacity to advance PIRA's cause, and not simply because they conformed to some traditional republican modus operandi. All of the components of the strategy were to be subject to constant scrutiny. This explicitly analytical approach was reflected in the republican press from the mid-1970s when Danny Morrison and Tom Hartley became joint editors of *Republican News*. In 1979, *An Phoblacht*, which circulated mainly in the South, was merged with the Northern based *Republican News* to produce a uniform Provisional perspective on events, and in 1981 was complemented by the periodical *Iris*, established with the same purpose in mind. The general tenor of the articles which appeared in these publications was more intellectual and less prone to repetitious sloganising. Emphasis was placed on continuous evaluation and tactical flexibility which mitigated the Provisionals' previous sense of infallibility. More stress was now laid on empathising with the people and adapting the strategy to take account of the specific context in which it was to be practised. In one of his 'Brownie' articles, Adams summed up this position:

> we should not suppose that we have the monopoly on truth. We should avoid jargon, we should remember that despite everything suffered by them [the nationalist community in general], new ideas must be carefully digested by many of our people and, finally, we must never forget that our ideology must be so shaped that it meets the needs of the Irish people and is not some pie-in-the-sky theory which bears no resemblance to Irish conditions or needs.[28]

Part of the Northerners' approach to gain greater public support was to be more specific about the nature of their political goals. They began to articulate an overtly socialist viewpoint, declaring their aim to be the creation of a democratic socialist state which would ensure that the Irish people gained 'complete political, cultural, economic and national control of their own country and all its resources'.[29] The Provisionals were careful to deny the Marxist label, instead Adams argued that such views embodied a more literal interpretation of the 1916 Proclamation 'which in itself was a radical document', because, Adams said, 'It talks about the wealth of Ireland belonging to the people of Ireland.'[30] This view still represented only the vaguest of aspirations, but the way to clarify the republican vision, it was felt, was by active involvement in community-based politics. Additionally, to stand any real chance of fulfilling the movement's objectives, the radicals believed that the politicisation process had to be extended beyond Northern Ireland. This was implied in Drumm's speech when he said that the conflict could not be 'fought exclusively on the backs of the oppressed in the Six Counties'. Two years later at Bodenstown, Gerry Adams was more explicit:

Today's circumstances and our objectives dictate the need for the building of an agitational struggle in the twenty-six counties. . . . It needs to be done now because our most glaring weakness to date lies in our failure to develop revolutionary politics and to build a strong political alternative to so-called constitutional politics.[31]

Therefore, the Provisionals felt that if they were ever to be serious contenders for power, then the process of politicisation would have to be an all-Ireland affair. The Provisionals now aspired, again in the words of Adams, to be more than 'merely a Brits-Out Movement'.[32]

One of the main features of the Northern radicals' perspective was their scepticism towards any thought of political accommodation with the unionists because they would always 'be loyal to Britain as the guardian of their privileges'.[33] To an extent, one could say that the Northerners were more realistic, more honest, about recognising the intractability of loyalist hostility by accepting that there would, according to the republican commentator Peter Dowling:

necessarily [be] increasing Protestant and Catholic disunity before the freedom struggle can be successful. There is no ducking the unfortunate fact of political life in Ireland today that the loyalists will become increasingly enraged as they see their Orange statelet of Protestant privilege being destroyed by Republican successes.[34]

Alternatively, these views could also be said to represent a more prejudiced and emotional reflection of the Northern nationalist experience, which was resentful of the injustices they felt they had suffered at Protestant hands over the previous fifty years. Either way, the overt enmity towards the loyalists appeared to manifest itself in practice with allegations that the Provisionals were now deliberately out to spread sectarian discord to maximise support in nationalist areas. For example, during the tense atmosphere of the Maze hunger strikes of 1981, the Provisionals were accused of exploiting, if not manufacturing, rumours of loyalist plans to overrun Catholic neighbourhoods.[35] There is also little doubt that the Provisionals did seek to satiate some of the sectarian emotion generated by the hunger strikes by killing the Unionist Member of Parliament, Robert Bradford, in November 1981 because, the Provisionals said, he was a 'propagator of anti-Catholic sectarian hatred',[36] and 'a prominent motivator of attacks on Catholics'.[37] The Provisionals produced little hard evidence to substantiate these claims.

The more strident view of loyalism, the greater emphasis on a socialist programme and the demand for increased political participation all brought the Northerners into dispute with the Southern leadership. Differences between the two factions were displayed openly in early 1979 when *An Phoblacht/Republican News* declared: 'We are out to set up a unitary, socialist Republic.'[38] This brought a terse rebuke from the leaders in Dublin who stated that the movement's objectives were 'clearly defined as the setting up of a Democratic Socialist Republic on Federal lines', and added that 'personal views to the contrary are not Republican policy'.[39] The point at issue was the concept of federalism as contained in the *Eire Nua* programme, PSF's official policy document. The idea of an Ulster parliament was anathema to many Northerners. Having experienced unionist rule, they did not want it perpetuated under a different guise. The scheme was viewed as a relic of the early years of PIRA's campaign, a political quick-fix to attract the Protestants into a united Ireland. The Northerners believed any compromise with loyalism would merely impede progress towards a socialist state. In any event, it was reasoned, the Protestants would no more accept a nine-county parliament in a federal state than a unified socialist republic, so why bother offering concessions at all? As Adams sought to stress:

> We must recognise that loyalists are a national political minority whose basis is economic and whose philosophy is neo-fascist, anti-nationalist and anti-democratic. We cannot, and we should not, ever tolerate or compromise with (by government structures or any other means) loyalism.[40]

It was a mark of the declining influence of the Dublin leadership that the provisions of *Eire Nua* had in fact been under siege from the late 1970s onwards and modified increasingly to reflect the leftist interpretation of the Northern radicals.[41] The commitment to federalism was voted down at the 1981 Ard Fheis and officially abandoned the following year. The quarrels over federalism, however, were a cover for an infinitely more divisive issue which stemmed from the idea of a thirty-two county struggle. In Northern Ireland PSF already had a significantly disaffected section of the population from which it could try to carve out a political constituency. This was not so evident in the South, which enjoyed a stable, functioning democracy. There was no question of military operations against the Republic. The IRA's Standing Order Number Eight, which had been in force for over thirty years, prohibited such actions in acknowledgement of the legitimacy of the Southern state in the eyes of most of its inhabitants. If PSF was to become a political organisation of any relevance in the South, it needed to work within the system. This raised the possibility of ending the policy of abstention from the Irish Republic's national assembly. For the radicals, who tended to view all means as tactics rather than principles, this posed no great problem, but with all the symbolic connotations of the 1969/70 split, the subject remained taboo for some years. What changed the situation were the hunger strikes of 1980 and 1981. Protests at the removal of political status had been going on inside the prisons since 1976, but had received scant attention from PSF. It was not until a non-Provisional grouping, the Relatives Action Committee (RAC), was formed to coordinate outside support that the protests gained PSF's outright backing.[42] The success the RAC had in generating public support, in particular getting the hunger striker, Bobby Sands, and later his agent, Owen Carron, elected to the seat of Fermanagh and South Tyrone, demonstrated the degree of latent sympathy for the republican cause. This persuaded the radicals that there was a sufficient basis for electoral participation, not just for the purposes of intervention to spotlight a particular issue, but as part of a long-term aim to build a strong political party 'as a necessary part of the revolutionary process'.[43] Electoral fortunes in the Irish Republic also appeared promising with the election of hunger strikers Kieran

Doherty and Kevin Agnew to the Irish parliament in the June general election. PSF's Ard Fheis in 1981 took the first step towards unwinding republican policy on abstention by voting to contest local elections in Northern Ireland and to take whatever seats won.

The tensions that the twin issues of abstention and federalism produced were considerable. The more traditional Southerners felt that too much politicisation would dilute republican ideology and even aid Britain's policy to normalise the situation in Northern Ireland. These fears were stimulated by the Northerners' deviations from the official policy, as for instance when *Republican News* announced that 'a revolutionary strategy does not rule out – as a secondary feature – the demand by people for state funding of jobs, housing, transport, education and health facilities'.[44] An idea of the antagonism which existed between the two factions was provided in November 1979 when the PSF leadership in Dublin issued a harsh statement declaring that 'a concerted campaign to distort the aims and objectives of Sinn Fein has been prosecuted by the enemies of the Republican Movement'.[45] The animosity continued to deepen. At the 1983 Ard Fheis delegates voted to allow PSF to contest the 1984 European elections and endorsed a proposal that would open the way for discussion on ending abstention. Having been rebuffed on both of these issues, O Bradaigh and O Conaill resigned from the PSF Executive. Both men had been fighting a rearguard for nearly eight years and their resignations marked the end of Southern domination of the movement's leadership.

On the surface, the more traditional elements seemed to have reason for their concern. All the talk of community politics and electoralism appeared to signify a slide into the sort of reformism of the despised Officials. Official Sinn Fein proclaimed that 'there was more to the struggle than getting rid of British troops', and that 'the struggle should not just be confined to the North', or become 'an elitist military struggle'.[46] To the traditionalists, the ideas emanating from the PSF radicals sounded ominously similar to such slogans. The Northerners were at pains to stress that they were not embarking on a road of compromise and apostasy. In their view, the British would never leave of their own accord and the loyalists would always resist moves towards Irish unity. 'For this reason', Danny Morrison asserted, 'republicans cannot subscribe to constitutional politics as the sole panacea for Ireland's major ailments or as a substitute for the political effectiveness of force.'[47]

THE ROLE OF THE MILITARY INSTRUMENT IN THE POLITICISATION PROCESS – THE LONG WAR AND THE TOTAL STRATEGY

The Northern radicals' perspective on politicisation influenced how they saw the role of armed force within the political process. The way they interpreted the conflict changed the premises upon which calculations of the utility of force were to be made. Theoretically, the military instrument was put in the same basket with all the other potential means at PIRA's disposal and evaluated on the basis of its functionality. As Adams declared: 'there is now a realisation in republican circles that armed struggle on its own is inadequate and that non-armed forms of political struggle are at least as important.'[48] Even so, there is little reason to think that the radicals ever doubted the value of armed force. Coming from the North they had been the ones most exposed to the militarising effects of the conflict and as a matter of temperament were likely to be committed to violence. In addition, the nature of their analysis inclined them to believe that Britain's presence could only be dislodged through arms. In 1976 Adams stated in the clearest terms that Britain had to be fought:

> The enemy allows us no choice. It is an armed struggle, because the enemy is armed. Because he protects and establishes his vested interests by force of arms . . . we must insist that freedom cannot be obtained and when obtained, maintained except by armed men.[49]

This was the one line of republican thought which continued to be expounded in the same belligerent fashion that had characterised much of the rhetoric of the early 1970s. For example in May 1980 the front page of *An Phoblacht/ Republican News*, proclaimed: 'There is only one message Thatcher and her Brits understand and that is the automatic type which comes out of the barrel of a gun.'[50] The intrinsic value of the armed struggle was never questioned. What was new in the Northerners' thinking was how this military component fitted into the overall context of the movement's strategy.

The factor which was to most affect the implementation of the military instrument was the notion of the 'long war'. On the surface it appeared a simple and straightforward approach but it was, in fact, a complex idea which embraced many facets and implicit assumptions. It was the central concept around which PIRA's strategy was formulated. The first, basic, assumption it embraced was the belief that because of the rigidity of British imperialism, PIRA's campaign would inevitably be protracted: 'the war to liberate and unify this country will be a bitter and long drawn out struggle. There is no quick solution to our British problem.' Therefore the Provisionals added: *'We are committed to and more importantly geared to a long term war'* (emphasis in original).[51] The first recommendation to prepare for a 'long term armed struggle' was contained in the *Staff Report* of 1977.[52] The overhaul of PIRA along cellular lines into a tighter and more efficient force was the initial step in the development of an organisation more suited to the rigours of a prolonged campaign. Even so, the long war idea was not a specific blueprint which delineated intermediate objectives to be achieved within an extended time span:

> The stress on the long term nature of the struggle was necessary to counter any complacency which was creeping in. So while the army is geared to a long struggle it is not necessarily pacing itself in the long term. It is seeking the complete demolition of British rule by the shortest possible route.[53]

So the long war idea acted as an internal stabilising device in order to prevent demoralisation by recognising that it was impossible to predict the date of a

British withdrawal. But the long war approach was much more than this. It was a looser, though more flexible and comprehensive arrangement, which allowed changing conditions and needs to influence, and be accommodated within, the movement's thinking. For example, the notion of the long war enabled the Provisionals to accept that armed force was not a decisive weapon and would have to be relocated within a broader plan. It was argued that to fight on a single military front against the superior resources of the British would be 'contributing to the isolation and eventual defeat of the republican struggle'.[54] By accepting that the nature of the campaign would be both lengthy and not exclusively reliant on the military instrument, the Provisionals had made available to themselves other avenues of resistance which could be manipulated to advance their cause, as the following statement implies:

> it needs to be said loudly and unequivocally that freedom, unity and the creation of conditions by which we can proceed to the democratic socialist republic will not be achieved by armed struggle alone, and that armed struggle of an evolutionary nature cannot even be sustained without popular, logistical back-up and support.[55]

The first important attribute of the long war idea in this respect was that it enabled the Provisionals to sustain a consistent level of military activity while providing time to develop these alternative forms of resistance, subsequent to their incorporation into the movement's strategic programme.[56]

Up until the reorganisation and politicisation of the movement, PIRA's strategy had been very much a mono-military approach. It was assumed military actions could themselves be politicising, stimulate support and generate propaganda, as well as have a direct pressurising effect on the British government. All these elements were considered to be linked and flowed from the source of military activity rather than as independent variables which deserved individual attention. The emergence of the long war approach marked a shift away from this position towards what can be described as a 'total strategy' where every facet of resistance was dealt with as a separate battleground to be exploited within the same war, thereby maximising the coercive pressure on the British government. The intention, as the 1980 Easter Statement from PIRA's leadership declared, was to 'tie together all aspects of nationalism and socialism and all the strands of rural and urban discontent into a surging wave of Republicanism'.[57] By treating different facets of the struggle as distinct units, the Provisionals could hope to mobilise the greatest amount of resources and involve the greatest number of people:

> Our resistance must be military, political, cultural, social and economic, at the same time. In that way we can involve all the people in our war against the British and collaborationist forces. Within that spectrum of resistance there is a place for everybody, and everybody can find his or her place. Everyone is equal in the struggle no matter what job they are doing: selling papers, collecting, picketing, leafletting [sic], carrying out an operation . . .[58]

The long war was the natural theoretical framework in which all the components of PIRA's strategy could be maintained. More specifically, it provided a mechanism to hold together the military and political elements to ensure that the two worked in tandem with each other. The military arm would work to keep the political situation in Northern Ireland in a state of flux, 'to frustrate the British aim of making the six counties governable through power-sharing type institutions'.[59] Meanwhile, other non-violent forms of involvement would be used to exploit the political vacuum created by the military campaign. For example, participation in elections would be designed to 'show clearly that people support radical republicanism and resistance to the British presence more than they support the collaborationist tendency'.[60] The Provisionals believed that the long war scenario would give them the opportunity to build up a non-constitutional alternative to those parties like the SDLP. Over time they could begin to undermine the SDLP's claim to be the 'sole voice of the nationalist people'.[61] So by chipping away at the SDLP's electoral base, they hoped to 'deny them [the SDLP] positions which they have used consistently to collaborate with and give credit to the British administration'.[62] The interlocking political and military sides of PIRA's campaign into a mutually supporting symbiosis was summed up neatly by Danny Morrison at the 1981 Ard Fheis: 'Who here really believes we can win the war through the ballot box? But will anyone here object, if with a ballot paper in this hand and an Armalite in this hand, we take power in Ireland?'[63]

Although PIRA's campaign was now conducted on a wide range of fronts, the Provisionals stressed that for those who were concerned that electoral involvement heralded a 'new tendency or departure, they can be assured that the military struggle will go on with all the energy at our disposal'.[64] Indeed, if one traces the specific role of the military instrument, it is clear that it remained at the heart of PIRA's strategic plans.

PIRA's campaign objective was still to wage a war of psychological attrition intended to 'disenchant the British people with their government's involvement in Ireland'.[65] The military ideas of the Northern radicals were distilled in what became PIRA's standard training manual known as the *Green Book*. The *Green Book* outlined the main military items of the campaign which were a 'war of attrition against enemy personnel' and 'a bombing campaign aimed at making the enemy's interest in our country unprofitable'. The immediate purpose was to make the 'Six Counties . . . ungovernable, except by colonial military rule.'[66] So PIRA's basic strategic concept of trying to demoralise British public opinion into accepting withdrawal, remained intact. The concept was merely redefined within the framework of the long war in a way which recognised that grinding down the resolve of the British government and public did not always have to centre around the effects of military action.

The pattern of PIRA's military activity from 1977 to 1983 reflected this change in emphasis. In this period, PIRA was known to be responsible for 298 deaths, compared to 598 between 1971 and 1976. The total number of shooting incidents for these same periods declined from 24,319 between 1971 and 1976 to 4,793 between 1977 and 1983, and bombings from 5,232 to 2,406. There was a trend away from the massive bombing campaigns that had characterised the early

1970s towards greater concentration against the security forces. The total number of security forces personnel killed from 1977 to 1983 remained high at 279 while the total number of civilian deaths fell to 328, compared to 1,235 over the preceding period. During this time, PIRA injected a wide diversity into its targeting policy ranging from, for example, businessmen and prison warders, to off-duty members of the security forces. Targets for PIRA's bombs included commercial premises, RUC stations, government offices and the occasional blasting of town centres.

The aim of this sort of campaign was to keep Northern Ireland on the political agenda, highlighting it as an unstable factor in UK politics. Explaining the rationale for the bombings in the province, a Provisional spokesman argued that it 'irritates our enemies' by forcing the British to pay compensation, driving away foreign investment, and garnering propaganda value by demonstrating PIRA's 'determination and co-ordination'.[67] These explanations reveal a significant divergence from the previous emphasis within PIRA's thinking. No longer was the military campaign directed at making Northern Ireland an unbearable financial and psychological burden. The accent was now placed on keeping military operations ticking over to sustain the 'irritation' factor. Although the costs may not be prohibitive, the hope was that they would be considered an annoying, inconvenient and, ultimately, unnecessary affliction.

While the belief that it was public opinion in Great Britain which could act as the main lever on the British government remained the main constant in PIRA's strategy, the Provisionals sought to add greater definition to this point. They argued that because the 'Brits are an imperialist army . . . there is little effective link between their demoralisation and the British public's attitude to the war'. For this reason, the 'necessity to bring the war in Ireland home to the British people' through periodic mainland bombing campaigns remained a critical component of the strategy.[68] Also, PIRA sought to extend its attacks beyond the British Isles to the continent, in particular, against British Army bases and personnel in Germany. These operations were to be geared primarily towards creating propaganda in order to keep 'international attention focused on Britain's dirty war in Ireland'.[69] Occasionally these operations were supplemented by spectacular attacks against prestigious targets. Perhaps the best known 'spectacular' of recent times was the assassination of Lord Mountbatten along with a number of friends and relatives when a bomb destroyed his boat off the coast of Mullaghmore, Co. Sligo, on 27 August 1979. The shock caused by this incident was heightened by the killing of eighteen soldiers on the same day in a double-bomb ambush at Warrenpoint, Co. Down. Spectaculars were intended to be more than just dramatic protests against the British presence in Northern Ireland, as a PIRA spokesman explained in the wake of the Mountbatten killings: 'When they've finished cursing, of course, and damning us, they'll have to question the value of continuing with their occupation of Ireland. Because that is why he died.'[70]

This type of statement signified a subtle, though important shift in PIRA's use of armed force. Military action was no longer regarded as a method of total coercion aimed at terrorising the British out of Northern Ireland but as an instrument of armed propaganda.[71] In other words, once the military act had drawn the attention of a potential audience, the Provisionals could then attempt to focus it on all the other manifestations of the nationalist rejection of British rule. The Provisionals could hope to point to the popularity of community politics, participation in cultural affairs, economic resistance and, most importantly, political endorsement of the armed struggle through the ballot box. The implication of statements such as the one above concerning the Mountbatten killings was that after the furore surrounding an operation would come what could almost be described, as an appeal to the 'good sense' of the public who would see that PIRA's violence was not the work of a few unrepresentative criminal elements but symptomatic of a wider, more popularly based discontent. Through these means, the Provisionals might establish their political credentials with other groups, such as those sections of the British Labour Party sympathetic to PIRA's aims, and who could have some influence over a future Labour administration. By the early 1980s it was clear that this was the direction in which the Provisionals were moving.[72]

The central assumption of PIRA's thinking was that, eventually, all the individual elements of the total strategy would coalesce into a critical mass that would produce a British decision to withdraw. As O Conaill specified, the aim was now to apply sufficient 'pressure onto the point where the British will see that to break the log jam the declaration of intent to withdraw is the really important thing'.[73] Disaffection with the financial cost of the propping up Northern Ireland, the inability to eradicate PIRA, the lack of consensus for internal solutions, loyalist recalcitrance and continual embarrassments inflicted on Britain's reputation abroad would, together, constitute a favourable political constellation for the Provisionals. The notion of unacceptable cost in this context would not arise solely from the expense and deprivations caused by a low level campaign of isolated military engagements, but from the prospect of simple relief from all the petty aggravations associated with the retention of Northern Ireland within the UK. The potential efficacy of this multi-faceted strategy can be depicted diagrammatically as in Figure 6.1. This can be contrasted with the previous strategic plan utilised by PIRA in the early 1970s in Figure 6.2. Figure 6.1 displays the complexity of the total strategy, spanning a whole series of measures designed to increase the pressure on the British, whereas in Figure 6.2 the military instrument was virtually the only mode of operation. As Figure 6.1 indicates, although the armed struggle was treated as one method along a continuum of insurgency resistance, it could still be seen as the motor of the entire strategy as it functioned both to publicise the conflict and as a coercive instrument in its own right, albeit on a limited scale, as well as remaining the most symbolic expression of republican resistance.

One of the main features of the total strategy was that it enabled the military instrument to be governed by calculations of its efficacy rather than ideological tradition. Republican symbolism would not affect PIRA's military decisions. For

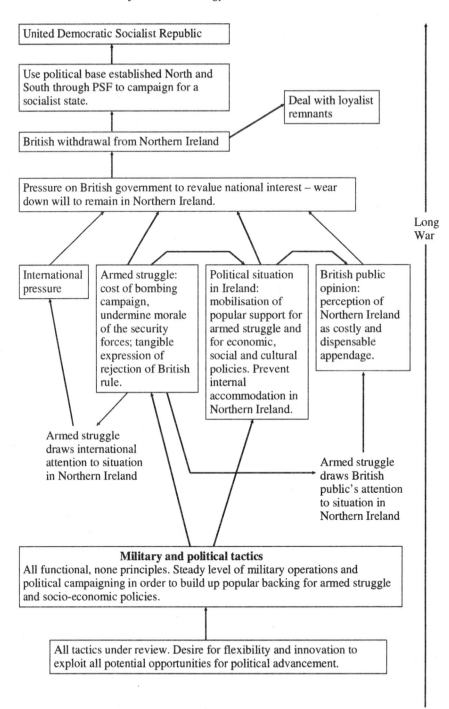

United Democratic Socialist Republic

Use political base established North and South through PSF to campaign for a socialist state.

Deal with loyalist remnants

British withdrawal from Northern Ireland

Pressure on British government to revalue national interest – wear down will to remain in Northern Ireland.

Long War

International pressure

Armed struggle: cost of bombing campaign, undermine morale of the security forces; tangible expression of rejection of British rule.

Political situation in Ireland: mobilisation of popular support for armed struggle and for economic, social and cultural policies. Prevent internal accommodation in Northern Ireland.

British public opinion: perception of Northern Ireland as costly and dispensable appendage.

Armed struggle draws international attention to situation in Northern Ireland

Armed struggle draws British public's attention to situation in Northern Ireland

Military and political tactics
All functional, none principles. Steady level of military operations and political campaigning in order to build up popular backing for armed struggle and socio-economic policies.

All tactics under review. Desire for flexibility and innovation to exploit all potential opportunities for political advancement.

Figure 6.1 The Provisional IRA's Total Strategy, 1977 onwards

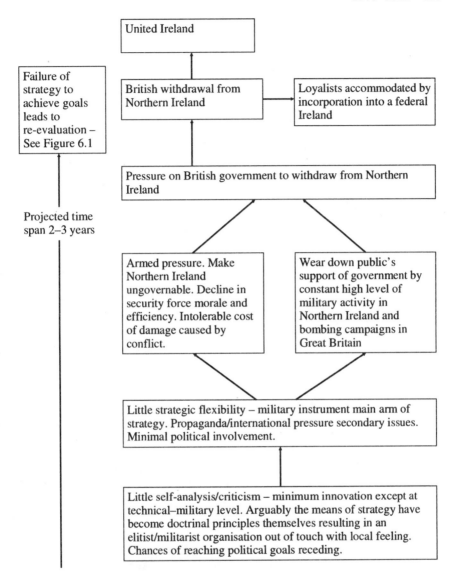

Figure 6.2 The Provisional IRA's Mono-Military Strategy, 1970–1976

example, PIRA would not consciously plan attacks to coincide with significant dates in the republican calendar, such as at Easter time or on the anniversary of the introduction of internment. The long war meant PIRA planned its attacks with care and in its own time. To restrict operations to either symbolic targets, such as the British Army, or to symbolic dates would not only seem an exercise in self-indulgent ideological posturing, but would allow the security forces to predict the nature and extent of PIRA's attacks. The security forces could take counter-measures and PIRA could suffer increased losses as a result. More fundamentally, to allow military activity to be dictated by the tokens of republican doctrine would have inhibited the proper functioning of armed force within the long war framework. Although attacks against the most obvious manifestations of the British presence, like the army, may have previously satisfied certain desires for revenge, the Provisionals now recognised that 'there is no guarantee that such a singular strategy would mean the realisation of all the factors instrumental in creating withdrawal'.[74] In other words, merely focusing on a narrow range of targets would dissipate the movement's stamina and actually diminish the pressure on the British.

The Provisionals emphasised that one of the consequences of the reorganisation into a smaller cell-based force geared for a long war was that there would be lulls in military activity for months at a time. The Provisionals acknowledged that these were caused mainly by problems of supply and intelligence.[75] The advantage of the total strategy was that when lulls occurred the momentum of the overall campaign could be carried by other elements of the strategy. This was a fundamental point which the Provisionals have been keen to highlight:

> it should be stressed that while there is a natural ebb and flow caused by logistical problems etc., it is a mistake to judge the intensity of the struggle using solely the level of operations as a guideline. While operational levels will fluctuate, political work in IRA base areas, education, recruitment, expanding the support base, all continue on a daily basis.[76]

If the armed struggle could now oscillate freely between periods of high and low activity without harming the impetus of the movement, then it was conceivable that the military arm could be consciously synchronised to suit the particular political circumstances. By the late 1970s there was already some evidence that PIRA was tailoring its operations for this purpose. The Glover report noted that the move away from large-scale commercial bombings, which often entailed a high risk to civilians, was probably undertaken because such attacks were politically damaging and alienated Catholic opinion.[77] The strongest indication that the military and political components were being alternated in order to derive maximum political advantage came in 1981 and 1982. During 1981, the Maze hunger strikes absorbed most of the republican movement's attention. Adams said that despite 'considerable popular demand for the IRA to take punitive action', PIRA eased back on its activities so as not to divert attention away from the growing political support the protests were receiving.[78] The Provisionals acknowledged the frustration felt by their supporters 'who believe that the IRA should pay the British government in kind for the deaths of comrades',[79] and in May 1981, after the deaths of the last hunger strikers, seemed to respond to this pressure in a burst of violence which left twenty-two dead by the end of the month. In October, with the Maze protests drawing to an end, further retribution was dispensed with a series of bombings in London. In Northern Ireland between September and November, thirty people lost their lives, among them Robert

Bradford MP. The next ten months saw another downturn in the violence with only fifty deaths, compared to almost 100 in the previous ten months. Similarly, the number of shooting incidents in 1982 fell dramatically to 382 from 815 in 1981 and explosions were down from 398 to 219. These figures can be interpreted as an attempt to reduce the level of violence in order to conserve the political support already gained in the run-up to the assembly elections, due in October, in which PSF was fielding candidates.

There is some debate as to whether the low levels of violence in 1981 and 1982 were attributable to a deliberate policy of restraint or to a more involuntary lapse caused by an increase in the number of arrests and the fact that the Maze protests had sapped most of the movement's energy.[80] There is also doubt as to whether the reduction in operations during the hunger strikes set a precedent for the coordination of political and military action. However, as the early years of the 1980s had demonstrated, by allowing the political face of the Provisionals to become more prominent, forward momentum could be retained despite a decrease in the level of military activity. The total strategy did enable the Provisionals to mobilise their resources more fully and to develop a more effective interchange between military and political tactics, which indicated both a more efficient use of armed force and a marked improvement in the quality of PIRA's strategic analysis.

FROM FERMANAGH AND SOUTH TYRONE TO WESTMINSTER – THE SUCCESS OF THE TOTAL STRATEGY

Just over a decade after the Provisionals' prospects appeared to have receded from the high watermark reached in the early 1970s, the early 1980s was also to prove a time of great trepidation for the movement. This time the effects would be felt on a political rather than a military front and, as such, would pose a wider, more serious threat to PIRA's opponents.

The years from 1981 to 1983 indicated the potential of the total strategy by marking the Provisionals' successful entry into electoral politics. The stimulus was provided by the victories of Bobby Sands and Owen Carron in the Fermanagh and South Tyrone by-elections of 1981. These events helped convince the Northern leaders, who had been working towards electoral participation, that a sufficient reservoir of alienated Catholic opinion existed to sustain a long-term political challenge. The elections in October 1982 to a new assembly, as part of Secretary of State James Prior's 'rolling devolution' initiative, provided the first chance to see how PSF's vote would fare. The outcome was acclaimed as a substantial advance for PSF, which had five of its twelve candidates elected on 10.1 per cent of the vote (64,191 first preference votes). PSF's impact was confirmed in the June 1983 general election when Gerry Adams was elected as abstentionist MP for West Belfast. The party raised its share of the vote in the province to 13.4 per cent (102,701 votes).

The two results were a triumph for PSF, especially as they represented a clear erosion of the SDLP's hold on the nationalist vote. PSF's result in 1983 constituted 42 per cent of the nationalist vote and led O Bradaigh to predict that PSF would overtake the SDLP within two years.[81] The common perception of PSF in this period was of a young, energetic and election-hungry party, a world away from the suspicious and lack-lustre attitudes that had characterised the movement's previous approach to most political matters. Moreover, its message of uncompromising nationalism contrasted favourably in the minds of many Catholics to the SDLP's continuing failure to deliver any power into nationalist hands. A MORI poll conducted in June 1984 revealed that those who voted for PSF perceived the party to be well-led, community based, and in touch with local feelings. Significantly, 84 per cent believed that one of PSF's main electoral assets was its ability to make the British take notice of nationalists. In this regard, the duality of force and politics was highly pertinent for PSF supporters, 70 per cent of whom agreed that violence could be justified to bring about political change.[82]

The degree of support for PSF not only gave the Provisionals themselves a huge boost in confidence but succeeded in attracting renewed external interest. Contacts with members of the British Labour Party had been increasing since the 1981 hunger strikes. In July 1983 Gerry Adams was received in London as a guest of Ken Livingstone, leader of the Greater London Council. Adams saw this as an opportunity to establish a dialogue with the British population so that republican ideas could be 'put to an audience ignorant of these views'.[83] These developments caused alarm in government circles in both London and Dublin. James Prior stated publicly his fear that the 'revolutionary' image of PSF might help it displace the SDLP.[84] This admission was a sign of how far the governments in Britain and Ireland had been thrown back on the defensive. For the first time in the current phase of the troubles they were faced with a counter-insurgency problem which extended beyond the bounds of mere security provision. A situation where there was no nationalist majority for any form of constitutional politics in Northern Ireland threatened to have a serious destabilising influence, because the basis for an internal solution would be rendered untenable. Adams declared that by undermining the SDLP, PSF could hope to establish 'a sort of republican veto'.[85] Concern at such a prospect led the London and Dublin governments to embark on a search for a political framework to contain the growth of PSF which was to lead eventually to the Anglo-Irish Agreement of 1985.

The progression of the Provisionals to this point was a testament to the mix of violence and politics contained in the long war/total strategy plan. For most of the 1970s physical force was regarded as functional, but it was also seen as an all embracing symbol of republican struggle and, as a result, largely autonomous of all other considerations. The attempt to connect the struggle with a semblance of popular legitimacy enabled PIRA to move away from the overt reliance on doctrinal symbolism to justify its existence. Now the republican attitude was to increase support for the movement and to ensure that PIRA's position was understood within the nationalist community. For example, the *Green Book* stated that 'we do not employ revolutionary violence without being able to illustrate that we have no recourse to any other means'.[86]

The recognition that violence should be treated more as a direct expression of political purpose helped to redress the previous republican deficiency in contextual analysis. The most significant step forward in this sense was the acceptance in the late 1970s that, with the protraction of the struggle, a change in direction was necessary which would, as a matter of course, affect the employment of the military instrument. This demanded an overhaul not just of the organisation, but more importantly, of the republican mentality itself. It meant an end to ideological elitism, a willingness to be more self-critical and to acknowledge that the struggle could no longer be built solely upon an armed conspiracy. Widening the struggle to include political participation presented a new set of challenges for the Provisionals. The essence of this position was summed up by Adams in one of his 'Brownie' articles:

> While it may be possible to struggle on without mass support, to be successful we must strive towards mobilising the maximum amount of people and enlisting their support, in a structured manner based on their needs and geared towards republican people's objectives. We cannot gain the republic without the people. We cannot do it on our own.[87]

These sorts of views represented a greater inclination to engage in a more sober assessment of the situation in which the movement found itself. This was seen most clearly in the Provisionals' attitude to the Protestant community, which recognised that loyalism was wholly incompatible with republican objectives. Also, the Provisionals came to accept that loyalism would not automatically fade away after a British withdrawal. The possibility of further extensive conflict was admitted, but they continued to argue that just 'how much blood is shed depends entirely on the British government'.[88] Less realistically in this respect, the Provisionals believed that a commitment to withdraw would also require the British to disarm all loyalist forces. In Morrison's words: 'We want a commitment that they will get out lock, stock and barrel. If they leave behind 30,000 armed loyalist in the UDR and RUC, that's a recipe for disaster'[89] – a view which tended to miss the point that the security forces had enough trouble trying to disarm a couple of hundred republicans. Disarming '30,000 armed loyalists' could prove slightly more problematic.

Overall, though, the long war made the Provisionals more sensitive to the dimensions of the conflict and more mindful of the limitations of their strategy. They strove to point out that PIRA's military strength should not be exaggerated or be subject to excessive rhetorical bravado, as the *Green Book* insisted, 'we do not claim that we are going to escalate the war if we cannot do just that'.[90] This contrasted with some of the wilder claims made for PIRA's military capabilities earlier in the 1970s. The experience of the 1970s underlined the basic reality of the relationship between PIRA and its more powerful adversary. The assessment of Britain's performance in the Falklands in 1982 rammed home the message to any wishful thinkers left in PIRA's ranks. One of the most lucid expositions of PIRA's strategy to have appeared in the republican press, 'Lessons of Malvinas' by Peter Dowling, put it succinctly: 'Given the obviously permanent (if slightly shifting) IRA/Britain imbalance of personnel, firepower and technology, the idea of getting rid of the British by purely military means is totally unrealistic.'[91]

The awareness of the extent of British military strength revealed the essence of the long war approach as a highly cautious strategy which aimed to avoid the provocation of counter-measures that could harm PIRA directly or further restrict the conditions in which it could operate, as happened with Operation Motorman for instance. This was why, for example, the killing of UDR and RUC members, on or off duty, presented such an attractive military option. They were low risk operations which the security forces could do little to stop. They did not transgress any scruples PIRA had about appearing sectarian. Yet such actions were sufficiently disparate and removed from the experience of people in the rest of the UK not to contribute to anything which might have incited the authorities into a crackdown. At the same time, these operations aided PIRA's purpose by keeping the military pot boiling in Northern Ireland while stirring up the Protestants. With sharpened feelings of contempt for the loyalists, the Provisionals believed they could play them off against the British by goading them into backlashes which would alienate opinion in Great Britain. Referring to the protests organised by Ian Paisley after the killing of Robert Bradford, Richard McAuley of PSF said: 'Provided the protests do not lead to civil war, they are not unwelcome. We believe they could bring forward a British withdrawal by three or four years, and in that sense they are useful.'[92]

The long war highlighted how attenuated the military instrument had become, certainly in comparison to the high level of operations in the early 1970s. PIRA's operations, even against its most favoured targets like the army and the RUC, now had to be conducted at a relatively low level. The interesting aspect of this situation was the extent to which the phenomenon of tacit bargaining appeared to be at work within the military dimension of the conflict. The notion of tacit bargaining deals with the idea that in war combatants may come to a mutual, though implicit, understanding to observe a degree of restraint to keep the conflict within certain boundaries.[93] It rested on the view that the British and PIRA had reached a level of military confrontation which both sides could tolerate without endangering their interests. PIRA could not escalate for fear it would provoke the British. The British could not do likewise without incurring domestic and international opprobrium. This was a view confirmed on the British side. A former British Army officer with experience in Northern Ireland once remarked:

> If an unwritten rule is put into play such as: stay with legitimate [i.e. security force] targets and we will play the game but go outside those then it is open season on the key men. This can have a useful effect of serving to contain the mad dogs.[94]

In other words, both sides had fought each other to a standstill with the resources each were prepared to commit. The most intriguing angle here was that the most crucial battlefield now appeared to take place *below* the military threshold.

The pivotal question for PIRA's strategy was, could it affect the correlation of forces between the two sides? The Falklands war provided a good foil to PIRA's campaign. The war was short and the moral issues relatively clear cut. As a consequence, the government enjoyed high levels of public support for its actions. These factors helped Britain to victory in 1982. The Provisionals' intention was to deny such favourable circumstances. By mounting a systematic campaign of minor military engagements, PIRA believed it could sufficiently lengthen the duration of the war to drive a psychological wedge through British society. Faced with so many *political* difficulties in dealing with a low level military threat, it was hoped that the authorities would be unable to avoid becoming embroiled in controversy. Eventually, dissensions over 'shoot-to-kill' allegations, hunger strikes, issues of civil liberties, law and order, etc. would adequately muddy the waters concerning the legitimacy of British involvement in Northern Ireland to destroy domestic consensus, and so undercut Britain's political will to stay.

Greater acceptance of the wide power differential with Britain was reflected in the moderation of the once frenetic tones of the movement's public language. Gone were the ideas of a fundamentally flawed opponent, and the more fanatical, cocksure self-belief. It was now accepted that nothing PIRA could do on its own could bring about the movement's objectives and that, at best, it could only exert indirect leverage over its adversary. The reality, as Peter Dowling emphasised, was that: 'however contradictory and unpalatable it may seem, the struggle to remove the British from here will only be brought to a successful conclusion at the behest of British public opinion stirred by the successful military actions of Irish republicans.'[95] The Provisionals seemed to have gained a firmer grasp on the simple, but essential, strategic axiom that the extent of the goals sought through warfare are usually made in proportion to the effort and resources devoted to the conflict. The Provisionals were under no illusions that the ambitious nature of their objectives required a concerted long-term collective effort on all fronts: 'There is work to be done. There is no magic formula. Only hard, intelligent building, consolidating and building again!'[96]

The most notable aspect of the total strategy was that it at least tried to address the problem of material inferiority. PIRA's philosophy, as Morrison said, was 'to keep all tactical options open, provided it never loses sight of the end result.'[97] In this way, the Provisionals could put far more factors into play and fight it out in arenas where the British did not possess any obvious pre-eminence. Using the military effort to undermine the stability of Northern Ireland, the movement could attract notoriety which it could use to further publicise its social, economic and cultural policies. Support for these policies, and by inference PIRA's armed struggle, as expressed through elections, could generate propaganda which could be used to gain sympathy abroad and discredit British involvement in Northern Ireland. In so doing, the Provisionals believed that the passage of time would gnaw away at the British psyche, and culminate in a decision to withdraw through exasperation.

The Provisionals could now see more clearly that the political effect of the campaign was the most crucial element which made the strategy efficacious, rather than the direct repercussions individual engagements may have had in the military field. Dowling's article, 'Lessons of Malvinas', stressed that every tactic should be scrutinised in the light of this requirement, adding that 'All actions should seek to unite and maximise nationalist support, and should be comprehensible to those supporters in the South who do not daily experience repression.'[98] It was to serve these goals that in 1978 PSF emerged as an overt organisation ready to publicly advocate republican policies. Previous to that, Morrison said, 'our politics had always been talked about and sold below the counter'.[99] PSF was now integral to the republican struggle. Adams stipulated that the 'party must be ideologically united on radical republican objectives and capable of formulating and implementing long-term and short-term strategies'.[100] Allowing PSF to campaign independently of the armed struggle, while being supportive of it, enabled the republican movement to move forward on a wide front and its message to be disseminated to the widest possible audience.

The advantage of the restructuring process was that the Provisionals were now able to be more precise about exploiting the propaganda effects of their campaign. This enhanced the overall strategy by allowing the movement to pack a greater political punch behind each military action. The total strategy did not overcome PIRA's deficiency in power, but it at least maximised its options, to make it a more potent coercive weapon than if it had relied purely on the military instrument. In this sense, the total strategy acted as a substitute for the risky pursuit of military escalation. By letting political initiatives back up military action, the Provisionals could portray themselves, both inside and outside Ireland, as a strong and popularly based movement. Thus, the Provisionals had the opportunity to build up their credibility and project an image of power without running the risk of either provoking damaging counter-measures or alienating public opinion, both of which were inherent in any decision to escalate.

THE EVOLVING STRATEGY

Looking with a longer historical view, the most significant feature about the adoption of the total strategy was that it represented an attempt to re-establish a sense of fluidity to Irish republican thinking. The movement itself had a fertile history of thinkers: Wolfe Tone, the Young Irelanders, Mitchel and Lalor through to Pearse, Connolly and Mellows. Yet this tradition, which had developed consistently since the late eighteenth century, had been halted in its tracks in the early 1920s.

The period from 1916 to 1921 was the golden age of republican struggle – a period of gallant sacrifice and military achievement. But it was swiftly followed by the disillusion of the Treaty settlement. The trauma of the civil war effectively froze the movement in a time warp which curtailed any further ideological development. Gerry Adams reckoned that the movement had been intellectually decapitated by the executions of 1916, which had delivered the leadership into the hands of 'non-republicans', such as Collins, Griffith and de Valera, and left the IRA as a traditionalist rearguard fighting against the betrayal of the ideals of 1916.[101] The more politically conscious socialist-republicans had always been present within the IRA, of course, but until the mid-1960s they were largely eclipsed by the traditionalists, and in any event, the bulk of them remained with the Officials when the movement split in 1969/70. While the Official IRA became a fully-fledged constitutional party, later in the 1980s dropping all references to its republican past and becoming simply the Workers' Party, the traditional intellectual enfeeblement of non-constitutional nationalism lived on in the Provisionals.

In many ways, the Northern radicals saw their dwindling fortunes in the mid-1970s as a symptom of the movement's general vacation of the political field to their opponents five decades earlier.[102] They wanted to reverse this trend and reinvigorate the movement. They believed this could be done by elaborating a republican doctrine that was relevant to contemporary circumstances and, there-fore, capable of attracting popular support. Essentially, the radicals wanted to make the strategy evolve once again in recognition that the politico-military battlefield upon which PIRA would continue to fight would be one of constant flux, demanding different solutions in response to changing conditions. In effect, it meant lifting the republican tradition out of being just that, a tradition, and moulding it into a developing political philosophy. This did not mean the collapse of the republican tradition. The radicals continued to draw on it for inspiration and legitimacy. For example, the *Green Book* stressed the Provisionals' 'direct lineal succession with the Provisional Government of 1916, the first Dail of 1919 and the second Dail of 1921'.[103] Similarly, the radicals reiterated that the doc-trines enunciated by past visionaries needed to be built on, not abandoned. At the 1979 Bodenstown commemoration, Adams declared: 'The teachings of Lalor, of Connolly, McSwiney, Mellows, Pearse and Theobald Wolfe Tone, up-dated if needs be to suit today's conditions, are the teachings of the Republican Movement.'[104]

Establishing an evolving strategy meant accepting that the context of the conflict would affect the employment of the methods of republican struggle, including the military instrument. This required that all aspects of the strategy be placed under constant review. This would ensure that the strategy would be analysis-led and not dictated by slogans or dogmas which had been elevated to positions of explicit importance within the republican tradition such that they interfered excessively with the process of strategic formulation.

The re-evaluation of the Provisionals' strategy undertaken by the Northern radicals could be said to have marked the rejuvenation of the movement from a period of decline and failure. The reassessment did not, however, resolve all of the anomalies in republican thinking. Although the Northern leaders succeeded in establishing the ascendancy of their brand of radical republicanism, the new strategy remained a careful and sometimes precarious balance between innova-tive modernism and traditionalism. The crucial aspect of the reassessment was that it brought far more coherence to the process of strategic formulation within the republican movement. The evolving strategy undoubtedly produced a more sophisticated and flexible base upon which the Provisionals could conduct their campaign. It also ensured that the movement could endure, and maybe prosper, into the next decade and beyond without suffering from the kind of wholesale political dislocation experienced in the mid-1970s. The essential point left hanging was that, if the Provisional IRA could now endure, what chance did the movement really stand of achieving its objectives with its revised strategy?

7 A continuing military enigma

The contradictory dynamics of the total strategy, 1983–1990

It was an open secret that the public upheavals in the republican movement caused by the politicisation process also caused ructions in PIRA's ranks. Dissension over practicalities centred on the relationship between peaceful political campaigning and the armed struggle. As PSF took on a more active role and rose to a position of more equal status with PIRA, it became clear that the two organisations would be in close competition for resources. The streamlining of the military organisation had reduced PIRA's operational costs, but PSF's political activities made heavy demands on the movement's finances. In the 1982 assembly elections, for example, PSF spent more money on its election campaign, over £27,000, than any of the rival parties.[1] Bishop and Mallie have said that by 1983 the cost of the party's advice centres was in the region of £300,000 per annum, while the general election campaign of that year had cost £30,000,[2] though other estimates have put the figure even higher at £137,000.[3] Either way, the financial burden was considerable. Suspicion of the politically go-ahead radicals was greatest among local PIRA activists who feared that the armed struggle would be run down and resources diverted to cater for PSF's schemes. According to Liam Clarke, this caution was shown in the spring of 1983 when a meeting of ASU operatives in Belfast gave the Northern radicals two years in which to demonstrate the continued effectiveness of their approach.[4] In the intervening years there were periodic press reports of arguments within PIRA about the lack of money to maintain a guerrilla war and particularly about the diminishing level of operations in Belfast.[5] In April 1985, four activists, including Ivor Bell, a former Army Council member and delegate to the 1972 talks with William Whitelaw, were expelled from PIRA after allegedly opposing the diversion of funds away from PIRA to finance PSF's campaign in the up-coming May local council elections, and for subsequently trying to mobilise support against the armalite and ballot box strategy.[6] There was even a suggestion that the explosion outside Harrods in December 1983, which killed five people, was the work of a faction deliberately out to disrupt contacts with the political left in Britain which Adams was trying to cultivate. Speculation was raised when PIRA said that the attack was 'not authorised by the Army Council'.[7] There was little proof that this or any other attack was intended to undermine Adams' position. PIRA later claimed that its statement was meant to convey that the Harrods bomb was a mistake caused by 'extremely difficult communications' and was not a repudiation of the bombing team concerned.[8]

The PSF leadership has always been careful to stress that the 'tactic of armed struggle is of primary importance'.[9] Martin McGuinness outlined the position thus: 'We recognise the value and limitations of electoral success. We recognise that only a disciplined armed struggle by the IRA will end British rule.'[10] Outright hostility within PIRA towards PSF appears to have been sporadic rather than coordinated and not symptomatic of any widespread antagonism towards the radicals. By 1986 any major doubts within PIRA had been sufficiently dispelled for an Army Council spokesman to announce that the movement 'has overcome many of the genuine fears that increased political activity would lead to a downgrading of the armed struggle'.[11]

Tensions within PSF did not dissipate so rapidly. Problems grew with evidence that PSF had reached its electoral peak in Northern Ireland. After three years of steady gains at the polls, the party's vote in the 1984 European election slipped to 91,476, down 11,000 votes on its performance in the 1983 general election. The decline was confirmed by the local elections in 1985. Despite winning a respectable fifty-nine council seats, PSF's showing fell to 11.8 per cent of the vote (75,686 first preference votes). Adams described the 1984 result a 'useful injection of reality'.[12] It was clear that the talk of overtaking the SDLP had been far too optimistic. Having reached an electoral peak in Northern Ireland, the PSF leadership now set its sights on electoral expansion into the Irish Republic. Ever since the early 1980s it had been PSF's intention to campaign on a thirty-two county basis, but events in Northern Ireland had, until then, absorbed its attentions. In the South, the party remained organisationally sluggish and devoid of real leadership. The situation was compounded by a widespread perception of PSF in the South as a single issue fringe group. Morrison admitted that PSF had 'to recognise . . . that the vast majority of people in the 26 counties consider the institutions of the state as being legitimate'.[13] This meant that if PSF was to be of any relevance in the South it would need to lift its policy of abstention from the Irish Dail, Leinster House, and campaign in the mainstream of Southern politics. With memories of the 1969/70 split still alive, it was an emotive issue, especially for older republicans who believed that abstentionism formed the cornerstone of the Provisionals' identity. PSF's leaders carefully prepared their ground. A PIRA Convention, held between September and October 1986, the first since 1970, renewed its commitment to the 'armed overthrow of British rule in Ireland', but also endorsed the radicals' plans by amending PIRA's constitution to allow the organisation to back non-abstentionist candidates.[14]

The PIRA Convention's support bolstered the PSF leadership when the motion to drop abstention came up for discussion at the 1986 Ard Fheis. Following an emotional, and sometimes acrimonious debate, the motion received the two-thirds majority necessary to permit the taking of seats at Leinster House. After the vote was taken, a number of those opposed to the change, amongst them O Conaill and O Bradaigh, walked out to form a new party, Republican Sinn Fein (RSF). RSF officially based its opposition on moralistic grounds about upholding allegiance to the 1916 Proclamation, the declaration of independence by the first Dail in 1919 and the non-recognition of 'British created institutions', which included the Dublin parliament.[15] The dimensions of the split need not be overplayed. The scale of the radicals' victory in the abstention debate, 429 votes to 161, was emphatic and displayed a real shift in opinion throughout the movement. In any case, it was widely known beforehand that a traditionalist rump would be unlikely to accept any decision to end abstentionism.

For all RSF's dogmatism and seeming concern for the preservation of the idealism of the past over progress in the present, some of the more practical arguments RSF levelled against the Provisionals' electoral policy were valid. Many of those who objected to the end of abstentionism could see the benefit that elections had brought in undermining the policy of criminalisation and in restricting the SDLP's room for manoeuvre, but in their view the moment recognition was given to the Southern state the movement would be fatally compromised. Inextricably they would be drawn into the system of wheeler-dealing which would eventually result in the implicit acceptance of all the panoply of state apparatus they despised: the police, the courts, security co-operation with Britain, etc. O Bradaigh put it this way: 'They will be signing their own extinction as revolutionaries not because they want to but because it cannot be otherwise.'[16] The bottom line was that electoral participation and an armed campaign were incompatible, as O Bradaigh argued: 'You cannot ride two horses at the same time.'[17]

One of the risks of dropping abstentionism was that, once the Southern state had been recognised as having legitimacy, where electoral participation is permissible, while the North was regarded as irreformable where armed struggle was a necessity, then PSF was in danger of creating two different parties to suit two different political systems – a de facto recognition of partition. The radicals denied these accusations. 'We need to keep our republican gut' and 'must never lose sight of our national objectives', Adams reminded his audience at the 1986 Ard Fheis.[18] The radicals' line, as expressed by *An Phoblacht/Republican News*, was that: 'Leinster House does corrupt. It corrupts corruptible people . . . the weak and vain, the insincere and the gombeen. It cannot corrupt a revolutionary.'[19] But this was self-refuting. If one professes to be a revolutionary who will refuse to participate in the political process, then why bother taking seats in parliament? 'I cannot see what they would do if they were elected to Leinster House,' pondered one pro-abstentionist councillor before the 1986 Ard Fheis.[20]

Whatever the impediment to PSF's political progress, abstention had been a vehicle for reducing some of the anomalies within republican thinking. Abstention was the hand-maiden of absolutism as it ensured that republican ideals remained untainted by influences in the wider political world. Once this principle was banished, republican ideology theoretically became more vulnerable to dilution by outside forces. Adams knew all along that there would be difficulties in this new approach. In 1983 he admitted: 'there are contradictions between our struggle and the political structure in the same way there are contradictions in Irish society.'[21] In saying this, Adams was perhaps more prescient than he might have wished, because the evolution of the military instrument from the early 1980s reflected the movement's attempts to grapple with the increasing rhetorical and practical contradictions that have emerged following the adoption of a higher political profile.

THE ARMALITE VERSUS THE BALLOT BOX

When the Provisionals abolished abstention in 1986 they claimed that simple vote-catching was not their sole intention. They recognised that support for violence would dissuade many people from voting for PSF. This was not seen as a barrier but as an opportunity both to develop the party organisation and to get their message across by using election campaigns and parliamentary seats as political platforms. As *An Phoblacht/Republican News* elucidated, electoral intervention was seen as consistent with their overall plans:

> Initially our solidarity with the armed struggle may cost us support among some sections of the non-republican populace. However, rather than com- promise or be evasive, republicans must explain the origins and correctness of physical force. We can then learn to live without the support of those to whom the armed struggle is an insuperable difficulty. It is something we have assessed. But we will also educate many into republicanism, into our analysis of the crisis in Ireland, into supporting republicanism and the republican struggle.[22]

Nevertheless, constant exhortations, not least from Adams himself, 'to move into the mainstream of political relevancy',[23] required there to be some compromise between the armed and peaceful political sides of the struggle. It was no good entering the electoral arena only to end up with a minuscule number of votes. Poor performances would hardly be consistent for an energetic organisation which believed itself capable of breaking the mould of Irish politics. In order not to alienate potential sympathisers it proved necessary for the armed struggle to be 'acceptable to the people on whose behalf it is carried out'.[24] Evidence of PIRA's attempts to make its campaign more tolerable to would-be supporters can be gleaned from some of the statistics for the violence that occurred in the mid-1980s. Tables 7.1 and 7.2 demonstrate how, since the late 1970s, PIRA has concentrated its attacks on security forces personnel. This was accompanied by a corresponding decrease in the number of bombings in urban areas and against commercial property which place civilians at greatest risk. This is reflected in both tables in the decline in civilian fatalities as a percentage of the total number of deaths recorded up to the mid-1980s. However, Table 7.3 indicates that there was little in PIRA's operational profile to signify that the level of attacks were adjusted to coincide with the elections which took place in the period. There were no depreciations in the rate of explosions or deaths of security force personnel in the run up to, or appreciations following, each of the elections concerned. Only in May 1985, the month in which local elections were held in Northern Ireland, was there a dip in the figures, but this is insufficient to establish any trend. The

Table 7.1 Yearly civilian fatalities* and percentage of total fatalities each year, 1969–1985

Year	Number	% of total fatalities
1969	13	86.7
1970	17	68.0
1971	93	53.8
1972	238	50.1
1973	127	50.4
1974	143	65.3
1975	171	69.8
1976	213	72.0
1977	47	42.3
1978	31	41.3
1979	27	25.0
1980	34	43.6
1981	34	30.9
1982	31	32.3
1983	28	35.9
1984	16	25.4
1985	15	28.3

Source: Compiled from data contained in *Irish Information Agenda*, London, Irish Information Partnership, 1987, Table B1viii, p. 4.

Note: *Excludes deaths of paramilitary suspects, political activists, elected representatives, prison officers, former members of security forces and unclassified deaths.

bulk of the statistical information up to the mid-1980s suggests that, with the exception of the hunger strike elections in 1981 when there was a reduction in the level of operations, the refinements in the employment of the military instrument applied *only* to PIRA's targeting policy, indicated by the clear preference for attacks on security force targets over civilian ones.

One explanation for the absence of any co-operation between PIRA and PSF during elections could be that, having reached an electoral ceiling in Northern Ireland (PSF's vote has stabilised around 80,000 to 90,000 votes for some years now), the movement felt that there was limited political mileage to be gained in further constraining PIRA's operations to facilitate PSF's electoral progress. If this was the case, then there seemed little to confirm the suspicions of the traditionalists that the military campaign had or was likely to become subordinate to PSF's political crusade.

Although the primacy of the military arm never appeared under threat, certain intellectual incongruities did emerge. This was most noticeable in PSF's attitude towards the Anglo-Irish Agreement, or Hillsborough Accord, concluded between the British and Irish governments in November 1985. To reassure unionists, the Agreement affirmed the current status of Northern Ireland, recognising the current

Table 7.2 Yearly security force and civilian fatalities caused by republican paramilitaries and percentage of total fatalities in each year, 1979–1986

a) *Security force fatalities*

Year	Number	% of total
1979	59	54.6
1980	27	34.6
1981	43	39.1
1982	41	42.7
1983	34	43.6
1984	28	44.4
1985	29	54.7
1986	24	45.3

b) *Civilian fatalities*

Year	Number	% of total
1979	19	17.6
1980	20	25.6
1981	22	20.0
1982	27	28.1
1983	15	19.2
1984	10	15.9
1985	13	24.5
1986	14	26.4

Source: Compiled from *Irish Information Agenda*, Table B1ii, pp. 3–4.

wish of the majority to remain part of the UK. Both governments reiterated that any change in Northern Ireland's constitutional position could only come about with the consent of the majority. For nationalists, the main provision of the Accord was the recognition of a wider Irish dimension through the establishment of an intergovernmental conference which granted the Dublin government a consultative role in the affairs of the province. Although PSF opposed the Agreement as yet another doomed attempt at an internal settlement, Adams stated in late 1985 that the Agreement's introduction had shown that the British could be moved by republican pressure: 'The equation is therefore a simple one: support for Sinn Fein equals concessions from the British.'[25] This argument was duly incorporated into PSF's campaign literature: 'Sinn Fein recognises that the Hillsborough Agreement has come about as a direct result of the electoral advances of Sinn Fein and the successes of the Republican Movement.'[26] This represented a straight trawl for votes with little regard for doctrinal consistency. By trying to claim credit for concessions to improve a system which the movement always said needed to be destroyed came dangerously close to

Table 7.3 Monthly fatalities of security forces and monthly rate of explosions, 1983–86

i) *Monthly fatalities of security forces*

	Jan.	Feb.	Mar.	Apr.	May	June	July	Aug.	Sep.	Oct.	Nov.	Dec.	Total
1983	3	3	2	3	2	2[a]	4	1	1	5	7	1	34
1984	5	1	3	2	8	2[b]	2	2	1	2	0	1	29
1985	0	13	3	1	4[c]	2	0	0	2	0	3	2	30
1986	3[d]	2	2	2	4	0	7	1	0	3	1	0	24

ii) *Monthly rate of explosions*

	Jan.	Feb.	Mar.	Apr.	May	June	July	Aug.	Sep.	Oct.	Nov.	Dec.	Total
1983	5	15	19	12	19	46[a]	23	18	44	17	26	22	266
1984	26	27	22	21	15	12[b]	16	19	13	11	4	7	193
1985	7	11	8	14	4[c]	11	14	32	32	8	5	17	163
1986	13[d]	7	5	13	15	7	5	25	9	26	22	26	172

iii) *Monthly rate of explosions of known republican paramilitary origin, 1984–1986*

	Jan.	Feb.	Mar.	Apr.	May	June	July	Aug.	Sep.	Oct.	Nov.	Dec.	Total
1984	26	25	22	20	15	12[b]	16	19	13	11	4	7	190
1985	7	11	8	14	4[c]	11	14	31	8	8	5	17	162
1986	13[d]	7	5	12	15	6	4	25	25	25	22	26	169

Source: Compiled from *Irish Information Agenda*, Table B7iii, p. 1.

Notes: [a] Month of Westminster general election.
[b] Month of European community elections.
[c] Month of local elections, Northern Ireland.
[d] Month of Unionist (anti-Anglo-Irish Agreement) by-elections.

undermining the argument that the Northern state was irreformable. There was some internal criticism of PSF's 'confused position of on the one hand opposing the Hillsborough Agreement but at the same time trying to claim credit for the benefits which might arise from it'.[27] The attempt to play it both ways was probably one reason why PSF failed to stimulate its electoral fortunes. After all, why should nationalists who favoured the Agreement vote for PSF which was, at heart, opposed to the Agreement when others like the SDLP were wholly supportive? The point was illustrated in the British general election of June 1987. PSF remained more or less static with 11.4 per cent of the poll in Northern Ireland, while in the Southern election in February the same year, PSF received a truly dismal 1.9 per cent.

The awkward balance of maintaining a revolutionary party on the one hand, while trying to juggle with the politics of popularity with the other, was one previously unknown area into which PSF was led by its decision to enter electoral politics. PIRA's emphasis on attacking members of the security forces was part of the process to make the movement more palatable to voters, as it was assumed that such attacks could be passed off as legitimate military targets. Such intentions counted for little, however, if attacks went wrong and ended up killing large numbers of civilians, as happened during the period from 1987 to 1990. The most notorious incident during this period was the Enniskillen bombing on Remembrance Day in November 1987 which killed eleven Protestants. The sectarianism evident in the choice of target, and the overtones of mendacity in trying to blame the explosion on British Army scanning equipment, compounded a public relations disaster for the Provisionals. The political effect of such mistakes often restricted PSF's capacity to expand beyond its core of support, as one PIRA spokesman commented after Enniskillen: 'Our central base can take a hell of a lot of jolting and crises. But the outer reaches are just totally devastated.'[28] In 1988 civilian fatalities comprised 31 per cent of PIRA's victims. They rose to 39 per cent in 1989.[29] The cost in terms of lost support for PSF was revealed in the local elections of May 1989. Although PSF's share of the vote at 11.3 per cent was only 0.1 per cent down on the 1987 general election, the party received 6,500 fewer votes than the 1985 local election and lost sixteen of its council seats. PSF councillor, Mitchel McLaughlin, acknowledged that 'IRA operations that went wrong did have an effect because in a sense Sinn Fein is held accountable at local level for all aspects of the republican struggle.'[30] This sort of statement was indicative of a degree of PSF irritation with the regularity of PIRA's errors and illustrated well the tension which existed between the armed struggle and PSF's desire to maximise its electoral potential. On a number of occasions since the early 1980s Adams reproved PIRA for its operational laxity. Following the European election in 1984 he warned:

> there are varying degrees of tolerance within the nationalist electorate for aspects of the armed struggle. . . . I think there is a need to refer to what I said at the 1983 Ard Fheis. That is that revolutionary force must be controlled and disciplined so that it is clearly seen as a symbol of our people's resistance.[31]

Adams never publicly condemned any PIRA operation, but his criticisms of PIRA were to become less coded from the late 1980s onwards as mistakes became more frequent and their negative impact on PSF's electoral prospects more evident. During his speech to the 1989 Ard Fheis, he addressed some of his remarks to members of PIRA: 'You have a massive responsibility. At times the fate of the struggle is in your hands. You have to be careful and careful again.'[32] The problem for PSF was that PIRA did not actually dissent from anything Adams said. According to a member of the GHQ staff: 'We will always be striving to place the struggle on ground which republicans can unhesitatingly, and without great difficulty, defend.'[33] The main reasons for the high rate of mistakes were historical and structural. Traditionally, PIRA units, particularly those in border areas, enjoyed a large degree of autonomy, more so since the introduction of the cell structure. ASUs were able to plan their actions with little reference to the higher echelons of PIRA's command. This was probably a strong factor in the Enniskillen bombing. Being an illegal conspiratorial organisation, PIRA found it hard to train recruits and test equipment, while financial constraints prevented it from obtaining the most up-to-date and reliable weaponry. As a consequence, there was an in-built propensity for mistakes to occur.[34]

The inherent risk of military mistakes helps to dispel the idea that PIRA operations in this period were designed to undermine specific diplomatic initiatives. There has been a tendency, in both the British and Irish press, to attribute motives of political timing to each major action. For example, the attack on the Conservative Party Conference at Brighton in October 1984 was said to be intended to destroy the prospects for increased co-operation in a forthcoming summit between Margaret Thatcher and Irish Prime Minister, Garret FitzGerald.[35] Such attributions were highly speculative and credited PIRA with a sense of omnipresence which it did not possess. PIRA was a small organisation, possibly 300 active service unit activists at most. It has had to function in conditions of strict security. Attacks could take weeks, if not months, to plan. Many of them have had to be called off. For example, PIRA admitted that out of eighteen bombing missions carried out between February and May 1983, eight had to be aborted either because the bombs failed to detonate properly or because they were located by the security forces.[36] In any case, spectacular operations, whether they go wrong or not, have tended to spur rather than hinder Anglo-Irish co-operation against PIRA. The Enniskillen bombing, for instance, enabled the Irish government to push a contentious extradition bill through the Dail. It was opportunism, not political coincidence, which was the guiding motive behind PIRA's attacks.

Fundamentally, the long war approach explicitly rejected such notions as offensives or political timing.[37] Ever since the introduction of the long war concept in the late 1970s, the aim has been to sustain a continuous level of attacks irrespective of political developments within or between the governments of Britain and Ireland. The following extract from an interview with a PIRA spokesman illustrates this point. It refers to two series of bombing and shooting incidents conducted by PIRA in Northern Ireland, the first in November 1978 and the second in April 1979, the month before the British general election.

> These attacks [the November 1978 attacks] were inaccurately described by the media as part of a winter offensive, as if we were trying to realise a short term goal or aim. This was not so. Similarly, what is happening now is not a pre-election blitz but is just a period of concerted activity in our overall struggle to destabilise British rule in Ireland.[38]

There are two deductions one can make both from an examination of PIRA's operational profile and from statements like those above. First, PIRA was unable to fight to prescription, that is, to make its attacks coincide with individual political events with any degree of regularity, and second, that it was impossible to fight an antiseptic, voter-friendly war. The second point in particular highlighted the underlying tension within the armalite and ballot box strategy. Could PSF credibly campaign on a range of economic and social issues, such as housing, jobs, investment and health, while PIRA helped destroy them? There were two telling incidents that underlined this query, noted by Liam Clarke in his own investigation. Both incidents involved PIRA bombing attacks on the Andersonstown Road RUC station, West Belfast, in which a number of surrounding houses were damaged. The first, in June 1983, happened the night before the Westminster election, leaving PSF activists to answer for PIRA's actions and advise residents on state compensation. Apparently, when Adams was canvassing the following morning he saw the bombing unit returning from the mission and shook his fist in anger at their car.[39] The second incident occurred the following year while PSF was leading a delegation to the Northern Ireland Housing Executive to complain about housing conditions in West Belfast.[40] These sorts of embarrassments did mark out certain lines of divergence between PIRA and PSF. They stemmed from differing perceptions rather than elementary disagreements over the movement's direction. As the commentator, Ed Moloney, pointed out, being at the sharp military end of the struggle, PIRA was inclined to see operations which went wrong and killed civilians as technical mistakes, resulting from faulty equipment, inadequate warning times and so on. PSF, on the other hand, saw such actions as conceptually flawed, believing that operations should never be carried out in areas, such as towns and cities, where there was a high risk to civilians.[41] For example, when asked in an interview whether he could really have been surprised that the Enniskillen bomb had caused civilian deaths after it had been placed in a position where civilians had always congregated, Adams replied: 'I think that was the stupid mistake, planting it there in the first place, the fact that it was a memorial service, the fact that all fatalities bar one were civilians.'[42]

It is clear that PSF did not count the cost of mistakes as missed opportunities to hit the security forces but in terms of damage to its political reputation and election prospects. On the other side of the coin, PIRA occasionally saw the restrictions it felt obliged to observe as posing a reverse propaganda threat. For example, in 1985 PIRA launched a series of bombings against Belfast city centre. PIRA felt that the British had used the reduced level of violence in urban areas as a 'propaganda platform' to attract investment and promote a 'facade of normality'. The intention of the bombings, as the Belfast Brigade's statement claiming responsibility for the attacks read, was to destroy these claims: 'There is no "normality". Such propaganda claims are false and today's attack is a potent demonstration of our determination to continue our struggle against the British colonial presence wherever and whenever the opportunity presents itself.'[43] Sentiments such as these contravened the political interests of PSF. Adams was aware of this difficulty. In 1987 he reminded PIRA that it had 'a major responsibility to ensure that the armed struggle was geared to republican goals'. He continued: 'It's when the IRA, as in Enniskillen, omits to take this into account that tragedies take place.'[44] Yet organisational, historical and temperamental factors showed PIRA's inability to fine tune the armed struggle to advance republican goals in the manner which Adams suggested. It was precisely this point, the fact that Adams and PSF did not appear to have any direct influence over PIRA's operational planning, which emphasised the central problem for Irish republican strategy; the issue of political control over the military instrument.

THE CONTRADICTIONS OVER POLITICAL CONTROL OF THE MILITARY INSTRUMENT

The question of political control over the use of violence has been a major reason why republican violence has sometimes been misapplied in the past. With the advent of the total strategy and the rise of PSF to a position of equivalence with PIRA, one might have expected some of the problems which existed in this area to start moving towards resolution. As the military instrument was considered incapable of shouldering the republican struggle alone and, therefore, to be accompanied by increased political activity, it followed that there should be some coordination of military and political means in order to optimise the level of resistance. This raised the larger question of how this coordination should be formed and controlled. Since war is an expression of political purpose to achieve certain ends through violence, it is to be expected that policy will affect the employment of the military instrument to ensure there is maximum movement towards the political objective. In theory, this should mean that the PSF leadership would oversee all aspects of the struggle. Although PSF would not necessarily take any interest in day-to-day military decisions, it would define the general thrust of military policy by laying down the boundaries of permissible action in war. PSF would thus be able to instruct PIRA on what military objectives it should seek and when to refrain from actions which might inhibit the advance towards the overall goal.

The complication here lay in trying to establish the exact relationship between PIRA and PSF. Ever since 1919 Sinn Fein and the IRA have maintained that they are separate organisations which share the same aspirations. Mutual agreement on aims, according to one PSF pamphlet in 1973, 'does not mean Sinn Fein has any control or say in Army policy and vice versa. Sinn Fein is simply a political organisation whose policy is the establishment of a 32-county socialist republic.'[45] Similarly, in the late 1980s, Adams declared: 'There isn't any organic relationship . . . Sinn Fein supports the right in particular circumstances to take up armed resistance.'[46] Such claims have always given some ground for scepticism. One might ask what was the rumpus over abstention all about. Why did the PSF leadership need to reassure its members that ending abstention would not lead to any diminution of the armed struggle? If there were no formal ties with PIRA, then PSF was in no position to answer for PIRA, as no PSF decision on abstention could have by itself altered PIRA's commitment to violence. The fact that PSF did answer for PIRA and always seemed well versed in the vocabulary of PIRA strategy implied a link which went beyond mere coincidence of objectives. The most conclusive evidence in recent times which revealed there to be more than a nodding acquaintance between PSF and PIRA was the case of Danny Morrison, PSF's director of publicity, who was convicted along with six others of the false imprisonment of Joseph Lynch, a police informer who had been lured to a house in West Belfast by PIRA to face interrogation. On a number of occasions Morrison's public utterances indicated a degree of familiarity with PIRA which suggested that he was empowered to act as some sort of de facto spokesman for the organisation. In December 1982 he is recorded to have stated that the Northern Ireland assembly was a 'sectarian forum' and a target for the Provisional IRA,[47] which indicated, at the very least that he was a conduit to convey PIRA's thinking. Having such a senior PSF figure gaoled as a result of direct participation in a PIRA operation was undoubtedly a major embarrassment for the republican movement.

Uncertainty over the nature of the connections between PIRA and PSF leads to the more serious accusation that PSF was not only linked, but subordinated to PIRA. Historically, there was no doubt that the IRA had been the senior member in the partnership. Adams had always tried to deny any 'monkey and organ grinder relationship with the IRA'. 'The suggestion that Sinn Fein would be running off to the IRA to ratify tactical and political decisions is nonsense.'[48] Yet it was the *Staff Report* of 1977 which stated: 'Sinn Fein should come under *Army organisers* at all levels . . . Sinn Fein should be radicalised *(under Army direction)*' (italics mine). This testified to the fact that the modern PSF organisation had its original terms of reference shaped by the Army Council. Although this did not prove that PSF continued to be submissive, there were instances which indicated that PSF still occasionally bowed to PIRA's influence. For example, Bishop and Mallie say that in 1985 the Belfast Brigade engineered the selection of their favoured candidate, Alex Maskey, for a Belfast council by-election, over Adams' first choice.[49] One could also point to the terms PIRA appeared to have extracted from PSF in return for endorsing the abolition of abstention, which included the over-turning of a pro-abortion motion passed in 1985 and a general toning down in PSF's socialist rhetoric.[50]

It was quite possible that the denials of association were mere legal niceties to prevent PSF's proscription. It was also clear that over the previous ten years PSF did move out of PIRA's shadow and gain greater control over its own affairs, though whether this made it wholly independent of PIRA is still a matter for debate. If there was no formal, organic link, then there was plenty of evidence of unofficial links and associations, possibly based on personal contacts, which permitted a degree of mutual understanding and informal co-operation. Certainly, the distinctly ad hoc fashion in which PSF believed it could rely on PIRA's assistance lent weight to this interpretation. In hoping that PIRA would help PSF at election times by reducing the number of operations, Morrison once said: 'We would like to think that the IRA would appreciate when to take an expedient holiday for a week.'[51] At other times, Adams sought to emphasise PSF's separation by distancing the party from PIRA: 'Sinn Fein does not unambiguously support the IRA, we support their right to engage in armed struggle. No-one should give unambiguous support to any organisation or institution.'[52]

Either way, separate or subordinate, PSF did not appear to receive the close co-operation that it may have wished from PIRA between 1983 and 1990, as evinced by the failure of Adams' strictures on avoiding mistakes to modify PIRA's operating procedures to any noticeable extent. Nor, from the information contained in Table 7.3, did PIRA seem to pay much attention to Morrison's call for undeclared ceasefires come elections. The political damage that this lack of coordination could inflict on PSF's progress, and the movement's prospects generally, was immense. The Harrods bomb, and later the Brighton bombing, did a great deal to erode the contacts which PSF had been trying to build up with the political left in Britain. Outright support from the broad left could never have been expected so long as PIRA's violence continued, but the sympathy of some on the far left might have been preserved if PIRA waged a restrained campaign.

Although the far left never extended its influence into government during the 1980s, such contacts could still have proved a useful bridgehead into British politics. Clumsy operations like the Harrods bombing placed sympathisers in a moral quandary over whether to support a movement that carried out operations which killed civilians. The Brighton bomb, on the other hand, had the effect of strengthening the Conservative government's image, something guaranteed to bring the Provisionals into contempt in the eyes of virtually all those on the left of British politics.[53]

The evidence suggests that there was little political guidance of the military instrument, either because PSF was a subsidiary arm of PIRA or, more likely, because PSF was a semi-detached organisation without any direct say in the use of violence. If this was the case, then it blew away the entire rationale concerning the armed struggle's relationship with the total strategy. How could the armed struggle be considered merely as one tactic to be used or discarded in accordance with its functionality if there was no political control over the application of force in the first place? Taking people like Adams at their word, and accepting that there were no formal PSF links with PIRA, then why should anyone have bothered listening to such a minor party and fellow traveller of the Provisional IRA? What would have been the point in talking to PSF about political settlements or ceasefires if it had no influence, apart from moral suasion, over PIRA. Even if PSF wanted an end to violence there seemed little it could have done to ensure that PIRA would stop. Instead, the regulation of the military instrument appeared to remain in the hands of the shadowy Army Council which was free to employ violence wherever it so chose, unaccountable to anyone beyond its own organisation.

The confusion at the heart of republican strategy left a series of questions about the movement's underlying attitude towards the practice of violence. Was the inability to impose control over the armed struggle, for all the talk of calculating it on the basis of its utility, symptomatic of a continuing sentimental attachment to physical force? Adams pronounced the armed struggle to be a 'morally correct form of resistance'. He also saw it as an effective form of resistance:

> the British Government rarely listens to the force of argument. It understands only the argument of force. . . . Armed struggle, however, is not merely a defensive reaction by an oppressed people. It sets the political agenda. Thus armed struggle can advance the overall struggle to the advantage of those in whose interest it is waged.[54]

This combination of moral approval and assertion, though rarely explanation, of the instrumentality of the armed struggle intimated an emotional affinity with the use of force. Physical force was not only one of the most important unifying factors in the movement, it appeared to be the only real feature which preserved the Provisionals' notoriety and identity. Indeed, Adams emphasised the commitment to the armed struggle as a means of differentiating the Provisionals from their rivals in the Officials:

For anyone who has eyes to see, it is clear that the Sticky leadership had abandoned the armed struggle as a form of resistance to British rule. . . . For our part, this leadership has been active in the longest phase of resistance to the British presence. Our record speaks for itself.[55]

When the Provisionals used the armed struggle in this manner to distinguish themselves from their political rivals, it casts doubt over whether the efficacy of physical force could ever be seriously challenged under the aegis of the total strategy without causing huge internal disruption. It suggests that force continued to be regarded as an unimpeachable facet of republican resistance. A contribution to the confidential PSF journal, *Iris Bheag*, a good guide to the feelings of local activists, argued: 'Without the war there would be no cutting edge. . . . This means calling off the armed struggle is not an option open to the Irish revolution.'[56] Such views exhibited an air of permanence regarding the military instrument. It is possible to speculate whether the loyalty to the campaign of violence professed by PSF's leaders was genuine or simply an implicit admission that they had no authority over PIRA and that the military instrument was, therefore, inherently uncontrollable. McGuinness once said: 'Sinn Fein would never consider any suggestion that it should dictate operational conditions to the men and women who engage in the legitimate armed struggle against the forces of British imperialism,'[57] thus leaving open the question as to whether this was a statement of voluntary restraint on the part of PSF or merely, as seems more probable, confirmation of a pre-existing fact.

The questions posed are difficult to answer with precision because of legal smoke-screens and clashing or insufficient evidence. The commitment to violence undoubtedly remained a complex mixture of motives, and with all the passionate symbolism and intensity of physical force in the republican tradition it is too much to expect even the radical politico-Provisionals to have treated the subject in an emotionally detached way. Yet the distinct impression persisted that there was still no meaningful political management of the use of violence. Although PIRA may not have wilfully ignored PSF's advice on military matters, it was evident that PIRA was free to reject it, if it so wished. Along with differing organisational structures, the traditionally dominant role of the IRA over Sinn Fein and the difficulty of imposing firm control over ASUs, it was patent that PIRA remained independent of any external authority. On more than one occasion this was openly stated. In 1983, for example, a member of PIRA's leadership proclaimed: 'The military struggle will not slow down to relate to Sinn Fein's political activity. If anything, subject to logistical considerations, the war is likely to be stepped up.'[58] More implicit assertions of autonomy from political constraints lived on through the 1980s in PIRA's continuing tendency to issue belligerently worded statements to 'carry on the struggle through 1984 until victory'[59] and by emphasising that the 'armed struggle will continue and continue while finding ways of intensifying the war'.[60]

The question of military autonomy has been a recurring problem in Irish republican strategy. The lack of a discernible political-military nexus within republican strategy underlined the curious nature of the movement with regard to the degree to which the military arm has consistently prevailed over political considerations and continued to regulate the republican struggle. To reiterate what Adams said, the armed struggle 'sets the political agenda'. But could the political agenda itself be regulated? The balance of the evidence suggests that this was still not possible as the military instrument under the Provisional IRA alone could not be guaranteed as a functional element in war to be deployed in a measured way under politically controlled conditions.

CONTRADICTIONS IN THE RHETORIC OF BRITISH WITHDRAWAL

The issue of political control is not something which exists in the abstract as a debating point for strategic commentators. Failure to accurately define the role of force in the political process can prevent the military instrument from being properly directed to achieve appropriate ends. At worst, this can lead to the indiscriminate application of violence in a manner which can hinder the attainment of objectives. Because low intensity warfare strategies often seek to use military engagements as a means of pressure rather than physical denial, their practitioners have to exercise considerable political caution in order to avoid both the wastage of scarce military resources and the provocation of enemy countermeasures which restrict the freedom to operate. The lack of effective political stewardship of PIRA still made it difficult to discern the exact purpose of armed force in relation to the main objective of effecting the removal of Northern Ireland from the UK. The chief task in attempting to discover the function of the military instrument in this respect lay in trying to detect, from private and public pronouncements, the decisive point at which the Provisionals believed military pressure should be applied to get the British to concede to their will. PIRA's *Green Book* appeared explicit. It categorised the 'main enemy' to be 'the establishment', which was defined as 'all those who have a vested interest in maintaining the present status quo in politicians, media, judiciary, certain business elements and the Brit war machine comprising the Brit Army, the UDR, RUC, Screws [prison officers], Civilian Searchers'.[61] The interests which this group had in perpetuating the status quo were seen to range variously from personal gain and economic exploitation to the desire to protect British security interests on the Western flank.[62] On a number of occasions the Provisionals tried to be more specific about the nature of their political enemy. In 1981 O Bradaigh proclaimed:

> What's meant by the expression "England" is the English ruling classes who have dominated and exploited the Irish people, and indeed, much of the world in their time and have also exploited their own working people as is clear from those who wish to study it [sic].[63]

According to PIRA's leadership, 'we do not intend to hold the British people responsible for their government's crimes in Ireland. Any attacks will be limited to the British political establishment and to military targets.'[64] In the main,

PIRA's actions remained consistent with such statements. Attacks in Northern Ireland have usually been aimed at intimidating those categories of people listed in the *Green Book* so that they desist from supporting the institutions of the state. Striking at figures in the political establishment has been one of the ways in which the Provisionals believed they could have an impact on governmental decision making. In the aftermath of the Brighton bombing, Adams declared that the operation had been successful in forcing the British to apply 'attention once again to what's happening in the Six Counties',[65] while Morrison argued that if the cabinet had been killed it would have produced a 'rethink in British political circles which would have led to a British withdrawal in a much shorter period'.[66]

Attacks against prestige political targets have remained a priority for the Provisionals, but because they were mostly well protected it was always unlikely that PIRA could have focused sufficient military pressure on this area to force a fundamental shift in British policy. For these sorts of reasons, in PIRA's view the pivotal factor in dislodging establishment interests in Ireland resided, not in altering the opinions of those in government, but in changing the perceptions of the British populace as a whole. During an interview in 1984, a PIRA spokesperson stated:

> Such a strategy relies on the premise that the British people do not support British government sponsored murder in Ireland, that they want their troops withdrawn from Ireland as indicated in opinion polls, and that they have the potential to eventually force the British government, because of the cost of the war or the attrition rate or because of demoralisation and war weariness, to withdraw from Ireland. Such a strategy requires the belief that if the British people really knew what was going on in their name they would support the right of the Irish people to self-determination.[67]

At first glance, the previous half-dozen quotations above appear to express a logical account of the function of the armed struggle within the total strategy framework. On closer inspection, however, they are confused, contradictory and, in some cases, self-refuting. In the first instance, if the argument runs that Britain is governed by an exploitative ruling class which maintains entrenched interests in Ireland, then why should the political establishment take any notice of what their own people say? The very notion of a ruling class means that the views of the majority have little or no influence on those who govern. Therefore, what was the point in hoping that public opinion would be able to affect policy towards Northern Ireland? The Provisionals themselves seemed implicitly to admit the dubiousness of this proposition in the passage quoted above by complaining that the British government was defying popular feeling as expressed through opinion polls. In order to rationalise away this analytical problem the Provisionals contradicted themselves by conceding that Great Britain was internally democratic, so ending up in even more of a rhetorical mess. By asserting that public attitudes could affect the definition of the national interest, the Provisionals were, in effect, acknowledging that the British people *were* responsible for the situation in

Ireland as it was they who allowed the actions of the political establishment to be perpetuated, through lack of interest if nothing else.

It followed that if the British polity was, in PIRA's opinion, underpinned by democratic consent, then it was the British people as much as their rulers who constituted the enemy. In spite of the disavowals, it was apparent that the Provisionals did harbour certain notions of mass British culpability. This has often been reflected when describing the rationale for mainland bombing campaigns: 'It's only when strikes are carried out in Britain that the complacency and indifference of the British people themselves becomes broken.'[68] Though the Provisionals were anxious to avoid civilian casualties, there was little doubt that a basic antipathy towards the British in general lurked beneath the surface of PIRA's rhetoric. The deliberate targeting of ordinary British citizens has appealed to the instincts of certain republican extremists. In the aforementioned interview, the Provisionals warned:

> What the British people have to realise is that because of their apathy towards Ireland, which is extremely frustrating, and because of British atrocities in Ireland, some oppressed Irish people and republican supporters, out of desperation, would view no-warning bombs as a way of shaking up the British people and their government.[69]

The comfort that the Provisionals drew from opinion polls conducted on the mainland can also be challenged. By their nature, opinion polls provide only a rough guide to public feelings and are prone to fluctuate, especially on complicated issues, and consequently tend to produce mixed findings. Like many political actors, the Provisionals have simply selected and accentuated those results which were the most favourable to their point of view. An extensive survey of British attitudes was revealed in a *Daily Express*-MORI poll in 1987. The findings provided some encouragement for the Provisionals, with 61 per cent wanting a withdrawal of troops (22 per cent for immediate withdrawal, 39 per cent for a phased withdrawal), against 34 per cent in favour of keeping the troops in the province for as long as necessary. Furthermore, 55 per cent agreed that the province was costing too much to maintain. However, attitudes were more divided when it came to political settlements, with 58 per cent favouring non-republican solutions, (29 per cent in favour of Northern Ireland remaining part of the UK and 29 per cent supporting independence), while Irish unity was the least favoured solution (27 per cent).[70]

Broadly, results from opinion polls have been ambiguous rather than conclusive. Even if polls reflect decisively against the retention of Northern Ireland as part of the state, it would still take a remarkable level of public cynicism to expel a consenting region of the UK. Such cynicism is simply not evident within British society. For example, in 1980 one poll recorded that 50 per cent of people would vote against Northern Ireland remaining in the UK. Yet two-thirds of those questioned said that it was for the people of Northern Ireland to determine their own future, with only 6 per cent believing that anyone elsewhere in the UK should be consulted.[71] Proceeding from thought to action is the true test of the intensity of public feelings on any issue. PIRA's campaign may have had a negative effect on popular regard for Northern Ireland, but this has been insufficient to override public attitudes towards the maintenance of certain democratic principles like that of regional consent.

When one examines the practicalities of a British withdrawal against the wishes of the majority in the province, or more specifically, against the will of the Protestant community, the prospect looks highly troublesome. Opinion surveys in Northern Ireland consistently register huge Protestant majorities in favour of remaining inside the UK, as high as 91 per cent of the community,[72] with one poll in the late 1970s revealing only 1.5 per cent Protestant support for a united Ireland.[73] The near monolithic nature of Protestant opposition when confronted with the united Ireland option suggests that the forcible incorporation of the province into an all-Ireland framework could well meet with considerable resistance. The question of the military balance is important here. The RUC is the second largest and most heavily armed police force in the UK with over 12,000 officers, including reserves. The Royal Irish Regiment (the former UDR merged with the Royal Irish Rangers) is the largest regiment in the British Army, with over 6,300 members. Being 90 per cent and 97 per cent Protestant in composition respectively, they can ultimately be treated as offshoots of the unionist community, and should they choose to resist the imposition of any initiative, would represent a formidable military bloc in themselves. Along with the UDA, UVF and other assorted loyalist factions, plus the number of Ulster people serving with regular Irish regiments in the British Army, the territorial reserves and other branches of the armed services, it is clear that the loyalist community is one of the most militarised in the world. In total, if one adds in all those who have passed through these organisations over a twenty year period since 1969/70 and include all the other licenced firearms holders in the province,[74] one is talking about a large body of people with military experience, access to weapons and control over the intelligence system and security apparatus. Should an anti-unionist solution be imposed on the province, it is difficult to envisage the Protestant community consenting to be disarmed. These arguments are not new and have been made by a number of commentators over the years.[75] It is not unrealistic to posit that massed and armed Protestant resistance could be numbered in tens and possibly hundreds of thousands, conceivably even out-numbering the entire regular British Army. Voluntary disarmament of the loyalist community is therefore an improbable notion, while physical suppression would be a hazardous undertaking. Suppression would also apply a double standard. If the British and republicans are prepared to countenance the extirpation of Protestant resistance, then Protestants could argue with equal force for the wholesale subjugation of the republicans. Overall, the military balance in Northern Ireland indicates that the imposition of any settlement remains potentially unenforceable if the Protestants choose to resist en masse. Further, if the British operate in Ireland on the basis of self-interest, as the Provisionals contend, then following this logic, Britain cannot be expected to fight a costly war against the Protestant community.

Aside from the question of whether it was in Britain's moral or physical power to deliver Protestant acquiescence, there was little to suggest that PIRA's actions, either in Northern Ireland or the mainland, could produce the intended effect of disillusioning both public and government to the extent where the disengagement of Northern Ireland from the UK was seriously contemplated. At best, this intention could be described as an assertion, at worst, a wholly discredited military objective. One of the most significant findings of the 1987 *Daily Express*-MORI poll was that only 3 per cent of respondents placed Northern Ireland as an urgent problem on their list of priorities. Moreover, 45 per cent believed the conflict to be a religious war. Only 6 per cent blamed the British Army for the trouble while a negligible 2 per cent thought that the border was a factor. 'Generally, the survey leaves an impression of apathy and contempt,' complained an article in *An Phoblacht/Republican News*, 'Ireland can still safely be kept at the very back of the election manifestos.'[76] Such comments, whether intended or not, were an indictment of the failure of PIRA's strategy. After two decades of violence the Provisionals' efforts, by their own admission, had produced no more than an air of impassive insouciance amongst the only group of people who they believed could have a significant degree of leverage over the British government. If one chose to follow the Provisionals' arguments, then one could say that they unwittingly hindered their own cause by desensitising the British public to the kind of low level military campaign which PIRA waged, thereby contributing to the air of general apathy which they so bitterly resented. In so doing, the Provisionals have helped to perpetuate the very conditions in which the 'ruling establishment's' activities in Ireland could flourish free from any popular inquiry.

Where did all this leave the Provisionals' strategy? There was scant consistency in PIRA's rhetoric on the subject, reflecting little methodical construction as to how the military instrument could be employed within the context of the total strategy to bring about the desired changes. This left the Provisionals looking both intellectually and physically vulnerable in the sense that they could neither field solid evidence for the effectiveness of their strategy, nor provide any adequate answer, should they actually succeed in encouraging the British to disengage, about how to survive, let alone overcome, the potential power of Protestant resistance. The lack of clarity in the mechanics of PIRA's strategy concealed a deeper flaw in the Provisionals' design. It would be fair to surmise that a confusion in rhetoric is also a symptom of a confusion in analysis. If so, this suggested that, despite the revisions in strategic thinking since the late 1970s, the Provisionals still did not possess a clear understanding of the role, efficacy and limitations of the armed struggle.

THE INEQUALITY OF POWER – PIRA'S ETERNAL DILEMMA

The imprecision with which the Provisionals regarded the function of the military instrument derived in part from the nature of the long war/total strategy. There is no question that the total strategy was a far more advanced theory than the outright military posture of the early 1970s. The aim was to yield absolute military potential for time, in the hope that over the long-term a reduced but steady level of operations, combined with political activities away from the military conflict, would eventually defeat British resolve to hold Northern Ireland within the United Kingdom. As outlined in Chapter 6, the strategy was a rarefied form of psychological attrition. Yet for all the refinement of the total strategy it has proved to be a paradoxical construct which failed to square with much of the Provisionals' rhetoric.

Although the military instrument was theoretically graded as a tactic within the total strategy, the Provisionals still recognised the unique pressurising and publicity-earning properties that a campaign of violence possessed compared to other methods of resistance. As a consequence, the Provisionals continued to extol the virtues of the armed struggle: 'The IRA by unrelenting armed struggle, has made [the British] foothold [in Ireland] a very costly one for the British establishment.'[77] It was plain that the Provisionals continued to regard physical force in this period between 1983 and 1990 as the key component in their campaign to obtain a British withdrawal. They pledged that 'attacks will continue and escalate until the final option is taken and Britain leaves Ireland for good'.[78] It can be argued, however, that if the armed struggle continued to play such a vital role for the Provisionals, why did they ever adopt a strategy and organisational system which scaled down the main coercive element by such an appreciable degree? Given the extent of infiltration by the security forces in the 1970s, it was quite obvious that PIRA could not have carried on with the battalion structure without jeopardising the survival of the movement. Yet a lot of the advantages and disadvantages of dropping the old structure and shifting to the cell system largely cancelled each other out. By reorganising into such a small force PIRA has been unable to sustain concerted offensives of the kind which did so much to destabilise Northern Ireland in the early 1970s. In addition, the reduction in the number of PIRA activists made it far easier for the security forces to concentrate their resources against known operatives, which left the movement just as vulnerable to losses in personnel as it had been under the old system. In particular, the increased monitoring and penetration of PIRA led to a rise in the number of counter-ambushes mounted by the security forces, most notably by the Special Air Service (SAS). Between 1978 and 1988, some thirty PIRA members were killed in SAS operations.[79] The period between 1983 and 1984, and between 1987 and 1988, were particularly severe as the Provisionals lost around fifteen and twenty members respectively to accidents and shoot-outs. The damage was felt not just in numerical terms but also in the loss of experience and seniority. For example, in May 1987 one of PIRA's most hardened units, the East Tyrone Brigade, was all but wiped out when eight of its men were killed in an SAS ambush during an attack on an RUC station at Loughall, Co. Armagh.[80] The move to the cell system thus made even modest losses hard to bear. Earlier, in the mid-1980s, when PIRA suffered heavy casualties with six personnel killed between November 1983 and June 1984, the Provisionals acknowledged that: 'By any standard, it is a high rate of attrition by a ruthless and undeniably sophisticated British enemy with far greater manpower and technical resources than the IRA has at its command.'[81]

One purpose of the long war/total strategy was to help deal with the problem of facing a stronger opponent. In particular, it was designed to overcome the danger of provoking a massive security crackdown which PIRA may not have been able to withstand. The intention was to offset the loss of direct military pressure by making greater political capital out of low level engagements in order to demonstrate growing political support in place of growing military momentum. However, the total strategy did not eliminate the escalation dilemma but merely displaced it to another dimension of the conflict. Any reasonably sophisticated counter-insurgent will view a conflict as a many sided confrontation, not simply one which exists on the military/security plane, and fashion responses accordingly. In other words, a counter-insurgent will usually have the potential to interdict what one may call an opponent's 'political escalation' just as effectively as military escalation. The political strides made by PSF in the early 1980s came as a shock to the British and Irish governments, but it spurred both governments to find more effective means of dealing with the republican political threat, the outcome being the Anglo-Irish Agreement. The Agreement could be seen as a response to stave off danger in the political field just as Operation Motorman was a reaction to the heightened military threat posed by the Provisionals in mid-1972. According to the Provisionals: 'The catalyst for the Hillsborough Treaty was undoubtedly a combination of the Brighton bomb and the electoral rise of Sinn Fein.'[82] This may have been true, but it was immaterial. The fact that the Anglo-Irish Agreement was a development which took place outside the military arena in response to a perceived political/security threat did not mean that PSF could expect to benefit politically from the introduction of a measure intended to stunt its growth.

Despite their attempts to claim credit for the introduction of the Anglo-Irish Agreement, the Provisionals always viewed the Anglo-Irish process as a piece of counter-insurgency aimed at 'putting a diplomatic veneer on British rule and injecting a credibility to constitutional nationalism so that British rule and its interests can be stabilised in the long-term'.[83] In 1985 the perceived dangers to the Provisionals' position initiated a debate within the movement on how to respond to the introduction of the Anglo-Irish Agreement. In the weeks before the signing of the Agreement, informed journalistic sources claimed that the Provisionals believed any London-Dublin agreement would initially be a trap to entice the movement to escalate its military campaign in order to try to kill off the deal (possibly by inciting unionist anger through a return to indiscriminate bombings) so providing the pretext for a security clampdown.[84] Such reports were endorsed following the signing of the Hillsborough Accord when the Provisionals stated their belief that the two governments were trying to create 'a climate in which coercive moves against Sinn Fein would be made possible'.[85] In fact, it seems that the Provisionals had settled on their response over a month before the signing of the Agreement, deciding that an intensification of violence was simply too risky. In October they outlined their intentions:

the IRA is stating that actions will not be carried out that are specifically aimed at dramatically undermining or wrecking the [Anglo-Irish] talks or summit. In this way, the IRA intends to expose the weaknesses of constitutional nationalism and strengthen the case that real gains – independence, peace with justice – can only be achieved through struggle and resistance, through expanding the revolutionary armed struggle of the Irish Republican Army![86]

The Anglo-Irish Agreement had thus scored its first success against the Provisionals by placing them in a double bind. They could have either escalated the conflict, which would have damaged their electoral support and justified a security clampdown, or they could have foregone a direct military challenge to the Anglo-Irish Agreement and risk losing the political initiative they had established over the past few years by allowing the benefits of the Agreement to materialise and appeal to the nationalist community. The effects of choosing the latter course of action were soon apparent in PSF's poor showing in the January 1986 by-elections. The Agreement was intended to curtail the rise in support for PSF and secure the position of the SDLP. The tactic was successful in this respect. Northern nationalists were supportive of the Agreement, even some PSF voters were initially sympathetic. According to one opinion poll, 22 per cent of PSF voters favoured the Agreement while 10 per cent were strongly supportive.[87] The erosion of PSF's electoral fortunes were confirmed by the 1989 local elections and by the European election of June the same year when PSF attained only 9.1 per cent of the vote.[88] The loss of political impetus following the Agreement's introduction gave the Provisionals cause for concern. One source admitted PSF's 'lack of ability to influence political events against a background of the Hillsborough Agreement', and added, 'as an organisation we have not been able to come to terms with the reality of the effects of Hillsborough within the nationalist community'.[89]

The Provisionals' fear of political marginalisation increased further in the late 1980s following the imposition of a series of media restrictions on the broadcasting of interviews with paramilitary organisations and their supporters. The restrictions were introduced in November 1988 as a response to an upsurge in PIRA activity earlier in the year which culminated in the killing of eight soldiers in a bomb attack on an army coach in August. Regulations of a similar kind had existed in the Republic of Ireland since 1976, though these prohibited rather than restricted the transmission of any paramilitary interviews. PSF frequently blamed these curbs for its electoral failures in the South. 'Censorship of Sinn Fein is a crucial factor in the Dublin establishment's campaign of disinformation and a central part of its effort to marginalise us,' claimed Adams after the disappointment of the 1987 election in the Irish Republic.[90] PSF became increasingly disturbed that sets of controls in both countries were hampering its ability to extend its message beyond its core of support. In 1989 PSF's publicity director, Danny Morrison, disclosed that inquiries to PSF's press centre from the British broadcasting media in the four months following the introduction of the restrictions had fallen to 110, compared to 471 in the preceding four months.[91]

Behind the worries about PSF's electoral prospects lay the Provisionals' anxiety that what they were witnessing in the developments in Anglo-Irish relations was the conjunction of forces lining up against them. Their view was that the Anglo-Irish Agreement was intended to push the unionists into a power sharing deal with the constitutional nationalists while the Irish government underpinned this process by 'policing the border' and 'supporting British initiatives'.[92] The Provisionals feared that political isolation would set the context for the 'Military and legal suppression of republicans'.[93] It was manifest from what the Provisionals said that they wanted a relaxed security regime in which to practise their strategy. They did not harbour any wistful notions about a harsher security regime somehow being of benefit to insurgents. One contributor to *Iris Bheag* warned the movement 'not to place hope in inadequate theories that resistance rises autonomously out of repression'.[94] Being strong advocates of the utility of the armed force, the Provisionals themselves were, conversely, also afraid of its power should they have felt threatened by their enemies with similar means.

The spectre of suppression and political oblivion prompted a wide debate inside PSF about how to tackle the movement's isolation from the political mainstream. Two internal conferences, one in 1986 and the other in 1987, concluded that the best way forward would be to develop a broad front by uniting other small pressure groups and parties around themes upon which all could agree, like the desire to expel Britain from Northern Ireland. Such a coalition would campaign on a wide range of economic, social and cultural issues in the South in order to 'polarise the people against the Free State government', and eventually build up the necessary base of support to 'undermine collaboration between the Free State and the Brits'.[95] One result of the new emphasis on coalition building was the banishment of some of the overt socialist idealism from PSF's propaganda. Danny Morrison even took some of his colleagues to task for using obscure socialist terminology which he believed inhibited public understanding of PSF's position. 'Introducing Marxist esperanto', he argued, 'is one sure way of keeping the revolution at bay.'[96] Adams also stressed the 'need to avoid ultra-republican positions'. He outlined the way in which the Provisionals should seek to broaden the appeal of the movement while keeping it firmly on republican lines:

> We have to proceed on the basis of the lowest possible common denominator and at the level of people's understanding. . . . We have to understand those who oppose us. We have to view all this in political terms and develop policies accordingly. The guiding light for such policies must be that they are based on general republican principles and that they bring us somewhere along the road towards our objectives, meeting the needs of the people and the particular conditions which exist.[97]

The most tangible sign of PSF's desire to establish its political credentials amongst a wider audience came in January 1988, when the party began a formal dialogue with the SDLP. PSF's goal in the talks was to engage the SDLP in an attempt to prioritise the issue of Irish unification by pressing the Irish government to launch a 'diplomatic offensive to secure national self-determination'.[98] PSF stated that the aim of its political struggle in Northern Ireland 'is to popularise opposition to British rule, and to extend that opposition into some form of broad anti-imperialist campaign. Our main political task is to turn opposition to British rule in Ireland into a political demand for national self-determination.'[99] In subsequent correspondence the SDLP made it clear that support for a joint initiative would be conditional on the ending of PIRA's campaign.[100] The logic of the broad front strategy certainly impelled the Provisionals in this direction since PSF's endorsement of violence was responsible for its isolation and pariah status on the Irish political scene. It remained conceivable that a cessation of the armed struggle might have enabled the movement to profit electorally, probably by picking up an increased vote from the political left. Those such as Gerry Adams recognised the obstacles that PIRA's campaign posed to PSF's involvement in broad front politics. For example, he agreed that a large measure of the nationalist population's support for constitutional parties 'rests upon their understandable aversion to the use of physical force and the consequences of physical force'.[101] But in a passage redolent of wanting it both ways, Adams stated:

> Such a movement should not be expected to restrict its support to any particular method of struggle. Therefore, while such a movement would in itself be a non-armed political movement it should not be expected to support armed struggle, nor for that matter, condemn it. Individual members would, as of right, have individual attitudes towards the use of armed struggle.[102]

This type of statement encouraged the impression that, from the Provisionals' own point of view, a broad front would merely have been an extravagant version of PSF which would itself would have remained something of an adjunct to PIRA. The ambiguity displayed towards the use of force within a possible broad front scenario reiterated all the suspicions about the movement's emotional attachment to violence and the inability, or unwillingness, of PSF to control the military instrument. The doubts surrounding this issue were confirmed during the talks with the SDLP when the Provisionals volunteered a curious description of the purpose of armed force. They began by offering a perfectly valid basis upon which to define the role of the military instrument within their strategy: 'Armed struggle is seen as a political option. Its use is considered in terms of achieving national political aims and the efficacy of other forms of struggle.'[103] After stating this, the Provisionals did not go on to elaborate the specific rationale for the use of force but immediately proceeded to give a moral justification:

> This need to wage an armed struggle arises from within the political experience of the Northern nationalist community. This experience has clearly taught them that the inherent undemocratic nature of the Union is maintained through the superior use of force by the British state; that the British state still acts against the democratic wish of the Irish people by its commitment to maintain the Union; and that Britain has no intention of withdrawing its political, military and economic interests from the Six Counties.[104]

Not only did the passage not follow logically from the statement which preceded it, but the imperative contained in the extract, the reference to the 'need to wage an armed struggle', was never explained. Furthermore, the reasoning in the excerpt was itself questionable and reinforced the view that the Provisionals had little comprehension of the functional value of armed struggle as the passage inadvertently undermined any subsequent explanation they may have sought to provide regarding the role of armed force in their campaign. The Provisionals argued that the British maintained the union through the 'superior use of force'. Yet, if the British were prepared to commit that superior level of force in the first place, then what possible use could PIRA's *inferior* force have been in challenging the might of British dominion?

The lack of coherence in the Provisionals' strategic pronouncements led the SDLP to ask, 'is the method more sacred than the cause?'[105] It was a question which neatly encapsulated the tensions between those arguments that the movement may have seen for keeping the armed struggle and those for dispensing with it for the sake of political progression. If the Provisionals ever chose to renounce violence in order to participate in mainstream politics, either as an independent entity or within a broad coalition, the movement risked losing its sense of identity and becoming submerged in a sea of other minor left-wing and republican groupings. On the other side, persistence with the campaign of violence merely underwrote the Provisionals' isolation by ensuring their exclusion from any part in the framing of a political settlement.

Reflecting on republican machinations since the early 1980s through to 1990, what the republican experience showed was the difficulty the movement had in trying to unify the demands for more effective participation with the hardline military exclusivism of the republican tradition. If anything, the Provisionals' manoeuvring between 1983 and the early 1990s highlighted the fact that the move to abandon abstention was conceived in haste without a great deal of consideration for the disruptive effects this was likely to have upon the internal cohesion of republican doctrine. The rush to bankroll its electoral gains, partly out of a desire to capitalise on the electoral successes of the hunger strikes, and partly out of fear at the possible impact of the Anglo-Irish Agreement on its level of support, seemed a sensible move at the time. The adoption of a strategy which emphasised political activity alongside a military campaign could be highly effective for the Provisionals if they enjoyed an expanding popular base. When the Provisionals decided to end abstention they were still riding on a wave of optimism regarding their electoral prospects. Since 1986, however, the Provisionals have experienced a reversal in their electoral fortunes, which was eventually to culminate in the symbolic loss of Gerry Adams' seat in West Belfast in the 1992 general election. In many ways this produced the worst possible outcome for the movement, as a contracting or stagnant political base merely generated negative publicity by demonstrating to the outside world that PIRA fought its war on a minority definition of nationalism. Yet the Provisionals still rigidly maintained the correctness of their position. The immobilism in their evaluation of the conflict in Northern Ireland was made evident during the first round of talks with the

SDLP which concluded in September 1988. Challenged to accept in principle that it was the deeply felt objections of Northern Protestants, and not malign British interference, which prevented Irish unification, Adams merely reasserted the fount of all republican belief: 'From the outset of the dialogue Sinn Fein has put the consistent republican and democratic view that the root cause of the conflict in Ireland is to be found in the British government's denial to the Irish nation of its right to national self-determination.'[106]

The polarised view of a straight fight between British imperialism and the forces of Irish freedom returns us to PIRA's central strategic problem which it faced in this period between 1983 and the early 1990s. No matter how the Provisionals tried to configure their strategy in relation to their attempts to balance the military and political components of their campaign, they simply did not possess the capacity to neutralise superior British power, nor unionist power. Whatever the merits of the total strategy, it aspired to reconcile two conflicting requirements. On the one hand, it endeavoured to preserve a degree of coercive military pressure. On the other, it tried to reduce reliance on military means in order to lower the risk that PIRA's violence would induce the British to take even sterner counter-measures against the movement. Although the total strategy did, on the whole, get the movement off the escalation hook, it should also be said that it got the British government off as well since the introduction of counter-insurgency measures were always likely to be politically contentious. In a sense, whether the Provisionals realised it or not, they were playing to the British tune. The efforts to ensure that PIRA's violence was not too provocative was itself a form of deference to British power. Indeed, one might say that it assisted the British goal of reducing the conflict to a so-called acceptable level of violence.

Having gone down the political road since 1983, the British were for the most part content to leave PSF to wrestle with its self-imposed dilemmas over how to establish its credibility within the mainstream of Irish political life. The confused and contradictory rhetoric which was generated trying to resolve the tensions within Irish republican strategic thinking still made it difficult to determine the exact function of the military instrument. It was an enigma for outside observers, and maybe, deep down, it was for the Provisionals themselves.

8 Ending the isolation?
Ending the violence?

Since 1989 there have been a further series of twists in Irish republican military and political activity. In many ways we are still trying to make sense of these events as they have yet to reveal their full significance. The years are often slow to yield the whole story and, inevitably, the more we enter the contemporary era the more impressionistic our analysis of PIRA's behaviour becomes. Interpretations become less reliant on solid evidence tempered by hindsight and far more on hunches and conjecture based on historical precedent.

On the surface, the Provisional IRA's campaign continued unabated. The most notable feature of PIRA's activities in recent years has been a renewed emphasis on attacks in England. The early 1990s saw a regular number of attacks against military installations and personnel in Great Britain, such as the bombing of army barracks and the shooting of armed service recruitment officers. The Provisionals also attacked overtly political targets. In 1990, for example, Ian Gow MP, an outspoken supporter of the unionist cause and vociferous opponent of the Provisional IRA, was killed by a car-bomb. The following year PIRA was able to launch a mortar attack in Whitehall which nearly hit a meeting of the British Gulf War cabinet.

From 1993 onwards PIRA's operations appeared to switch to more public targets. The Provisionals started bombing railway lines and stations and busy shopping districts. One of the most horrific attacks occurred in the northern English town of Warrington on 20 March 1993 when two bombs exploded in the town centre, killing two young boys. According to one PIRA spokesperson the rationale for the emphasis on commercial and public targets was to overload the British economy by disrupting daily life through the bombing of shopping thoroughfares, central London stations and so on.[1] The Provisionals also made use of hoax bomb threats to routinely cause security alerts all over the commuter rail and underground network, in the south-east of England in particular. The financial impact of PIRA's operations could be considerable. For instance, in May 1993 one massive bomb in Bishopsgate, in the heart of the City of London which killed one person, was estimated to have caused nearly £800 million in damage.[2]

The campaign against targets in Great Britain has been fully consistent with declared PIRA policy to visit the 'consequences' of the 'Irish war upon [British] national territory'.[3] For, in the words of one Provisional IRA source, 'England is the belly of the beast and that is where it hurts most.'[4] What was intriguing about PIRA's military actions was that they took place on a rapidly shifting political background which, in the past few years since 1989, centred around a number of press reports which suggested that the Provisionals were engaged in a debate between hardliners and more pragmatic elements who believed that a military impasse had been reached and that the movement should call a ceasefire, to allow PSF to participate in the constitutional mainstream.[5] Talk about a 'hawk–dove' contest had been an on-off subject for debate in knowledgable circles for a couple of years and speculation about the Provisionals calling off the armed struggle seemed for much of the time to be exaggerated. The possibility of a PIRA ceasefire was often based on the less than solid assumption that the Provisionals were increasingly war weary; that they were now disenchanted by the failing prospects for their armed campaign, having realised that the British government would hold firm and not give way to armed threats.[6] The optimistic belief was that the Provisionals might now be prepared to talk rather than shoot their way out of their predicament. Speculation was fuelled by conciliatory sounding language issuing from PSF. In March 1992 Gerry Adams spoke of the 'ballot box in one hand and the armalite in the other' being an 'outdated' slogan.[7] PSF press officer, Richard McAauley, seemed even more explicit: 'We're not going to realise our full potential as long as the war is going on in the north and as long as Sinn Fein is presented the way it is with regard to armed struggle and violence.'[8] Taken in isolation such statements did suggest a shift in republican thinking away from the armed struggle. At the end of an internal PSF conference in 1990 Martin McGuinness declared, 'We want an end to the armed struggle.' It looked like an emphatic statement of intent, but, as always one must be careful to read further and in historical context: 'But it must be an honourable end,' McGuinness continued, 'A British commitment to a programme of withdrawal will bring an honourable settlement for everyone.'[9] Aspects of the rhetoric may have been reworded to sound more emollient but the fundamental objective and analysis which underpinned the use of force remained firmly intact, as Mitchel McLaughlin made clear at the same conference:

> The British government continues to act against the wishes of the majority of Irish people by a commitment to maintain partition. . . . While this remains the British position then, regrettably, so will the anti-imperialist struggle in Ireland find armed struggle a valid option.[10]

Republicans denied that there was any change in the movement's thinking about the utility of physical force and consistently refuted the possibility of a ceasefire. McGuinness called the speculation the product of 'lazy journalism' which he described as 'less than useless' because 'it engenders futile, wishful thinking'.[11]

Equally, the notion of a hawk–dove split seemed inflated. Theories about divisions between moderates and hardliners have been far from new and prompted one PIRA spokesperson to comment: 'There have been so many "hawks and doves" let loose that it is a wonder we can walk the streets for bird droppings.'[12] Gerry Adams called the media speculation concerning the 'direction of republican politics' as no more than 'mischief making' and stated the movement's position thus:

> Yes, there is debate going on in Sinn Fein and among republicans in general. In fact there are debates going on all the time among republicans. There are discussions about the ongoing struggle, about policy matters, about the unionists and, most importantly, about the process by which peace can be established in this island.[13]

Indeed, it was this process of internal debate which was far more significant than any talk about a PIRA ceasefire in the early 1990s. Those who felt that the shifts and nuances in PSF's stance were a prelude to a cessation of PIRA violence were, for a time at least, mistaken. What the profile of events tended to indicate was that the various fluctuations in PSF's position over the previous couple of years had been less concerned with questioning the efficacy of armed struggle and more a case of manoeuvring to prevent political marginalisation. On 30 April 1991, following months of delicate negotiations between individual political parties and Peter Brooke, the Secretary of State for Northern Ireland, inter-party talks on the political future of the province got underway at Stormont. Getting the main constitutional parties to negotiate with each other face-to-face was a considerable achievement, this being the first time since the Sunningdale conference in 1973 that serious cross-party talks had been held. PSF was excluded from the talks as it refused to renounce support for the violence of PIRA, a pre-condition for participation. The prospect from 1990 onwards of being shut out from inter-party talks, or worse, being sidelined completely if the negotiations did manage to produce an internal settlement, appears to have worried PSF sufficiently to cause its leaders to take steps to make the party more agreeable to the political mainstream. Some of these steps entailed adopting a more conciliatory tone and even putting some rhetorical distance between PSF and the armed struggle. Although the first set of inter-party talks ended without agreement in July 1991, the process of cross-party dialogue established by Peter Brooke, and maintained by his successor, Sir Patrick Mayhew, continued to preoccupy much of PSF's energies.

The fear of political exclusion produced a mood of what can be called neo-realism within the republican movement. This has been expressed in two particular ways. The first was that PSF became more specific about the measures it saw as necessary to bring the conflict to an end. Rather than any sudden British pull-out, PSF said that it envisaged a more long-term process which as a first step involved a commitment by the British government to end partition and to encourage the unionist population to accept the goal of Irish unity. Part of this process, PSF acknowledged, would involve negotiations among all shades of opinion in Northern Ireland and a formal role for the Irish government which would co-operate with the implementation of these steps.[14] The second feature of the neo-realism was the willingness to admit that in many respects PSF was not strong enough by itself to effect all its aims and that its interests could best be served as part of a broader nationalist alliance pressurising for British withdrawal.

This line of thought was made clear by Gerry Adams in his presidential address to the 1994 PSF Ard Fheis: 'Irish republicans, by ourselves, simply do not possess the political strength to bring about these aims. While that situation obtains, it must continue to influence the political and strategic thinking of Irish republicans.' The focus of republican politics, according to Adams, should be on 'attempting to reconstruct a broader, deeper, sustainable Irish political consensus'. This consensus should be based on the unity of nationalists both North and South. 'Every effort must be made to harness this energy,' Adams said, 'to build upon it, and to direct it in a way which will advance the peace process and secure a negotiated settlement based on democratic principles.'[15]

It was against this background that the attempt to manoeuvre out of the political shadows and to move within a wider nationalist coalition, while retaining violence as a limited pressurising instrument, seemed to be the guiding principle behind republican actions. In this respect the movement was attempting a variation of the broad front idea. Instead of seeking an alliance with ostensibly small leftward leaning political groupings, the republican movement embarked on something more ambitious, by aiming to establish a modus vivendi with the forces of constitutional nationalism.

The high point for the Provisionals' efforts to forge a common nationalist agenda without having to forego the use of violence was reached toward the end of 1993, following a series of meetings between the SDLP leader, John Hume, and Gerry Adams. The Hume–Adams talks began in April 1993 at the instigation of a group of clerics who had originally been responsible for bringing together the two leaders in 1988. The premise of the talks seems to have been to work out how nationalist differences could be accommodated, and how such a common platform could be represented at an all-party conference which it was envisaged could be convened to frame a political settlement, and at which PSF would be included in return for a commitment by PIRA to end its violence.

Towards the later part of 1993 there was talk of a so-called peace process which was aiming to establish some sort of common nationalist position acceptable to republicans which would induce PSF to participate in the constitutional realm. The contents of the Hume–Adams dialogue were presented to the Irish government on 7 October 1993, though the details have, as yet, not been made public by the participants themselves. It was widely thought that the proposals revolved around the idea that the Provisionals would end their campaign in return for a declaration by the British government that it had no long-term interest in Ireland, that it recognised the right of the Irish people to self-determination as a whole, and that it would undertake to persuade the unionists to give their consent to these proposals.[16] For a while it seemed that the Provisionals were responsive to this agenda and that a commitment to abandon the armed campaign might be secured. Optimism was fuelled by statements from the Provisional IRA in early October 1993 that the Hume–Adams dialogue 'could provide the basis for peace'.[17] Adams himself derived much kudos, and international media attention, with his air of moderation and declared willingness to take any proposals from his talks with Hume to the Provisional IRA with the recommendation that the organisation review the continuation of the armed struggle.[18] The public stature of Adams as a prospective man of peace was undoubtedly raised by his high profile contacts with John Hume, and this genuinely wrong-footed both the British and Irish governments. The two governments were already operating in something of a policy vacuum on Northern Ireland (and arguably had been since the Anglo-Irish Agreement of 1985) and, suddenly, the Hume–Adams initiative appeared to contain the only proposals of any significance on the political scene. As a consequence, both governments felt reluctant to dismiss any plans arising from the talks out of fear of being seen as inflexible.

Even so, the ease both with which the initiative could be disrupted and the motives of the Provisionals' participation in the peace process thrown into question was revealed later in October 1993 when a bomb explosion in a fish shop in the Shankill Road, in Protestant West Belfast, killed ten people, including the PIRA bomber himself. Not only did the bombing touch off a frenzied round of loyalist revenge killings, but was the prelude to an extraordinary series of political contortions. At first, the Shankill bombing undercut Adams' standing as a peace-maker and provided the pretext for the British and Irish governments to back away from the Hume–Adams plan. The British Prime Minister, John Major, made it clear that he would not respond to the Hume–Adams initiative: 'I have no intention of doing that and the people of Ulster would not want me to do so.'[19] Major was later to state that the prospect of including the Provisionals in any peace talks would 'turn my stomach'.[20] On the face of it, the Hume–Adams plan had been buried under a blanket of condemnation.

Gerry Adams's initial reaction to the Shankill Road bomb also appeared to be one of shock and regret. 'I don't think that what happened, no matter what the intentions, can be excused,' he said.[21] Having come as close as any republican leader had to condemning a specific IRA action, Adams' subsequent behaviour seemed highly contradictory when he acted as one of the pall-bearers at the funeral of the PIRA member blown up while planting the bomb. Paying so public a tribute to the person responsible for derailing his efforts to reach agreement with the SDLP was widely interpreted as a brazenly cynical gesture. It suggested that the Provisionals' participation in the dialogue with Hume was little more than a propaganda exercise to embarrass the British and Irish governments rather than a sincere attempt to end the conflict.

Another interpretation of Adams' behaviour was that they were the actions of someone involved in a delicate balancing act of trying to be conciliatory and wishing to engage in a genuine dialogue, but without alienating the more militant grass-roots republicans who would take some convincing that the contents of the Hume–Adams package were sufficiently beneficial to warrant a cessation of PIRA's campaign.[22] This interpretation implicitly accepted the possibility of the existence of a peace faction within the Provisionals who were involved in a gradual and complex process of educating the movement into a more flexible frame of mind which would have as its end the eventual renunciation of violence. It was this assessment of the internal state of the Provisional IRA, that a moderate faction may be in the ascendant which would contemplate an end to PIRA's military campaign, that captivated those in the SDLP like John Hume. The assumption here seems to have been that the electoral path down which PSF embarked in the early 1980s contained its own logic and inner dynamic, propelling the movement in a certain, predestined direction that would lead inevitably to the questioning of the utility of violence. First came the trade-off between physical force and electoral campaigning which the adoption of the ballot box and armalite strategy necessarily entailed. In time, this gave rise to a politically conscious section of republicanism acutely sensitive to the limits of violence and cognisant of the need to fashion a realistic political platform in order to strike deals with the Irish government and, in the long-term, with the British themselves. This necessitated enhancing republican negotiating strength through the formation of informal alliances with more mainstream nationalist parties and embracing neo-realistic rhetoric which accepted that the process of British withdrawal was likely to be a complicated, drawn-out business and which should, if at all possible, be based on the widest measure of popular consent across Ireland, including that of the unionist population of Ulster. It was this point of consent which was crucial. As soon as the principle of unionist consent was acknowledged the rationale for the use of violence would fall away as one would not now be seeking to coerce anybody into conceding to a political objective with which they otherwise would not have agreed. Thus the way could be opened for the abandonment of violence. This was the line of reasoning which seemed to transfix the SDLP. Subsequent events were to show that this perception of the republican movement's evolving position was not just held by the SDLP but was, to a significant degree, shared by the British government as well.

THE SECRET TALKS

In late November 1993 a series of press reports in Northern Irish newspapers claimed that meetings had taken place between PSF representatives and British officials. These reports gathered sufficient momentum in the public domain to force the British government to admit that it had been involved in prolonged secret discussions with the Provisionals. The revelation of the talks seemed to come out of the blue and caused surprise in British and Irish political circles and fury in the unionist community. In fact there had been rumours and intimations of contacts throughout the previous year. In July 1993 James Molyneaux, the leader of the Ulster Unionist Party, insisted that the British government had been in secret communication with the Provisionals, although this was vehemently denied by the Northern Ireland Office.[23] Even further back, in January, the Northern Ireland Secretary, Sir Patrick Mayhew, in a speech to the Rotary Club of Belfast, hinted that there may have been a degree of informal contact with the Provisionals when he stated: 'There is no way out. I believe the Provisional leaders increasingly realise this and many of them wisely want to stop. They face further fruitless years dragging their children into equal misery.'[24] The intimation contained in Sir Patrick Mayhew's speech that, even in very early 1993, he was somewhat familiar with the evolution of PIRA's thinking about the futility of violence is reinforced when one refers to the British version of the text of the exchanges between the two sides. According to the British, the dialogue was initiated by the Provisionals who communicated a message from Martin McGuinness, PSF's vice-president, on 22 February 1993, which read:

> The conflict is over but we need your advice on how to bring it to a close. We wish to have an unannounced ceasefire in order to hold a dialogue leading to peace. We cannot announce such a move as it will lead to confusion for the volunteers because the press will misrepresent it as surrender. We cannot meet Secretary of State's public renunciation of violence, but it would be given privately as long as we were sure that we were not being tricked.[25]

The riddle here is that the Provisionals denied ever sending this message and protested that it was 'counterfeit'.[26] Adjudicating whether the Provisionals did send, or were likely to have ever sent, such a message is an exceedingly difficult task. Part of the dispute arises from the fact that the messages were conveyed, not in written form, but orally. Unless the conversations between the British and PSF discussants were recorded, there must be a questionmark placed over the accuracy of the transcript of the talks. If the text was composed from notes or summaries of verbal exchanges then the scope for distortions and misrepresentations was large. Indeed, in the rancorous public bickering between the British government and PSF following the disclosure of the secret talks, Sir Patrick Mayhew was forced to admit to eighteen typing errors in the British version. Another area for suspicion about the precision with which messages were imparted is simply that based on past rhetoric; a statement beginning 'The conflict is over but we need your advice on how to bring it to a close' is such a profoundly un-IRA thing to say.

Furthermore, the origins of the dialogue itself are clouded by obscurity. Apparently the talks arose out of long-established informal lines of communication. On the British side, it is not clear whether talks were initiated and conducted through channels which had full official backing. The person on the British side who handled the talks was Michael Oatley, a former MI6 officer who had built up a number of contacts with the republican movement during his service in Northern Ireland which stretched back over the previous twenty years. At the time of the secret talks in 1993, Oatley was working in the private sector and so presumably enjoyed no official standing as a government representative. How much authority did Michael Oatley have? Whether he was acting at the behest of the British authorities or on his own initiative is not fully evident. Overall, it seems that the 1993 dialogue had no formal beginning but simply emerged from the darkness and into the gloom.

If the British government and republican movement had been in indirect contact with each other for a number of years then the obvious question is, at what point did the informal talks become an official dialogue? If this question was not addressed by either side at the outset, then disagreement over the exact terms of reference of the talks was bound to result. How one evaluates the significance of a dialogue managed through informal channels by individuals whose official credentials are unknown is problematic. Thoughts and feelings may be conveyed in private which can never be acknowledged publicly as statements of official positions. This may be one reason for the controversy over whether the 'conflict is over' message was ever sent. One side may simply have communicated a misleading impression to the other in the preliminary stages of the talks. After all, the assertion that the 'conflict is over' could well hold different meanings for the British and Provisionals depending on the background context upon which the remarks may have been made. The British may well have interpreted any such message in terms of a willingness by PIRA to lay down its arms in exhaustion. On the other hand, if the British had, for one reason or another, given the impression to the Provisionals that their will was faltering and that they would be prepared to reach a compromise, then any phrase issuing from the republican side acknowledging the conflict might be drawing to a close takes on a very different complexion because the Provisionals might have thought it was the British who were on the verge of surrendering.

Whatever the truth concerning who said what, a dispute over the opening message provided an astonishingly ill-defined premise for the dialogue which suggests that both the British and republicans were talking at cross-purposes right from the start. This is reflected strongly in the subsequent messages which display an element of confusion and crossed lines. It is evident that both parties were communicating with very different agendas in mind. As a result, it is not clear what, in the end, the talks were about or in which direction they were leading. The British version of the text indicates that they were reacting to PIRA's alleged desire to end violence. Accordingly, the British regarded the secret contacts as a means of offering advice on how best to initiate a process which would see an end to hostilities. During the talks the British signalled their willingness to enter exploratory talks on a range of issues which would lead to the inclusion of PSF in constitutional negotiations. All along, the British stressed that any formal negotiations could only commence after a substantial reduction in PIRA's violence had taken place. It was accepted that any cessation of violence would, at first, be unannounced, after which the British envisaged PSF's 'progressive entry' into negotiations with the other constitutional parties in Northern Ireland.[27] The British balanced the demand for the cessation of PIRA's campaign with the assurance that: 'No political objective which is advocated by constitutional means could properly be excluded from discussion in the talks process.'[28] The British further affirmed that a united Ireland would not be ruled out as a possible outcome of the constitutional talks so long as this was based on the consent of the people in Northern Ireland.

The Provisionals, by contrast, were unmoved by these proposals and wished to jump way ahead of the British position. The tenor of the messages from the republican movement reflected an eagerness to appoint representatives and begin formal talks. One message from the Provisionals communicated on 10 May is full of procedural questions relating to how and when to 'proceed without delay to the delegation meetings'.[29] For the British, the cessation of PIRA's campaign was the essential prerequisite before any movement towards the opening of a formal dialogue could take place. The unresponsiveness of the Provisionals to this line of thinking drew an increasingly impatient British reaction. In one message, dated 5 May 1993, the British reiterated: 'Events on the ground are crucial, as we have consistently made clear. We have not received the necessary private assurance that organised violence had been brought to an end.'[30]

Not only did the two sides not comprehend each other's terms of reference for entering the dialogue in the first place, but they also clashed over the possible progression of future negotiations. The British government argued that its objective in any negotiations was to reach an 'agreed accommodation, not an imposed settlement, arrived at through an inclusive process in which the parties are free agents'.[31] The British message continued:

> The British Government does not have, and will not adopt, any prior objective of 'ending of partition'. The British Government cannot enter a talks process, or expect others to do so, with the purpose of achieving a predetermined outcome, whether the 'ending of partition' or anything else.[32]

The Provisionals took issue with this assessment, interpreting the refusal of the British to agree to any pre-ordained outcome as a 'commitment to uphold the unionist veto'.[33] Instead, the Provisionals asserted that: 'The route to peace in Ireland is to be found in the restoration of the Irish people of our right to national self-determination',[34] which anyone familiar with the IRA vernacular will know is long-hand for British withdrawal.

Despite the mutual incomprehension evident in the messages, what they do illustrate clearly is that the idea of ending the campaign of violence in return for the promise of inclusion in the constitutional process was nowhere on the Provisionals' agenda. They continually evaded the question of giving a prior assurance of a cessation of violence. In May 1993, the Provisionals declared they need not give any undertaking since both sides had 'proceeded to this stage without assurance',[35] of any kind, then presumably they should continue to place faith in the other's good intentions without qualification. Later in August, the Provisionals again side-stepped the issue, claiming that '[a]s for events on the ground' it was now the loyalist paramilitaries who were responsible for most of the violence, the presupposition of which that the UFF and the UVF, and not PIRA, that should be suppressed.[36] Such responses hardly accorded with the British proposals for PSF to exchange the armed struggle for a place at the peace table. Clearly, the Provisionals had other ideas in mind when they involved themselves in the secret contacts.

So how should this rather muddled episode be interpreted? First, it is possible to delineate a consistent line of thinking in PIRA's pronouncements, which at one level were indicative of an increasingly sophisticated approach to political engagement. One possible intellectual gloss which can be placed on the Provisionals' motions is that they wanted to communicate to the British that they did want to see an end to violence and had firm, well-thought out views about how this could be achieved. In this sense, the Provisionals were trying to convince the British that their military campaign was not aimless, unpurposive bloodshed driven by a fixation with physical force, but by a clear set of political objectives, which if attained, would see the end of republican violence. Thus, one message from the Provisionals of 22 July sought to outline their overall understanding of the turmoil in Northern Ireland and how it could be ameliorated:

> British sovereignty over the six counties, as with all of Ireland before partition, is the inherent cause of political instability and conflict. This must be addressed within the democratic context of the right to national self-determination if the cause of the instability and conflict is to be removed.[37]

If PIRA's participation in the secret talks was to show that its military activity was solidly directed politically, then this did demonstrate an advance on its previous attitude towards dealing with the British. It seems that the Provisionals were attempting to learn from the mistakes made in the 1972 and 1975/76 ceasefires when the vagueness of their political platform gave rise to the impression that the movement was committed to violence for its own sake, without guidance and control, and without any definite ideas as to how the conflict could be brought to an end. Necessarily, the result of this negative image closed down potential lines of contact with the British. Here, in the secret talks of 1993, the Provisionals were seeking to counteract any such impression. From the assessment that the cause of the violence sprang from 'British sovereignty over the six counties', the Provisionals went on to enunciate a series of steps which both sides could usefully perform to help bring the conflict to an end. In the message of 22 July, the Provisionals benignly perceived their own role to be to 'assist' the British in the 'establishment of, and to support, a process which, with due regard for the real difficulties involved, culminates in the exercise of that right [of 'national self-determination'] and the end of your jurisdiction'.[38] So far as 'regard for the real difficulties' were concerned, the function of the British government was to 'play a crucial and constructive role in persuading the unionist community to reach an accommodation with the Irish people'.[39]

The second point one may observe is that while the secret contacts indicated some degree of political development, they also appeared to demonstrate the limits of this progression. In particular, the talks displayed the peculiar attitude the republican movement has exhibited towards the concept of negotiation in the past. On the one hand, the Provisionals wanted to prove that they were political sophisticates who had well-constructed arguments, positions and proposals. On the other hand, the notion that these arguments and positions, which informed the overall goal of PIRA's military campaign, could be tempered through a bargaining process which might lead to the moderation of political objectives, based on the power realities in Northern Ireland as they exist between the forces of unionism and nationalism and between British and PIRA military capabilities, still seemed as alien to the republican mind as it ever had been. In this respect, republicanism had not changed since the 1972 talks with William Whitelaw.

Negotiations were not really negotiations. They were simply discussions about the mechanics of British disengagement. The Provisionals claimed in their communication of 22 July that Irish unity was inevitable if the Irish people as a whole are allowed to express their views. It was the denial of this 'right to national self-determination' which lay at the root of the violence. Consequently, the Provisionals saw their campaign as a symptom and not a cause of the conflict. If the British removed the barrier to 'national self-determination' by 'persuading the unionist community' to reach an accommodation in an all-Ireland context, then the source of the conflict would be purged and violence would cease. What all this meant was that the underlying military threat remained: if the British did not undertake to withdraw, the killing would go on. The basic message in republican strategy was the same as it always had been, the only difference being that it now took much longer to say it.

THE DOWNING STREET DECLARATION

Assessing the overall significance of the secret talks is not easy. What is clear is that the Provisionals were not on the verge of a ceasefire. Evidently, what PIRA was trying to do was to strike up direct negotiations with the British government without ending its campaign. From PIRA's standpoint there was no imperative to cease its campaign. Why should it, when its armed struggle had, in propaganda terms, gained them a degree of recognition as a negotiating partner, thereby exposing the British government's denials of contact, and all the 'turn my stomach' rhetoric about not talking to terrorists as bogus and deceitful. The length to which PIRA was indulged through special channels of communication, and the apparent toleration of freelancing intermediaries, did point to a degree of befuddlement towards the organisation in official British circles. Admittedly, the British position in the talks remained one of consistent scepticism throughout, and nothing that was said differed from officially declared policy, but then quite why all this required the need for secrecy is still a mystery.

Although the PIRA–British contacts of 1993 are revealing in a number of ways, charting as they do the growing political suppleness of the Provisionals in the presentation of their rationale for the armed struggle, they were, perhaps, less important as a factor in themselves and have greater meaning when placed in the context of the events which followed the revelation of the talks.

The final messages of the secret British–PIRA dialogue were sent in November. The last few exchanges were inconclusive and it was not clear how or why contact was broken, or if it ever was. What was more transparent was that the trigger for subsequent events was the public disclosure of the secret contacts themselves. The first acknowledgement of the existence of the contacts came from the republican side. According to one source, the reason for exposing the dialogue was the Provisionals' annoyance at a speech by John Major at the Mansion House in London, in which he stated that PSF would be able to enter the talks process in return for the permanent cessation of PIRA violence. In the republican view, the British were arrogantly laying down demands to which the Provisionals had to conform: 'They were saying "These are the preconditions for talking" yet they had just stopped talking to us after a long time.'[40]

The disclosure of the secret dialogue caused severe discomfort to the British government, as the Provisionals no doubt intended, especially after so many vociferous official denials of contact. Yet the revelation of the talks acted as a spur for both the British and Irish governments to take the political offensive. A flurry of diplomatic activity in late 1993 culminated in the announcement of the Downing Street declaration on 15 December 1993. This was a joint statement by the two governments. It was one of the most comprehensive statements of official attitudes towards Northern Ireland and aimed to outline the framework for a negotiated settlement, entice PSF into the constitutional fold and end the conflict.[41]

The Downing Street declaration can be said to have resulted from the conjunction of three main influences. First, the British government may well have been reacting to cover its embarrassment at the exposure of its secret contacts with PIRA and have decided that the best form of defence was attack by seizing the political initiative in an effort to deflect criticism of its conduct. Second, in a similar way, the preceding months had seen the Hume–Adams plan dominating the political scene. In the absence of any agreed British–Irish position on the province, both governments may well have spotted an opportunity to fill their own policy void. Finally, despite the inconclusive nature of the secret talks, both governments continued to harbour the belief that the IRA – or at least a section of it – could be induced to give up violence. Elements of both the Hume–Adams plan and the secret talks were evident in the declaration, which promised that PSF would be allowed to join negotiations on the future political arrangements for Northern Ireland in exchange for a permanent halt to PIRA's violence. It also placed on record the British government's willingness to accept a united Ireland as a possible result of any negotiations. Such a formula, it was hoped, would appeal to moderates in PSF or, if not, would at least place the movement in a dilemma as to how to respond to the declaration without appearing rejectionist. This intention was made apparent by John Major when he said: 'We have an option for peace. Whether that option is picked up lies with the men of violence, not with us.'[42] There was no doubting that by itself the declaration was regarded by republicans, in Martin McGuinness' words, as 'worthless'.[43] The promise of entry into open-ended negotiations was simply not enough to tempt them. They wanted evidence of 'real movement' in the direction of an eventual British withdrawal, towards something like joint sovereignty, before any end to PIRA's campaign could be contemplated. Although republicans recognised that while the declaration did contain a 'nationalist shadow', it upheld the status quo by reaffirming that any change in Northern Ireland's position could only come about with the consent of the majority of the people there; thus giving the 'unionists the food and the nationalists the aroma'.[44] In this sense, the declaration was seen as a 'slap in the face' which merely offered republicans 'the conditions under which they may capitulate to the unionist veto'.[45]

Despite the basic antipathy felt towards the Downing Street declaration, the republican movement had to tread carefully. A straight rejection of the declaration by PSF would have risked alienating the goodwill, both in Ireland and elsewhere, built up by Adams' moderate, statesmanlike, manoeuvrings. As a consequence, the Provisionals adopted the most logical course open to them – prevarication. Instead of repudiating the declaration outright, Adams called on the British government to clarify sections of the document. In addition, PSF set up its own so-called Peace Commission to take soundings from grass-roots republican opinion about the declaration. Both moves were widely interpreted by critics of the movement as mere stalling tactics.

During this period of intensive political activity spanning the Hume–Adams' talks, the revelation of the secret PIRA–British contacts and the Downing Street declaration, the Provisionals' military campaign continued apace. If the Provisionals' political moves in this period are read in conjunction with their military activities, then it is possible to piece together the outline of a politico-military bargaining process taking place within republican strategy. Interpreting republican manoeuvrings in a very broad manner, one can discern one general line of approach within the Provisionals' thinking. This approach was one in which the Provisionals were prepared to entertain an end to their violence, but their willingness to discuss the terms under which they would renounce violence was itself contingent on opening up a direct line of dialogue with the British before a complete cessation of the fighting. To this extent, the Provisionals felt that maintaining a substantial level of military operations would sustain coercive pressure to induce Britain to begin a dialogue while, at the same time, displaying that the movement was not acting out of weakness when indicating its potential willingness to discuss the terms of a ceasefire. What was interesting here was that it appeared that the principle of being seen to have established a dialogue *before* ending the fighting was the paramount concern of Provisionals, rather than the detailed substance of any dialogue itself. Having fought their way to this position with the British, the Provisionals might have been prepared to conclude that this was a satisfactory point to end the military campaign in favour of peaceful political efforts to attain their goals.

This broad interpretation of republican thinking is supported if one looks at the PIRA's political and military actions during the period. For example, in March 1994, PIRA mounted three mortar bombing attacks on Heathrow airport in the space of five days. On the surface this audacious series of attacks appeared to herald the rejection of the declaration and to confirm the movement's basic militant disposition. This interpretation was substantiated by Adams' ominous sounding comments in the wake of the first bombing that: 'The causes of the conflict are still on-going. Every so often there will be a spectacular to remind the world.'[46] However, after the third attack on Heathrow, the Provisionals issued a statement which not only claimed responsibility for the bombings but also offered a detailed commentary on the evolving republican attitude to the political developments over the preceding four months. Part of the statement read:

The continued opportunity for peace should not be squandered. There is an urgent need to re-focus attention and to move the peace process forward. We, our supporters and activists have a vested interest in achieving a just and lasting peace in Ireland. We are prepared to be flexible in exploring the potential for peace. All concerned should leave no stone unturned.[47]

The bombings and the statement seemed to send contradictory signals. On one level, the attacks on Heathrow appeared to be a forewarning of the impending rejection of the Downing Street declaration. Yet, at another level, the statement indicated that the movement was interested in maintaining the momentum which might lead to the peaceful resolution of the conflict. Above all, the statement signified a desire on the Provisionals' part to re-establish some form of contact with the British. The fact that the mortar attacks on Heathrow were accompanied by a detailed announcement of the republican position suggests more than any recent PIRA military operation that this desire to create an opportunity for talks with the British was the specific intention of the violence. The Provisionals also tried mixing their military pressure with political initiatives to encourage the British government to move away from its no-contact approach to PSF. For example, on 5 April PIRA began a three-day ceasefire, the intention of which, Gerry Adams declared was to provide 'the opportunity for Sinn Fein and the London government to remove the clarification road block so that the peace process can move forward'.[48] The adeptness with which the Provisionals combined political and military initiatives displayed a level of sophistication which succeeded in increasing the political pressure on the British. John Major dismissed the seventy-two hour truce as merely 'playing on people's emotions',[49] but others, such as the SDLP, urged that it demonstrated a genuine willingness to exhibit flexibility and should be taken seriously.

Although the Downing Street declaration initially wrong-footed the Provisionals, they played their hand well. The call for clarification enabled PSF first, to avoid rejection of the declaration, second, to re-establish a formal dialogue with the British, and third, to try to extract more concessions by playing on the hope that a little more movement in its direction would be sufficient to gain a ceasefire. PSF's stance successfully forced the underlying divergencies in British and Irish government attitudes into the open. The Irish were much more receptive to PSF's request for clarification. In order to smooth the path for the Provisionals, the Irish premier, Albert Reynolds, went so far as to remove the eighteen-year-old broadcasting ban on the movement in January 1994 and to suggest that a peace settlement would result in an amnesty for those convicted of paramilitary offences. Pressure to provide some form of response also built up within British opposition circles. Despite the initial British resistance to clarify the declaration, the need to maintain a unified policy position with the Irish was seen as imperative, without which the declaration would be in danger of coming apart at the seams. Eventually the British felt moved to respond to PSF's overtures.

On 13 May 1994 PSF submitted a list of questions it wanted clarified to the Irish government which passed it on to the British. The questions tabled by PSF concerned, inter alia, a number of areas revolving around Britain's long-term view of the province's future, including the steps 'which would follow the "starting point" established by the Downing Street declaration', and the time frame envisaged for a settlement to be reached. PSF also asked about the extent to which the unionists would have 'a veto on constitutional change' and enquired about the process which will lead to the 'demilitarisation' of the conflict.[50]

All along the British suspected that PSF's intentions in calling for clarification were little more than a ploy to draw the government into negotiations. Nevertheless, the British agreed to provide a commentary on PSF's questions rather than address specific points of dispute. In a twenty-one page document published on 19 May the British government dismissed most of PSF's questions, many of which the government argued were matters for negotiation once PIRA violence had ended. The government did, however, confirm that no political objective would be excluded from the negotiating agenda and gave a reassurance that PSF did not have to accept the Downing Street declaration as a basis for entering talks, but reiterated that this could only come after the renunciation of violence. The document ended by placing the ball firmly back in PSF's court: 'Sinn Fein ask: What comes next? Certainly no further playing for time. If the joint declaration is the starting point for the peace process the next step is for violence to end for good.'[51]

Following the publication of the British reply, the pressure was now on the Provisionals. All the straws in the wind indicated that PSF would at last feel compelled to do what it had always wanted, to repudiate the declaration once and for all. The dilemma of how to respond was enunciated by one republican who stated: 'We'll have to keep the peace process alive, yet stress that the British haven't offered enough.'[52] This was exactly how PSF chose to react when a conference of 500 delegates met in Letterkenny, Co. Donegal on 24 July. The conference rejected key elements of the declaration, describing them as 'negative and contradictory'. The Provisionals agreed that the declaration was a step forward, but that it was not enough to end the violence. In Gerry Adams' words, PIRA would continue to 'take its own counsel'.[53]

So ended, apparently, one of the most tortured episodes in recent Northern Ireland politics. With the Downing Street declaration all but dead and buried, there seemed little else left to do except to pick over the debris of yet another failed initiative. The Provisionals had displayed considerable political acumen. They were able to manipulate skilfully the political agenda, mixing the language of moderation with military pressure to force the pace of events. The British government had felt moved to shift ground on the political front to the point of acknowledging publicly that it would not stand in the way of a united Ireland. The other significant propaganda dividend to accrue, especially from the round of secret contacts with the British, was to make the Provisionals look like legitimate negotiating partners. The strategy of procrastination paid off well in this respect, making both the British and Irish governments look foolish as they sat waiting around for PSF to deliver its verdict on the Downing Street declaration. The British, in particular, were compromised by the situation, especially when John

Major declared that the road to peace was 'in Gerry Adams' hands',[54] which seemed to pay a remarkable compliment to the Provisionals' stature, besides being something of an implicit abrogation of responsibility for the overall security situation in Northern Ireland.

Having been treated both by the SDLP and, so it later emerged, by the British as partners in dialogue, then witnessing the two governments conclude the Downing Street declaration, and then being publicly anointed as the people who held the key to peace, must have fortified the Provisionals' belief in the effectiveness of their strategy. Would the movement have progressed this far without the motor of violent pressure to push forward the political agenda? Ordinarily, there was little room to doubt how this question would play in the republican mind as anything other than a vindication of the military campaign and green light to carry on.[55]

For sure the Provisionals achieved many small victories in this period, but as a propaganda and strategic episode, it was also a mixed blessing. The Downing Street declaration and its subsequent clarification by the British did, in the end, call PSF's bluff. It challenged the Provisionals to live up to the widespread hopes that the movement had undergone a sea-change of opinion and would be prepared to swap the armed struggle for negotiation. The rejection of the declaration following PSF's conference in Letterkenny, revealed the outward moderation as little more than a facade, thus exposing the movement to bitter criticism from those whose expectations had been punctured. Moreover, the grounds for rejecting the declaration raised the question as to what exactly the Provisionals really wanted to achieve by continuing its military campaign. One of the elements in the Hume–Adams proposals was that for PIRA to cease its violence, the British would have to end their constitutional guarantee to the unionists and undertake to become 'persuaders' for a united Ireland. The issue of the unionist 'veto' was, according to Adams, raised 'time and again' at the conference as a principle reason for turning down the declaration.[56] So was republican violence now just about trying to get the British to move on a point of wording to act as persuaders? Gerry Adams' comments in the weeks following the Downing Street declaration that 'If the republican struggle needs to continue for the next 25 years, then so be it'[57] suggested that this might indeed be the case. To the Provisionals this may have seemed logical. To others outside the movement, it was insanely disproportionate.

The oddity in the republican position, as evinced in the repudiation of the Downing Street declaration, was that while railing against the so-called unionist veto, the Provisionals also reiterated their belief that the consent of the unionists was essential to any final settlement. Therefore, unionists were free to give their consent, so long as they consented to a united Ireland. A novel interpretation of the notion of consent. Republican views on unionist agreement were even more ambiguous if one took into account other pronouncements on the issue. If 'the British state was to take up the republican idea and become "persuader" of the unionists, then how exactly would it "persuade" them? At what point would persuasion be interpreted as coercion?' asked one republican minded writer rhetorically.

Yet the British state could, without much difficulty, genuinely persuade, as distinct from coerce, the British public into democratically deciding that the north of Ireland was no longer to come under the political tutelage of Britain – whereas currently the people of the north can undemocratically veto the democratic expression of the British public that their government can withdraw in response to a democratic mandate.[58]

This piece of logic added yet another twist to republican thinking. Leaving aside the difficulty of imagining a British government trying to physically coerce its own public on anything, the essential ambiguity in the passage was just who, in the republican view, were the unionists. The assumption contained in the passage was that the British populace at large were the unionists and all that needed to be done was to convince them of the value of a united Ireland and suddenly a domestic consensus for withdrawal would be created. Northern Protestant concerns form only one small part of British opinion and can be safely dismissed if they happen to conflict with overall domestic views. As the passage spelled out, the Northern unionist viewpoint is undemocratic. So, in other words, republicans actually refuted the concept of loyalist consent. Loyalist consent was obviously desirable, but loyalists had no *right* of consent.

In the end, beneath the conciliatory haze and the linguistic acrobatics, the same forces at work within republicanism were readily identifiable. Gerry Adams' reaction in the aftermath of PSF's rejection of the Downing Street declaration, that the 'peace process' was still alive and that it was merely the 'nuts and bolts of British withdrawal'[59] that need to be decided, indicated the limits to any supposed new thinking. The same uncompromising belief in ridding Ireland of British influence and the failure to square the circle of unionist hostility remained deeply entrenched, as did the ever pervasive shadow of violence.

THE CEASEFIRE

The convoluted series of events of 1993 and 1994 did display the Provisionals' enhanced adroitness in terms of political tactics. In particular, the willingness to build minor fire-breaks into the military campaign, such as the seventy-two hour ceasefire, as a means of exerting political pressure on Britain over the clarification issue, demonstrated the confidence the movement possessed to interchange peaceful and violent action. As an advance in the movement's strategic thinking, the events of the preceding two years did show the growing intellectual innovation within the movement. As an advance to a realistic solution to the Northern Ireland conflict, however, it appeared just another step on the road to nowhere.

In the days following PSF's formal rejection of the Downing Street declaration, the party never looked so isolated and out of touch with popular feeling both in Ireland and abroad. A torrent of criticism rained down on PSF from all quarters, including from normally sympathetic Irish-American circles, the expectations of whom had been dashed by the dismissal of the declaration.

Within two weeks of PSF's Letterkenny conference, rumours started to spread that the Provisionals were preparing the ground for a ceasefire. As the rumours gathered pace, PSF did little to play down the speculation. It was known that Gerry Adams' contacts with John Hume continued despite the setback of PSF's stance on the Downing Street declaration. Referring to the possibility of a cessation of violence, the two men issued a statement claiming: 'we believe that the essential ingredients of such a strategy may now be available. We are convinced that significant progress has been made in developing the conditions necessary for this negotiated peace to occur.'[60] What was meant by 'significant progress' was unclear. Scepticism about the seriousness of republican motives was rife. The ceasefire rumours could easily be decoded merely as a cynical attempt to claw back the propaganda initiative after the stinging rebukes the movement received in the wake of the rejection of the Downing Street declaration.[61] Moreover, PIRA's military campaign continued with bombing attacks on Brighton and Bognor Regis, two coastal resorts in southern England, which increased the leeriness towards republican intentions.

On 31 August 1994 the Provisional IRA declared an unconditional and indefinite ceasefire.

> Recognising the potential of the current situation and in order to enhance the democratic process and to underline our definitive commitment to its success, the leadership of the IRA have decided that as of midnight Wednesday, August 31st, there will be a complete cessation of military operations.[62]

So began the Provisional IRA's statement. The ceasefire announcement produced scenes of jubilation in nationalist areas of Belfast, while provoking brooding suspicion in the loyalist community and general bemusement all round. A degree of bafflement was justified. PIRA's decision was puzzling, leaving many questions unanswered. One question was over timing. Why, having shortly before spurned the Downing Street declaration as a basis for peace, suddenly turn around and announce a ceasefire? What were the underlying motivations for the announcement? Was the ceasefire a permanent renunciation of violence? It is not possible at this point in time to evaluate the full import of these questions. The months and years ahead will eventually unveil the full significance of events. While acknowledging the current insufficiency of detailed information, it is possible to make one or two observations.

The question of the timing of the ceasefire announcement is still something of a mystery. Was it simply a gesture aimed at winning back public acclaim after the appallingly bad publicity suffered by the movement following its repudiation of the Downing Street declaration? If so, then this would place a large query over the sincerity of PIRA's intent, and raise numerous other disputes concerning how lasting the halt to its violence would really be. Certainly, there was an imperative to win back public favour. It is known that the influential Irish-American lobby, traditionally sympathetic to PIRA's cause, was expecting a pay-back, especially after pressing successfully for Gerry Adams to be granted a visa to enter the United States on a mission to supposedly publicise the 'peace process'. The rejection of the Downing Street declaration went down badly in Irish-American political circles and must have weighed as one factor in the Provisionals' thinking.[63] On the other hand, a ceasefire was a dramatic step for the Provisionals to have taken merely on the grounds of a propaganda stunt. Looking at the antecedents of the ceasefire does suggest that the purpose of the Provisionals extended beyond short-term expediency. In January 1994, shortly after the proclamation of the Downing Street declaration, one opinion poll conducted among PSF supporters indicated that there was 38 per cent 'strong approval' for the declaration, with only 4 per cent disapproving.[64] Assuming that this was an accurate reflection of PSF opinion, then present within the party was a substantial faction willing to embrace the declaration as a basis for ending the violence. As the commentator, David McKittrick, has noted, PSF's rejection of the declaration was probably never intended as a categorical repudiation. It was a qualified response which, while refusing to endorse the document in full, was prepared to accept it as a formula for further discussion.[65] In addition, it was reported that Gerry Adams had met the leaders of PIRA before the Letterkenny conference when he is said to have discussed the idea of a ceasefire.[66] All this suggests that the ceasefire was a pre-planned move and not just a straight piece of opportunism in response to an immediate need to seize back the propaganda high ground. From here, the questions over the Provisionals' behaviour merge into a twilight of half-plausible explanations and guesswork. If the ceasefire plan was contrived before the Letterkenny conference, then what were the reasons which governed PIRA's thinking?

In the loyalist community the prevailing suspicion was that PIRA's ceasefire had been the result of a secret deal to pressure unionists into accepting a united Ireland. The weeks leading up to the ceasefire had seen some further movement in the British government's position over the 1920 Government of Ireland Act. Section 75 of the Act asserted the Westminster parliament's supreme authority over Northern Ireland. The government indicated that it was prepared to replace section 75 with a clause allowing a change in the status of Northern Ireland if a majority in the province so wanted.[67] Although unionists fulminated against this apparent concession, its significance cannot be overrated. As the British government was at pains to point out, the provisions of the 1920 Act had been over-written a number of times by subsequent legislation. Legislation and international treaties from the Anglo-Irish Treaty of 1921 to the Hillsborough Agreement of 1985 had already enshrined the principle of change by consent[68] which, in fact, shored up the unionist right to dissent from a united Ireland. Although nationalists had demanded revisions to the 1920 Act, nevertheless amending section 75 would, in effect, be a rather meaningless formality and could hardly be represented as a sign of a secret deal with the Provisionals, symptomatic of British backsliding on the union. John Major went out of his way to stress that: 'We held no secret talks to arrange this ceasefire, struck no secret deals, made no secret promises and accepted no conditions.'[69] Unionist wariness remains, especially in the light of the British government's mendacious denials of contacts with the Provisionals the previous autumn. Even so, the risks, not to say sheer folly, for any democratic government to conclude secret deals behind the backs of elected politicians, along with the widespread knowledge of seething alienation felt within the loyalist population over the ceasefire and a litany of other perceived injustices visited upon them,[70] would seem to rule out the possibility of a surreptitious bargain having been struck.

If the notion of a secret deal between the British and the Provisionals can be discounted as a convincing reason for PIRA's ceasefire, what are we left with? A backstage pact between the forces of Irish nationalism would seem a more plausible explanation for PIRA's decision. The idea of a pan-nationalist front, encompassing the militant republicanism of PSF, the Irish political establishment and the constitutional nationalism of the SDLP, with the Irish–American lobby in tow, to exert pressure on Britain and the unionists represents a compelling argument.[71] This view of the Provisionals' motives is given substance in comments made by Gerry Adams on 29 August 1994, when he declared: 'I am satisfied that Irish nationalism, if properly mobilised and focused at home and internationally, now has sufficient political confidence, weight and support to bring about the changes which are essential to a just and lasting peace.'[72] The Provisionals' may well have reckoned that advancement towards republican goals could, for the time being, be served best through a cross-nationalist consensus. The quid pro quo for the foundation of the nationalist alliance was the Provisionals' formal renunciation of violence. The meeting between Gerry Adams, John Hume and Irish Prime Minister Albert Reynolds in Dublin on 6 September, where the three men were pictured clasping hands in cordial amity (much to the horror of both the unionists and the British government), suggested strongly that some sort of accord was established to push forward a nationalist agenda.

There was another dimension to the Provisionals' decision to halt their campaign. The Provisionals are militarists. They recognise the utility of armed force in politics. They always have done, and in all probability, will continue to do so. If the ceasefire is genuine and the Provisionals calculated that their interests are now to be more effectively pursued through non-violent means, then correspondingly, there must have been an equal and opposite calculation in the decline in the value of the military instrument. A number of factors could have weighed on the republican mind. The reality of the military position, as the Provisionals half acknowledged, was that for years the armed struggle against the security forces had stalemated. PIRA's shift to the cell-system and adoption of the total strategy back in the late 1970s was an implicit acceptance of this fact. The security forces had contained the violence and, as a consequence, the armed struggle was having less and less impact on the public consciousness, long inured to years of PIRA activity. The military stalemate was compounded by the increasingly obvious isolation PSF was suffering; cast adrift from any wider nationalist consensus as a consequence of its adherence to the armed struggle. The military campaign underwrote PSF's pariah status and the prospect of being trapped permanently within a political ghetto was surely a crucial factor for republican contemplation. There was one further consideration which the Provisionals would be more loath to admit, but which nevertheless must have been significant: that is, for the previous two years PIRA had been out-gunned by the loyalist paramilitaries. At the time of the ceasefire, the body count for 1994 stood at twenty-three victims as a result of actions by republican groups to thirty-three at the hands of the combined forces of the UVF and UFF.[73] The preceding few years had seen the loyalist groups growing in military strength, feeding off Protestant discontent which has been rising ever since the Anglo-Irish Agreement of 1985. Just as in the early 1970s, the Catholics were exposed as highly vulnerable. One difference between the nature of the loyalist campaign of the 1970s and that of the 1990s was that it became more discriminate. Loyalist paramilitaries began to target figures connected with PSF: party members, local councillors and their families. Additionally, by 1993 the UVF's bomb-making capability had started to revive and loyalists were increasingly mounting bombing and shooting raids across the border into the Irish Republic.[74] Whether PIRA cared to concede the point, the actuality was that by the time of the ceasefire announcement, its violence had been checked.

When the Provisionals issued their statement proclaiming a complete cessation of military operations few commentators spoke of an IRA surrender. On the contrary, no-one expected the Provisionals to lay down their arms and disband their military organisation. For a non-state actor, the Provisional IRA maintained a substantial military capability. It had been known for some time that the movement was supplied with enough arms and recruits to keep it going for years to come.[75] Nevertheless, the truth was that by the time of PIRA's ceasefire, the organisation's overall military position was one of relative decline. Talk of a surrender may be wrong. But one can make a distinction between surrender and *strategic failure*. Physical exhaustion to the point of capitulation, that is surrender, is not a pre-requisite for strategic failure, which is the inability to attain designated ends with chosen means. And the Provisionals were clearly suffering from the latter. Their military campaign, and indeed, their whole strategic construct up to August 1994, arguably never posed any serious threat to the status quo. Quite the reverse, PIRA's armed struggle probably detracted from republican goals, solidifying the status quo, by further polarising sectarian divisions in Northern Ireland, thereby making the prospect of reaching a solution which the Provisionals might find acceptable even more remote.

If the Provisionals arrived at their ceasefire announcement on the basis of the declining functionality of their military campaign, then this provided the firmest evidence that the armed struggle was subject to a strategic calculus within republican thinking; for the Provisionals would have been seen to fulfil the essential strategic precept that if the ends are proving unobtainable, policy makers will have to reform their strategy either by changing the means or moderating the objectives.

The precise motives for PIRA's ceasefire have yet to emerge. If the republican movement has made the specific strategic calculation to adjust its means by giving up violence, it may yet prove an inspired move, simultaneously removing the obstacle preventing republican participation in mainstream politics and drawing the sting of its more powerful loyalist paramilitary adversaries, who now had the onus placed on them to match PIRA's ceasefire.

Whether the Provisionals will be able to extract all the potential advantages to be had from moving into the hitherto unexplored avenues of peaceful political conduct hinges on the question: does the PIRA ceasefire amount to a permanent end to its violence? This question itself turns on two other points: 1) How sincere are the Provisionals? Are they genuinely committed to a peaceful resolution of the conflict? Or are they merely using the ceasefire as a temporary tactic, intending to retain the option of returning to the armed struggle if they are not satisfied with any progress made in constitutional talks?; 2) Can the Provisionals control their own members in the ceasefire, especially in the event of provocation from loyalist paramilitaries?

The first issue concerning the sincerity of PIRA's ceasefire was the immediate point of contention following the Provisionals' announcement on 31 August. The fundamental precondition set out in the Downing Street declaration for PSF's entry into constitutional talks was that both governments must be assured that the renunciation of violence was permanent. The Provisional IRA's statement made no reference to a permanent end to violence but to a 'complete cessation of military operations'. While the Irish government was eager to endorse PIRA's announcement as sufficient confirmation that PIRA's violence had ended for good, the British were less convinced and demanded that the Provisionals state whether 'complete' meant permanent. The Northern Ireland Secretary, Sir Patrick Mayhew, was insistent that: 'This is not just a piece of pedantry about a particular word. What lies behind it is that any talks that may take place shall not take place under the implied threat that violence could start again.'[76] The British said they were prepared to accept any form of words which indicated that violence was over once and for all.[77] Gerry Adams, in a supposed attempt to clarify the situation and assure all sides that violence was over, asserted that: 'When the IRA says it has called a "complete cessation of military operations", that is what it means.'[78] Which actually clarified nothing. It merely fuelled the suspicion that the Provisionals were being evasive. 'It's such a simple thing to put right, so easy to say,' said Sir Patrick Mayhew, 'When people refuse, you wonder why.'[79] The reason for PSF's refusal could well have something to do with not being seen to be dictated to by the British; gestures and symbolism being everything to republicans. Alternatively, the more pessimistic, and more likely, explanation for the evasion is simply that the Provisionals are hedging their bets and are refusing to tie the hands of future republican leaders to a policy of non-violence in perpetuity. Evidence for this view resides in the forlorn hope that the Provisionals will scale down their military organisation. Indications are that, just because the ceasefire is in operation, the movement will not stop functioning in its efforts to procure arms and gather intelligence.[80] One might ask, if the ceasefire does mean the end of PIRA's armed campaign, wherein lies the need to maintain the military side of the movement? In all probability, the Provisionals will try to wring the maximum concessions out of the British through negotiations, and revert back to the armed struggle if and when they fail to get all they want. In the words of one Belfast republican, the 'armed struggle is a tactic not a principle, and a ceasefire can be a tactic too'.[81]

Against the pessimistic scenario that PIRA's ceasefire is only a temporary political tactic, one can raise a counter-argument. It might be contended that in declaring a ceasefire the republican leadership has crossed the Rubicon and there may well be no going back. A protracted ceasefire is fraught with dangers for the movement. Republican leaders must be aware of the pitfalls awaiting them should a return to the armed struggle be deemed necessary. Quite simply, people get used to peace. Taking up violence again could well be a propaganda disaster, and at the very least, provide the pretext for a severe security clampdown on the movement. Even if the Provisionals manage to keep their military organisation well-oiled during the ceasefire, this does not mean that it will not also suffer a degree of depreciation. PIRA activists will, if the ceasefire lasts long enough, get out of practice. The security forces will have more opportunities to increase their surveillance and infiltration of the movement, exactly as happened during the 1975 truce. This line of argument may seem forceful, but one can always say that the movement has travelled this road before in the 1975/76 truce and still survived, just.

The other major point of concern, illustrated most graphically in the ceasefire of 1975, is the issue as to whether the movement possesses the necessary cohesion to control its own members. The experience in 1975/1976 revealed deep fissures in the movement, with some PIRA units refusing to accept the ceasefire. At this point in time there seems to be concurrence that PIRA will not face the same sorts of internal disputes as it did in 1975 and 1976. A large part of the rationale for the organisational changes implemented after the debacle of the 1975 truce was to impose greater discipline over the movement. The shift within the leadership in the late 1970s towards the group of Northerners under Gerry Adams and Martin McGuinness ensured that PIRA has been much more closely tied to its own base of support. Doubtless there were voices raised against the ceasefire by hardline elements, but the current leadership by all accounts enjoys sufficient trust at local level to contain any internal opposition.[82]

Of less certainty is how the Provisionals might react in the face of attempted loyalist provocation. During PIRA's truces in 1972 and 1975, a rise in loyalist violence, especially the systematic campaign of sectarian attacks against Catholics, goaded PIRA units to break the ceasefire and retaliate in kind against Protestants. In 1994, unionist suspicions of PIRA's motives for calling a ceasefire ensured that the loyalist paramilitaries did not follow suit and declare an end to their own military campaigns. In the first two days after PIRA's announcement, the UFF killed a young Catholic man and the UVF placed a car-bomb outside PSF's offices in West Belfast. For the time being, however, the Provisionals have shown themselves willing to ride out any loyalist attacks. PSF councillor, Tom Hartley, declared in the wake of the UVF bombing of PSF's offices that 'we will not be intimidated by the loyalist death squads nor will we be deflected from the peace process'.[83] Whether this sense of self-restraint will persist in the face of any determined loyalist onslaught has at this point in time yet to be seen. It could be argued that the Provisionals might even welcome a degree of loyalist pro-vocation, particularly if it meant that the bulk of the effort of the security forces would be deployed trying to neutralise their paramilitary rivals. For the immediate future, however, these concerns appear academic, because on 13 October 1994, the loyalist paramilitaries declared their own ceasefire, but warned that: 'The permanence of our ceasefire will be dependent completely upon the continuing cessation of all nationalist violence. The sole responsiblity for a return to war lies with them.'[84]

The way ahead in the aftermath of both the PIRA and loyalist ceasefires is a path strewn with obstacles. The politicians, including any peace-minded republicans, have yet to prove that they can chart the course to an overall settlement. The fundamental cause of the conflict – the dispute over which jurisdiction Northern Ireland should belong to – remains unresolved and will continue to do so until there is a shift in the hitherto unmovable positions of each side. If there is to be any prospect of, in the words of PIRA's ceasefire statement, 'a just and lasting settlement', the Provisionals will probably have to embrace the corollary of its strategic decision to switch their means away from violence, and moderate their political objectives. There is no certainty republicans are prepared to do this. In a rally on 14 August 1994 to mark the twenty-fifth anniversary of the deployment of British troops on the streets of Northern Ireland, Gerry Adams decreed, 'British troops must go, the unionist veto must go, partition must go.'[85] Irish republicanism has not changed its basic outlook. The differences between the sides in the Northern Ireland conflict look as intractable as ever.

The future contains such a range of complexity that the outcome of any constitutional negotiations on Northern Ireland is impossible to predict at this stage. But it is possible to say one thing in relation to the evolution of republican strategic thinking. Republicans are creatures of tradition. They do not undergo dramatic ideological conversions. Irish republicans will never formally renounce violence as a political instrument. So long as their goals remain unfulfilled, so will the rationale for armed struggle exist. 'The struggle is not over. It has entered a new phase,'[86] so says Gerry Adams. The Irish republican conception of the political environment is one of war and conflict. The struggle goes on; it may be peaceful, it may be violent, but it will always be war.

Conclusion

This study has attempted to understand and dissect the Irish republican strategic perspective in order to determine how the movement has seen its aims being advanced through the employment of armed force. Reference to strategic theory has been used to help analyse the judgments exercised by the movement on this issue. In one sense it is difficult to reach any definitive conclusions, not least as a consequence of the recent period of fluidity in Northern Irish politics which may just herald the end of PIRA's campaign of violence. Even so, the conflict itself will not be over until there is an overall political solution acceptable to the majority of people in both the contending communities in Northern Ireland. In the absence of a formal political settlement the potential will always exist, despite the current IRA ceasefire, for a reversion to hostilities. While this remains the case, the role of the military instrument in Irish republican strategic thinking will continue to unfold. Future developments will, therefore, necessarily modify the interpretations set down here. However, by looking at the overall process of the republican movement's strategic formulation as it has evolved, we can make some historically valid generalisations.

The pattern of Irish republican military activity has been very diverse. Over the decades the movement has embraced an assortment of low intensity war techniques, ranging from anti-colonial guerrilla warfare in the early twentieth century, terrorist bombings of Britain in the late 1930s, rural insurgent war in the 1956–62 border campaign, through to a social revolutionary strategy of the 1960s and the largely urban guerrilla campaign in the early 1970s, ending up in the present with a dual military/electoral strategy.

The constant factor in IRA's strategic history has been the commitment to the absolutist convictions of republican ideology. These affect how republicans interpret methods of resistance and guide the assumptions they make about their chosen strategies. It is a process which has sometimes led republicans to devise strategies on faulty analysis. The ardent belief in the utility of physical force has often obstructed the IRA from recognising when its strategies *have been* successful in fulfilling their potential, as in 1921 and 1972 when the British were pressured by republican violence to open a dialogue with the movement. The inability to think in terms of compromise made it difficult for the movement to detect the limited utility of its violence and prevented the IRA from moving ahead in stages. Instead, the IRA has frequently squandered positions of temporary military advantage by persisting with a particular strategy even though it has exhausted its potential. In the past when this happened, a process appeared to be set in train whereby ideological symbolism came to dominate over the careful evaluation of the function of armed struggle. In these circumstances, the military instrument became uncontrollable as the ideological attachment to physical force started to fulfil its own inner dynamic, even if such actions, as evinced in the sectarian war in the mid-1970s, were regressive in relation to the movement's stated goals. Faced with the defeat of its strategy, the IRA proceeded to search for another way in which to reformulate the armed struggle. As a result, the history of the IRA has been marked, not by a stolid persistence with a single unsuccessful strategy, so much as a tradition of poor strategic analysis which has often caused the movement to over-estimate the ability of its means to overcome far more powerful adversaries.

Even so, deeply held ideological principles can be challenged if they are deemed to impede the progress of the republican movement, though this has invariably caused great unrest within republicanism. It is easy to see why internal disruption has taken place over the issue of abstention as it was the key factor which inter-related with all the other doctrinal precepts. It has insulated the movement from corrupting external influences, preserved the idea of the nationalist vanguard and sustained the perceived virtues of the armed struggle, though, as the 1986 RSF split revealed, it is not always the doctrinaire hardliners who remained in the ascendant.

Overall, the process of strategic change within the republican movement has been both capricious and volatile. Although the republican tradition is inward looking, it has shown itself capable of self-criticism and this has permitted the movement to change or modify its strategy, though usually within very limited bounds. Whether such changes have necessarily enhanced the movement's ability to achieve its goals is open to question, but they have enabled the IRA to adapt and survive. Yet for all the military instrument's many incarnations, and in spite of the republicans' vigorous and assertive public facade that they are pre-destined to win, the over-riding need to endure in the face of adversity has resulted in the IRA's strategic tradition being characterised more by insecurity than certainty and continuity.

The substantive revisions wrought by the Northern radicals in the late 1970s was certainly a product of the desperate insecurity induced by the disastrous 1975 ceasefire, but it did appear to herald a serious attempt to rectify some of the deficiencies in republican strategic analysis. Theoretically, the re-evaluation has shifted the traditional perspectives of the movement by placing the military instrument in a wider context where the value of all available means are considered without favour, while the abandonment of abstention suggests a determination to end any sense of elitism, with the movement now prepared to submit itself to the electorate for popular endorsement. Fundamentally, the re-evaluation sought to reject any idea that the maxims of the past should regulate republican activity in the present. Martin McGuinness said in 1985 that part of the process of reinvigoration lay in the willingness of many republicans to 'discard many of the myths that nourished our movement, myths that had, objectively, become fetters'. McGuinness continued:

> As a national movement we are still learning but at least republicans can now admit that there are unthinking republicans, and that we cannot expect uncon- ditional and uncritical support because of Easter 1916 or just because a majority of Irish people voted for Sinn Fein in 1918. Any support that Sinn Fein gains must be earned through a coherent revolutionary political programme. By accepting that fact we remove the danger implicit in all liberation struggles, that a blind desire for freedom can become an irrational dash into reaction and despair.[1]

The modern republican leadership now seems keenly aware of the trends and nuances of the movement's history. The leadership appears particularly sensitive to the stultifying effects that a self-conscious invocation of an ideological tradi- tion can have in preventing the movement from adapting to changing conditions which has, in the past, trapped the movement in a debilitating cycle where initial military success is followed by marginalisation and defeat. It was a theme that Adams was anxious to stress at the 1986 Ard Fheis: 'Our experience teaches us that as a group we are often successful when we have a flexible approach. We are at our weakest when we are forced into a static political position where the more powerful forces of imperialism can be employed to isolate us.'[2] This statement, more than any other, explains republican behaviour over recent years. The effort to avoid being cornered by the 'forces of imperialism' has led into the sorts of political trade-offs with constitutional parties in Ireland, culminating in PIRA's ceasefire of 31 August 1994.

In spite of the evident desire to adopt a more flexible approach to the process of strategic formulation through the constant re-examination of the relevance of policies, the utility of the means and the validity of beliefs, there is little to suggest that the movement's central assumption has been challenged from within. The perception of the Northern Irish conflict as a problem of colonial British interference remains firmly in place as the cornerstone of republican analysis. 'The fundamental aim', Adams proclaimed in a speech in April 1988, 'has always been to get Britain to abandon its partition policy and adopt instead a policy of reunifying Ireland – that is withdrawing from Ireland and handing over sover- eignty to an all-Ireland government.'[3] This constitutes the basic mental frame around which PIRA has sought to construct a viable strategy, but it also sustains other traditional facets of republican belief. It has driven the perception of the armed struggle as the most effective means of forcing Britain out.

The Provisionals' colonial exegesis also governs the movement's disposition towards Ulster Protestants, who are still perceived as 'hopelessly reliant on Britain' and regarded by the British purely 'in terms of their place in the political and strategic interests of British imperialism'.[4] As a national minority who make up only twenty per cent of Irish people they are not entitled to a 'veto over national independence'.[5] The movement's offhand dismissal of loyalism was once summed up by Danny Morrison: 'There is nothing we can do to convince them and I think it pointless to waste energy trying.'[6]

The tone of republican statements on the nature of unionism has softened a little in recent years. At a cultural conference in September 1992 PSF's Northern chairman, Mitchel McLaughlin, accepted that: 'Over the years the slogan "Brits out" has been allowed to come in a very real way for many of the unionist tradition to mean them, when in fact republicans never, at any time, meant that but it was never made clear.'[7] This was a line echoed by Adams in 1994 when he stressed that he wanted to 'assure northern Protestants, that the republican demand for British withdrawal is not aimed at them. It is directed at the British government's control in Ireland.'[8] The problem is that PIRA's campaign *is* aimed at them. It is the vast bulk of the Protestant community who solidly support 'the British government's control in Ireland' and help maintain it through recruitment to the local security forces.[9] To argue, as Adams has in the past, that 'if there are five UDR men lined up by the IRA there is no question of asking which of these five are Protestant and which are Catholics'[10] is either disingenuous or naive when over 90 per cent of the locally recruited security forces are drawn from the Protestant community. The objective truth about PIRA's campaign, whatever that might be, is irrelevant. It is a question of interpretation. The cold logic of PIRA's colonial analysis may mean that it makes no religious distinctions in its targeting policy. The point is that the Protestants interpret the killing of members of the RUC and UDR as deliberate acts of sectarian genocide. PIRA's record both in the sectarian war in the mid-1970s and in more recent times, with operations such as the Enniskillen bombing and the assassination of unionist politicians, renders the Provisionals secular incantations highly suspect.

The rejection of loyalism as a phenomenon of any durable significance sits uneasily with the nature of Protestant/unionist power as revealed over the past twenty years in Northern Ireland, with, for instance, the rise of the Protestant paramilitaries which did so much to undermine PIRA's strategy in the early 1970s and the Ulster Workers Council strike in 1974. It also ignores the fact that it is Protestants who continue to dominate much of the security apparatus. The general disregard for the Protestant viewpoint tends to uphold the charge of crypto-sectarianism. The position of the Northern Protestant community represents an ideological blindspot for the republican movement. Republicans may be able to show a degree of empathy for the unionist/Protestant way of thinking but they can never acknowledge its legitimacy. For if they do, the whole republican intellectual edifice, their strategic construct, everything they have been fighting for over twenty-five years, collapses. The commentator, David McKittrick, has written that 'Sinn Fein represents the last expression of the failure of Irish nationalism to come to terms with Unionism.'[11] A product of this failure is that PIRA has conducted its military operations in a manner which has fuelled the Protestant siege mentality and reinforced Protestant political cohesion by keeping the unionist community alarmed and armed. The extent to which PIRA's campaign has militarised the loyalists and retrenched their hostility towards Irish nationalism must put a serious questionmark over whether PIRA could survive in any vacuum created by a British withdrawal. Republican rhetoric on the Protestant-loyalist position has moderated slightly in recent years. It remains to be seen if this heralds a willingness to compromise on deeply held convictions about the nature of loyalism. Certainly, it is debatable whether a heightened appreciation of loyalist sensibilities played any part in the decision to declare the ceasefire in August 1994. If the Provisionals have concluded that killing Protestants does not enhance their cause, then this indeed is a step forward.

Until the Provisionals demonstrate a preparedness to compromise on deeply held ideological convictions, there must still be a query placed over the extent to which the republican movement has embraced new thinking. The republican journey since the mid- to late 1980s may have led the movement into the hitherto unchartered waters of political engagement with the forces of Irish constitutionalism, but this does not necessarily mean that fundamental positions have changed. In a speech delivered in 1986, Martin McGuinness sought to elaborate on the new, progressive bearing of the republican leadership by describing how the movement's historical tradition should be squared with the need to maintain a forward looking, energetic and politically mature organisation capable of responding to popular concerns, acknowledging its own problems and accepting criticism:

> In 14 years' time we will be in the 21st century and the struggle of our past, no matter how heroic, no matter how tragic, will have limited relevance. Of course, we must remember Irish history. As republicans we possess a continuity of vision and of action that stretches back to 1798 and beyond. But the Ireland Wolfe Tone lived in bears only a historical relationship to the Ireland of today and of tomorrow. Every time we refuse to consider new options, to engage in revolutionary self-criticism, to examine the politics and the aspirations of the Irish people, we betray reality. And republicans of all people, should never be afraid to face the real world. . . . However, one of our political failings, and one that still must be combated, is our apparent readiness to dismiss evaluations of the movement that conflict with our own views.[12]

The passage encapsulates the essence of an evolving movement, drawing inspiration from the past but continually seeking to refine its analysis and methods. However, the limits to the revisionist process were clearly marked out earlier in the speech when McGuinness attacked the 'rewriting of history by West Britons and British propaganda'.[13] The presumption seemed to be that only republicans were entitled to review history when it suits them, while everyone else should conform to a rarefied traditional view. In fact, the speech underlines the dichotomy in republican political thinking. At one level, the Provisionals attempt to project the image of a consummate rational actor operating in the 'real world', untutored by the myths of the past and dispassionately assessing alternative courses of action. Yet at the same time, the Provisionals have so often tried to evade essential questions of the 'real world' which impinge on the issue of strategic formulation, such as the nature of the British presence, the limited effectiveness of republican means and the scope of Protestant hostility.

The lengths to which the Provisionals have gone to avoid addressing sensitive areas in order to maintain the parameters which underpin their analysis has made their pronouncements about the validity of the military instrument both shallow and inconsistent. Part of the problem in trying to detect any firm comprehension of the role of the military instrument is that ever since the early 1970s the Provisionals have cited so many theories and theorists in support of their campaign that it is difficult to know exactly what they believe. The Provisionals' propaganda is often full of references to, amongst others, the theories of Mao, Marighela, Taber, Guevarra, Clausewitz and Liddell Hart.[14] *Iris Bheag*, the PSF journal which is largely for internal consumption, is regularly interspersed with excerpts from the writings of military practitioners, third world leaders and revolutionary theorists.[15] The pamphlet, *Notes for Revolutionaries*, contains an extensive list of inspiring strategic proverbs from almost every major military thinker since Sun Tzu in the second century BC.[16] The inclusion of such dictums may only be designed to enthuse the movement with revolutionary ardour. But, ultimately, their rhetorical usage in the Provisionals' literature seems a symptom of PIRA's own confusion. The Provisionals tend to quote these strategic theorists and their aphorisms out of thin air without giving due regard to the fact that strategies and philosophies of war are highly divergent, often at complete odds with each other. Clausewitzian theory is not the same as that of Liddell Hart. Mao all but contradicts Marighela. There is no attempt to assemble these disparate pieces of information into any systematic theory or plan.

One might suspect that the closer one examines the evidence surrounding PIRA's military rhetoric the more it would converge into a sense of uniformity. It does not. It splays out into a form of strategic chaos where every piece of rationalising information is extracted to give the impression of the skilful appreciation and exploitation of the military instrument. The end product is one where it is extremely hard to pin down the Provisionals to any coherent statement of strategic intent. In 1989, Danny Morrison stated that 'when it is politically costly for the British to remain in Ireland, they'll go ... it won't be triggered until a large number of British soldiers are killed and that's what's going to happen'.[17] This appears to be the only discernible core of republican military doctrine; hit the British hard enough and they will eventually give up. It is simple, crude, theoretically it may even be true, but totally beyond PIRA's demonstrable capacity to achieve in practice.

The lack of any credible definition of the role of the armed struggle casts doubt as to how far the Provisional IRA has changed its basic outlook since the movement's reorganisation in the late 1970s. In May 1987, McGuinness declared that 'the IRA is now a real people's army' which 'has broken with militarism' and 'with elitism'.[18] It is debatable whether the politicisation of the movement has banished elitism and turned PIRA into an army of the people, or even if it was ever intended to. Just after he was elected MP for West Belfast, Gerry Adams argued: 'The IRA does not need an electoral mandate for armed struggle. It derives its mandate from the presence of the British in the six counties.'[19] But how could the Provisionals profess to be a 'people's army' without regard to some form of quantifiable mandate? There was a strong sense here in which the Provisionals appeared to be seeking to use elections as a propaganda ploy to claim political backing for their campaign while, in fact, retrenching their own emotional commitment to the use of violence. One editorial in the republican press in April 1985 stated that: 'Sinn Fein, by popularising political and cultural resistance and by defending the right of the IRA to wage war, has consolidated and made permanent the sympathetic base from which the armed struggle is launched.'[20] So, according to such a view, the use of force is not a direct function of popular approval, but a pre-existing historic right of resistance which happens to be acknowledged by a certain level of electoral support. If this assessment is accurate, then the principles which supposedly underwrite the entire politicisation process are little more than a pretence to suggest that the armed struggle is a carefully selected and reasoned instrument of policy, when, in truth, it is an independent variable unconstrained by reference either to external sources of legitimacy or serious analysis of its utility.

The long war approach adopted in the late 1970s is a perfect self-justifying strategic framework. It allows the movement to proceed in tandem with an intellectual rationale which excuses present failure with the promise of future success. *Tiocfaidh ar la* – our day will come – is more than a meaningless republican slogan. Even so, one perceptible thread in the history of the republican movement after 1921 is that the desire to preserve a distinct ideo-military entity often appears to have been placed at a higher premium than the willingness to consider whether military action has necessarily been the best way to advance republican goals. We can say that this may be one factor which has caused the republican movement, at points in its history, to misapply the military instrument. There are occasions when PIRA's mask of rationality does appear to slip which, implicitly at least, reveals the incentive to maintain the armed struggle to be less than directly functional in any strategic sense. For example, in 1978 a senior member of PIRA's leadership was asked during an interview whether the fighting of the past decade had been worth the cost. 'Of course not,' he replied, 'Virtually nothing has been achieved.' He went on: 'We can't give up now and admit that men and women were sent to their graves died for nothing.'[21] These sentiments were echoed nine years later in an editorial in *An Phoblacht/Republican News* commemorating the 1916 Easter rising: 'the struggle goes on, not out of any sham emotionalism but out of duty both to those who have died and future generations and out of the recognition that peace and prosperity depends on victory being achieved.'[22] Neither of the two statements attempted to address how the continuation of the armed struggle could achieve victory, but perhaps they did illustrate that the primary motivation for the republican movement to carry on is simply that it always has carried on, not out of sham emotionalism, but certainly out of genuine emotionalism.

The totality of Irish republican violence is the product of immensely complex social and historical factors. The entire Irish republican military experience cannot be reduced to a few trite strategic equations. The one general point this inquiry indicates, though, is that the movement's employment of the military instrument has often been conditioned by particular cultural reflexes which do not always accord with the norms of strategic theory. All this is not to say that in the current atmosphere, where the IRA ceasefire prevails, republican thinking has not modified certain ideas about the armed struggle. The point is that only the progression of any constitutional negotiations involving republican represent-atives will truly reveal the extent of any reassessment. Until that time, it is too early to pontificate on the removal of the gun from Irish republican politics.

So what does all this tell us about the current state of Irish republican strategic thinking? Twenty-five years after taking up arms in defence of a long tradition of physical force nationalism, the Provisional IRA still has not been able to resolve its inner contradictions. The Provisionals' rhetoric still seems to pull in two different directions. Asked to state how far the republican cause had been advanced after two decades of campaigning, Gerry Adams claimed that the British were being brought closer to withdrawal in that the 'option of withdrawal is becoming more of an issue' for British public opinion.[23] This is generally consistent with PIRA's less restrained declarations that its resistance 'will finally sever the British stranglehold over our country'.[24] The way Adams sees things, initiatives like the Downing Street declaration of December 1993 represent:

> a slow and painful process of England's disengagement from her first and last colony, Ireland. It may be a small step, as was the Hillsborough Agreement of 1985 – which leaving aside justifiable republican criticisms – gave Dublin, for the first time, a 'foot in the door' in the Six Counties.[25]

However, these statements do not square with other aspects of the Provisionals' analysis which have, for instance, described the Hillsborough Agreement as copperfastening partition. The Provisionals reject the notion put forth by the SDLP that the British government is neutral with regard to the political future of Northern Ireland. In Danny Morrison's view: 'I just don't see how the SDLP can say the Brits are neutral, given the lengths to which the Brits are prepared to go to maintain their presence in the North.'[26]

So which of the arguments is true? Either the British are getting ever closer to withdrawal or else they are putting in great efforts to bolster their control over Northern Ireland. Both cannot be right. Republicans seem to hold concurrent, but opposing, views. On the one hand republicans interpret events as representing a slow process of British disengagement, whereas, on the other, their mistrust of British motives makes them see all British actions as a series of correctives to accommodate nationalist opinion with the aim of strengthening Britain's hold over the province. This apparent contradiction unveils the tension in Irish repub-lican thinking between the outward expressions of self-assurance that events are moving their way and the unconscious sense of insecurity they have of the power-reality of their position in relation to their limited capacity to influence political developments.

Mitchel McLaughlin, PSF's Northern chairman, captured the essence of the paradox in republican strategic thinking: 'The only thing you will find among republicans is an absolute certainty that they will win, even when objective reality tells them it's not going to be in their lifetime.'[27] The belief that events are moving relentlessly their way, combined with the 'reality' that the inevitability of a republican victory will not occur in their lifetime (or anybody else's lifetime) forms the mental disjunction in Irish republican thinking which separates certainty from insecurity. This intellectual weakness illustrates what is perhaps the republican movement's greatest psychological vulnerability. Republican ideology is teleological – it sees an end to history. Republicans see history as one of continuous advance to a pre-destined goal. But the nature of historical change is rarely this simple. History does not necessarily advance with inevitability in any direction. In certain respects the progression of events can be interpreted in a cyclical way in the sense that one can trace forms and patterns in historical development which display parallels from one era to the next. The Irish republican strategic experience bears testament to this cyclical element in historical development. Irish republicans construct their strategy in which to practise armed resistance. However, persistence with a particular strategy, even though it may have outlived its usefulness, has often led to the domination of ideological symbolism over strategic decision making which has made the movement's violence appear disconnected from political motivation. In turn, this has led to missed opportunities and political marginalisation. Faced with defeat, the IRA searches around for a more effective strategy in which to recast the military instrument. In the course of searching, aspects of republican ideology have been challenged, though often at the expense of a damaging split. It is this cyclical element which appears to represent the process of strategic change within the republican movement, rather than one of inexorable advance towards victory. Whether the 1994 ceasefire represents a break in this cycle and a fundamental change in the composition of republican strategy is still not clear, but one thing is for sure, Irish republicans cannot tolerate any thought that their goal is receding or may never be reached. There may be setbacks and wrong turnings but these are occasional and temporary, and will not stop the march of progress. To acknowledge that events move in any other direction except towards the ultimate republican vision would be history in reverse. To accept any such possibility would probably finish the movement; for if a psychological pebble is dislodged, it may start a landslide.

Notes

INTRODUCTION – DEVELOPING A STRATEGIC APPROACH TO THE IRISH REPUBLICAN MOVEMENT

1 M. Howard, *The Causes of Wars*, London, Counterpoint, 1983, p. 36.
2 B. Liddell Hart, *Strategy: The Indirect Approach*, London, Faber, 1967, p. 335.
3 T.C. Schelling, *Arms and Influence*, New Haven, Mass., Yale University Press, 1966, p. 2.
4 C. von Clausewitz, *On War*, M. Howard and P. Paret (trans. and eds), Princeton, N.J., Princeton University Press, 1984, p. 87.
5 Ibid., p. 75.
6 Ibid., pp. 75–80.
7 T.C. Schelling, *The Strategy of Conflict*, Cambridge, Mass., Harvard University Press, 1980, p. 5.
8 Clausewitz, op. cit., p. 81.
9 See K. Holsti, *International Politics: A Framework of Analysis*, Englewood Cliffs, N.J., Prentice Hall, 1977, pp. 3–25.
10 A. Wolfers, *Discord and Collaboration*, Baltimore, Johns Hopkins University Press, 1962, pp. 82–83.
11 F. Lopez-Alves, 'Political crises, strategic choices, and terrorism: the rise and fall of the Uruguayan Tuparmaros', *Terrorism and Political Violence*, vol. 1, April 1989, no. 2, p. 204.
12 Ibid., p. 204.
13 Clausewitz, op. cit., p. 87.
14 Ibid., p. 87.
15 Ibid., p. 87.
16 Quoted in P. Paret, *Clausewitz and the State*, Princeton, Princeton University Press, 1985, p. 354.
17 J. Bowyer Bell, *The Secret Army*, Dublin, Poolbeg, 1989, pp. 447–463.
18 Ibid., p. 454.

1 THE IRISH REPUBLICAN MILITARY MIND – THE EVOLUTION OF A STRATEGIC TRADITION

1 See P. Gibbon, 'Orange and green myths', *Fortnight*, August 1972.
2 *Eire Nua*, PSF news sheet, n.p., January 1977.
3 Quoted in G. Adams, *A Pathway to Peace*, Cork, Mercier, 1988, p. 48.
4 S.O.D., 'Wolfe Tone and today', *The United Irishman*, June 1949.
5 G. Adams, *Towards a Strategy for Peace*, Letter to J. Hume, PSF Document no. 1, PSF–SDLP Talks, 14 March 1988, p. 1.

6 J. Hope, 'Why England occupies Ireland', *An Phoblacht*, 5 April 1978.
7 Adams, *A Pathway to Peace*, p. 10 and pp. 32–33.
8 Quoted in J. Froude, *The English in Ireland in the Eighteenth Century*, vol. III, London, Longmans, Green & Co., 1895, p. 18.
9 The Constitution of the United Irishmen (1797) in C. Carlton (ed.), *Bigotry and Blood: Documents on the Ulster Troubles*, Chicago, Prentice Hall, 1977, p. 46.
10 Quoted in J. Brennan, 'The philosophy of Tone', *An Phoblacht*, 18 June 1932.
11 Quoted in P. MacAonghusa and L. O Reagain (eds), *The Best of Wolfe Tone*, Cork, Mercier, 1972, p. 46.
12 J. Carty, *Ireland from the Great Famine to the Treaty, 1851–1921*, Dublin, C.J. Fallon, 1951, p. 30.
13 G. Adams, *The Politics of Irish Freedom*, Dingle, Co. Kerry, Brandon, 1986, p. 165.
14 See *Republican News*, 16 February 1973.
15 'Daithi O Conaill television interview', *Republican News*, 30 November 1974.
16 See L. O Broin, *Revolutionary Underground*, Dublin, Gill & Macmillan, 1976, pp. 27–29 and T. Corfe, *The Phoenix Park Murders*, London, Hodder & Stoughton, 1968, pp. 135–136.
17 P. Tynan, *The Irish Invincibles and Their Times*, London, Chatham & Co., 1894, p. 430, cited in T. Corfe, 'Political assassination in the Irish tradition', in A. O'Day and Y. Alexander (eds), *Terrorism in Ireland*, London, Croom Helm, 1984, p. 112.
18 See M. Bourke, *John O'Leary*, Tralee, Co. Kerry, Anvil, 1967, p. 145.
19 *Republican News*, 5 February 1977.
20 See D. O'Neil, *Three Perennial Themes of Anti-Colonialism: The Irish Case*, Denver, Monograph Series in World Affairs, University of Denver, vol. 14, book 1, 1976, p. 112.
21 J. Hutchinson, *The Dynamics of Cultural Nationalism*, London, Allen & Unwin, 1987, pp. 104–105.
22 Quoted in P. Pearse, *Ghosts*, Part VII, reprinted in *An Phoblacht*, 1 October 1926.
23 P. Pearse, *Ghosts*, Parts I–III, reprinted in *An Phoblacht*, 17 September 1926.
24 Ibid.
25 Adams, *The Politics of Irish Freedom*, p. 62 and see also p. 88.
26 Quoted in E. Norman, *A History of Modern Ireland*, London, Allen Lane, The Penguin Press, 1971, p. 123.
27 T. Garvin, *Nationalist Revolutionaries in Ireland, 1858–1928*, Oxford, Clarendon, 1987, pp. 149–157.
28 E. de Valera, 'The work before Ireland', *An Phoblacht*, 15 January 1926.
29 J. Bennett introduction to S. Cronin and R. Roche, *Freedom the Wolfe Tone Way*, Tralee, Co. Kerry, Anvil, 1973, p. 67.
30 *An Phoblacht/Republican News (AP/RN)*, 18 February 1982.
31 Quoted in R. Kee, *The Green Flag*, London, Weidenfeld & Nicolson, 1972, p.306.
32 S.O.D., 'Wolfe Tone and today', *United Irishman*, June 1949.
33 J. O'Leary, *Recollections of Fenians and Fenianism*, vol. II, Shannon, Irish University Press, 1968, pp. 242–243.
34 Pearse, *Ghosts*, Parts I–III.
35 Ibid.
36 J. Devoy, *Recollections of an Irish Rebel*, Shannon, Irish University Press, 1969, p. 186.
37 See R. O Bradaigh, 'What is Irish republicanism?', in *Irish Independent*, 9 December 1970.
38 P. Pearse, *Ghosts*, Parts IV–V, reprinted in *An Phoblacht*, 24 September 1926.
39 Quoted in T. Dunne, *Wolfe Tone: An Analysis of his Political Philosophy*, Cork, Tower, 1982, p. 60.
40 Quoted in J. Connolly Heron (ed.), *The Words of James Connolly*, Cork, Mercier, 1986, p. 79.

41   Quoted in M. Elliott, *Partners in Revolution*, London, Yale University Press, 1982, p. 371.
42   Quoted in M. O Dubhghaill, *Insurrection Fires at Eastertide*, Cork, Mercier, 1966, p. 133.
43   *Eire Og*, PSF newsheet, West Belfast, vol. 2, no. 4, n.d. (c. 1975).
44   *The Volunteer*, PSF, Lurgan, 9 April 1977.
45   S. O'Kelly, 'The United Irishmen were republicans', *United Irishman*, July/August 1948.
46   See R. Kearney, 'The IRA's strategy of failure', in M. Hederman and R. Kearney (eds), *The Crane Bag*, Dublin, Wolfhound, 1982, pp. 700–702.
47   'Father John Kenyon: his views on physical versus moral force', *United Irishman*, September 1948.
48   Quoted in E. Hull, *A History of Ireland and Her People*, vol. II, London, Harrap, n.d., p. 338.
49   M. de Buitleir, 'The tradition of physical force', Part 2, *An Phoblacht*, 21 April 1934.
50   Quoted in Norman, op. cit., p. 124.
51   Quoted in p. O'Hegarty, *A History of Ireland Under the Union, 1801–1922*, London, Methuen, 1952, p. 346.
52   'Dustin', 'The neology of a military campaign', *Republican News*, 10 April 1976.
53   Sinn Fein, 'Constitutionalism and Sinn Fein', *Sinn Fein Pamphlets*, no. 5, n.p., n.d. (c. 1912–1916), p. 2.
54   T. MacSwiney, *Principles of Freedom*, Chapter 3, reprinted in *United Irishman*, February 1962.
55   See L. O Broin, *Fenian Fever*, London, Chatto & Windus, 1971, pp. 210–217.
56   Quoted in Carty, op. cit., p. 27.
57   Devoy, op. cit., p. 250.
58   M. de Buitleir, 'The tradition of physical force', Part 1, *An Phoblacht*, 7 April 1934.
59   *AP/RN*, 15 April 1982.
60   *AP/RN*, 28 August 1986.
61   *Belfast Telegraph*, interview with R. O Bradaigh, reprinted in *An Phoblacht*, September 1971.
62   Quoted in C. Townshend, *Political Violence in Ireland*, Oxford, Clarendon, 1983, p. 32.
63   Quoted in K. Short, *The Dynamite War: Irish American Bombers in Victorian Britain*, Dublin, Gill & Macmillan, 1979, p. 38.
64   From *Weekly Union*, 10 July 1880, cited in M. Davitt, *The Fall of Feudalism in Ireland*, London, Harper, 1904, p. 433.
65   Quoted in *The Volunteer*, PSF, Derry, August 1974.
66   Beechmount Correspondent, 'The question of physical force', *An Phoblacht*, 19 January 1973.
67   J. Fintan Lalor, *Irish Felon*, no. 4, reprinted in L. Fogarty (ed.), *James Fintan Lalor*, Dublin, Talbot, 1918, p. 107.
68   For a critical view of Pearse in this regard see X. Carty, *In Bloody Protest*, Dublin, Able, 1978.
69   Quoted in R. Dudley Edwards, *Patrick Pearse*, London, Victor Gollanz, 1977, p. 179.
70   McSwiney, op. cit.
71   Le Traolach, 'Connolly's charter championed by IRA', *An Phoblacht*, September 1972.
72   See C. von Clausewitz, *On War*, M. Howard and P. Paret (trans. and eds), Princeton, N. J., Princeton University Press, 1984, pp. 596–597 and p. 601.
73   P. Pearse, *Political Writings and Speeches*, Dublin, Talbot, 1952, p. 268.
74   S. MacStiofain, *Memoirs of a Revolutionary*, Edinburgh, Gordon Cremonsi, 1975, p. 258.

75 Pearse, *Ghosts*, Parts I–III.
76 L. MacLiam, 'Republicans will continue struggle for national liberation', *Republican News*, 20 March 1976.
77 L. McCaffrey, *The Irish Question, 1800–1922*, Lexington, University of Kentucky Press, 1968, pp. 68–69.
78 Quoted in R. Comerford, *Charles J. Kickham*, Dublin, Wolfhound, 1979, p. 47.
79 See ibid., pp. 131–132.
80 D. Breatnach, 'The republican ethic', *An Phoblacht*, July 1970.
81 Pearse, *Political Writings and Speeches*, p. 105.
82 Quoted in *The Irish Times*, 23 April 1973.
83 S. O Riain, *Provos: Patriots or Terrorists?*, Dublin, Irish Book Bureau, 1974, p. 35.
84 J. Bennett in Cronin and Roche, op. cit., p. 65.
85 J. Connolly, 'Socialism and nationalism', *Shan van Vocht*, January 1897 reprinted in P. Beresford Ellis (ed.), *James Connolly: Selected Writings*, London, Pluto, 1988, p. 122.
86 See J. Boyle, 'Connolly, the Citizen Army and the rising', in K. Nowlan (ed.), *The Making of 1916*, Dublin, Stationary Office, 1969, pp. 66–67.
87 Le Traolach, 'Connolly's charter championed by IRA', *An Phoblacht*, September 1972.
88 J. Connolly, 'Physical force in Irish politics', *Workers Republic*, 22 July 1899, reprinted in Beresford Ellis, op. cit., p. 208.
89 P. Flynn, 'What is Irish republicanism?', *AP/RN*, 11 October 1980.
90 Quoted in McAonghusa and O Reagain, op. cit., p. 46.
91 O Riain, op. cit., p. 7.
92 D. O Conaill, Bodenstown speech, *An Phoblacht*, July 1970.
93 Pearse, *Political Writings and Speeches*, p. 104.
94 O Riain, op. cit., p. 8.
95 E. de Valera, 'Save Ulster for Ireland', *An Phoblacht*, 4 December 1925.
96 See Adams, *The Politics of Irish Freedom*, p. 116.
97 P. MacLogain 'Partition: its causes and consequences', *United Irishman*, May 1948.
98 Ibid.
99 Ibid.
100 *Freedom Struggle in Ireland*, Dublin, PSF, n.d. (c. mid-1973), p. 3.
101 Adams, *The Politics of Irish Freedom*, pp. 124–125.
102 Ibid., p. 116.
103 *The Belfast Telegraph*, 24 June 1987, cited in A. Guelke, *Northern Ireland: The International Perspective,* Dublin, Gill & Macmillan, 1988, p. 32.
104 Adams, *A Pathway to Peace*, p. 11.
105 see P. O'Malley, *The Uncivil Wars*, Belfast, Blackstaff, 1983, pp. 287–299.
106 Adams, *A Pathway to Peace*, p. 11.
107 M. de Buitleir, 'The tradition of physical force', Part 2, *An Phoblacht*, 21 April 1934.
108 *AP/RN*, 5 November 1981, cited in O'Malley, op. cit., p. 288.
109 *AP/RN*, 28 August 1986.
110 SDLP Document no. 1, PSF–SDLP Talks, 17 March 1988, p. 4.
111 Document no. 4, PSF–SDLP Talks, 1988, reprinted in *The Irish Times*, 19 September 1988.
112 D. Morrison, Bodenstown speech, *AP/RN*, 27 June 1981.
113 See T. Ireland, *Ireland Past and Present*, New York, G.P. Putnam's & Sons, 1942, p. 222.
114 P. Johnson, *Ireland: Land of Troubles*, London, Eyre Methuen, 1980, p. 76.
115 See M. Tierney, *Modern Ireland Since 1850*, Dublin, Gill & Macmillan, 1978, pp. 87–89.
116 *Scenario for Peace*, Dublin, PSF, May 1987, p. 2.

117 J. Bennett, *The Northern Conflict and British Power*, Irish Sovereignty Movement Pamphlet, no. 1, 1973, p. 12.
118 J. Bennett in Cronin and Roche, op. cit., pp. 20–21.
119 Adams, *The Politics of Irish Freedom*, p. 124.

2 TRANSITIONS IN IRISH REPUBLICAN STRATEGY – THE DEVELOPMENT OF THE MILITARY INSTRUMENT FROM THE EASTER RISING TO THE CIVIL WAR

1 'The inheritors of 1916', *AP/RN*, 3 April 1986.
2 R. O Bradaigh, 'What is Irish republicanism?', *The Irish Independent*, 9 December 1970.
3 Proclamation of the Republic of Ireland, 1916, reprinted in A. Mitchell and P. O'Snodaigh (eds), *Irish Political Documents, 1916–1949*, Dublin, Irish Academic Press, 1985, p. 17.
4 P. Pearse, *Ghosts*, Parts I–III, *An Phoblacht*, 17 September 1926.
5 J. Connolly, Statement at court martial, 9 May 1916, reprinted in O. Dudley Edwards and B. Ransom (eds), *James Connolly: Selected Political Writings*, New York, Grove Press, 1974, p. 378.
6 Quoted in C. Duff, *Six Days to Shake an Empire*, London, J.M. Dent & Sons, 1966, p. 225.
7 See for example the protest pamphlet J. Sweetman, *Ireland and Conscription*, Dublin, no stated publisher, n.d. (c. 1917).
8 For an assessment of Sinn Fein's transformation into a republican minded party see M. Laffan, 'The unification of Sinn Fein in 1917', *Irish Historical Studies*, vol. XVII, March 1971, pp. 353–379.
9 See *The Ethics of Sinn Fein*, Dublin, Sinn Fein, September 1917, p. 5.
10 *Sinn Fein Election Manifesto*, 1918, reprinted in Mitchell and O'Snodaigh, op. cit., p. 48.
11 Dail Eireann address to the free nations of the world, 21 January 1919, reprinted in Mitchell and O'Snodaigh, op. cit., p. 59.
12 Captain W., 'IRA in 1922', *An Phoblacht*, 25 March 1927.
13 See M. Tierney, *Eoin MacNeill*, F.X. Martin (ed.), Oxford, Clarendon, 1988, p. 165 and p. 190.
14 Quoted in C. Townshend, *Political Violence in Ireland*, Oxford, Clarendon, 1983, p. 243.
15 See ibid., pp. 289–290.
16 Quoted in G. Hayes-McCoy, 'A military history of the rising', in K. Nowlan (ed.), *The Making of 1916*, Dublin, Stationery Office, 1969, p. 300.
17 T. Hachy, *Britain and Irish Separatism*, Washington D.C., Catholic University Press of America, 1977, p. 195. See also D. Lynch and F. O'Donoghue, *The IRB and the 1916 Uprising*, Cork, Mercier, n.d., p. 32.
18 See T. Gray, *The Irish Answer*, London, Heinemann, 1966, pp. 61–65 and T. Bowden, *The Breakdown of Public Security*, London, Sage, 1977, pp. 84–88.
19 G. Hayes-McCoy, 'The conduct of the Anglo-Irish war', in T. Desmond Williams (ed.), *The Irish Struggle*, London, Routledge & Kegan Paul, 1966, pp. 60–61.
20 Quoted in S. O'Mahoney, *Frongoch: University of Revolution*, Dublin, FDR Teoranta, 1987, p. 67.
21 *An t-Oglach*, 31 January 1919, reprinted in A. Hepburn (ed.), *The Conflict of Nationality in Modern Ireland*, London, Edward Arnold, 1980, pp. 112–113.
22 Statement by Lord Curzon to Parliament, 20 October 1920, reprinted in Mitchell and O'Snodaigh, op. cit., p. 85.
23 J. O'Beirne Ranelagh, *A Short History of Ireland*, Cambridge, Cambridge University Press, 1983, p. 194.

24 See M. McManus, *Eamon de Valera*, London, Victor Gollanz, 1944, p. 63.

25 See L. Deasy, *Towards Free Ireland*, Dublin, Mercier, 1973, pp. 154–168.

26 See C. Townshend, *The British Campaign in Ireland, 1919–1921*, Oxford, Oxford University Press, 1975, pp. 113–114.

27 M. Foot, 'Revolt, rebellion, revolution, civil war: the Irish experience', in M. Elliott-Bateman *et al.*, *Revolt to Revolution*, Manchester, Manchester University Press, 1974, p. 183.

28 M. Collins interview, *Freeman's Journal*, 22 April 1921, reprinted in Mitchell and O'Snodaigh, op. cit., p. 103

29 Quoted in P. Beaslai, *Michael Collins and the Making of a New Ireland*, vol. II, London, Harrap, 1926, p. 383.

30 T. Barry, *Guerrilla Days in Ireland*, Tralee, Co. Kerry, Anvil, 1971, p. 26.

31 Captain W., 'IRA in 1922', *An Phoblacht*, 25 March 1927.

32 D. Boyce, *Englishmen and Irish Troubles: British Public Opinion and the Making of a New Ireland, 1918–1922*, London, Johnathan Cape, 1972, p. 85.

33 See for example, 'Police burn town in County Meath – explosion in Cork', *The New York Times*, 28 September 1920, reprinted in Mitchell and O'Snodaigh, op. cit., pp. 82–84.

34 Boyce, op. cit., pp. 51–53.

35 Ibid., pp. 61–82.

36 Quoted in S. Cronin, *The McGarrity Papers*, Tralee, Co. Kerry, Anvil, 1972, p.103.

37 Quoted in ibid., p. 101.

38 See J. Bowyer Bell, *The Secret Army*, Dublin, Poolbeg, 1989, p. 24.

39 Townshend, *The British Campaign in Ireland*, p. 180.

40 O. MacDonagh, *Ireland*, Englewood Cliffs, N.J., Prentice Hall, 1968, p. 88.

41 Quoted in Cronin, op. cit., p. 103.

42 Quoted in L. O Broin, *Michael Collins*, Dublin, Gill & Macmillan, 1980, p. 84.

43 T. Bowden, 'Ireland: decay of control', in Elliott-Bateman, op. cit., pp. 225–226.

44 See Townshend, *Political Violence in Ireland*, p. 353.

45 See D. Boyce, 'Water for the fish: terrorism and public opinion', in Y. Alexander and A. O'Day (eds), *Terrorism in Ireland*, London, Croom Helm, 1984, p. 153.

46 Townshend, *The British Campaign in Ireland*, pp. 203–204.

47 MacDonagh, op. cit., p. 87.

48 E. Holt, *Protest in Arms*, London, Putnam, 1960, p. 355.

49 F.S.L. Lyons, *Ireland Since the Famine*, London, Weidenfeld & Nicolson, 1971, p. 425.

50 Barry, op. cit., p. 207.

51 Townshend, *The British Campaign in Ireland*, p. 193.

52 E. O'Malley, *The Singing Flame*, Dublin, Anvil, 1992, p. 15.

53 Quoted in K. Griffith and T. O'Grady, *Curious Journeys: An Oral History of Ireland's Unfinished Revolution*, London, Hutchinson, 1982, p. 247.

54 Quoted in M. Hopkinson, *Green Against Green*, Dublin, Gill & Macmillan, 1988, p. 9.

55 See Lyons, op. cit., pp. 442–443.

56 'Republican strength – where it really lies', *The Free State*, 22 April 1922.

57 Oath of Allegiance to Dail Eireann, 20 August 1919, reprinted in Mitchell and O'Snodaigh, op. cit., p. 66.

58 *The Plain People*, 28 May 1922.

59 E. de Valera, 'Save Ulster for Ireland', *An Phoblacht*, 4 December 1925.

60 'Things to think about – the Oath', *The Plain People*, 9 April 1922.

61 Ibid.

62 'Is the Free State a step towards the republic?', *The Nation*, no. 5, 1922 (c. mid-1922).

63 'The "trust to luck" policy', *The Free State*, 4 March 1922.

64   E. de Blaghd, 'The Fenian faith', *The Free State*, 18 March 1922.
65   'Fidelity or foolishness?', *The Free State*, 29 July 1922.
66   Ibid.
67   Captain W., 'IRA in 1922', *An Phoblacht*, 25 March 1927.
68   'Will the English come back?', *The Nation*, no. 2, 1922.
69   Quoted in R. Kee, *The Green Flag*, London, Weidenfeld & Nicolson, 1972, p. 719.
70   Quoted in F. Pakenham, *Peace by Ordeal*, London, Jonathan Cape, 1935, p. 331.
71   E. de Valera, 'The work before Ireland', *An Phoblacht*, 15 January 1926.
72   'The nation's will', *The Free State*, 4 March 1922.
73   Ibid.
74   'Fidelity or foolishness?', *The Free State*, 29 July 1922.
75   'What the people think about the delegation', *The Free State*, 22 April 1922.
76   'The gamblers and the dangers of their game', *The Free State*, 4 March 1922.
77   Correspondence from E. de Valera to D. Lloyd George, 28 June 1921, reprinted in Mitchell and O'Snodaigh, op. cit., p. 113.
78   Ibid., 30 September 1921, p. 115.
79   E. de Valera, 'Save Ulster for Ireland', *An Phoblacht*, 4 December 1925.
80   Quoted in Griffith and O'Grady, op. cit., p. 266.
81   'Civil war the greater evil', *The Nation*, no. 2, 1922.
82   'The gamblers and the dangers of their game', *The Free State*, 4 March 1922.
83   Ibid.
84   E. de Valera, Speech in Kilarney, 18 March 1922, in M. Moynihan (ed.), *Speeches and Statements by Eamon de Valera 1917–1973*, Dublin, Gill & Macmillan, 1980, pp. 103–104.
85   P. O Gallachobair, 'By what authority?', *Eire: The Irish Nation*, no. 7, Dublin, Irish Nation Committee, 1922, p. 3.
86   O'Malley, op. cit., p. 171.
87   Beaslai, op. cit., vol. II, p. 401.
88   O'Malley, op. cit., p. 80.
89   'Civil war will pay the jobbers', *The Nation*, no. 6, 1922.
90   'Republican strength – where it really lies', *The Free State*, 22 April 1922.
91   'Futility', *The Irish People*, 23 July 1922.
92   Ibid.
93   'Irregular idealism', *The Irish People*, 23 July 1922.
94   See Hopkinson, op. cit., p. 230 and p. 236.
95   *The Plain People*, 9 April 1922.
96   *Republic of Ireland*, 29 June 1922.
97   Quoted in J. Curran, *The Birth of the Irish Free State*, Alabama, University of Alabama Press, 1980, p. 231.
98   'The war against gun rule', *The Irish People*, 16 July 1922.
99   'The IRA stands true', *The Plain People*, 9 April 1922.
100   'The Responsibility!', *Republic of Ireland* (Scottish edition), 28 October 1922.
101   'To the Free State soldiers', *Republic of Ireland* (Scottish edition), 28 October 1922.
102   'The people and guerrilla tactics', *The Free State*, 29 July 1922.
103   E. de Blaghd, 'The Fenian faith', *The Free State*, 18 March 1922.
104   Ibid.
105   Free State proclamation of military courts and offer of amnesty, 10 October 1922, reprinted in Mitchell and O'Snodaigh, op. cit., pp. 148–150.
106   *The Responsibility*, IRA Publicity Department, September 1922, p. 4.
107   'Khaki or green?', *An Long – War Sheet*, no. 1, 4 October 1922.
108   Kee, op. cit., p. 744.
109   O'Malley, op. cit., p. 145.
110   Speech by W. Cosgrave at the opening of the Free State Parliament, 11 September 1922, reprinted in Mitchell and O'Snodaigh, op. cit., pp. 144–145.

111 O Gallchobhair, op. cit., p. 3.
112 E. de Valera, Declaration at End of Civil War, reprinted in Mitchell and O'Snodaigh, op. cit., p. 163.
113 S. O Riain, *Provos: Patriots or Terrorists?*, Dublin, Irish Book Bureau, 1974, p. 23.
114 Quoted in G. Adams, *A Pathway to Peace*, Cork, Mercier, 1988, p. 54.
115 Quoted in E. Neeson, *The Civil War in Ireland*, Cork, Mercier, 1966, p. 197.
116 Quoted in Hopkinson, op. cit., p. 229.
117 C. von Clausewitz, *On War*, M. Howard and P. Paret (trans. and eds), Princeton, N.J., Princeton University Press, 1984, p. 99.

3 POLITICAL CONTROL VERSUS THE AUTONOMOUS MILITARY INSTRUMENT – IRISH REPUBLICAN STRATEGY FROM THE CIVIL WAR TO THE 1970s

1 Quoted in K. Nowlan, 'Dail Eireann and the army: unity and division', in D. Williams (ed.), *The Irish Struggle*, London, Routledge & Kegan Paul, 1966, p. 69.
2 *An t-Oglach*, 31 January 1919, reprinted in A. Hepburn (ed.), *The Conflict of Nationality in Modern Ireland*, London, Edward Arnold, 1980, p. 112.
3 C. Townshend, *Political Violence in Ireland*, Oxford, Clarendon, 1983, pp. 331–332.
4 *An t-Oglach*, 31 January 1919, in Hepburn, op. cit., p. 112.
5 Quoted in T. Hachy, *Britain and Irish Separatism*, Washington D.C., Catholic University Press of America, 1977, p. 269. It should be noted here that there were certain advantages in keeping the Dail and the IRA separate. Inter alia, it avoided the danger of the republican leadership being decapitated by arrests.
6 Quoted in J. Carty, *Ireland from the Great Famine to the Treaty, 1951–1921*, Dublin, C.J. Fallon, 1951, p. 202.
7 Nowlan, op. cit., p. 70.
8 Quoted in L. O Broin, *Michael Collins*, Dublin, Gill & Macmillan, 1980, p. 68.
9 Quoted in R. Kee, *The Green Flag*, London, Weidenfeld & Nicolson, 1972, p. 661.
10 M. Hopkinson, *Green Against Green*, Dublin, Gill & Macmillan, 1988, p. 41.
11 R. O'Connor, statement to press, 26 April 1922 cited in D. Macardle, *The Irish Republic*, London, Victor Gollanz, 1937, p. 725.
12 Macardle, op. cit., p.721.
13 Statement of the Executive of the Irish Republican Army, 28 March 1922, reprinted in F. O'Donoghue, *No Other Law*, Dublin, Irish Press, 1954, p. 330.
14 E. de Valera, Memorandum to IRA executive, 12 October 1922, reprinted in A. Mitchell and P. O'Snodaigh (eds), *Irish Political Documents*, Dublin, Irish Academic Press, 1985, p. 146.
15 Ibid., p. 147.
16 Quoted in P. Beaslai, *Michael Collins and the Making of a New Ireland*, London, Harrap, vol. 1, 1926, p. 369.
17 E. Neeson, *The Civil War in Ireland*, Cork, Mercier, 1966, p. 184.
18 Quoted in M. McInerney, *Peadar O'Donnell*, Dublin, O'Brien Press, 1974, p. 71.
19 Quoted in ibid., p. 72.
20 Hopkinson, op. cit., pp. 128–129.
21 Captain W., 'IRA in 1922', *An Phoblacht*, 25 March 1927.
22 'The army and its task', *An Phoblacht*, 29 October 1926.
23 Quoted in Earl of Longford and T. O'Neill, *Eamon de Valera*, London, Hutchinson, 1970, p. 210.
24 Quoted in R. Fanning, '"The rule of order": Eamon de Valera and the IRA, 1923–40', in J. O'Carroll and J. Murphy (eds), *De Valera and His Times*, Cork, Cork University Press, 1983, p. 161.

25   Draft agenda for IRA convention, 20 November 1925, cited in J. Bowyer Bell, *The Secret Army*, Dublin, Poolbeg, 1989, p. 53.
26   'Force as a means towards Irish freedom', *The Nation*, 14 January 1928.
27   'Army council statement', *An Phoblacht*, 3 June 1927.
28   Ibid.
29   See 'Oglaigh Na h-Eireann [Irish Volunteers] – manifesto to the Irish people', *An Phoblacht*, 14 January 1933.
30   'The army council state basis for unity', *An Phoblacht*, 2 September 1933.
31   H. Patterson, *The Politics of Illusion*, London, Hutchinson Radius, 1989, p. 46.
32   'What Mellows wrote in Mountjoy', *An Phoblacht*, 19 May 1934.
33   Democratic programme of Dail Eireann (1919), reprinted in Mitchell and O'Snodaigh, op. cit., pp. 59–60.
34   'What Mellows wrote in Mountjoy', *An Phoblacht*, 19 May 1934.
35   Patterson, op. cit., pp. 28–29 and p. 44.
36   The programme of Saor Eire (1931), reprinted in Mitchell and O'Snodaigh, op. cit., p. 185.
37   See The Republican Congress manifesto (1931) reprinted in ibid., pp. 208–210.
38   M. O'Donnell, 'Who fights and runs', *An Phoblacht*, 25 March 1927.
39   Ibid.
40   G. Gilmore, 'The revolutionary task', *An Phoblacht*, 30 April 1932.
41   Ibid.
42   See E. Rumpf and A. Hepburn, *Nationalism and Socialism in Twentieth Century Ireland*, Liverpool, Liverpool University Press, 1977, pp. 91–93.
43   IRA ultimatum to British government, 12 January 1939, reprinted in Mitchell and O'Snodaigh, op. cit., pp. 220–221.
44   T. Ireland, *Ireland Past and Present*, New York, G.P. Putnam's & Sons, 1942, p. 690.
45   Quoted in S. Cronin, *The McGarrity Papers*, Tralee, Co. Kerry, Anvil, 1972, p. 167.
46   *The New York Times*, 11 February 1940.
47   *The Daily Herald*, 10 February 1940.
48   See *The Manchester Guardian*, 9 February 1940.
49   Fanning, op. cit., pp. 169–170.
50   Quoted in *The Daily Express*, 19 February 1940.
51   See *The Daily Telegraph*, 8 January 1940.
52   Quoted in T. Ryle Dwyer, *Irish Neutrality and the USA, 1939–1947*, Dublin, Gill & Macmillan, 1977, p. 21.
53   'Moral sanction for revolution', *An Phoblacht*, 29 October 1926.
54   'IRA attitude towards Britain', *An Phoblacht*, 31 March 1928.
55   M. Twomey, 'The task of the IRA', *An Phoblacht*, 3 December 1932.
56   'Oglaigh Na h-Eireann – manifesto to the Irish people', *An Phoblacht*, 14 January 1933.
57   Adjutant General, IRA, official statement to all ranks, 31 January 1933, reprinted in *An Phoblacht*, 4 February 1933.
58   S. Cronin, *Irish Nationalism*, Dublin, Academy Press, 1980, p. 160.
59   'The army council manifesto', *An Phoblacht*, 22 April 1933.
60   Ibid.
61   S. Cronin, *The McGarrity Papers*, p. 162.
62   See C. Foley, *The Legion of the Rearguard*, London, Pluto, 1992, p. 179.
63   Sinn Fein, *National Unity and Independence Programme*, Dublin, n.d. (c. late 1920s/early 1930s), p. 2.
64   Ibid.
65   See B. Purdie, *Politics in the Streets*, Belfast, Blackstaff, 1990, p. 41.
66   'Sinn Fein victory', *United Irishman*, June 1955.
67   'Revolt in the north', *United Irishman*, January 1957.
68   J. McGarrity (pseudonym), *Resistance: The Story of the Struggle in British Occupied Ireland*, n.p., Irish Freedom Press, n.d. (c. 1957/1958), p. 38.

69 *Handbook for Volunteers of the Irish Republican Army: Notes on Guerrilla Warfare*, n.p., IRA GHQ, 1956, pp. 5–6.
70 See ibid., pp. 19–21.
71 McGarrity, *Resistance*, p. 38.
72 *Handbook for Volunteers*, p. 12.
73 McGarrity, *Resistance*, pp. 54–55.
74 *Handbook for Volunteers*, p. 16.
75 'Freedom fighter', *United Irishman*, February 1957.
76 P. MacLogain, 'Presidential address', *United Irishman*, December 1958.
77 'Easter message', *United Irishman*, May 1957.
78 'Resistance to British rule in Ireland today', *United Irishman*, May 1958.
79 P. MacLogain, 'Presidential address', *United Irishman*, December 1958.
80 'Resistance to British rule in Ireland today', *United Irishman*, May 1958.
81 Bowyer Bell, op. cit., pp. 328–329.
82 'Britain must withdraw her forces', *United Irishman*, January 1958.
83 'Resistance statement', *United Irishman*, January 1959.
84 S. Cronin, 'The authority of history is behind fight in the north', *United Irishman*, June 1959.
85 Irish Republican Publicity Bureau (IRPB) statement, 26 February 1926, reprinted in *United Irishman*, March 1962.
86 Interview with C. Goulding, *This Week*, 31 July 1970.
87 Ibid.
88 R. Johnston, '1916 and its aftermath', *United Irishman*, April 1966.
89 R. Johnston, 'Whither Ireland?', *United Irishman*, October 1965.
90 Interview with C. Goulding, *This Week*, 31 July 1970.
91 D. Breatnach, 'Realism', *United Irishman*, September 1963.
92 C. Goulding, statement (1972) in R. Sweetman, *On Our Knees: Ireland 1972*, London, Pan, 1972, p. 141.
93 Ibid., p. 142.
94 See, for example, R. MacEoin, 'An economic resistance movement', *United Irishman*, October 1964.
95 C. Goulding, 'We can go it alone', *United Irishman*, November 1966.
96 See ibid.
97 G. Gilmore, 'The revolutionary task', *An Phoblacht*, 30 April 1932.
98 Quoted in McInerney, op. cit., p. 148.
99 G. Adams, *The Politics of Irish Freedom*, Dingle, Co. Kerry, Brandon, 1986, p. 10.
100 Patterson, op. cit., p. 87.
101 R. Johnston, 'Whither Ireland?', *United Irishman*, October 1965.
102 Ibid.
103 *An Phoblacht* (CRA), January 1967.
104 Ibid.
105 *An Phoblacht* (CRA), May/June 1967.
106 S. MacStiofain, *Memoirs of a Revolutionary*, Edinburgh, Gordon Cremonesi, 1975, p. 104.
107 *An Phoblacht* (CRA), January 1967.
108 Interview with C. Goulding, *This Week*, 31 July 1970.
109 T. Meade, 'No longer well-meaning political simplicists', *United Irishman*, November 1966.
110 C. Goulding, 'There will be a fight', *United Irishman*, September 1965.
111 Patterson, op. cit., p. 96.
112 Copy of the IRA political and military plan, reprinted in The Government of Northern Ireland, *Violence and Civil Disturbance in Northern Ireland*, Report of Tribunal of Inquiry, Cmd. 566, vol. 2, Belfast, Her Majesty's Stationery Office, April 1972, p. 48.

113 Ibid., p 50.
114 Statement from the Irish Republican Publicity Bureau, 23 May 1971, reprinted in ibid., p. 52.
115 Interview with C. Goulding, *This Week*, 31 July 1970.
116 T. Meade, 'No longer well-meaning political simplicists', *United Irishman*, November 1966.
117 Ibid.
118 S. Garland, Bodenstown speech, *United Irishman*, July 1968.
119 T. Meade, 'No longer well-meaning political simplicists', *United Irishman*, November 1966.
120 Goulding Statement in Sweetman, op. cit., p. 144.
121 T. Meade, 'No longer well-meaning political simplicists', *United Irishman*, November 1966.
122 Copy of the IRA political and military plan, reprinted in *Violence and Civil Disturbance in Northern Ireland*, op. cit., p. 47.
123 Ibid., p. 47.
124 S. Garland, Bodenstown speech, *United Irishman*, July 1968.
125 T. MacGiolla, Bodenstown speech, *United Irishman*, July 1969.
126 Interview with C. Goulding, *This Week*, 31 July 1970.
127 Ibid.
128 Ibid.
129 See P. Walsh, *From Civil Rights to National War: Northern Ireland Catholic Politics 1964–1974*, Belfast, Athol, 1989, pp. 36–38.
130 See Purdie, op. cit., pp. 149–151.
131 Goulding statement in Sweetman, op. cit., p. 143.
132 'Unionism and Paisley – an analysis', *United Irishman*, November 1966.
133 'Civil rights now!', *United Irishman*, September 1968.
134 'Republican Clubs plan future action', *United Irishman*, October 1968.
135 E. McCann, *War and an Irish Town*, London, Pluto, 1980, p. 35.
136 'Unionists fear civil rights', *United Irishman*, October 1968.
137 Quoted in Cronin, *Irish Nationalism*, p. 190.
138 See 'Resistance', *United Irishman*, September 1969.
139 'The IRA in the 70s', *United Irishman*, January 1970.
140 See MacStiofain, op. cit., pp. 130–137.
141 Irish Republican Publicity Bureau (IRPB), statement 28 December 1969, reprinted in *An Phoblacht*, February 1970.
142 See Cronin, *Irish Nationalism*, p. 196.
143 *An Phoblacht* (CRA), May/June 1967.
144 *An Phoblacht* (CRA), January 1967.
145 *An Phoblacht* (CRA), October 1967.
146 Ibid.
147 MacStiofain, op. cit., p. 134.
148 Ibid., p. 113.
149 Quoted in P. Bishop and E. Mallie, *The Provisional IRA*, London, Heinemann, 1987, p. 92.
150 C. Goulding, IRA statement, *United Irishman*, September 1969. The original report was carried in *The Irish Times*, 19 August 1969.
151 See J. Mounter, 'Doubts on role of IRA in Belfast gun battles', *The Times*, 27 August 1969.
152 MacStiofain, op. cit., pp. 125–127.
153 T. MacGiolla, Speech to 1968 Sinn Fein Ard Fheis, reprinted in *United Irishman*, January 1969.
154 See C. de Baroid, *Ballymurphy and the Irish War*, London, Pluto, 1990, pp. 37–38.
155 Quoted in Cronin, *Irish Nationalism*, p. 204.
156 Adams, op. cit., p. 8.

157 G. Adams, 'Adams on republicanism and socialism', *Fortnight*, September 1983.
158 Ibid.
159 Statement issued subsequent to a meeting of the PSF Caretaker Executive 17 January 1970. This statement was reprinted in *An Phoblacht*, February 1970.
160 Ibid.
161 'Unionism and Paisley – an analysis', *United Irishman*, November 1966.
162 Ibid.
163 J. (Sean) Garland, 'Building revolution', *United Irishman*, May 1971.
164 Ibid.
165 'IRA New Year statement', *United Irishman*, January 1972.
166 Quoted in *The Irish Times*, 9 July 1971, cited in Hepburn, op. cit., p. 190.
167 'Para HQ blasted at Aldershot', *United Irishman*, March 1972.
168 Goulding statement in Sweetman, op. cit., p. 147.
169 Patterson, op. cit., pp. 140–141.
170 'In the shadow of a gunman', Part 1, *Magill*, April 1982.
171 See ibid. See also Part 2, *Magill*, May 1982.

4 THE MILITARY ASCENDANCY – THE PROVISIONAL IRA ON THE OFFENSIVE, 1970–1972

1 S. MacStiofain, *Memoirs of a Revolutionary*, Edinburgh, Gordon Cremonesi, 1975, p. 138.
2 Minutes of the Sinn Fein Provisional Committee, 17 January 1970. These minutes comprise the handwritten notes of Ruairi O Bradaigh.
3 Ibid.
4 MacStiofain, op. cit., p. 146.
5 Ibid., p. 146.
6 See D. Hamill, *Pig in the Middle*, London, Methuen, 1985, pp. 72–73.
7 See *The Sunday Times* Insight Team, *Ulster*, London, Penguin, 1972, p. 204.
8 See for example R. Moss, 'The security of Ulster', in *Conflict Studies*, London, Institute for the Study of Conflict, November 1971, p. 18.
9 C. de Baroid, *Ballymurphy and the Irish War*, London, Pluto, 1990, pp. 57–58.
10 *Freedom Struggle by the Provisionals*, n.p., PSF, n.d. (c. 1973), p. 25.
11 See J. Sluka, *Hearts and Minds, Water and Fish: Support for the IRA and INLA in a Northern Irish Ghetto*, Greenwich, Conn., JAI Press, 1989, pp. 270–275.
12 P. Bishop and E. Mallie, *The Provisional IRA*, London, Heinemann, p. 114.
13 C. Cruise O'Brien, *States of Ireland*, London, Hutchinson, 1972, pp. 205–207.
14 See F. Burton, *The Politics of Legitimacy*, London, Routledge & Kegan Paul, 1978, pp. 68–127, especially p. 106.
15 'IRA versus the Provisionals', *The Observer*, 14 February 1971.
16 D. Mansfield and T. Rogerson, 'IRA in Northern Ireland', in B. O'Neill et al., (eds), *Political Violence and Insurgency*, Arvada, Colorado, Phoenix, 1974, p. 130.
17 I. McAllister, *The Northern Ireland Social Democratic and Labour Party*, London, Macmillan, 1977, p. 98.
18 P. Walsh, *From Civil Rights to National War: Northern Ireland Catholic Politics, 1964–1974*, Belfast, Athol, 1989, p. 57.
19 Interview with R. O Bradaigh, *This Week*, 16 August 1970.
20 PSF Statement, *An Phoblacht*, February 1970.
21 D. O Conaill, Bodenstown speech, *An Phoblacht*, July 1970.
22 *Belfast Telegraph* interview with R. O Bradaigh, reprinted in *An Phoblacht*, September 1971.
23 See for example, 'Protestant dog ready to bite', *The Sunday Times*, 24 August 1969.
24 *Belfast Telegraph* interview with R. O Bradaigh, reprinted in *An Phoblacht*, September 1971.

25 'Our aims and methods', *An Phoblacht*, March 1970.
26 S. MacStiofain, statement in R. Sweetman, *On Our Knees*, London, Pan, 1972, p. 156.
27 Quoted in *The Times*, 7 April 1970.
28 MacStiofain, *Memoirs of a Revolutionary*, p. 146.
29 Bishop and Mallie, op. cit., p. 135.
30 Quoted in *The Irish Times*, 18 March 1971.
31 S. MacStiofain, statement from Army Council, *Republican News*, 30 October 1971.
32 Figures for shootings and bombing incidents (including devices defused) from *Irish Information Agenda*, London, Irish Information Partnership, 1987, Table B7i, For deaths, Table B1vi, p. 1 and Table 1 in W. Flackes and S. Elliott, *Northern Ireland: A Political Directory*, Belfast, Blackstaff, 1989, p. 411.
33 'Resist, resist, resist', *Republican News*, 4 September 1971.
34 M. McGuire, *To Take Arms*, London, Macmillan, 1973, p. 74.
35 Ibid., pp. 74–75.
36 Quoted in Bishop and Mallie, op. cit., p. 140. See also Burton, op. cit., p. 82.
37 Quoted in *The Times*, 30 July 1971.
38 *Belfast Telegraph* interview with R. O Bradaigh, reprinted in *An Phoblacht*, September 1971.
39 *Republican News*, April 1971.
40 Ibid.
41 D.G. Boyce, 'Water for the fish', in Y. Alexander and A. O'Day (eds), *Terrorism in Ireland*, London, Croom Helm, 1984, p. 166.
42 Quoted in K. Kelley, *The Longest War*, London, Zed, 1982, p. 153.
43 MacStiofain, *Memoirs of a Revolutionary*, p. 243.
44 Ibid., p. 243.
45 *Freedom Struggle by the Provisionals*, p. 34.
46 *The Irish Times*, 20 December 1971.
47 Burton, op. cit., pp. 82–83.
48 Ibid., p. 83.
49 RUC Statistical Information, Belfast, RUC Information Office, 1989.
50 RUC information supplied by letter, 14 June 1990. Yearly statistics on recruitment are published in the *Chief Constable's Annual Report*, Belfast, RUC. See also C. Ryder, *RUC: A force Under Fire*, London, Methuen, 1989, p. 127.
51 McGuire, op. cit., pp. 34–35.
52 Quoted in J. MacAnthony, 'Gun glory', *The Guardian*, 14 August 1971.
53 M. Turner, 'Living with bombs', *Fortnight*, 1 October 1971.
54 See table in T. O'Hanlon, *The Irish: Portrait of a People*, London, Andre Deutsch, 1976, p. 241.
55 T. Coogan, *The IRA*, London, Fontana, 1987, p. 471.
56 'Bring our boys home', *Republican News*, 2 October 1971.
57 *The Daily Telegraph*, 11 October 1971.
58 *Republican News*, 2 January 1972.
59 R. O Bradaigh, *Our People: Our Future*, Dublin, PSF, 1973, p. 24.
60 MacStiofain, op. cit., p. 241.
61 See McAllister, op. cit., p. 103.
62 See Flackes and Elliott, op. cit., pp. 402–404 and Hamill, op. cit., p. 65.
63 See 'The balance of military forces', in *The Ulster Debate*, London, Institute for the Study of Conflict, 1972, p. 53.
64 P. Janke, 'Ulster: a decade of violence', *Conflict Studies*, no. 108, June 1979, pp. 18–19. See also Appendix 1 in M. Arthur, *Northern Ireland: Soldiers Talking*, London, Sidgwick & Jackson, 1987, p. 255.
65 McGuire, op. cit., pp. 110.
66 'Dail Uladh – IRA: step towards a political solution', *An Phoblacht*, September 1971.

67   See *Freedom Struggle by the Provisionals*, p. 44.
68   *The Irish Times*, 11 March 1972.
69   McGuire, op. cit., p. 100.
70   See *The Observer*, 26 March 1972.
71   See C. Keena, *A Biography of Gerry Adams*, Cork, Mercier, 1990, p. 14.
72   MacStiofain, op. cit., p. 241. See also p. 258.
73   *An Phoblacht*, April 1972.
74   MacStiofain, op. cit., p. 261.
75   Ibid., p. 269.
76   Deaths through violence, 1969–72: 679. Deaths through road accidents, 1969–72: 1,205. Source: RUC Statistics.
77   Bishop and Mallie, op. cit., p. 132.
78   Quoted in R. Fisk, 'Both IRA wings say: "We fight on"', *The Times*, 3 April 1972.
79   'No truce on these terms', *Republican News*, Easter Sunday, 1972.
80   *Freedom Struggle by the Provisionals*, p. 67.
81   MacStiofain, op. cit., pp. 281–283.
82   Keena, op. cit., p. 20.
83   W. Whitelaw, *The Whitelaw Memoirs*, London, Aurum, 1989, pp. 99–100.
84   Ibid., p. 100.
85   J. Cahill, Bodenstown speech, *An Phoblacht*, July 1971.
86   Quoted in K. McCool, 'Valuable lesson in British duplicity', *AP/RN*, 6 August 1987.
87   Quoted in J. Bowyer Bell, *The Secret Army*, Dublin, Poolbeg, 1989, p. 384.
88   MacStiofain, op. cit., p. 285.
89   D. Breatnach, 'The republican ethic', *An Phoblacht*, July 1970.
90   Quoted in McCool, op. cit.
91   'Provisionals call off ceasefire after army clash in Belfast', *The Times*, 10 July 1972.
92   Quoted in *The Irish Press*, 9 July 1972.
93   '1am: UDA puts loyalists on war footing', *The Guardian*, 11 July 1972.
94   MacStiofain, op. cit., p. 294.
95   Ibid., p. 295.
96   S. Winchester and S. Hoggart, '11 dead, 100 hurt in hour of bombs', *The Guardian*, 22 July 1972.
97   Quoted in *The Daily Telegraph*, 22 July 1972.
98   Hamill, op. cit., pp. 107–113.
99   P. Chippindale, 'Motorman's slow drive', *The Guardian*, 26 August 1972.
100 'Whitelaw: I won't meet IRA again', *The Sunday Times*, 23 July 1972.
101 Whitelaw, op. cit., p. 101.
102 Quoted in G. McKnight, *The Mind of the Terrorist*, London, Michael Joseph, 1974, p. 74.
103 Ibid., p. 75.
104 McGuire, op. cit., p. 73.
105 See D. Coyle, 'Provisional IRA hints at modified truce conditions', *The Financial Times*, 5 April 1972.
106 McGuire, op. cit., pp. 104–105.
107 M. McGuire, 'I accuse Sean MacStiofain', *The Observer*, 3 September 1972.
108 See S. Winchester, 'Belfast Provisionals want no truck with a truce', *The Guardian*, 20 July 1972.
109 Quoted in Bishop and Mallie, op. cit., p. 152.
110 McGuire, *To Take Arms*, p. 145.
111 Ibid., p. 128.
112 Ibid., p. 147.
113 See M. Holland, 'Why IRA broke the truce', *The Observer*, 16 July 1972.
114 M. McGuire, 'I accuse Sean MacStiofain', *The Observer*, 3 September 1972.
115 'Sean MacStiofain reads message from Provisional Government', *Republican News*, 10 November 1972.

116   M. McGuire, 'I accuse Sean MacStiofain', *The Observer*, 3 September 1972.
117   Quoted in Kelley, op. cit., p. 186.
118   I. Rowan and G. Kemp, 'Why bombing goes on', *The Sunday Telegraph*, 2 April 1972.

5 THE EROSION OF PROVISIONAL IRA STRATEGY, 1972–1977

1   Quoted in G. McKnight, *The Mind of the Terrorist*, London, Michael Joseph, 1974, p. 68.
2   *Irish Information Agenda*, London, Irish Information Partnership, p. 2 of Table B1vi.
3   See A. Guelke, *Northern Ireland: The International Perspective*, Dublin, Gill & Macmillan, 1988, p. 64.
4   For a survey of loyalist paramilitary strategies see A. Aughey, 'Sectarian conflict, 1972–1977', in K. Jeffery (ed.), *The Divided Province*, London, Orbis, 1987, pp. 80–85.
5   M. Dillon and D. Lehane, *Political Murder in Northern Ireland*, London, Penguin, 1973, p. 101.
6   See S. Loughran, 'The working class of the Falls and Shankill are all Irish', *Republican News*, 23 February 1973.
7   S. O Rian, *Provos: Patriots or Terrorists?*, Dublin, Irish Book Bureau, 1974, p. 17.
8   'Motiveless murders work of British Army squads', *Republican News*, 9 March 1974.
9   'British murder gangs step-up campaign', *Republican News*, 2 February 1973.
10   Dillon and Lehane, op. cit., pp. 292–318.
11   Ibid., p. 318. Republicans both then and since have alleged that loyalist paramilitaries and the security forces routinely collude in attacks on republican targets. Evidence for this charge is patchy. For an assessment see S. Bruce, *The Red Hand*, Oxford, Oxford University Press, 1992, pp. 199–207 and pp. 273–276.
12   'Invitation to the UDA', *Republican News*, 16 February 1973.
13   Dillon and Lehane, op. cit., pp. 75–90.
14   D. O Conaill, quoted in *The Irish Times*, 14 July 1973.
15   Quoted in F. Burton, *The Politics of Legitimacy*, London, Routledge & Kegan Paul, 1978, p. 101.
16   M. McGuire, 'I accuse Sean MacStiofain', *The Observer*, 3 September 1972.
17   Interview with S. Loughran, *Andersonstown News*, 18 January 1975.
18   'Freeman' (D. Fennell), 'For whom is the revolution', *An Phoblacht*, 14 March 1975.
19   Quoted in *The Daily Telegraph*, 19 April 1976.
20   S. Hoggart, 'Wilson blows open IRA battle plans', *The Guardian*, 14 May 1974.
21   According to Colin Wallace, a former British Army information officer, the interpretation of the documents was intentionally slanted as part of an army disinformation exercise, *The Media Programme*, Channel 4, 29 April 1990.
22   'Republican plans', *People's News*, PSF, North Belfast, 19 May 1974.
23   Quoted in P. Hetherington, 'Scorched earth key to terror tactics', *The Guardian*, 14 May 1974.
24   Ibid.
25   J. Holland, 'The third battalion at home', *Hibernia*, 2 July 1976.
26   Dillon and Lehane, op. cit., p. 247.
27   Quoted in G. Wansell, 'Defector who finds life too quiet', *The Times*, 22 February 1973.
28   *Fortnight*, 29 October 1971.
29   M. McGuire, *To Take Arms*, London, Macmillan, 1973, p. 95.

30 Ibid., p. 135.
31 Quoted in *The Daily Telegraph*, 25 November 1972.
32 S. MacStiofain statement, in R. Sweetman, *On Our Knees*, London, Pan, 1972, p. 157.
33 'Behind the assassinations', *Hibernia*, 25 October 1974.
34 D. Brown, 'Why sectarian blood greases the Provisionals' path', *The Guardian*, 7 January 1976.
35 See R. Ned Lebow, 'The origins of sectarian assassination: the case of Belfast', in A. Olson and D. Buckley (eds), *International Terrorism*, Wayne, N.J., Avery, 1980, pp. 43–44.
36 P. Eddy and C. Ryder, 'Seven bloody days in Ulster', *The Sunday Times*, 4 February 1973.
37 'MacMoney', 'Bandit country', *Fortnight*, 23 January 1976.
38 L. MacLiam, 'Republicans must rely on their own strength and unity of purpose', *Republican News*, 6 March 1976.
39 G. Adams, *Peace in Ireland: A Broad Analysis of the Present Situation*, Long Kesh, PSF, 1976, p. 14.
40 'Ulsterisation', *The Volunteer*, Lurgan, PSF, 7 May 1977.
41 Adams, op. cit., p. 11.
42 'London bombings', *The Voice*, West Belfast, PSF, 5 February 1977.
43 M. Holland, 'Why Britain is still the prime target', *The Observer*, 13 February 1977.
44 'Ulsterisation', *The Volunteer*, Lurgan, PSF, 7 May 1977.
45 *Der Spiegal* interview with S. Twomey, reprinted in *The Daily Express*, 20 November 1973.
46 See T. Thornton, 'Terror as a weapon of political agitation', in H. Eckstein (ed.), *Internal War*, New York, Collier-Macmillan, 1964, p. 81.
47 P. Arnlis, 'Nature of strategy, politics, revolution, British withdrawal', *Republican News*, 27 March 1976.
48 Ibid.
49 P. Chippindale, 'The time bomb that blew up IRA', *The Guardian*, 15 November 1973.
50 P. Arnlis, 'Nature of strategy, politics, revolution, British withdrawal', *Republican News*, 27 March 1976.
51 See P. Chippindale, 'Gunning for the upper classes', *The Guardian*, 29 November 1973.
52 Quoted in K. Kelley, *The Longest War*, London, Zed, 1982, p. 242.
53 See P. Chippindale, 'Capital punishment', *The Guardian*, 19 March 1976.
54 Quoted in P. Chippindale, 'Gunning for the upper classes', *The Guardian*, 29 November 1973.
55 This interview was reprinted in *Republican News*, 30 November 1974.
56 See 'Why Provos brought terror to Britain', *The Sunday Times*, 23 November 1974.
57 See for example, 'Angry MPs pledge support for "no appeasement" promise', *The Times*, 23 November 1974.
58 Home Secretary's broadcast on emergency measures, 25 November 1974, London Press Service (Verbatim Service), 228/74, 26 November 1974.
59 See 'The guilty men', *Fortnight*, April 1991.
60 D. Brown, 'Taking stock of the Provos', *The Guardian*, 3 December 1974.
61 P. Chippindale, 'Army fears that more is to come', *The Guardian*, 23 November 1974.
62 *Sunday Press* interview with D. O Conaill, reprinted by Irish Republican Information Service (IRIS), 6 December 1974.
63 Ibid.
64 M. Rees, *Northern Ireland: A Personal Perspective*, London, Methuen, 1985, pp. 176–177.

65   Ibid., pp. 180–181.
66   W.D. Flackes and S. Elliott, *Northern Ireland: A Political Directory*, Belfast, Blackstaff, p. 412 and 415.
67   'IRA split by struggle for power', *The Sunday Telegraph*, 22 December 1974.
68   'Death of a ceasefire', *The Sunday Times*, 19 December 1974.
69   'Ceasefire extended to 16th January', *Republican News Evening Edition*, 2 January 1975.
70   'Army statement on ceasefire', *Republican News*, 25 January 1975.
71   'Army council want negotiations', *Republicans News Evening Edition*, 22 January 1975.
72   Rees, op. cit., p. 248.
73   *Republican News*, 19 April 1975.
74   Quoted in K. Myers, 'IRA peace by stealth?', *The Observer*, 22 December 1974.
75   'Peace by ordeal', *Republican News*, 5 July 1975.
76   See Rees, op. cit., pp. 154–155.
77   Quoted in 'Death of a ceasefire', *The Sunday Times*, 19 December 1974.
78   'Peace by ordeal', *Republican News*, 5 July 1975.
79   Interview with S. Costello, *The Starry Plough*, April 1975.
80   Kelley, op. cit., p. 232.
81   See 'The republican feud', *Fortnight*, November 1975.
82   J. Holland, 'Provo police in action', *Hibernia*, 14 November 1975.
83   *Republican News*, 23 February 1974.
84   'Congratulations to the IRA', *Eire Og*, West Belfast, PSF, 18 October 1975.
85   'Ceasefire crumbles as IRA blasts Belfast buildings', *The Daily Telegraph*, 10 April 1975.
86   'Christmas message from the Belfast brigade', *Republican News*, 28 December 1975.
87   'MacMoney', 'Bandit Country', *Fortnight*, 23 January 1976.
88   *The Observer* Foreign News Service, No. 34806, 1 May 1976.
89   'IRA interview', *Iris*, April 1981.
90   L. MacLiam, 'IRA aims are clear cut', *Republican News*, 29 May 1974.
91   Interview with S. Loughran, *Andersonstown News*, 18 January 1975. See also P. Bishop and E. Mallie, *The Provisional IRA*, London, Heinemann, 1987, p. 220.
92   See I. Rowan, 'Why Rees moved to reassure the Provisionals', *The Sunday Telegraph*, 27 July 1975.
93   PIRA Easter statement 1975, Dublin, March 1975.
94   *An Phoblacht*, 28 February 1975.
95   *Republican News*, 2 January 1972.
96   *An Phoblacht*, 4 January 1974.
97   'Provisionals confident of victory', IRIS, 3 February 1977.
98   Source: Northern Ireland Attitude Survey, in E. Moxon-Browne, *Nation, Class and Creed in Northern Ireland*, Aldershot, Gower, 1983, p. 116.
99   'Republican army pledge – we fight on', *Republican News*, 13 March 1976.
100 'We want our country', *Republican News*, 2 June 1973.
101 *Republican News*, 24 August 1974.
102 R. O Bradaigh, 'British disengagement now inevitable', IRIS, 24 October 1975.
103 *Nation*, West Belfast, PSF, 4 January 1976.
104 *The Volunteer*, West Belfast, PSF, December 1976.
105 'We are winning', *Republican News*, 9 April 1977.
106 'Victory for the IRA', *An Phoblacht*, July 1972.
107 'We are winning', *Republican News*, 9 April 1977.
108 'British army starts withdrawal', *Republican News*, 8 December 1974.
109 *Eire Nua*, PSF journal, January 1977.
110 'We want our country', *Republican News*, 2 June 1973.

111 Quoted in 'Victory is ours for the taking', *An Phoblacht*, 19 October.1973.
112 Quoted in *The Ulster Newsletter*, 20 September 1976.
113 See Guelke, op. cit., p. 205.
114 E. Davis and R. Sinnott, *Attitudes in the Republic of Ireland Relevant to the Northern Ireland Problem*, Dublin, ESRI, 1979, p. 88.
115 P. Arnlis, 'Nature of strategy, politics, revolution, British withdrawal', *Republican News*, 27 March 1976.
116 D. McCusker, 'No future without freedom', *Republican News Evening Edition*, July 1973.
117 'Dustin', 'The neology of a military campaign', *Republican News*, 10 April 1976.
118 C. Lambe, 'British go home', *Republican News*, 23 June 1973.
119 *An Phoblacht*, 14 September 1973.
120 See R. Jervis, *Perception and Misperception in International Politics*, Princeton, N.J., Princeton University Press, 1976, esp. pp. 288–315 and pp. 382–406.
121 See for example D. Larson, *Origins of Containment: A Psychological Explanation*, Princeton, N.J., Princeton University Press, 1985, pp. 46–47.
122 T. Nelis, 'Guerrilla warfare', *Republican News*, 13 July 1974.
123 'The Provos', *Eire Og*, 16 October 1975.
124 Quoted in *The Ulster Newsletter*, 2 February 1976.
125 Flackes and Elliott, op. cit., Table 5, p. 415.

6 THE EVOLUTION OF PIRA'S TOTAL STRATEGY, 1977–1983

1 P. Arnlis, 'The Brit withdrawal', *Republican News*, January 1977.
2 See Table 1, in W.D. Flackes and S. Elliott, *Northern Ireland: A Political Directory*, Belfast, Blackstaff, 1989, p. 411.
3 See for example, 'Irish targets for Irish republicans', *Fortnight*, November 1983.
4 See *Republican News*, 28 February 1976.
5 *A Broader Base: The Need for Local Involvement*, Dublin, PSF, 1974, p. 2.
6 See P. Bishop and E. Mallie, *The Provisional IRA*, London, Heinemann, 1987, p. 250.
7 *Staff Report*, PIRA, c. 1977, reprinted in L. Clarke, *Broadening the Battlefield*, Dublin, Gill & Macmillan, 1987, pp. 251–253.
8 See 'The IRA shifts to new type of terrorism', *The Christian Science Monitor*, 6 August 1973.
9 *Northern Ireland: Future Terrorist Trends*, Ministry of Defence, 2 November 1978, reprinted in S. Cronin, *Irish Nationalism*, Dublin, Academy, 1980, p. 342.
10 D. Morrison, in M. Collins (ed.), *Ireland After Britain*, London, Pluto, 1985, p. 84.
11 See G. Adams, *The Politics of Irish Freedom*, Dingle, Co. Kerry, Brandon, 1986, p.150.
12 G. Adams, Bobby Sands Memorial Lecture, 5 May 1985, reprinted in *Iris*, July 1985.
13 Interview with member of PIRA leadership, *Magill*, August 1978.
14 Text of the PSF Memorandum to the Gardner Committee, reprinted in *Fortnight*, 10 January 1975.
15 R. Debray, *A Critique of Arms*, vol. I, London, Penguin, 1977, p. 134.
16 P. Arnlis, 'The Brit withdrawal', *Republican News*, January 1977.
17 *Staff Report*, in Clarke, op. cit., p. 253.
18 'Brownie' (G. Adams), 'Active republicanism', *Republican News*, 1 May 1976.
19 'Brownie', 'Revolutionary rules', *An Phoblacht/Republican News (AP/RN)*, 7 June 1982.
20 *Notes for Revolutionaries*, Belfast, PSF, 1982, p. 45.
21 Adams, *The Politics of Irish Freedom*, p. 58 and p. 150.

22 'Brownie', 'The republic a reality', *Republican News*, 29 November 1975.
23 See M. Oppenheimer, *The Urban Guerrilla*, London, Penguin, 1970, p. 59.
24 'Vindicator', 'Theory and practice', *Republican News*, 26 February 1977.
25 J. Drumm, Bodenstown speech, *An Phoblacht*, 15 June 1977.
26 Quoted in *The Christian Science Monitor*, 6 August 1973.
27 *Republican News*, 30 April 1975.
28 'Brownie', 'Revolutionary rules', *AP/RN*, 7 June 1982.
29 Army Council statement, *Republican News*, 28 January 1978.
30 *Hibernia* interview with G. Adams, reprinted in *AP/RN*, 3 November 1979.
31 G. Adams, Bodenstown speech, *AP/RN*, 26 June 1979.
32 Ibid.
33 P. Dowling, 'This we will maintain', *Republican News*, 26 November 1977.
34 P. Dowling, 'The British presence, partition and Protestant privilege', *AP/RN*, 22
    October 1981.
35 See D. McKittrick, 'Atkins accuses IRA of fomenting sectarian conflict', *The Irish
    Times*, 1 May 1981. See also Clarke, op. cit., pp. 150–151.
36 'War news', *AP/RN*, 19 November 1981.
37 'IRA: why we shot Bradford', *AP/RN*, 19 November 1981.
38 'Struggle on all fronts', *AP/RN*, 10 February 1979.
39 PSF press release, Dublin, 12 February 1979.
40 Quoted in *AP/RN*, 5 November 1981.
41 See 'The move to the left', *Magill*, September 1980.
42 See 'The politics of the H-Block', *Magill*, December 1980.
43 IRA spokesperson, 'We are here to stay', *AP/RN*, 1 April 1982.
44 *Republican News*, 10 June 1978.
45 *Statement of Aims*, Dublin, PSF, 25 October 1979.
46 T. MacGiolla, *The Struggle for Democracy, Peace and Freedom*, Dublin, Official
    Sinn Fein, 1975, p. 2.
47 D. Morrison, 'The Provos will not lay down their arms', *Fortnight*, December 1982.
48 Adams, *The Politics of Irish Freedom*, p. 64.
49 'Brownie', 'Active republicanism', *Republican News*, 1 May 1976.
50 'Only one message', *AP/RN*, 24 May 1980.
51 'IRA geared to a long war', *Republican News*, 9 December 1978.
52 *Staff Report*, in Clarke, op. cit., p. 252.
53 'IRA interview', *Iris*, April 1981.
54 'Build and consolidate', *AP/RN*, 3 June 1982.
55 Ibid.
56 See J. Barton, 'Long Kesh and the long war', *The Leveller*, no. 26, May 1979.
57 *AP/RN*, 12 April 1980.
58 Interview with PIRA spokesperson, *Iris*, July/August 1982.
59 Interview with PIRA spokespersons, *Magill*, July 1983.
60 'The IRA attitude to elections', *Iris*, November 1981.
61 'Peace and war', *AP/RN*, 7 October 1982.
62 Quoted in *The Irish News*, 3 November 1981.
63 Quoted in 'By ballot and bullet', *AP/RN*, 5 November 1981.
64 'The IRA attitude to elections', *Iris*, July/August 1982.
65 'IRA interview', *Iris*, April 1981.
66 Quoted in T. Coogan, *The IRA*, London, Fontana, 1987, p. 693.
67 'IRA interview', IRIS, 11 August 1979.
68 *Notes for Revolutionaries*, pp. 45–46.
69 Ibid., pp. 49–50.
70 Quoted in N. Kirby, 'IRA say Mountbatten killing will not be the last', *The Irish
    Times*, 1 September 1979.
71 See Adams, op. cit., p. 64.

72 See E. Moloney 'Where are the Provos going?', *Fortnight*, May 1983.
73 Quoted in P. O'Malley, *The Uncivil Wars*, Belfast, Blackstaff, 1983, p. 284.
74 *Notes for Revolutionaries*, pp. 48–49.
75 'IRA interview', IRIS, 11 August 1979.
76 Interview with PIRA spokesperson, *Iris*, July/August 1982.
77 *Northern Ireland: Future Terrorist Trends*, in Cronin, op. cit., p. 347.
78 Adams, op. cit., p. 86.
79 'IRA attitude on H-Block', *AP/RN*, 5 September 1981.
80 See Bishop and Mallie, op. cit., p. 294.
81 R. O Bradaigh, 'Election a turning point', *AP/RN*, 16 June 1983.
82 See E. Moxon-Browne, 'Alienation: the case of Catholics in Northern Ireland', in M. Slann and B. Schecterman (eds), *Multi-Dimensional Terrorism*, Boulder, Colorado, Westview, 1987, p. 105.
83 G. Adams, in M. Collins (ed.), *Ireland After Britain*, London, Pluto, 1985, p. 2.
84 'Prior fears rise of Sinn Fein', *The Financial Times*, 14 November 1983.
85 Interview with G. Adams, *Magill*, July 1983.
86 Quoted in Coogan, op. cit., p. 688.
87 'Brownie', 'Revolutionary rules', *AP/RN*, 7 June 1982.
88 Quoted in O'Malley, op. cit., p. 284.
89 D. Morrison, interview in *Marxism Today*, December 1981, cited in A. Aughey, 'Political violence in Northern Ireland', in H.H. Tucker (ed.), *Combating the Terrorists*, New York, Facts on File, 1988, p. 90.
90 Quoted in Coogan, op. cit., p. 688.
91 P. Dowling, 'Lessons of the Malvinas', *AP/RN*, 8 July 1982.
92 Quoted in 'Paisley's action day cheers republicans', *The Daily Telegraph*, 23 November 1981.
93 See T.C. Schelling, *The Strategy of Conflict*, Cambridge, Mass., Harvard University Press, pp. 53–67 and pp. 74–77.
94 Quoted in J. Adams, et al., *Ambush*, London, Pan, 1988, p. 89.
95 See P. Dowling, 'Lessons of Malvinas', *AP/RN*, 8 July 1982.
96 'Build and consolidate', *AP/RN*, 3 June 1983.
97 Morrison, in Collins, op. cit., p. 93.
98 P. Dowling, 'Lessons of Malvinas', *AP/RN*, 8 July 1982.
99 Morrison, in Collins, op. cit., p. 89.
100 'Brownie', 'Revolutionary rules', *AP/RN*, June 1982.
101 Adams, *The Politics of Irish Freedom*, p. 39.
102 Ibid., p. 47.
103 Quoted in Coogan, op. cit., p. 685.
104 G. Adams, Bodenstown speech, *AP/RN*, 26 June 1979.

7 A CONTINUING MILITARY ENIGMA – THE CONTRADICTORY DYNAMICS OF THE TOTAL STRATEGY, 1983–1990

1 C. Keena, *A Biography of Gerry Adams*, Cork, Mercier, 1990, p.107.
2 P. Bishop and E. Mallie, *The Provisional IRA*, London, Heinemann, 1987, p. 312.
3 See J. Adams, *The Financing of Terror*, Sevenoaks, New English Library, 1986, p. 166.
4 L. Clarke, *Broadening the Battlefield*, Dublin, Gill & Macmillan, 1987, p. 22.
5 See M. Holland, 'Why did IRA attack Brighton?', *The Sunday Press*, 7 October 1984.
6 'Provo split', *New Hibernia*, May 1985. See also *The Sunday Times*, 20 April 1985.
7 PIRA statement, reprinted in *The Irish Times*, 19 December 1983.
8 Interview with PIRA spokesperson, *AP/RN*, 5 January 1984.

9   G. Adams, *The Politics of Irish Freedom*, Dingle, Co. Kerry, Brandon, 1986, p. 64.
10   M. McGuinness, 'We will never be slaves again', *AP/RN*, 28 June 1984.
11   Quoted in 'The ballot and the bomb', *Magill*, July 1986.
12   Interview with G. Adams, *AP/RN*, 21 June 1984.
13   Interview with D. Morrison, *Magill*, September 1984.
14   *AP/RN*, 16 October 1986.
15   *Republican Bulletin*, RSF, 2 November 1986.
16   Quoted in G. Barry, 'The bullet or the ballot?', *The Sunday Tribune*, 26 October 1986.
17   Quoted in 'In the shadow of the gunmen', *The Guardian*, 28 January 1989.
18   G. Adams, 'Presidential address', in *The Politics of Revolution*, Dublin, PSF, 1986, p. 13.
19   *AP/RN*, 6 November 1986.
20   Quoted in 'The Armalite and the Dail', *The Sunday Tribune*, 14 September 1986.
21   Quoted in E. Moloney, 'Gunmen were doing their duty – Adams', *The Irish Times*, 19 December 1983.
22   *AP/RN*, 6 November 1986.
23   Adams, *The Politics of Irish Freedom*, p. 152.
24   M. McGuinness, 'We will never be slaves again', *AP/RN*, 28 June 1984.
25   Interview with G. Adams, *The Hillsborough Deal: Stepping Stone or Mill Stone?*, Dublin, PSF pamphlet, December 1985.
26   *Sinn Fein Policy Document*, Dublin, PSF, 1987, p. 14.
27   'Denis the Menace', 'Needs of the struggle', *Iris Bheag*, internal PSF discussion journal, no. 4, November 1987, p. 3.
28   Quoted in D. McKittrick, 'IRA's toll of civilian deaths grows despite public stance', *The Independent*, 13 April 1989.
29   *Fortnight*, March 1990.
30   Interview with M. McLaughlin, *AP/RN*, 25 May 1989.
31   Interview with G. Adams, *AP/RN*, 21 June 1984.
32   G. Adams, *Presidential Address, 84th Ard Fheis*, Dublin, PSF, 1989, p. 4.
33   'IRA interview', *AP/RN*, 26 January 1989.
34   E. Moloney, 'Mistaken strategy', *Fortnight*, May 1989.
35   See for example, *The Guardian*, *The Irish Press*, *The Irish News*, 13 October 1984 and *The Sunday Press*, 14 October 1984.
36   'A constant level of resistance', *Iris*, July 1983.
37   Even when PIRA's attacks do seem to coincide with political events, the republican movement rarely acknowledges any link. PIRA's bombing of the Baltic Exchange in the City of London, which killed three people, on 10 April 1992, might have seemed a classic case of a symbolic attack coinciding as it did with the results of the British general elections. However, *AP/RN's* reportage of the attack did not refer to the election in any form. See 'Massive explosion in City of London', *AP/RN*, 16 April 1992.
38   Quoted in 'Unprecedented casualties', *AP/RN*, 21 April 1979.
39   Clarke, op. cit., p. 227.
40   'Big test for ballot box supporters', *New Hibernia*, April 1985.
41   E. Moloney, 'Mistaken strategy', *Fortnight*, May 1989.
42   Interview with G. Adams, *The Last Post*, December 1987.
43   'IRA shatter "normality" facade', *AP/RN*, 20 June 1985.
44   Interview with G. Adams, *The Irish Press*, 23 November 1987.
45   'Why Sinn Fein?', *The Volunteer*, Lurgan, PSF, 2 February 1973.
46   Interview with G. Adams, *Magill*, August 1988.
47   Diary of events, *Fortnight*, January 1993.
48   Interview with G. Adams, *Magill*, August 1988.
49   Bishop and Mallie, op. cit., p. 304.

50 Clarke, op. cit., p. 231.
51 Quoted in P. Bishop, 'A gunmen cleans up his act', *The Observer*, 17 April 1983.
52 Interview with G. Adams, *The Last Post*, December 1987.
53 See K. Toolis, 'The British left after Brighton', *Fortnight*, November 1985.
54 Adams, *Presidential Address*, 1989, pp. 3–4.
55 G. Adams, 'Presidential address', *The Politics of Revolution*, Dublin, PSF, 1986, p. 11.
56 Sean Doite, 'After Enniskillen', *Iris Bheag*, no. 5, December 1987, p. 13.
57 M. McGuinness, 'We will never be slaves again', *AP/RN*, 28 June 1984.
58 Interview with PIRA spokesperson, *Magill*, July 1983.
59 Interview with PIRA spokesperson, *AP/RN*, 5 January 1984.
60 'Until Britain tires', *Sceal*, Newry, PSF, 29 September 1988.
61 Quoted in T. Coogan, *The IRA*, London, Fontana, 1987, pp. 691–692.
62 See Adams, *The Politics of Irish Freedom*, pp. 96–97.
63 Interview with R. O Bradaigh, *Iris*, April 1981.
64 Interview with PIRA spokespersons, *Magill*, July 1983.
65 'Adams says bombing had calculated aim', *The Irish Times*, 15 October 1984.
66 Quoted in 'RUC withhold comment on SF interview', *The Irish Times*, 15 October 1984.
67 PIRA interview, *AP/RN*, 5 January 1984.
68 D. O Conaill, quoted in P. O'Malley, *The Uncivil Wars*, Belfast, Blackstaff, 1983, p. 287.
69 PIRA interview, *AP/RN*, 5 January 1984.
70 *The Daily Express*, 10 February 1987.
71 *The Guardian*, 22 December 1980.
72 *New Society*, 6 September 1979.
73 E. Moxon-Browne, *Nation, Class and Creed in Northern Ireland*, Aldershot, Gower, 1988, p. 24.
74 In 1988 there were 125,904 licensed firearms in Northern Ireland. See *Chief Constable's Annual Report*, Belfast, HMSO, 1988, p. 26.
75 See K. Boyle and T. Hadden, *Ireland: A Positive Proposal*, London, Penguin, 1985, pp. 25–27.
76 H. MacThomas, 'British public says "no"', *AP/RN*, 12 February 1987.
77 *AP/RN*, 3 March 1988.
78 'Taking stock', *AP/RN*, 24 April 1986.
79 See Appendix A, J. Adams, et al., *Ambush*, London, Pan, 1988, pp. 191–192.
80 'Tyrone group one of most active', *The Irish Times*, 11 May 1987.
81 'A war of sacrifice and attrition', *Iris*, August 1984.
82 *Iris*, October 1987.
83 G. Adams, 'Presidential address', *AP/RN*, 7 November 1985.
84 See E. Moloney, 'Provos wait for the Anglo-Irish offensive', *Fortnight*, 21 October 1985.
85 'Attempt to isolate republicans', *AP/RN*, 21 November 1985.
86 'IRA not to be drawn,' *AP/RN*, 3 October 1985.
87 *Fortnight*, October 1986.
88 *Fortnight*, July/Aug. 1989.
89 'Denis the Menace', 'Needs of the struggle', *Iris Bheag*, no. 4, November 1987.
90 Interview with G. Adams, *The Irish People* (USA), 7 March 1987.
91 D. Morrison, *Ireland: The Censored Subject*, Dublin, PSF, 1989, pp. 9–10.
92 *Hillsborough – The Balance Sheet 1985–88: A Failure*, Dublin, PSF, 1989, p. 13.
93 Ibid., p. 13.
94 'Paxo', 'A question about Enniskillen', *Iris Bheag*, no. 5, December 1987, p. 16.
95 'Tonto', 'The internal conference – some reflections', *Iris Bheag*, no. 1, 1987, pp. 5–6.

96 D. Morrison, 'Bad language (1)', *Iris Bheag*, no. 3, 1987, pp. 7–8.
97 'A bus ride to independence and socialism' speech given to PSF internal conference 1986 in G. Adams, *Signposts to Independence and Socialism*, Dublin, PSF, 1988, p. 16.
98 G. Adams, *Towards a Strategy for Peace*, letter to J. Hume, PSF document no. 1, PSF–SDLP Talks, 14 March 1988, p. 20.
99 Ibid., p. 5.
100 J. Hume, letter to G. Adams, SDLP document no. 1, PSF–SDLP Talks, 18 March 1988, p. 5.
101 G. Adams, *A Pathway to Peace*, Cork, Mercier, 1988, p. 62.
102 Ibid., p. 77.
103 Adams, *Towards a Strategy for Peace*, p. 7.
104 Ibid., p. 8.
105 SDLP statement on end of PSF–SDLP Talks, *The Irish Times*, 6 September 1988.
106 PSF statement on end of PSF–SDLP Talks, *The Irish Times*, 6 September 1988.

8 ENDING THE ISOLATION? ENDING THE VIOLENCE?

1 *The Guardian*, 11 February 1993
2 *The International Express*, 28 April–4 May 1993.
3 PIRA statement issued after the bombings of a Warrington gas works and Camden High Street, north London, on 26 and 27 February 1993 respectively. Quoted in *The Weekly Telegraph*, week ending, 7 March 1993.
4 Quoted in *The International Express*, 8–14 April 1993.
5 See for example, C. Ryder, 'IRA supporters debate calling end to violence', *The Daily Telegraph*, 23 March 1990.
6 See *The Economist*, 20 November 1993.
7 Troubles chronology, *Fortnight*, May 1992.
8 Quoted in R. Wilson, 'Time for magnanimity', *Fortnight*, September 1992.
9 'Determined and committed to success', *AP/RN*, 5 April 1990.
10 'Confronting British power in the 1990s', *AP/RN*, 5 April 1990.
11 M. McGuinness, 'A majority . . . on the island . . . are in favour of unification', *Fortnight*, April 1990.
12 Interview with GHQ spokesperson, Oglaigh na-hEireann, *AP/RN*, 28 June 1990.
13 'Planning for peace in the '90s', *AP/RN*, 29 March 1990.
14 See *Towards a Lasting Peace in Ireland*, manifesto Westminster election, Belfast, PSF, April 1992.
15 G. Adams, 'There is one way – and that is forward', *AP/RN*, 3 March 1994.
16 *The Irish Times*, 27 September 1993.
17 Quoted in Troubles chronology, 3 October 1993, *Fortnight*, November 1993.
18 *The Irish Times*, 2 October 1993.
19 Quoted in *The Weekly Telegraph*, 27 October 1993.
20 Quoted in Reuter report, *The Straits Times*, 3 November 1993.
21 Quoted in *The Weekly Telegraph*, 27 October–2 November 1993.
22 'The burdens of Ulster', *The Economist*, 30 October 1993.
23 *Sunday Life*, 11 July 1993. It is conceivable that James Molyneaux had been kept informed about the secret contacts by official British sources all along.
24 Quoted in 'Provisionals "want way out"', *The Weekly Telegraph*, 20–26 January 1993.
25 Disputed PIRA message, 22 February 1993, text of PIRA–British exchanges, reprinted in *The Weekly Telegraph*, 8–14 December 1993.
26 Quoted in ibid.
27 British message, 19 March 1993, in ibid.

28 Ibid.
29 PIRA message, 10 May 1993, in ibid.
30 British message, 5 May 1993, in ibid.
31 British message, 19 March 1993, in ibid.
32 Ibid.
33 PIRA message, 22 July 1993, in ibid.
34 Ibid.
35 PIRA message, 10 May 1993, in ibid.
36 PIRA message, 14 August 1993, in ibid.
37 PIRA message, 22 July 1993, in ibid.
38 Ibid.
39 Ibid.
40 Quoted in M. O'Doherty, 'Shh . . . SF', *Fortnight*, December 1993.
41 Text of Downing Street declaration, reprinted in *The Weekly Telegraph*, 22–28 December 1993.
42 Quoted in ibid.
43 Quoted in 'Major warns IRA of isolation', *The Weekly Telegraph*, 5–11 January 1994.
44 A. McIntyre, 'Not worth the paper', *Fortnight*, February 1994.
45 Ibid.
46 Quoted in 'Three IRA attacks on airport', *The Weekly Telegraph*, 16–22 March 1994.
47 Quoted in Reuter report, *The Straits Times*, 15 March 1994.
48 Quoted in Agence France Press report, *The Straits Times*, 5 April 1994.
49 Ibid.
50 Quoted in P. Johnston and C. Randall, 'Mayhew warned of Ulster trap', *The Daily Telegraph*, 16 May 1994.
51 Quoted in P. Johnston, 'A critical point for Irish peace', *The Daily Telegraph*, 20 May 1994.
52 Quoted in S. Breen, 'Wrong again', *Fortnight*, June 1994.
53 R. Savill and R. Shrimsley, 'Ulster peace deal rejected by Sinn Fein', *The Weekly Telegraph*, 27 July–2 August 1994.
54 Quoted in P. Johnston, 'Hardliners reject Ulster peace push', *The Weekly Telegraph*, 9–15 August 1994.
55 See H. Patterson, 'Wishful thinking', *Fortnight*, April 1994.
56 R. Savill and R. Shrimsley, 'Ulster peace deal rejected by Sinn Fein', *The Weekly Telegraph*, 27 July–2 August 1994.
57 Quoted in 'IRA told time is running out', *The Weekly Telegraph*, 12–18 January 1994.
58 A. MacIntyre, 'Not worth the paper', *Fortnight*, February 1994.
59 Quoted in Troubles chronology, 25 July 1994, *Fortnight*, September 1994.
60 Quoted in Reuter/*New York Times* report, *The Straits Times*, 30 August 1994.
61 See 'Believe it or not', *The Economist*, 20 August 1994.
62 PIRA statement reprinted in 'At last?', *The Economist*, 3 September 1994.
63 See K. Cullen, 'Wearing thin', *Fortnight*, September 1994.
64 Ulster Marketing Survey for Independent Television News, cited in M. O'Doherty, 'Ourselves plus', *Fortnight*, February 1994.
65 D. McKittrick, 'N. Ireland: After the killings, hopes of peace', *The Straits Times*, 7 September 1994.
66 *The Irish Press*, 3 August 1994, cited in Troubles chronology, *Fortnight*, September 1994.
67 'Britain ready to launch trade-off with Dublin', *The Weekly Telegraph*, 31 August–6 September 1994.
68 See 'Rula Law', 'Excuse me, I'm a lawyer', *Fortnight*, September 1994.

69 Quoted in Reuter/*New York Times* report, *The Straits Times*, 5 September 1994.
70 See S. Bruce, 'Fear and loathing', *Fortnight*, September 1994.
71 See N. Stack, 'Come off it – Gerry Adams is definitely no Nelson Mandela', *The Business Times*, 17–18 September 1994.
72 Quoted in D. McKittrick, 'N. Ireland: After the killings hopes of peace', *The Straits Times*, 7 September 1994.
73 From *USA Today* report, *The Straits Times*, 3 September 1994.
74 According to a report in the *Irish Independent*, 11 August 1994, Irish army documents warned of the growing loyalist paramilitary threat to the Irish Republic. Cited in Troubles chronology, *Fortnight*, September 1994.
75 See for example D. McKittrick, 'Semtex in terrorist armoury is key to growing threat', *The Independent*, 31 December 1988.
76 Quoted in 'The battle to make the real peace out of the ceasefire', *International Express*, 8–14 September 1994.
77 At the time of writing the British government were inching their way towards a formal recognition of PIRA's ceasefire as permanent. See 'Peace deal with IRA is close', *The Weekly Telegraph*, 14–20 September 1994.
78 Quoted in Reuter/Associated Press report, *The Straits Times*, 2 September 1994.
79 Quoted in Reuter report, *The Straits Times*, 3 September 1994.
80 See for example 'But the Provos keep up their arms supplies', *International Express*, 8–14 September 1994.
81 Quoted in S. Breen, 'No surrender', *Fortnight*, September 1994.
82 See ibid.
83 Quoted in Reuter/Associated press report, *The Straits Times*, 6 September 1994.
84 Reuter report, *The Straits Times*, 14 October 1994.
85 Quoted in R. Wilson, 'Don't hold your breath', *Fortnight*, September 1994.
86 Quoted in D. Pedersen, 'Slouching toward peace', *Newsweek*, 12 September 1994.

CONCLUSION

1 M. McGuinness, 'Discarding the fetters of republican myth', *Fortnight*, 3 March 1985.
2 G. Adams, 'Presidential address', *The Politics of Revolution*, Dublin, PSF, 1986, p. 9.
3 'Freedom – much more than the right to vote', speech delivered in April 1988, in G. Adams, *Signposts to Independence and Socialism*, Dublin, PSF, 1989, p. 5.
4 *AP/RN*, 14 July 1988.
5 G. Adams, *A Pathway to Peace*, Cork, Mercier, 1988, p. 41.
6 D. Morrison, in M. Collins (ed.), *Ireland After Britain*, London, Pluto, 1985, p. 92.
7 Quoted in 'Beyond ideology', *Fortnight*, October 1992.
8 G. Adams, 'There is only one way – and that is forward', *AP/RN*, 3 March 1994.
9 See S. Bruce, *The Red Hand*, Oxford, Oxford University Press, 1992, p. 278.
10 G. Adams, *The Politics of Irish Freedom*, Dingle, Co. Kerry, Brandon, 1986, p. 120.
11 D. McKittrick, 'Decades of violence in a world of stalemate', *The Independent*, 14 August 1989.
12 M. McGuinness, *Bodenstown 1986*, text of oration to annual Wolfe Tone commemoration, London, Wolfe Tone Society, 1986.
13 Ibid.
14 Examples of allusions to such theorists in the early/mid-1970s can be found in the following: *An Phoblacht*, 1 February 1974 (Liddell Hart), *Republican News*, 29 May 1974 (reference to Clausewitzian theories), *Republican News*, 13 July 1974 (Taber and Mao), *The Volunteer*, Derry, August 1974 (Taber), *Eire Og*, 18 October 1975 (reference to Marighela's theories), and *Republican News*, 8 January 1977 (Taber).

15 See for example, *Iris Bheag*, nos. 2, 3, 4, 5 (1987) and 6, 8, 12 (1988).

16 *Notes for Revolutionaries*, Belfast, PSF, 1982, pp. 27–40.

17 '*Playboy* Interview: the IRA', reprinted in *Magill*, March 1989.

18 M. McGuinness, 'The right to freedom', Bobby Sands Memorial Lecture, 10 May 1987, reprinted in *AP/RN*, 28 May 1987.

19 Interview with G. Adams, *Magill*, July 1983.

20 *AP/RN*, 25 April 1985.

21 Interview with PIRA spokesperson, *Magill*, August 1978.

22 *AP/RN*, 16 April 1987.

23 Quoted in p. O'Malley, *Northern Ireland: Questions of Nuance*, Belfast, Blackstaff, 1990, p. 57.

24 Easter message from the leadership of the republican movement, *AP/RN*, 19 April 1990.

25 G. Adams, 'There is only one way – and that is forward', *AP/RN*, 3 March 1994.

26 Quoted in O'Malley, op. cit., p. 59.

27 Quoted in M. O'Doherty, 'A distant victory', *New Statesman and Society*, 5 June 1992.

Bibliography

IRISH REPUBLICAN MATERIAL (IRA, PIRA/PSF, OIRA/OFFICIAL SINN FEIN, INLA/IRSP, RSF – INCLUDING PRO-TREATY IRA, 1921–1922)

Irish republican newspapers and periodicals

An Long – War Sheet
An Phoblacht, anti-Treaty IRA, 1920s–1930s.
An Phoblacht, Committee for Revolutionary Action, 1960s.
An Phoblacht, PIRA/PSF.
An Phoblacht/Republican News, PIRA/PSF.
Iris
Iris Bheag
The Nation, anti-Treaty, 1922.
Republican Bulletin
Republican News
Republican News Evening Edition
Republic of Ireland
The Free State
The Irish People
The Irish People, USA
The Last Post
The Plain People
The Starry Plough
The United Irishman

Local Irish republican newssheets

Eire Nua, n.p., probably Belfast, PSF.
Eire Og, Andersonstown, West Belfast, Hall-Petticrew PSF Cumann.
Nation, Clonard, West Belfast, Peader de Blaca/Tony Lewis/Danny O'Neill/Tom McCann/Clonard Martyrs PSF Cumainn.
The People's News, North Belfast, PSF North Belfast Comhairle Ceantir.
Sceal, Newry, South Down, John Mitchel and Newry Martyrs PSF Cumann.
The Voice, Moyard, West Belfast, O'Rawe-Bryson PSF Cumann.
The Volunteer, Andersonstown, West Belfast, PSF.
The Volunteer, Derry, PSF.
The Volunteer, Lurgan, Co. Armagh, PSF.

Other Irish republican news services

Irish Republican Information Service
PSF press releases
PSF statements

Irish republican pamphlets, booklets and manifestos

A Broader Base: The Need for Local Involvement, Dublin, PSF, 1974.
A Scenario For Peace, Dublin, PSF, 1987.
Adams, G., *Peace in Ireland: A Broad Analysis of the Present Situation*, Long Kesh nr. Belfast, PSF, 18 September 1976.
——, *Presidential Address*, 84th Ard Fheis, Dublin, PSF, 1989.
——, *Signposts to Independence and Socialism*, Dublin, PSF, 1988.
Bennett, J., 'The Northern conflict and British power', *Irish Sovereignty Movement Pamphlet*, no. 1, 1973.
'Constitutionalism and Sinn Fein', *Sinn Fein Pamphlets*, no. 5, n.p., Sinn Fein, n.d. (c. 1912–1916).
Clar, Ard Fheis Agenda, Sinn Fein, March 1926.
Easter Statement 1975, Dublin, PIRA, March 1975.
Freedom Struggle by the Provisionals, n.p. (probably Dublin), PSF, n.d. (c. 1973).
Freedom Struggle in Ireland, Dublin, PSF, n.d.
Handbook for Volunteers of the Irish Republican Army: Notes on Guerrilla Warfare, n.p., IRA GHQ, 1956.
Hillsborough – The Balance Sheet, 1985–88, Dublin, PSF, 1989.
McGarrity, J., *Resistance: The Story of the Struggle in British Occupied Ireland*, n.p., Irish Freedom Press, n.d. (c. 1957).
MacGiolla, T., *The Struggle for Democracy, Peace and Freedom*, Dublin, Repsol, 1975.
McGuinness, M., *Bodenstown '86*, London, Wolfe Tone Society 1986.
Morrison, D., *Ireland: The Censored Subject*, Dublin, PSF, 1989.
National Unity and Independence Programme, Dublin, Sinn Fein, n.d. (c. late 1920s/early 1930s).
Notes for Revolutionaries – A Collection of Notes, Quotes, Poems and Songs on all Aspects of the Republican Struggle, Belfast, PSF, 1982.
O Bradaigh, R., *Our People: Our Future*, Dublin, PSF, 1973.
O Gallachobair, P., 'By what authority?', *Eire: The Irish Nation*, no. 7, Dublin, Irish Nation Committee, 1922.
O Riain, S., *Provos: Patriots or Terrorists?*, Dublin, Irish Book Bureau, 1974.
Sinn Fein Policy Document 1987, Dublin, PSF, 1987.
Statement of Aims, Dublin, PSF, 25 October 1979.
The Hillsborough Deal: Stepping Stone or Millstone?, Dublin, PSF, 1985.
The Politics of Revolution, Dublin, PSF, 1986.
Towards a Lasting Peace in Ireland, manifesto Westminster election, Belfast, PSF, April 1992.

Memoirs, collections of speeches, documents and statistics

Adams, G., *A Pathway to Peace*, Cork, Mercier, 1988.
——, *The Politics of Irish Freedom*, Dingle, Co. Kerry, Brandon, 1986.
Barry, T., *Guerrilla Days in Ireland*, Tralee, Co. Kerry, Anvil, 1972.
Cronin, S., *The McGarrity Papers*, Tralee, Co. Kerry, Anvil, 1972.
Davis, E.E. and Sinott, R., *Attitudes in the Republic of Ireland Relevant to the Northern Ireland Problem*, Dublin, Economic and Social Research Institute, 1979.

Davitt, M., *The Fall of Feudalism in Ireland, or the Story of the Land League Revolutions*, London, Harper, 1904.

Deasy, L. *Towards Free Ireland: The West Cork Brigade in the War of Independence*, Dublin, Mercier, 1973.

Devoy, J., *Recollections of an Irish Rebel*, Shannon, Irish University Press, 1969.

Edwards, O. Dudley and Ransom, B. (eds.), *James Connolly: Selected Political Writings*, New York, Grove, 1973.

Ellis, P. Beresford (ed.), *James Connolly: Selected Writings*, London, Pluto, 1988.

Hepburn, A.C. (ed.), *The Conflict of Nationality in Modern Ireland*, London, Edward Arnold, 1980.

Heron, J. Connolly (ed.), *The Words of James Connolly*, Cork, Mercier, 1986.

Irish Information Agenda, London, Irish Information Partnership, 1987.

MacStiofain, S., *Memoirs of a Revolutionary*, Edinburgh, Gordon Cremonesi, 1975.

McGuire, M., *To Take Arms: A Year in the Provisional IRA*, London, Macmillan, 1973.

Mitchell, A. and O'Snodaigh, P. (eds.), *Irish Political Documents, 1916–1949*, Dublin, Irish Academic Press, 1985.

Moxon-Browne, E., *Nation, Class and Creed in Northern Ireland*, Aldershot, Gower, 1983.

Moynihan, M. (ed.), *Speeches and Statements by Eamon de Valera*, Dublin, Gill & Macmillan, 1980.

O'Donoghue, F., *No Other Land*, Dublin, Irish Press, 1954.

O'Leary, J., *Recollections of Fenians and Fenianism*, Shannon, Irish University Press, 1968.

O'Malley, E., *The Singing Flame*, Dublin, Anvil, 1992.

Pearse, P., *Political Writings and Speeches*, Dublin, Tabbott, 1952.

Rees, M., *Northern Ireland: A Personal Perspective*, London, Methuen, 1985.

Whitelaw, W., *The Whitelaw Memoirs*, London, Aurum, 1989.

OFFICIAL DOCUMENTS

The Government of Northern Ireland, *Violence and Civil Disturbance in Northern Ireland*, Report of Tribunal of Inquiry, Cmd. 566, vol. 2, Belfast, Her Majesty's Stationery Office, 1972.

UNPUBLISHED CORRESPONDENCE AND DOCUMENTS

Minutes of Sinn Fein Provisional Committee, 17 January 1970.

Statistics on fatalities caused by violence and road accidents since 1969, and total terrorist charges since 1976, up to 22 June 1989, RUC Information Office, Belfast.

PUBLISHED CORRESPONDENCE

Adams, G., *Towards a Strategy for Peace*, PSF Document No. 1, PSF–SDLP Talks, Letter to J. Hume, 14 March 1988.

Hume, J., Letter to G. Adams, SDLP Document No. 1, PSF–SDLP Talks, 17 March 1988.

These and other items in the PSF–SDLP Talks between January and September 1988 were later published as a compendium, *The Sinn Fein/SDLP Talks*, Dublin, PSF, 1989.

NEWSPAPERS AND PERIODICALS

Andersonstown News
Fortnight

Hands Off Ireland
Hibernia
Irish Independent
Magill
New Hibernia
New Society
Newsweek
The Business Times
The Christian Science Monitor
The Daily Express
The Daily Herald
The Daily Telegraph
The Economist
The Guardian
The Financial Times
The Independent
The International Express
The Irish News
The Irish Press
The Irish Times
The Leveller
The Manchester Guardian
The Nation, Fianna Fail
The New Statesman and Society
The New York Times
The Observer
The Straits Times
The Sunday Press
The Sunday Telegraph
The Sunday Times
The Sunday Tribune
The Times
The Ulster Newsletter
The Weekly Telegraph
This Week

SELECT READING LIST

Baroid, C. de, *Ballymurphy and the Irish War*, London, Pluto, 1990.
Bowyer Bell, J., *The Secret Army: The IRA, 1916–1979*, Dublin, Poolbeg, 1989.
Bishop, P. and Mallie, E., *The Provisional IRA*, London, Heinemann, 1987.
Boyce, D.G., *Nationalism in Ireland*, London, Croom Helm, 1982.
Boyle, K. and Hadden, T., *Ireland: A Positive Proposal*, London, Penguin, 1985.
Bruce, S., *The Red Hand*, Oxford, Oxford University Press, 1992.
Burton, F., *The Politics of Legitimacy: Struggles in a Belfast Community*, London, Routledge & Kegan Paul, 1978.
Clarke, L., *Broadening the Battlefield: The H-Blocks and the Rise of Sinn Fein*, Dublin, Gill & Macmillan, 1987.
Coogan, T.P., *The IRA*, London, Fontana, 1987.
Dillon, M. and Lehane, D., *Political Murder in Northern Ireland*, London, Penguin, 1973.
Edwards, R. Dudley, *Patrick Pearse: Triumph of Failure*, London, Victor Gollanz, 1977.
Elliott, M., *Partners in Revolution: The United Irishmen and France*, London, Yale University Press, 1982.

——, *Wolfe Tone: Prophet of Irish Independence*, London, Yale University Press, 1989.

Flackes, W.D. and Elliott, S., *Northern Ireland: A Political Directory, 1968–1988*, Belfast, Blackstaff, 1989.

Foley, C., *Legion of the Rearguard*, London, Pluto, 1992.

Foster, R., *Modern Ireland 1600–1972*, London, Allen Lane: The Penguin Press, 1988.

Garvin, T., *Nationalist Revolutionaries in Ireland, 1858–1928*, Oxford, Clarendon, 1987.

Griffith, K. and O'Grady, T., *Curious Journeys: An Oral History of Ireland's Unfinished Revolution*, London, Hutchinson, 1982.

Guelke, A., *Northern Ireland: The International Perspective*, Dublin, Gill & Macmillan, 1988.

Hamill, D., *Pig in the Middle: The Army in Northern Ireland, 1969–1984*, London, Methuen, 1985.

Hederman, M.P. and Kearney, R., *The Crane Bag: Book of Irish Studies*, Dublin, Blackwater, 1982.

Hopkinson, M., *Green Against Green: The Irish Civil War*, Dublin, Gill & Macmillan, 1988.

Kee, R., *The Green Flag: A History of Irish Nationalism*, London, Weidenfeld & Nicolson, 1972.

Keena, C., *A Biography of Gerry Adams*, Cork, Mercier, 1990.

Kelley, K.J., *The Longest War*, London, Zed, 1982.

McAllister, I., *The Northern Ireland Social Democratic and Labour Party*, London, Macmillan, 1977.

Macardle, D., *The Irish Republic*, London, Victor Gollanz, 1937.

MacDonagh, O., *Ireland*, Englewood Cliffs, N.J., Prentice Hall, 1968.

Mansergh, N., *The Irish Question, 1840–1921*, London, Longmans, Green & Co., 1965.

McInerney, M., *Peadar O'Donnell: Irish Social Rebel*, Dublin, O'Brien, 1974.

Neeson, E., *The Civil War in Ireland*, Cork, Mercier, 1966.

Nowlan, K. (ed.), *The Making of 1916: Studies in the History of the Rising*, Dublin, Stationery Office, 1969.

O'Brien, C. Cruise, *States of Ireland*, London, Hutchinson, 1972.

O Broin, L., *Fenian Fever: An Anglo-American Dilemma*, London, Chatto & Windus, 1971.

——, *Michael Collins*, Dublin, Gill & Macmillan, 1980.

——, *Revolutionary Underground: The Story of the Irish Republican Brotherhood, 1858–1924*, Dublin, Gill & Macmillan, 1976.

O'Carroll, J.P. and Murphy, J.A. (eds.), *De Valera and His Times*, Cork, Cork University Press, 1983.

O'Hanlon, T.J., *The Irish: Portrait of a People*, London, Andre Deutsch, 1976.

O'Mahoney, S., *Frongoch: University of Revolution*, Dublin, FDR Teoranta, 1987.

O'Malley, P., *The Uncivil Wars: Ireland Today*, Belfast, Blackstaff, 1983.

——, *Northern Ireland: Questions of Nuance*, Belfast, Blackstaff, 1990.

Patterson, H., *The Politics of Illusion: Republicanism and Socialism in Modern Ireland*, London, Hutchinson Radius, 1989.

Short, K.R.M., *The Dynamite War: Irish American Bombers in Victorian Britain*, Dublin, Gill & Macmillan, 1979.

Sweetman, R., *On Our Knees: Ireland 1972*, London, Pan, 1972.

Townshend, C., *Political Violence in Ireland: Government and Resistance Since 1848*, Oxford, Clarendon, 1983.

——, *The British Campaign in Ireland, 1919–1921: The Development of Political and Military Policies*, Oxford, Clarendon, 1975.

Index